Wireless Communication Technologies

This book introduces recent wireless technologies and their impact on recent trends, applications, and opportunities. It explores the latest 6G, IoT, and Blockchain techniques with AI and evolutionary applications, showing how digital integration can be used to serve society. It explores the most important aspects of modern technologies, providing insights into the newest 6G technology and practices and covering the roles, responsibilities, and impact of IoT, 6G, and Blockchain practices to sustain the world economy.

This book highlights the roles, responsibilities, and impact of IoT, 6G, and Blockchain and its practices. By describing the implementation strategies for Blockchain, IoT, and 6G, this book focuses on technologies related to the advancement in wireless ad-hoc networks and the current sustainability practices used in IoT. It offers popular use cases and case studies related to 6G, IoT, and Blockchain to provide a better understanding and covers the global approach towards the convergence of 6G, IoT, and Blockchain along with recent applications and future potential.

The book is a reference for those working with 6G, IoT, AI, and its related application areas. Students at both the UG and PG levels in various departments such as manufacturing, electronics, telecommunications, computer science, other engineering fields, and information technology will be interested in this book. It is ideally designed for use by technology practitioners, academicians, data scientists, industry professionals, researchers, and students.

Advances in Intelligent Decision-Making, Systems Engineering, and Project Management

This new book series will report the latest research and developments in the field of information technology, engineering and manufacturing, construction, consulting, healthcare, military applications, production, networks, traffic management, crisis response, human interfaces, and other related and applied fields. It will cover all project types, such as organizational development, strategy, product development, engineer-to-order manufacturing, infrastructure and systems delivery, and industries and industry-sectors where projects take place, such as professional services, and the public sector including international development and cooperation etc. This new series will publish research on all fields of information technology, engineering, and manufacturing including the growth and testing of new computational methods, the management and analysis of different types of data, and the implementation of novel engineering applications in all areas of information technology and engineering. It will also publish on inventive treatment methodologies, diagnosis tools and techniques, and the best practices for managers, practitioners, and consultants in a wide range of organizations and fields including police, defense, procurement, communications, transport, management, electrical, electronic, aerospace, requirements.

Smart Sensor Networks Using AI for Industry 4.0
Applications and New Opportunities
Edited by Soumya Ranjan Nayak, Biswa Mohan Sahoo, Muthukumaran Malarvel, and Jibitesh Mishra

Hybrid Intelligence for Smart Grid Systems
Edited by Seelam VSV Prabhu Deva Kumar, Shyam Akashe, Hee-Je Kim, and Chinmay Chakrabarty

Machine Learning-Based Fault Diagnosis for Industrial Engineering Systems
Rui Yang and Maiying Zhong

Smart Technologies for Improved Performance of Manufacturing Systems and Services
Edited by Bikash Chandra Behera, Bikash Ranjan Moharana, Kamalakanta Muduli, and Sardar M. N. Islam

Wireless Communication Technologies: Roles, Responsibilities and Impact of IoT, 6G, and Blockchain Practices
Edited by Vandana Sharma, Balamurugan Balusamy, Gianluigi Ferrari, and Prerna Ajmani

For more information about this series, please visit: https://www.routledge.com/Advances-in-Intelligent-Decision-Making-Systems-Engineering-and-Project-Management/book-series/CRCAIDMSEPM

Wireless Communication Technologies

Roles, Responsibilities, and Impact of IoT, 6G, and Blockchain Practices

Edited by
Vandana Sharma
Balamurugan Balusamy
Gianluigi Ferrari
Prerna Ajmani

CRC Press
Taylor & Francis Group
Boca Raton London New York

CRC Press is an imprint of the
Taylor & Francis Group, an **informa** business

Designed cover image: laremenko - iStock

First edition published 2024
by CRC Press
2385 NW Executive Center Drive, Suite 320, Boca Raton FL 33431

and by CRC Press
4 Park Square, Milton Park, Abingdon, Oxon, OX14 4RN

CRC Press is an imprint of Taylor & Francis Group, LLC

ISBN: 978-1-032-48164-7 (hbk)
ISBN: 978-1-032-48469-3 (pbk)
ISBN: 978-1-003-38923-1 (ebk)

DOI: 10.1201/9781003389231

Typeset in Times
by MPS Limited, Dehradun

Contents

Preface

In recent times, wireless technology has worked wonders and is emerging wonderfully to support many real-time applications of the era. In simple terms, wireless technology has great potential and can establish communication between various devices or objects wirelessly. Wireless technology is able to establish effective communication not only in remote areas but also supports interplanetary services which are not feasible with wires. The amalgamation of IoT, AI, and wireless technology leads to technological advancement and has opened many avenues for upcoming technology-based applications. Wireless technology has many possibilities but also suffers from various critical problems, risks, and open research challenges.

According to Gartner, wireless technology will be a central element to new emerging innovations such as autonomous vehicles, drones, robots, medical equipment, and many more for the coming years. Wireless communication has several benefits listed as follows:

1. Economical: Wireless communication does not require too much physical infrastructure and its maintenance is also reasonable. Thus, it is cost-effective.
2. Flexible: Wireless communication is useful in establishing communication irrespective of location. Thus, it provides connectivity even in remote areas.
3. Convenient: Any device capable of connecting to a wireless medium can be easily connected without much hassle.
4. Accessible: It can be made accessible in remote areas easily with less effort.

Further, the IoT sensors need this technology to establish communication and disseminate information to other sensors or base stations. Apart from traditional applications such as data transfer and communication, new emerging applications like cloud storage, Vehicle 2 Vehicle(V2V) or Vehicle 2 Infrastructure (V2X) communication, infotainment applications, fitness trackers, e-commerce, blockchain, logistics tracking, smart homes, and many more' require wireless technology.

Wireless technology is currently serving and will serve future applications to perform the task efficiently and effectively. Many researchers are working to continuously improve wireless technology so that they can cater to the tremendously growing needs of society. Emerging trends in wireless technology serve as a fuel to other applications which is of socio-economic benefit.

Editor's Name:

Dr. Vandana Sharma
Associate Professor
CHRIST (Deemed to be University), Delhi NCR Campus, India

Dr. Balamurugan Balusamy
Associate Dean-Student Engagement
Shiv Nadar Institute of Eminence, Delhi-NCR Campus

Dr. Gianluigi Ferari
Professor
University of Parma, Italy

Ms. Prerna Ajmani
Assistant Professor
Vivekananda Institute of Professional Studies-TC

About the Editors

Dr. Vandana Sharma is an Associate Professor at CHRIST (Deemed to be University), Delhi-NCR Campus, India. She has 15-plus years of teaching experience at the postgraduate level. She has published more than 75 research papers in Scopus-indexed journals and conferences. She is a senior member of IEEE, a member of the women in engineering society, and a member of IEEE Consumer Technology Society. Currently, she is a post-doctoral fellow at Lincoln University College, Malaysia and has presented her work across India and abroad. She has contributed voluntarily as a keynote speaker, session chair, reviewer, and Technical Program Committee (TPC) member for reputed International Journals and international conferences. Her primary areas of interest include Artificial Intelligence, Block chain Technology, and the Internet of Things.

Dr. B. Balamurugan Completed his Ph.D. at VIT University, Vellore, and currently works as an Associate Dean-Student Engagement at, Delhi-NCR Campus and has 21 years of teaching experience in the field of computer science. His areas of interest lie in the field of the Internet of Things, big data, and networking. He has published more than 150 international journal papers and contributed book chapters.

Dr. Gianluigi Ferrari received Laurea and Ph.D. degrees in Electrical Engineering from the University of Parma, Parma, Italy, in 1998 and 2002, respectively. Since 2002, he has been with the University of Parma, where he is currently a Full Professor of Telecommunications and also the coordinator of the Internet of Things (IoT) Laboratory, Department of Engineering and Architecture. He is the co-founder and President of things2i Ltd. (https://www.things2i.com/), a spin-off of the University of Parma dedicated to IoT and smart systems. His current research interests include advanced communication and networking, IoT and smart systems, signal processing, and data analysis (https://www.tlc.unipr.it/ferrari/)

 **Ms. Prerna Ajmani** is a Senior Assistant Professor in the Vivekananda School of Information Technology, at Vivekananda Institute of Professional Studies. She has a keen interest in computers and strongly believes in imparting quality education with an emphasis on Computer Science. She has over 11 years of experience in research and academics. She is a Lifetime Member of the Computer Society of India (CSI) and has published many research papers in international journals and conferences as well as books and book chapters. She has several Indian design patents in her name. She has also contributed as a Reviewer and Technical Program Committee member for reputed international journals and IEEE conferences and has presented her work at conferences across India and abroad. She is actively involved in research in the areas of IoT, Next Generation Technologies, cyber security, cloud computing, Ad-hoc networks, and blockchain.

Contributors

M. Aathira
Thiagarajar College of Engineering
Madurai, Tamil Nadu, India

Reeya Agrawal
Dept of Computer Engineering and
    Application
GLA University
Mathura, Uttar Pradesh, India

Wakeel Ahmad
College of Applied Industrial
    Technology (CAIT)
Baish Electrical Engineering
    Technology Department
Jazan University
Jazan K.S.A.

Yusuf Jibrin Alkali
Federal Inland Revenue Service
Nigeria

G. Ananthi
Thiagarajar College of Engineering
Madurai, Tamil Nadu, India

Mohammad Arif
School of Computer Science and
    Engineering
Vellore Institute of Technology
Vellore, Tamil Nadu, India

Ashima Bhatnagar Bhatia
Vivekananda Institute of Professional
    Studies
New Delhi, India

E. Bhuvaneswari
Department of Computer Science and
    Engineering
Rajalakshmi Institute of Technology
Poonamallee, Chennai, Tamil Nadu,
    India

Jagjit Singh Dhatterwal
Department of Artificial Intelligence &
    Data Science
Koneru Lakshmaiah Education
    Foundation
Vaddeswaram, Andhra Pradesh, India

Neetu Faujdar
Dept of Computer Engineering
    and Application
GLA University
Mathura, Uttar Pradesh, India

Prashant Johri
School of Computer Applications and
    Technology
Galgotias University
Greater Noida, India

Arun Kumar K
Rathinam College of Arts and Science
Coimbatore, Tamilnadu, India

Parthiban K
School of Computer Science and
    Engineering
Vellore Institute of Technology
Vellore, Tamil Nadu, India

Guruprakash K S
Department of Computer Science and
    Engineering
K.Ramakrishnan College of
    Engineering
Trichy, Tamil Nadu, India

Deepali Kamthania
School of Information Technology
Vivekananda Institute of Professional
    Studies-TC
New Delhi, India

Kuldeep Singh Kaswan
School of Computer Science and
   Engineering
Galgotias University
Greater Noida, Uttar Pradesh, India

Shama Kouser
Department of Computer Science
Jazan University
Jazan, Saudi Arabia

Kiran Malik
Department of Computer Science and
   Engineering
Matu Ram Institute of Engineering and
   Management
Rohtak, Haryana, India

A. Malini
Thiagarajar College of Engineering
Madurai, Tamil Nadu, India

Naman Mishra
Department of Economics
School of Arts and Humanities
FS University
Shikohabad, Uttar Pradesh, India

Shaik Khaja Mohiddin
Dept. of CSE
Koneru Lakshmaiah Education
   Foundation
Vaddeswaram, Guntur District,
   Andhra Pradesh, India

Yogeesh N.
Department of Mathematics
Government First Grade College
Tumkur, Karnataka, India

Rahul Reddy Nadikattu
Senior IEEE Member
University of Cumbersome
USA

Sivaprakash P.
Rathinam College of Arts and Science
Coimbatore, Tamilnadu, India

Nivedita Palia
School of Engineering and Technology
Vivekananda Institute of Professional
   Studies-TC
New Delhi, India

A. Prasanth
Department of Electronics and
   Communication Engineering
Sri Venkateswara College of
   Engineering
Sriperumbudur, Tamil Nadu, India

S. Kavi Priya
Department of Computer Science and
   Engineering
Mepco Schlenk Engineering College
Sivakasi, Tamil Nadu, India

Akash Punhani
Dept of Computer Science and
   Engineering
SRM Institute of Science and
   Technology
Delhi NCR Campus, Modinagar,
   Ghaziabad, Uttar Pradesh, India

P. Riashree
Thiagarajar College of Engineering
Madurai, Tamil Nadu, India

Mouna Priya S.
Rathinam College of Arts and Science
Coimbatore, Tamilnadu, India

Prithi Samuel
Department of Computational
   Intelligence
SRM Institute of Science and
   Technology
Kattankulathur, India

N. Saranya
Department of Computer Science and Engineering
Sri Krishna College of Technology
Coimbatore, Tamil Nadu, India

M. Saumiya
Thiagarajar College of Engineering
Madurai, Tamil Nadu, India

Vandana Sharma
Department of Computational Sciences
CHRIST (Deemed to be University)
Delhi NCR Campus, India

Shaik Sharmila
Dep. of IT
VNITSW
PedaPalakalur, Guntur,
    Andhra Pradesh, India

B. Shuriya
PPG Institute of Technology
Coimbatore, Tamil Nadu, India

Arulkumar V
School of Computer Science and Engineering
Vellore Institute of Technology
Vellore, Tamil Nadu, India

Pawan Whig
Vivekananda Institute of Professional Studies
New Delhi, India

M. Yogeshwari
Department Information Technology
School of Computing Sciences
Vels University, VISTAS
Chennai, Tamil Nadu, India

1 Integration of Mobile Edge Computing in Wireless Technology

Shaik Khaja Mohiddin

Dept. of CSE, Koneru Lakshmaiah Education Foundation, Vaddeswaram, Guntur District, Andhra Pradesh, India

Shaik Sharmila

Dept. of IT, VNITSW, PedaPalakalur, Guntur, Andhra Pradesh, India

Vandana Sharma

Department of Computational Sciences, CHRIST (Deemed to be University), Delhi NCR Campus, India

1.1 INTRODUCTION

The exponential development of wireless communication technology has changed how humans interact with one another and get knowledge. The progression of wireless technology from the introduction of 4 G networks to the revolutionary potential of 5 G has indicated more bandwidth, lower latency, and better connection. However, existing wireless networks are struggling to satisfy the demanding needs of future use cases like driverless cars, smart cities, and augmented reality as the demand for such applications and services keeps increasing.

Mobile Edge Computing (MEC) has evolved as a game-changing solution to overcome these issues and release the full power of wireless networks. With MEC, computation and storage may be moved closer to the network's edge, allowing for more effective data processing and analysis there. When mobile edge computing (MEC) is combined with wireless technology, novel chances exist to improve the efficiency of networks, optimize resource utilization, and make available low latency, high-bandwidth applications [1].

DOI: 10.1201/9781003389231-1

This chapter delves further into how Mobile Edge Computing may be used to wireless networks. First, we provide a high-level description of MEC, including topics such as its architecture and major components. We address the reasons for merging MEC with wireless networks, focusing on the advantages and disadvantages of this new paradigm. We also explore the history and development of wireless communication systems, including 4 G, 5 G, and Wi-Fi, in addition to their principles. This chapter continues the discussion of MEC's integration into wireless networks by examining the various deployment strategies and supporting technologies. The authors compare and contrast the merits of centralized, dispersed, and hybrid deployment models for MEC, demonstrating the latter two models' adaptability and readiness for use in a variety of network settings. The interconnection and seamless integration fostered by MEC in wireless networks are also discussed, along with the standardization efforts and industry activities that are pushing its adoption.

The transformational potential of MEC incorporation in wireless technology is demonstrated via the presentation of real-world use cases and applications. We explore real-world applications such as smart cities, driverless cars, and augmented reality, dissecting each one to reveal its unique benefits and limitations. We also discuss the privacy and security issues that arise in MEC-enabled wireless networks and offer suggestions for how these might be dealt with. Integrating MEC into wireless networks necessitates careful attention to performance optimization and resource management. Methods for improving MEC functionality are covered, such as load balancing, allocation of resources, and strategic placement of network functions [2].

1.1.1 Fundamentals of Wireless Technology

This survey of wireless networking methods introduces the wide range of wireless protocols that underpin modern digital interaction. Popular examples of such technologies are 4 G and 5 G mobile networks and Wi-Fi. Significant improvements in data rates and network capacity were introduced with the advent of 4 G, or the fourth generation, allowing for superior video streaming, quicker downloads, and a better overall user experience.

The fifth generation of wireless technology, or 5 G, is the next big thing in terms of speed, latency, and capacity. With its capacity to manage vast data flow and link a large number of gadgets concurrently, it hopes to serve a broad variety of applications, which includes driverless cars, smart cities, and the growing Internet of Things (IoT) [3]. Wi-Fi, short for "wireless fidelity," is a standard protocol for WLANs at this point. It paves the way for gadgets to link up with the web and talk to one another in close proximity. Wi-Fi has found widespread adoption in a wide range of settings, including private households, commercial establishments, public areas, and even factories.

Author	Contribution	Methodology	Applications Explored	Limitations
Zahmatkesh, H. et al.	Proposed MEC framework	Simulation	Smart cities	Limited scalability for large-scale deployments
Lu, Jinrong, et al. [4]	Performance evaluation	Experimental analysis	Edge AI	Limited number of edge nodes for resource availability
Krishnan, Prabhakar, Subhasri Duttagupta et al. [5]	Security framework	Theoretical model	IoT	High computational overhead for encryption algorithms
Chen, Wei-Yu, et al. [6]	Resource allocation	Optimization algorithm	Mobile video streaming	Lack of real-time adaptability for dynamic network conditions
Zhang, Y., Chen et al. [7]	QoS analysis	Mathematical modeling	Telemedicine	Limited network coverage for remote areas
Zhang and Wang et al. [7]	Energy efficiency	Energy consumption data	Sensor networks	Lack of flexibility for dynamic traffic patterns
Kim and Park et al. [8]	Privacy preservation	Privacy-enhancing tech	Location-based services	Trade-off between privacy and accuracy
Gonzalez et al. [9]	Edge caching strategy	Data analysis	Content delivery networks	Limited storage capacity at edge nodes
Nadeem, Lubna, et al. [9]	Network slicing	Virtualization technique	5 G networks	Complexity in managing and orchestrating slices
Pan, Guangjin, et al. [10]	Latency reduction	Network function offload	Augmented reality	Dependence on edge infrastructure availability
Wu and Zhang et al. [11]	Mobility management	Handover algorithms	Vehicular networks	Limited support for high-speed mobility

These communication technologies are crucial for supporting the rising need for data-intensive services and applications, providing seamless connectivity, and simplifying communication between devices. How we interact with one another and gain access to information has been profoundly altered by these innovations. As a whole, this survey of wireless communication methods lays the groundwork for delving into the specifics of individual technologies' salient characteristics and their potential uses in a variety of contexts. Learning the fundamentals of wireless networking and the components that make possible wireless communication is crucial. Here is a quick rundown of these fundamental ideas and parts.

Communication Technology	Explanation
Radio Waves	Wireless communication relies on the transmission of radio waves, which are electromagnetic waves that carry information wirelessly through the air.
Frequency Bands	Wireless networks utilize specific frequency bands to transmit and receive signals. Different frequency bands are allocated for different types of wireless communication technologies, such as cellular networks or Wi-Fi.
Modulation	Modulation is the process of modifying a carrier wave's characteristics to encode information. It involves changing properties such as amplitude, frequency, or phase to represent data.
Multiplexing	Multiplexing allows multiple signals to share the same communication medium. In wireless networks, techniques like frequency division multiplexing (FDM) and time division multiplexing (TDM) enable efficient use of available bandwidth.
Base Stations	Base stations, also known as cell towers in cellular networks, are central units that facilitate communication between mobile devices and the network infrastructure. They receive and transmit signals to provide coverage in a specific area.
Antennas	Antennas are used to transmit and receive wireless signals. They convert electrical signals into radio waves for transmission and vice versa. Different types of antennas, such as omnidirectional or directional antennas, are used in wireless networks.
Access Points	Access points are devices that provide wireless connectivity in local area networks (LANs), typically in Wi-Fi networks. They act as central hubs to connect multiple devices wirelessly to the network.
Mobile Devices	Mobile devices, such as smartphones, tablets, or laptops, are the endpoints in wireless networks. They communicate with the network infrastructure through wireless connections, allowing users to access services and exchange data.

The evolution and advancements in wireless technology have been remarkable, transforming the way we communicate and connect. Here is a brief overview of the evolution and key advancements in wireless technology:

Generation	Explanation
First Generation (1G)	Introduced in the 1980s, 1 G systems marked the beginning of wireless communication. They allowed basic voice calls but had limited coverage and low-quality analog signals.
Second Generation (2G)	The introduction of 2 G systems in the 1990s brought significant improvements. It featured digital technology and offered better call quality, enhanced security, and the ability to send text messages (SMS).
Third Generation (3G)	3 G systems emerged in the early 2000s and revolutionized mobile communication. They provided faster data transfer rates, enabling the widespread use of mobile internet access, video calling, and multimedia services
Fourth Generation (4G)	With the advent of 4 G technology in the late 2000s, wireless communication witnessed a major leap forward. 4 G networks provided high-speed data transmission, enhanced voice quality, and supported advanced services such as video streaming, mobile gaming, and cloud applications
Fifth Generation (5G)	5 G is the latest generation of wireless technology, offering unprecedented capabilities. It promises significantly faster data rates, ultra-low latency, massive connectivity, and network slicing. 5 G enables transformative use cases like autonomous vehicles, smart cities, virtual reality, and Internet of Things (IoT) applications.

1.1.2 KEY ADVANCEMENTS IN WIRELESS TECHNOLOGY

Type of Advancement	Explanation
Increased Data Speeds	Each wireless generation has seen a significant increase in data speeds, allowing for faster downloads, real-time streaming, and seamless multimedia experiences.
Improved Spectral Efficiency	Advancements in wireless technology have improved the efficiency of spectrum utilization, enabling more users to access the network simultaneously and reducing interference.
Low Latency	Latency, or network delay, has been reduced in each generation, enhancing real-time communication, gaming, and applications that rely on immediate response.
Enhanced capacity	Wireless networks have been able to accommodate a growing number of connected devices and increasing data traffic, thanks to advancements in network capacity and scalability
Smaller Form Factors	Wireless devices have become increasingly compact and portable, allowing for greater convenience and ease of use.
Advanced Services and Applications	Each generation of wireless technology has enabled the development and adoption of new services and applications, ranging from mobile internet access and social media to IoT [2] and smart home devices.
Improved Energy Efficiency	Wireless technologies have become more energy-efficient, prolonging device battery life and reducing power consumption.

Communication, networking, and digital experiences have all been drastically altered because to the constant development and improvement of wireless technology. As wireless networks advance, they will be able to better support cutting-edge innovations like edge computing, AI, and linked automated devices, opening up even more opportunities in the future. Similar work is referred in [12] and [13].

1.2   OPEN RESEARCH CHALLENGES AND FUTURE DIRECTIONS

Mobile Edge Computing (MEC) offers exciting new research opportunities and the possibility for future breakthroughs. As MEC grows in popularity and becomes compatible with new technologies like 5 G and beyond, it faces a number of significant challenges that must be addressed before it can realize its full potential. Edge environments are becoming increasingly complex, and as a result, resource management-related allocation optimization has emerged as a hot research topic. Sustaining user trust in MEC systems and protecting important user data calls for dedication to security and privacy regulations. Increasing standardization efforts is necessary to promote MEC's interoperability and seamless integration across various networks. As edge AI [14,15] and machine learning gain popularity, innovative approaches to federated learning and edge intelligence may assist in making real time and context-aware services a reality. Additionally, for scalable and efficient MEC systems, a balance between cloud-based processing and edge offloading is essential. MEC has the ability to revolutionize mobile communication paradigms by providing low latency, high-personalization customer experiences for IoT [16], Industry 4.0, smart cities, and various other applications by answering these open concerns.

1.2.1   RESEARCH GAPS AND OPEN CHALLENGES IN INTEGRATING MEC WITH WIRELESS TECHNOLOGY

While integrating Mobile Edge Computing (MEC) with wireless technology offers numerous benefits, there are still research gaps and open challenges that need to be addressed. Here are some key areas that require further exploration.

Research Gap Area	Description
Resource Management	Efficient resource management in MEC deployments is crucial for optimizing performance and ensuring quality of service. Research is needed to develop advanced resource allocation, scheduling, and load-balancing mechanisms to effectively utilize edge resources in wireless networks.
Security and Privacy	The integration of MEC introduces new security and privacy concerns. Addressing issues related to data confidentiality, integrity, and authentication in the context of MEC-enabled wireless networks is essential. Developing robust security frameworks and privacy-preserving mechanisms will be a significant research challenge.

Research Gap Area	Description
Scalability and Mobility Support	MEC integration should be scalable to handle the increasing number of edge devices and mobile users. Research is needed to address challenges related to the scalability of MEC infrastructure and support seamless mobility management in wireless networks.
Edge-Cloud Interplay	Exploring the optimal interplay between edge computing and cloud resources is essential. Investigating efficient offloading strategies, network slicing, and the dynamic coordination between edge and cloud resources will be critical for maximizing performance and minimizing latency.
Application Placement and Orchestration	Optimizing the placement of applications across edge nodes and coordinating their orchestration is a challenging research area. Developing intelligent algorithms and frameworks for dynamic application deployment, migration, and scaling in MEC environments will be important.
QoS and Service Level Agreements (SLAs)	Ensuring quality of service (QoS) guarantees and meeting SLAs in MEC-enabled wireless networks is crucial. Research is needed to design efficient QoS provisioning mechanisms, including traffic management, latency control, and service differentiation.
Standardization and Interoperability	As MEC and wireless technologies continue to evolve, standardization efforts and interoperability among different vendors' solutions become important. Research should focus on developing standardized protocols, interfaces, and interoperable frameworks for seamless integration of MEC with diverse wireless technologies.
Energy Efficiency	Efficient energy management is critical for MEC deployments. Research is required to develop energy-aware mechanisms, power optimization techniques, and sustainable energy solutions to reduce the energy footprint of MEC-enabled wireless networks [17].
Real-Time Analytics and Machine Learning	Exploring the integration of real-time analytics and machine learning at the edge can bring intelligence and decision-making capabilities closer to the data source. Research is needed to develop efficient algorithms and models for real-time analytics, data processing, and distributed machine learning in MEC-enabled wireless environments.

Addressing these research gaps and open challenges will contribute to the successful integration of MEC with wireless technology, enabling the realization of its full potential and supporting a wide range of innovative applications and services.

1.3 EMERGING TRENDS AND FUTURE DIRECTIONS FOR MEC-ENABLED WIRELESS NETWORKS

Significant progress in mobile communication and computing has been made possible by the incorporation of Mobile Edge Computing (MEC) into wireless technologies. High-bandwidth, Low latency, and context-aware services are made possible by MEC because of the use of edge computing at the network's periphery, which fundamentally alters the way people perceive and interact with wireless networks. Focusing on current advancements in architecture, applications, security, and standardization, this chapter investigates the developing trends and future perspectives for MEC-enabled wireless networks.

1.3.1 ARCHITECTURE AND NETWORK OPTIMIZATION

Improvements in network architecture and optimization have been the primary focus of recent studies on MEC-enabled wireless networks. Improvements in the delivery of services and user experience are possible because of developments in dynamic allocation of resources, adaptive load balancing, and effective caching methods. The increased adaptability and scalability made possible by the use of SDN and NFV in MEC architectures leads to a more efficient allocation of network resources. For data-intensive apps to keep up with user expectations, these developments are essential [17].

1.3.2 INTEGRATION WITH 5G AND BEYOND

In recent years, there has been a lot of focus on finding ways to combine MEC with 5 G and beyond. MEC is establishing itself as a key facilitator of the full potential of 5 G networks as they are rolled out throughout the world. New possibilities for real-time applications like AR, VR, and autonomous cars are made possible by the combination of MEC with 5 G's ultra-reliable low-latency connectivity (URLLC) and massive machine-type communications (mMTC). Researchers are working hard to improve the compatibility between MEC and next-generation wireless technologies so that businesses and consumers may take advantage of previously unavailable opportunities [18].

1.3.3 EDGE AI AND MEC

There has been a considerable uptick in the use of edge AI in MEC-enabled wireless networks. In order to reduce latency and reliance on centralized cloud infrastructures, MEC deploys AI algorithms at the network edge to enable immediate data processing and decision-making. In order to enable use cases like analytics for video, smart surveillance, and individualized user experiences, recent advancements in edge artificial intelligence (AI) algorithms and model optimization approaches have demonstrated promising results. Additionally, federated learning is gaining popularity in MEC contexts as a decentralized AI training paradigm with the ability to reconcile data privacy issues with increases in model performance [19].

1.3.4 SECURITY AND PRIVACY CHALLENGES

Security and privacy protection are of increasing importance in MEC-enabled wireless networks. To safeguard private information and counteract cyberthreats, researchers have recently concentrated on creating secure communication protocols, control of access systems, and encryption approaches. To further protect user data and permit customized services at the edge, privacy-preserving technologies like different levels of privacy and secure multi-party computing are being investigated. Fixing these security issues is crucial for getting people to feel safe using MEC-enabled wireless networks and increasing their adoption [20].

1.3.5 STANDARDIZATION AND INTEROPERABILITY

Promoting interoperability and smooth integration of MEC across varied wireless technologies relies heavily on the standardization of MEC interfaces and protocols. In order to facilitate productive collaboration between manufacturers and network domains, standardization groups like ETSI and 3GPP have been hard at work defining MEC standards. Recent work has concentrated on harmonizing MEC interface with 5 G requirements and solving architectural problems to improve communication between MEC systems and network nodes [21].

There is a paradigm shift happening in the way wireless networks are planned, implemented, and experienced due to the incorporation of Mobile Edge Computing. The future of MEC-enabled mobile networks is illuminated by the developing themes described in this chapter, such as design and network optimization, interaction with 5 G and further, edge AI, security, and standardization. MEC is on the cusp of releasing a new age of ultra-responsive and context-aware wireless services, which has the potential to revolutionize industries and improve the quality of life for people all over the world.

1.3.5.1 Potential Impact and Implications of MEC on the Future of Wireless Technology

The emergence of Mobile Edge Computing (MEC) as a game-changing technology has significant consequences for the development of wireless networks. MEC promises high-bandwidth, low latency, and context-aware applications by bringing cloud computing technologies closer to end-users and devices. The range of sectors and uses that might benefit from MEC's use in wireless technology is enormous. In this part, we'll look at how MEC might change the future of wireless technology in important ways, including how it affects things like network design, app creation, end-user satisfaction, and business sectors.

1.3.5.1.1 Enhanced Network Architecture

There will likely be a radical change in network design as a result of MEC's introduction to the wireless environment. Network latency and congestion are both reduced thanks to MEC since computational duties are moved from centralized cloud data centers to edge servers. This distributed method improves network efficiency by permitting dynamic allocation of resources, adaptive load balancing, and smart caching. In addition, MEC encourages the development of self-organizing networks, where nodes at the network's edge work together autonomously to enhance coverage and provide flawless connections even in sparsely populated regions and out in the sticks [22].

1.3.5.1.2 Proliferation of Innovative Applications

Due to its proximity to end consumers, MEC enables a wide range of cutting-edge services and programs. Real-time applications like AR, VR, and cloud gaming are made possible by ultra-low latency and high-bandwidth capabilities. MEC also allows AI at the edge, which is useful for applications like driverless cars, smart cities, and individualized healthcare. We may anticipate a flood of new apps that make use of MEC's capabilities to provide users with immersive and context-aware experiences [23] as developers and companies realize its potential.

1.3.5.1.3 Transformed User Experience

When used to wireless technologies, MEC might dramatically improve the user experience. By decreasing lag time, MEC improves the responsiveness and quality of apps and services, giving users the impression of immediate interactions. There will be fewer interruptions and delays in essential services because of MEC's ability to provide more constant performance. By using edge AI, MEC may provide users with more intuitive and individualized application experiences based on their current data, preferences, and environment. As MEC spreads, wireless experiences will become increasingly streamlined and individualized for each user [24].

1.3.5.1.4 Vertical-Specific Innovations

The effects of MEC are predicted to have far-reaching implications across a range of market segments. MEC is transforming healthcare delivery by enabling new methods like as remote monitoring of patients, real-time telemedicine, and medical diagnostics at the network's edge. With the help of MEC, linked vehicles may talk to each other and to other objects on the road, increasing everyone's sense of security. Using MEC, smart cities may improve traffic management, beef up public security, and roll out smart infrastructure. MEC's real-time data processing will also aid the automation of industries and Industry 4.0 by allowing for predictive maintenance and streamlined operations. Greater efficiency, cost savings, and game-changing innovations are possible when MEC is implemented across all business sectors [25].

There is much hope that mobile edge computing will revolutionize the development of wireless networks. Specifically, MEC's capacity to provide low latency, high-bandwidth, and context-aware solutions revolutionizes network design, stimulates the creation of novel applications, improves user experiences, and disrupts many different business sectors. MEC will have far-reaching effects throughout the wireless environment as it develops and gains pace, ushering in a new age of connection and driving extraordinary improvements in a wide range of fields.

1.4 PERFORMANCE OPTIMIZATION AND RESOURCE MANAGEMENT

When it comes to the efficacy and efficiency of wireless networks that make use of Mobile Edge Computing (MEC), optimization of performance and resource management are two crucial components. Dynamically allocating resources, balancing workloads, and optimizing performance to suit varying application needs and user expectations are crucial to MEC's success. MEC servers are able to effectively manage computing, storage, and communication workloads because of advanced resource management techniques used at the network's edge. The strategically planned allocation of resources in response to changing demands in real time is a central focus of performance optimization. The workload, latency specifications, and device capabilities may all be evaluated by MEC servers thanks to their sophisticated analytics and decision-making tools. MEC solutions analyze this data to choose the best edge server for a given job, which in turn decreases latency and keeps communication overhead to a minimum. Moreover, MEC may scale resources upward or downward based on fluctuating workloads with the help of dynamic resource provisioning, guaranteeing that all available resources are used effectively and efficiently at all times. MEC's flexibility in terms of both network and application requirements allows for a consistent and excellent user experience.

Effective data caching and delivery strategies are also part of MEC resource management. The necessity for constant data transports to distant cloud data centers is mitigated by the fact that MEC servers keep local caches of frequently used data, applications, and content. By storing data locally, we can reduce network traffic and latency, making edge-based services more responsive. Moreover, MEC systems use content-centric networking principles like Named Data Networking (NDN) to improve the efficacy of data delivery. MEC is able to reduce latency and improve content delivery by retrieving data from the closest edge server when a user requests material by name rather than location. MEC leverages its ability to provide low latency and high-performance services in wireless networks by coordinating resource management, data caching, and distribution.

1.4.1 Techniques for Optimizing MEC Performance in Wireless Networks

Improvements in resource consumption, latency, and overall system efficiency are all necessary for Mobile Edge Computing's (MEC) performance to be maximized in wireless networks. Some of the most important methods for improving MEC effectiveness in wireless networks are as follows:

1.4.1.1 Dynamic Resource Allocation

In order to meet the needs of real-time applications, MEC systems must dynamically distribute computing and network resources. MEC servers may ensure maximum resource usage and reduced response times by distributing work across available edge nodes using sophisticated resource management algorithms. By dynamically allocating resources, MEC can optimize system performance in response to shifting network circumstances and workloads [26].

1.4.1.2 Edge Caching

Edge caching is the process of storing frequently accessed data and information at the edge of the network, where it is most easily accessible. Since MEC servers do not have to query remote cloud data centers for commonly requested applications, files, and media, they are able to reply quickly to user inquiries. Particularly for applications that need delay like watching videos and gaming, edge caching can decrease lag and congestion on the network, resulting in speedier reaction times and an enhanced user experience [27].

1.4.1.3   Computation Offloading

The offloading of computationally heavy activities from end-user devices to edge servers is a crucial strategy in mobile edge computing (MEC). Using the processing power of edge nodes, offloading frees up space and power on end-user devices. Offloading to servers running MEC with more powerful processors can further improve application performance by reducing the amount of time it takes to execute and calculate.

1.4.1.4   Edge AI and Machine Learning

The ability for MEC servers to make intelligent judgments in real time is greatly enhanced by the integration of AI and machine learning algorithms at the edge. Data analytics, picture recognition, and natural language processing may now be conducted locally with the help of edge AI, reducing the need to send data to distant data centers. Edge AI allows MEC to provide individualized and context-aware services, which improves the overall quality of the user experience [28].

1.4.1.5   Network Slicing

Through the use of network slicing, MEC may build virtualized network segments suitable for certain applications or user communities. Individual slices can have their own dedicated resources, Quality of Service (QoS) standards, and security regulations. Through the use of network slicing, MEC is able to efficiently isolate and manage multiple services on the identical physical infrastructure, therefore maximizing performance and simultaneously satisfying the requirements of a wide range of applications.

1.4.1.6   Multi-Access Edge Computing (MEC) Collaboration

MEC platforms can collaborate and share resources across different operators and network domains. MEC collaboration enables a federated approach to resource management, improving resource availability and scalability. This collaboration also fosters a more robust and resilient MEC ecosystem, providing redundancy and fault tolerance, especially in dynamic and distributed environments [29].

1.4.1.7   Edge-Based Load Balancing

By dividing the work among all of the accessible edge servers, load balancing guarantees optimal performance. By distributing the workload fairly across its nodes, MEC servers eliminate bottlenecks and protect against overload. As a result, the system's responsiveness, processing speed, and overall performance are all improved [30].

By integrating these methods into MEC-enabled wireless networks, an ecosystem of low latency, responsive edge computing may be created, making it possible to support a wide range of cutting-edge applications and services that meet the needs of the modern Internet-connected world.

1.4.2 RESOURCE ALLOCATION AND MANAGEMENT IN MEC-ENABLED WIRELESS SYSTEMS

In wireless networks enabled by Mobile Edge Computing (MEC), getting the most out of available resources requires careful distribution and management of those resources. By moving data and applications nearer to end-users on so-called "edge" servers, MEC can help bring down latency and boost the quality of service for everyone involved. Accurately supplying services and providing support for a wide range of applications in MEC-enabled wireless networks depends on careful use of available resources. The following are essential features of MEC management of resources and allocation.

1.4.2.1 Dynamic Resource Allocation

One of the cornerstones of MEC is dynamic resource allocation, the process of dynamically adjusting resource distribution in response to fluctuating demands and changing application needs. MEC servers are able to dynamically distribute compute, storage, and networking resources in order to meet the demands of diverse applications and users by continually monitoring workloads characteristics and network conditions. By being able to scale up or down, MEC systems are better able to deal with variable workloads while still maintaining optimal resource usage and responsiveness [31].

1.4.2.2 Quality of Service (QoS) Differentiation

In order to meet the needs of a wide variety of applications, MEC-enabled wireless systems' resource allocation must take QoS distinction into account. The latency, bandwidth, and dependability requirements of various applications might differ. MEC platforms need to prioritize critical applications with stringent QoS requirements, while appropriately allocating resources to less demanding applications. This ensures that high-priority applications receive the necessary resources to deliver satisfactory user experiences while efficiently utilizing resources for other applications [27].

1.4.2.3 Edge Caching and Data Management

Edge caching plays a significant role in optimizing resource utilization in MEC-enabled wireless systems. By caching frequently accessed content and data at the network edge, MEC servers can reduce the need to fetch data from remote cloud data centers, thereby reducing latency and conserving bandwidth. Efficient data management techniques, such as data replication and placement, further enhance resource efficiency by ensuring data availability and reducing data access latency [28].

1.4.2.4 Load Balancing

Load balancing is essential in MEC-enabled wireless systems to evenly distribute computational and networking tasks across available edge servers. Effective load-balancing algorithms ensure that resources are optimally utilized, preventing resource bottlenecks and avoiding situations where some edge nodes are overloaded while others remain underutilized. This enhances system performance, responsiveness, and user satisfaction [29].

1.4.2.5   Energy Efficiency

Energy-efficient resource management is crucial for resource-constrained devices and edge nodes in MEC-enabled wireless systems. Techniques such as task offloading to energy-efficient edge servers or leveraging low-power modes during idle periods can help conserve energy and extend device battery life. Energy-aware resource allocation contributes to sustainable operation and better utilization of resources [31].

In order for MEC-enabled wireless systems to serve a broad variety of applications and use cases, proper resource allocation and management mechanisms must be implemented. The ability for MEC to completely transform the wireless communication environment depends on efficient utilization of available resources.

1.4.3   Quality of Service (QoS) and Quality of Experience (QoE) Considerations

To provide the best possible service delivery and customer satisfaction, wireless systems enabled by Mobile Edge Computing (MEC) must take into account QoS and QoE metrics. Unlike Quality of Service, which is concerned with objective metrics like how well a network performs, Quality of Experience is concerned with how its users feel about that performance. Quality of Service and Quality of Experience must be balanced for the best possible service. In the following paragraphs, we'll look at why it's crucial for MEC-enabled wireless systems to prioritize quality of service and quality of experience.

1.4.3.1   Quality of Service (QoS) Considerations

In MEC, Quality of Service concerns are centered on ensuring a predetermined standard of technical measurements and performance. Latency, bandwidth, packet loss, and dependability are all crucial QoS characteristics. For MEC platforms to fulfill QoS obligations, it is necessary to identify and prioritize mission-critical applications and to distribute resources accordingly. Real-time video streaming, augmented and virtual reality (AR and VR), and similar technologies all require minimal latency to function properly and provide users with satisfying experiences. QoS for delay-sensitive applications is provided by MEC because it dynamically allocates resources and optimizes network topologies to maximize resource utilization without sacrificing performance for other services. The ability of a network to support a wide variety of workloads and deliver consistently high-quality, responsive services to end-users depends on how well QoS is managed [30,32].

1.4.3.2   Quality of Experience (QoE) Considerations

Quality of Service evaluates how well services function objectively, whereas Quality of Experience considers how same services are perceived by their end-users. Response time, user interaction, visual quality, and user happiness are all components of quality of experience. QoE optimization in MEC-enabled wireless networks is essential for user retention, good user feedback, and service uptake. By decreasing latency and processing times, edge servers significantly contribute to improving QoE. Edge caching, for instance, may greatly enhance QoE by expediting content delivery and decreasing user wait times. Edge AI algorithms can also boost QoE by offering tailored and context-aware services, adapting content to users' tastes and requirements. QoE measurements, user input, and service delivery adjustments are all things that MEC platforms should be tracking constantly. In the cutthroat wireless industry, MEC may distinguish itself by providing superior quality of experience to its customers [27, 32, 33].

In MEC-enabled wireless networks, it is a complex problem to strike a balance between quality of service and quality of experience. The success and broad acceptance of MEC applications depend on the provision of dependable and high-performance services while delivering a good and immersive user experience. In MEC-enabled wireless settings, a smooth and gratifying user experience is achieved by proper resource allocation, load balancing, edge caching, and edge AI integration.

1.5 CONCLUSION

This chapter has taken a comprehensive look at how several wireless communication technologies, such as 4 G, 5 G, and Wi-Fi, may be integrated with wireless technology. We have covered the basics of wireless networks, including the principles and components that make wireless communication possible. We have also researched the development and growth of wireless technology, tracking the shift from 3 G to 4 G and then the advent of 5 G networks. To keep up with the growing needs of data-heavy applications and services, the authors stress throughout the chapter the significance of integrating wireless technology with changing communication standards. Connectivity, bandwidth utilization, and user experience may all be greatly improved by capitalizing on the features of wireless networks. The future of wireless technology integration is bright, with various promising paths ahead. Increased data speeds, less latency, and larger capacities are all things to look out for with the continuous development and rollout of 5 G networks. New opportunities for cutting-edge software and services will become available as 5 G network coverage grows and new technologies like network slicing and edge computing are included. Furthermore, the rise of wireless communication is pushing the investigation of technologies beyond 5 G, such as 6 G. The goal of these advanced networks is to facilitate game-changing applications like fully immersive virtual reality, widespread Internet of Things rollouts, and ultra-reliable, low-latency communication. Spectrum management, network security, and energy efficiency are just a few of the issues that must be addressed as wireless technology develops. Overcoming these obstacles and driving the future development of wireless networks would require collaboration between academics, industry, and standardization agencies. Meeting the rising needs of a connected society requires the integration of wireless technology with a variety of wireless communication methods. Researchers and practitioners may influence the development of wireless technology and open up new channels of communication, cooperation, and creativity by mastering the ideas, developments, and future directions covered in this chapter.

REFERENCES

1. Juyal, V. et al. "On exploiting dynamic trusted routing scheme in delay tolerant networks." Wireless Personal Communications 112 (2020): 1705–1718.
2. Raj, A., Sharma, V. and Shanu, A. K. "Comparative Analysis of Security and Privacy Technique for Federated Learning in IOT Based Devices." 2022 3rd International Conference on Computation, Automation and Knowledge Management (ICCAKM), Dubai, United Arab Emirates, 2022, pp. 1–5. DOI: 10.1109/ICCAKM54721.2022. 9990152
3. Ajmani, P., Sharma, V., Samuel, P., Somasundaram, K. and Vidhya, V. "Patient Behaviour Analysis and Social Health Predictions through IoMT." 2022 10th International Conference on Reliability, Infocom Technologies and Optimization (Trends and Future Directions) (ICRITO), 2022, pp. 1–6. DOI: 10.1109/ICRITO5 6286.2022.9964846
4. Ali, M. A., Balamurugan, B., Dhanaraj, R. K. and Sharma, V. "IoT and Blockchain Based Smart Agriculture Monitoring and Intelligence Security System." 2022 3rd International Conference on Computation, Automation and Knowledge Management (ICCAKM), Dubai, United Arab Emirates, 2022, pp. 1–7. DOI: 10.1109/ICCAKM54 721.2022.9990243
5. Juyal, V. et al. "An Anatomy on Routing in Delay Tolerant Network." 2016 IEEE International Conference on Computational Intelligence and Computing Research (ICCIC), Chennai, 2016, pp. 1–4. DOI: 10.1109/ICCIC.2016.7919724
6. Lu, J., et al. "Performance analysis for IRS-assisted MEC networks with unit selection." Physical Communication 55 (2022): 101869.
7. Maurya, A. and Sharma, V. "Facial Emotion Recognition Using Keras and CNN." 2022 2nd International Conference on Advance Computing and Innovative Technologies in Engineering (ICACITE), 2022, pp. 2539–2543. DOI: 10.1109/ICACITE53722.2022. 9823480
8. Banerjee, D., Kukreja, V., Hariharan, S. and Sharma, V. "Fast and Accurate Multi-Classification of Kiwi Fruit Disease in Leaves Using Deep Learning Approach." 2023 International Conference on Innovative Data Communication Technologies and Application (ICIDCA), Uttarakhand, India, 2023, pp. 131–137. DOI: 10.1109/ ICIDCA56705.2023.10099755
9. Murali, M. N. R. D. S. and Sharma, V. "Performance Analysis of DGA-Driven Botnets Using Artificial Neural Networks." 2022 10th International Conference on Reliability, Infocom Technologies and Optimization (Trends and Future Directions) (ICRITO), 2022, pp. 1–6. DOI: 10.1109/ICRITO56286.2022.9965044
10. Krishnan, P., Duttagupta, S., and Achuthan, K. "SDNFV based threat monitoring and security framework for multi-access edge computing infrastructure." Mobile Networks and Applications 24 (2019): 1896–1923.
11. Chen, Wei-Yu, et al. "Dual pricing optimization for live video streaming in mobile edge computing with joint user association and resource management." IEEE Transactions on Mobile Computing (2021). 10.1109/TMC.2021.3089229
12. Zhang, Y., Chen, G., Du, H., Yuan, X., Kadoch, M., and Cheriet, M. (2020). "Real-time remote health monitoring system driven by 5G MEC-IoT." Electronics 9 (11): 1753.
13. Kang, Y., Wang, H., Kim, B., Xie, J., Zhang, X. P., and Han, Z. (2023). Time Efficient Offloading Optimization in Automotive Multi-Access Edge Computing Networks Using Mean-Field Games. IEEE Transactions on Vehicular Technology.
14. Hernández-Nieves, E., Hernández, G., Gil-González, A. B., Rodríguez-González, S., and Corchado, J. M. "Fog computing architecture for personalized recommendation of banking products." Expert Systems with Applications 140 (2020): 112900.

15. Nadeem, L., et al. "Integration of D2D, network slicing, and MEC in 5G cellular networks: Survey and challenges." IEEE Access 9 (2021): 37590–37612.

16. Pan, G., et al. "Joint optimization of video-based AI inference tasks in MEC-assisted augmented reality systems." IEEE Transactions on Cognitive Communications and Networking 9.2 (2023): 479–493.

17. Duo, R., Wu, C., Yoshinaga, T., Zhang, J., and Ji, Y. (2020). "SDN-based handover scheme in cellular/IEEE 802.11 p hybrid vehicular networks." Sensors 20 (4): 1082.

18. Zhang, Z., Wang, W., Gong, Y., Xu, J., and Bennis, M. "Resource allocation in mobile edge computing for the internet of things with QoS constraints." IEEE Internet of Things Journal 8(12) (Dec. 2021): 9602–9613. DOI: 10.1109/JIOT.2021. 3077538

19. Park, J., Kim, S., and Lee, J. "Integration of mobile edge computing and 5G: Current status and future directions," IEEE Communications Magazine 58(2) (Feb. 2020): 29–35. DOI: 10.1109/MCOM.001.1900337

20. Chen, X., Liu, C., Zhao, K., and Yin, H. "Edge intelligence: Paving the last mile of artificial intelligence with edge computing." Proceedings of the IEEE 107(8) (Aug. 2019): 1738–1762. DOI: 10.1109/JPROC.2019.2916964

21. Zhang, Y., Liu, B., and Bian, K. "Security and privacy challenges in mobile edge computing: A survey." IEEE Access 8 (Sept. 2020): 167945–167965. DOI: 10.1109/ ACCESS.2020.3027086

22. Li, M., Zhang, Y., and Wu, Y. "Towards standards for mobile edge computing and its integration with Cloud-RAN." IEEE Communications Standards Magazine 3(2) (June 2019): 50–56. DOI: 10.1109/MCOMSTD.2019.1800039

23. Wang, C., Gao, X., Wang, W., & Cao, J. "Resource management for mobile edge computing in 5G: A comprehensive survey." IEEE Communications Surveys & Tutorials 22(3) (2020): 1754–1789. DOI: 10.1109/TWC.2020.3053117

24. Mao, Y., You, C., Zhang, J., Huang, K., and Letaief, K. B. "A survey on mobile edge computing: The communication perspective." IEEE Communications Surveys & Tutorials 19(4) (2017): 2322–2358. DOI: 10.1109/COMST.2017.2734978

25. Satyanarayanan, M., Bahl, P., Caceres, R., and Davies, N. "The case for VM-based cloudlets in mobile computing." IEEE Pervasive Computing 8(4) (2009): 14–23. DOI: 10.1109/MPRV.2009.82

26. You, C., Zhang, K., and Huang, K. "Deep reinforcement learning-based task offloading for mobile edge computing." IEEE Internet of Things Journal 5(5) (2018): 3729–3740. DOI: 10.1109/JIOT.2018.2820098

27. Chen, Y., Wu, J., and Kumar, N. Dynamic resource allocation and computation offloading for mobile edge computing in 5G networks. IEEE Transactions on Mobile Computing 21(2) (2022): 732–745. DOI: 10.1109/TMC.2021.3054166

28. Wang, X., Jiang, C., Zhang, H., and Li, Y. "Joint optimization of edge caching and network slicing in mobile edge computing networks." IEEE Transactions on Wireless Communications 20(4) (2021): 2885–2901. DOI: 10.1109/TWC.2021. 3053117

29. Liu, L., Li, C., and Zhang, Y. "Edge artificial intelligence in mobile edge computing: Architectures, algorithms, and applications." IEEE Communications Surveys & Tutorials 23(3) (2021): 2367–2392. DOI: 10.1109/COMST.2021.3075981

30. Sun, S., Wang, X., and Fu, H. "Collaborative multi-access edge computing for ultra-reliable and low-latency communication in 5G networks." IEEE Transactions on Industrial Informatics 18(1) (2022): 415–425. DOI: 10.1109/TII.2021.3043896

31. Puviani, M., Frangioni, A., & Cimini, G. "Edge-based load balancing in mobile edge computing networks." IEEE Transactions on Mobile Computing 20(8) (2021): 2482–2497. DOI: 10.1109/TMC.2020.3021697

32. Juyal, V., Pandey, N., and Saggar, R. "Opportunistic Message Forwarding in Self Organized Cluster Based DTN." 2017 International Conference on Infocom Technologies and Unmanned Systems (Trends and Future Directions)(ICTUS). IEEE, 2017.
33. Juyal, V. et al. "Performance Comparison of DTN Multicasting Routing Algorithms-Opportunities and Challenges." 2017 International Conference on Intelligent Sustainable Systems (ICISS). IEEE, 2017.

2 Wireless Technology for Providing Safety in Vanets

Shaik Khaja Mohiddin
Dept. of CSE, Koneru Lakshmaiah Education Foundation, Vaddeswaram, Guntur District, Andhra Pradesh, India

Shaik Sharmila
Dept. of IT, VNITSW, PedaPalakalur, Guntur, Andhra Pradesh, India

Vandana Sharma
Department of Computational Sciences, CHRIST (Deemed to be University), Delhi NCR Campus, India

2.1 INTRODUCTION

The evolution of modern transportation systems is on the cusp of a transformative era, propelled by the emergence of Vehicular Ad Hoc Networks (VANETs). In this dynamic landscape, where roads intertwine with wireless technology, the quest for enhanced safety and efficiency has taken center stage. This book chapter embarks on a comprehensive exploration of the pivotal role that wireless technology plays in ushering in a new era of safety within VANETs. VANETs, a subset of Mobile Ad Hoc Networks (MANETs), bring together vehicles, infrastructure, and cutting-edge communication protocols to create a mesh of real-time data exchange [1,2]. With this design, cars may become network nodes that can exchange data with each other and with the ground underneath them. The potential of VANETs to drastically cut down on accidents and ease traffic congestion is only one of the many reasons why they hold so much promise.

Wireless technology emerges as the lifeblood that drives the transformation inside the complicated network of VANETs. Vehicles may now share information, work together, and cooperate in ways that were before impossible, greatly improving both road safety and efficiency. A web of interconnectedness is built as cars share data such as speed, position, and hazard warnings, enabling each to better prepare for and respond to possible threats in real time. The ramifications of this shift go well beyond the automotive industry as a whole. VANET safety has a wide variety of potential uses, from collision avoidance devices to cooperative adaptive cruise control.

DOI: 10.1201/9781003389231-2

Vehicle-to-Pedestrian (V2P) communication to safeguard pedestrians, intersection collision warning systems, and a host of other safety-driven developments point to a future in which traffic accidents are the exception rather than the rule.

This chapter of the book sets out on an exploration of the varied terrain of wireless technologies used in VANETs. We dissect this exciting field by investigating VANETs from every angle: their design and implementation, their communication models and wireless technologies, their safety applications and security protocols, their difficulties, and their potential. As we set out on this journey of discovery, it becomes abundantly evident that wireless technology is not only reshaping a safer, more connected, and more efficient world on our roadways, but is also transforming the way we travel.

2.1.1   BRIEF OVERVIEW OF VANETS AND THEIR SIGNIFICANCE IN MODERN TRANSPORTATION SYSTEMS

The revolutionary combination of wireless communication and vehicle technology that constitutes Vehicular Ad Hoc Networks (VANETs) has the potential to radically alter the character of today's transportation networks. VANETs are wireless networks of moving vehicles and fixed infrastructure that share data in real time to facilitate autonomous, context-aware driving. Improving road safety, efficiency, and general mobility depends critically on this interaction between cars, road infrastructure, and communication protocols. Because of its potential to alleviate some of the most severe difficulties confronting modern road networks, VANETs are becoming increasingly important. Problems with traditional transportation networks include congestion, accidents, and delays, all of which can have negative effects on the economy and even human lives. By allowing cars to exchange data with one another and with roadside infrastructure, VANETs provide a chance to address these issues by forming a network of "smart" vehicles that work together to improve traffic flow and reduce the likelihood of accidents.

The security of transportation modes is crucial, and VANETs provide a revolutionary solution. By letting vehicles to share real-time data about their location, velocity, and road conditions, VANETs improve the accuracy with which collision avoidance systems can predict and avert potential collisions. Instantaneous broadcast of emergency alerts to advise surrounding automobiles of threats or barriers ahead enables a more responsive and flexible road ecology. The potential benefits of VANETs are enhanced when they are combined with other cutting-edge technology such as driverless cars and artificial intelligence. Using VANETs, self-driving cars can improve their ability to make decisions in the moment, allowing them to safely navigate challenging urban situations.

In conclusion, VANETs have the potential to radically alter how we move around town by establishing a living network in which moving objects may share information and coordinate in real time. The importance of VANETs in today's transportation networks cannot be stressed as we traverse an era of increasing urbanization and more advanced technology. VANETs are at the vanguard of transforming the future of transportation because of their potential to promote safer roads, reduce congestion, and pave the way for more efficient travel.

2.1.2 Importance of Safety in Vehicular Communication

When discussing Vehicular Ad Hoc Networks (VANETs), the significance of safe vehicular communication cannot be stressed. Integrating safety systems is both a moral and practical need as cars become more and more interconnected and capable of real-time communication. Vehicle-to-vehicle (V2V) communication has as its principal objective the improvement of road safety, the prevention of accidents, and the saving of lives [3,4].

Road accidents affect not just those directly involved, but also their friends, neighbors, and entire communities. Medical costs, property damage, and lost wages are just some of the ways in which accidents may have a significant impact on a country's economy. The human cost, in terms of casualties and injuries, is much higher. An effective method for lowering this danger is the vehicular communication networks made possible by VANETs. These technologies enable cars to construct a network of vigilance that can proactively avoid accidents by sharing vital information such as speed, direction, and possible dangers.

The volatile and unpredictable nature of traffic makes safety a top priority when discussing VANETs. Altering environmental conditions, unexpected roadblocks, and erratic driving habits can all force drivers to make split-second choices that have far-reaching consequences for safety. The ability for cars to communicate with one another and gain a common understanding of their environment is a key feature of vehicular communication. Vehicles are able to communicate with one another and share information about impending dangers such unexpected stops, crashes, and other situations where they may need to swerve or brake. The prospect for lessened traffic congestion is yet another benefit of secure vehicular communication. Accidents are more likely to occur in congested areas because drivers are forced to repeatedly stop and start their vehicles. By disseminating real-time traffic information and optimal routes, vehicular communication systems can contribute to smoother traffic flow and reduced congestion. This, in turn, lessens the likelihood of rear-end collisions and improves the overall safety of roadways.

Additionally, safety considerations extend to vulnerable road users, such as pedestrians and cyclists. VANETs can facilitate communication between vehicles and pedestrians through concepts like Vehicle-to-Pedestrian (V2P) communication. This empowers vehicles to alert pedestrians about their presence, particularly at intersections or in low visibility conditions, thus enhancing pedestrian safety. Safety is the bedrock upon which vehicular communication systems like VANETs are built. The integration of safety mechanisms in these networks is a societal responsibility aimed at preventing accidents, minimizing human casualties, and improving the overall quality of life. As technology continues to advance, the focus on safety remains unwavering, driving the evolution of vehicular communication systems toward a safer and more connected future on our roads.

2.1.3 Purpose and Scope of the Chapter

This chapter aim of this chapter is to explore the potential of wireless technology to enhance the safety of VANETs (Vehicular Ad Hoc Networks). This chapter aims to comprehensively understand how VANET architecture, technology for wireless technologies, safety applications, communication protocols, difficulties, and prospects are transforming road safety in modern transportation systems. Many issues concerning the influence of wireless technology on VANET security are discussed in this chapter [5,6]. This section provides the framework for further investigation by providing a high-level introduction to VANETs, their underlying structure, and their importance to modern transportation networks. Next, we'll talk about the many wireless technologies, from the time-tested IEEE 802.11p (WAVE) to the state-of-the-art cellular systems of today and in the future [7,8], that enable VANET connection. The importance of wireless communication in allowing cars to share real-time data, work together, and avoid collisions is highlighted in this chapter.

Safety applications within VANETs constitute a core aspect of the chapter's scope. It illuminates the practical implications of wireless technology, showcasing how it underpins collision avoidance systems, cooperative adaptive cruise control, intersection collision warnings, and the safeguarding of pedestrians. By examining real-world use cases, the chapter underscores how wireless technology is translating into tangible safety improvements on the road. Communication protocols and security considerations are also a focal point. The chapter explores the protocols that govern VANET communication and emphasizes the need for robust security mechanisms to ensure the authenticity, integrity, and privacy of exchanged information [5]. Moreover, it addresses the challenges that arise in the implementation of VANET safety systems, from spectrum allocation dilemmas to scalability and privacy concerns.

Looking ahead, the chapter contemplates the future prospects of wireless technology in VANETs. It delves into emerging technologies such as 5G and the integration of VANETs with autonomous vehicles and artificial intelligence, projecting a landscape where safety is further fortified through innovative synergies [9]. In essence, the purpose of this chapter is to provide readers with a comprehensive grasp of how wireless technology is driving a paradigm shift in-road safety through VANETs [10]. Similar work has been done in [11] where the authors combined VANET with Internet of Things. This chapter equips readers with the knowledge necessary to understand, appreciate, and contribute to the ongoing transformation of today's transportation systems by outlining the scope of wireless technology's impact on VANET architecture, protocols, challenges, communication, applications, and future directions.

2.2   VANET ARCHITECTURE AND COMMUNICATION MODELS

VANETs are a subset of MANETs that provide two-way communication between vehicles and fixed infrastructure. There are three primary channels of information exchange in VANET design. VANETs are a subset of MANETs that provide two-way communication between vehicles and fixed infrastructure. There are three primary channels of information exchange in VANET design (Figure 2.1) (Table 2.1).

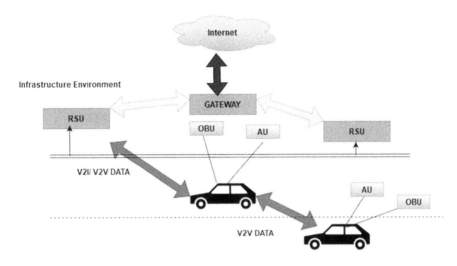

FIGURE 2.1   VANET architecture [12].

TABLE 2.1
Type of Communication Comparison

S.No.	Type of Communication	Description
1	Vehicle-to-Vehicle (V2V) Communication	V2V technology allows for two-way, direct communication between moving vehicles. This form of communication is required for usage in really real-time security systems. When automobiles are able to talk to one another, they may exchange information about their speeds and locations, which might greatly enhance road safety. If a vehicle detects an imminent collision and applies the brakes unexpectedly, it can send a signal to other vehicles to warn them.
2	Vehicle-to-Infrastructure (V2I) Communication	In V2I communication, automobiles and roadside facilities share information with one another. Some examples of this sort of infrastructure are traffic signals, road signage, toll booths, and in-road sensors. V2I communication is useful for optimizing traffic signals, managing traffic flow, and informing vehicles of road hazards, delays, and alternate routes. One way in which real-time traffic data is used to improve traffic flow and decrease congestion is by adjusting the timing of traffic lights
3	Vehicle-to-Everything (V2X) Communication	V2X is an expanded type of communication that goes beyond just Vehicle-to-Vehicle (V2V) and Vehicle-to-Infrastructure (V2I) to also include interactions with pedestrians (Vehicle-to-Pedestrian, or V2P) and other vehicles (Vehicle-to-Other, or V2O), such as bicycles and motorcycles. The goal of V2X is to establish an all-encompassing ecosystem for traffic control and road safety. Pedestrians can be warned of oncoming automobiles using V2P communication, while motorists can be made aware of vulnerable road users like bicyclists through V2O communication.

2.2.1 COMMUNICATION MODELS: BROADCAST, UNICAST, MULTICAST, AND GEOCAST

In VANETs, various communication models are used to transmit data among vehicles and infrastructure (Table 2.2).

2.3 WIRELESS TECHNOLOGIES ENABLING VANET SAFETY

Wireless technologies play a pivotal role in enhancing safety and communication within Vehicular Ad-Hoc Networks (VANETs), which are crucial for modern intelligent transportation systems. Below, an in-depth overview of each of the mentioned wireless technologies and their roles in ensuring VANET safety.

1. **IEEE 802.11p (WAVE - Wireless Access in Vehicular Environments):**
   - IEEE 802.11p, a standard under the Wireless Access in Vehicular Environments (WAVE) framework, is designed explicitly for VANETs. It operates in the 5.9GHz band and offers Dedicated Short Range Communication (DSRC) [13].
   - DSRC based on IEEE 802.11p is highly suitable for safety-critical applications, providing low latency, high-reliability communication among vehicles and infrastructure components. It facilitates vehicle-to-vehicle (V2V) and vehicle-to-infrastructure (V2I) communication.
   - Key safety applications include collision avoidance, traffic signal pre-emption, and cooperative awareness messages (CAMs) sharing real-time data on vehicle position, speed, and status.
2. **Cellular Technologies (e.g. 4G, 5G, and Beyond) in VANET Safety:**
   - Cellular technologies, including 4G LTE and 5G, offer an extended communication infrastructure for VANETs. They provide wider coverage and connectivity beyond DSRC's short range [14].
   - 4G LTE enables Vehicle-to-Infrastructure (V2I) communication, supporting applications like traffic management, navigation, and emergency services.
   - 5G and beyond are expected to revolutionize VANETs with ultra-low latency, high bandwidth, and massive device connectivity. They are well-suited for latency-sensitive safety applications like autonomous driving and cooperative collision avoidance.
3. **Emerging Technologies: 5G Vehicle-to-Everything (V2X) Communication:**
   - 5G V2X communication is a subset of 5G technology designed for VANETs. It enables vehicle-to-everything connectivity, encompassing V2V, V2I, vehicle-to-pedestrian (V2P), and vehicle-to-network (V2N) communication [11].
   - 5G V2X offers incredibly low latency (in the millisecond range), high reliability, and the capacity to handle massive device connectivity. These attributes are crucial for real-time safety-critical applications, such as autonomous driving, where split-second decisions are essential.

TABLE 2.2
A Comparison of Communication Models

S.No.	Type of Communication Model	Description	Use in VANETs	Security
1	Broadcast	In a broadcast communication model, a vehicle or infrastructure unit sends data to all nearby vehicles or infrastructure nodes	Broadcast is commonly used for safety-critical messages in V2V communication. Emergency warnings, such as sudden braking or accidents, are broadcasted to nearby vehicles to ensure that all potentially affected vehicles receive the alert.	This model is ideal for safety-critical messages that require immediate attention from nearby vehicles. It ensures that potentially affected vehicles are quickly alerted to hazards, improving overall road safety
2	Unicast	Unicast involves one-to-one communication, where data is transmitted from one vehicle or infrastructure node to a specific recipient.	Unicast can be used for less time-sensitive messages, such as navigation instructions or data exchange between specific vehicles and infrastructure units.	Unicast is useful for non-critical communication and data exchange. It can be employed for non-urgent updates and information sharing among vehicles and infrastructure units.
3	Multicast	Multicast is a one-to-many or few-to-many communication model, where data is sent to a selected group of vehicles or infrastructure nodes.	Multicast is useful for applications where a specific group of vehicles or infrastructure units needs to receive certain information. For example, a group of vehicles traveling together in a convoy can use multicast to share information among themselves.	Multicast is suitable for scenarios where specific groups of vehicles need to receive the same information simultaneously, such as coordinated maneuvers or convoy communication
4	Geocast	Geocast is a location-based communication model that delivers data to vehicles or infrastructure nodes within a specific geographic area.	Geocast is valuable for applications where information needs to be distributed to vehicles in a particular region. For instance, roadwork information can be geocast to vehicles approaching a construction zone.	Geocast is valuable for targeted information dissemination in specific geographic areas, which can be crucial for managing localized events like accidents or roadwork.

4. **Comparison of Different Wireless Technologies:**
   - Latency: IEEE 802.11p (DSRC) is known for its ultra-low latency, making it suitable for time-sensitive safety applications. Cellular technologies like 5G provide low latency as well, but the exact latency depends on network congestion and other factors.
   - Reliability: IEEE 802.11p and 5G V2X are designed with high reliability in mind, crucial for safety-critical applications. Cellular technologies offer robust reliability but may vary based on network conditions [15].
   - Coverage: IEEE 802.11p has a limited range, best suited for localized VANETs. Cellular technologies, especially 5G, provide broader coverage, making them suitable for urban and interurban VANETs.

2.4   CHALLENGES AND FUTURE DIRECTIONS IN VANET COMMUNICATION

Vehicular Ad-Hoc Networks (VANETs) hold great promise for improving road safety, traffic management, and overall transportation efficiency. However, they also face several challenges and opportunities for future development.

1. **Spectrum Allocation and Coexistence Challenges:**
   - *Limited Spectrum*: VANETs rely on dedicated radio frequencies for communication. The limited available spectrum poses challenges, especially as the number of connected vehicles increases. Competing with other wireless services for spectrum allocation is an ongoing issue.
   - *Coexistence with Other Wireless Systems*: Ensuring that VANETs can coexist with other wireless communication systems such as Wi-Fi and cellular networks is essential. Interference between different communication technologies can lead to disruptions in VANET communications.
   - *Dynamic Spectrum Access*: Future VANETs may benefit from technologies like dynamic spectrum access, which allows vehicles to opportunistically use available spectrum bands without causing interference. This requires regulatory changes and efficient spectrum management.

2. **Scalability Issues:**
   - *Efficient Communication*: As the number of vehicles on the road increases, the VANET must efficiently manage communication between a large number of vehicles. Scalability is crucial to maintain the low latency and reliability required for safety-critical applications.
   - *Network Overhead*: The management of routing tables, addressing, and message dissemination becomes more complex with a larger number of vehicles. Developing scalable routing algorithms and efficient protocols is essential.

3. **Privacy Concerns and Data Protection:**
   - *Location Privacy*: VANETs inherently involve the exchange of location and movement data. Protecting the privacy of drivers and passengers is a significant concern. Unauthorized access to this data can lead to tracking, profiling, and security risks.
   - *Secure Data Sharing*: Ensuring the security and integrity of data shared within VANETs is paramount. Protecting against cyberattacks and unauthorized access to critical safety-related information is an ongoing challenge.
   - *Anonymous Authentication*: Future VANETs may need to incorporate mechanisms for anonymous authentication, allowing vehicles to participate in communications without revealing their identity.

4. **Integration with Emerging Technologies:**
   - *Autonomous Vehicles*: VANETs play a crucial role in the communication between autonomous vehicles (AVs) for coordinated maneuvers and enhanced situational awareness. Integrating VANETs with AVs requires robust communication protocols and standards to ensure the safety of self-driving vehicles.
   - *AI and Machine Learning:* Using artificial intelligence, VANETs can anticipate traffic, optimize routes, and make split-second judgments. Machine learning algorithms may improve traffic management and safety by analyzing data from sensors and infrastructure.
   - *Edge Computing*: When linked into VANET infrastructure, edge computing can increase real-time data processing and decrease latency, enabling for speedier decisions to be made under duress.

2.5 COMMUNICATION PROTOCOLS AND STANDARDS IN VANETS

When it comes to safety-related applications, communication in Vehicular Ad-Hoc Networks (VANETs) must adhere to strict rules and standards. A summary of some important protocols and standards follows (Table 2.3).

2.5.1 SECURITY CONSIDERATIONS IN VANET COMMUNICATION

Security is a critical aspect of VANET communication, particularly for safety applications. Several security measures are essential as follows:

1. **Authentication:**
   - Vehicles and infrastructure must authenticate themselves to prevent unauthorized access and malicious entities from injecting false data.
   - Cryptographic techniques like digital signatures and public-key infrastructure (PKI) are commonly used for authentication.

TABLE 2.3

Comparison of Communication Protocols

Communication Protocol	Description	Use Case	Advantage
ETSI ITS-G5	ETSI (European Telecommunications Standards Institute) ITS-G5 is a set of European standards specifically developed for VANETs. It is based on IEEE 802.11p and adapts it to European regulatory requirements.	ETSI ITS-G5 is widely used for safety-critical applications in Europe, such as collision avoidance, traffic signal information exchange, and cooperative awareness messages (CAMs) dissemination.	It ensures interoperability among vehicles and infrastructure, making it suitable for cross-border travel within Europe.
IEEE 802.11p	IEEE 802.11p, often referred to as Wireless Access in Vehicular Environments (WAVE), is a standard designed for wireless communication in VANETs. It operates in the 5.9GHz band.	IEEE 802.11p is primarily used for safety applications in North America and some other regions. It supports V2V and V2I communication for applications like emergency braking warnings and intersection collision avoidance.	Its low latency and high reliability characteristics make it suitable for time-critical safety applications.
Cellular V2X (C-V2X):	Cellular V2X is an umbrella term for vehicular communication using cellular networks, particularly 4G LTE and 5G technologies. C-V2X can be further divided into two modes: direct communication (PC5) and network communication (Uu).	C-V2X offers a broader range of applications beyond safety, including infotainment, traffic management, and remote vehicle diagnostics. It can complement traditional VANET technologies.	C-V2X leverages the extensive cellular infrastructure and can provide broader coverage. It is adaptable to various use cases and can support both safety-critical and non-safety applications.

2. **Encryption:**
   - To protect the privacy and integrity of data exchanged in VANETs, encryption is crucial. It ensures that only authorized recipients can access and understand the data.
   - Advanced encryption standards (AES) and secure key management are employed to encrypt data.
3. **Message Integrity:**
   - Ensuring the integrity of safety-critical messages is vital. Any tampering with messages can have severe consequences.
   - Hash functions and message authentication codes (MACs) are used to verify message integrity.

2.5.2 QUALITY OF SERVICE (QoS) REQUIREMENTS FOR SAFETY-CRITICAL APPLICATIONS

Safety-critical applications in VANETs demand specific QoS requirements to ensure timely and reliable communication.

1. **Low Latency:** Safety messages must be delivered with minimal delay to support real-time decision-making, such as collision avoidance.
2. **High Reliability:** Communication must be highly reliable to avoid communication breakdowns during critical situations.
3. **Prioritization:** Safety-critical messages should be prioritized over non-critical ones to ensure they receive immediate attention.
4. **Redundancy:** Redundant communication paths are often employed to guarantee message delivery even in the presence of network disruptions.
5. **Scalability:** QoS mechanisms should be scalable to accommodate a growing number of vehicles on the road.

Balancing these QoS requirements with the constraints of the communication protocols and standards is a significant challenge in VANET design to ensure the effectiveness of safety applications in dynamic vehicular environments.

2.6 SAFETY APPLICATIONS AND USE CASES IN VANETS

Vehicular Ad-Hoc Networks (VANETs) are at the forefront of enhancing road safety through various applications and use cases. Here, we'll explore some of the critical safety applications enabled by VANETs (Table 2.4).

2.7 CASE STUDIES AND REAL-WORLD IMPLEMENTATIONS

These real-world examples highlight the various ways in which VANETs may be used to improve transportation safety, traffic management, and general efficiency. As the advantages of cooperative vehicular communication become clearer, VANET technology is projected to advance further (Table 2.5).

TABLE 2.4

Safety Application Comparisons

Application	Description	Working	Benefits
Collision Avoidance Systems	Collision avoidance systems leverage VANETs to enable real-time communication between vehicles, allowing them to exchange information about their speed, position, and trajectory. This information helps vehicles anticipate and avoid potential collisions [16]	When a vehicle detects a hazardous situation, such as sudden braking or an obstacle in its path, it broadcasts a warning message to nearby vehicles. These messages include critical data such as vehicle speed, direction, and location. Vehicles receiving these warnings can then take evasive action to prevent accidents	Collision avoidance systems reduce the likelihood of rear-end collisions, side collisions, and accidents at intersections. They enhance overall road safety by providing drivers with early warnings and additional time to react to potential threats.
Cooperative Adaptive Cruise Control (CACC) and Platooning	CACC and platooning are advanced traffic management and safety applications that rely on VANETs. CACC allows vehicles to maintain a safe following distance based on real-time communication with the leading vehicle, while platooning involves a group of vehicles traveling closely together in a coordinated manner [17,18].	Vehicles in a platoon maintain a constant and safe gap by adjusting their speed and distance according to data received from the leading vehicle. This coordination results in improved traffic flow, reduced congestion, and better fuel efficiency.	CACC and platooning enhance safety by reducing the likelihood of rear-end collisions and promoting smoother traffic flow. They also contribute to fuel savings and reduced emissions due to improved aerodynamics in platoons.

Intersection Collision Warning Systems and Red Light Violation Prevention	These safety applications focus on preventing accidents at intersections, where many accidents occur due to red light violations and poor visibility [19,20].	When approaching an intersection, vehicles having VANET technology can communicate with one another to share information. Warning messages are delivered to advise other motorists if one is likely to run a red light or if there is a risk of accident at an intersection.	Red light running incidents can be reduced by using an intersection collision warning system, which also increases safety for all drivers. Drivers are warned of impending danger so they can take the necessary precautions.
Pedestrian Safety through Vehicle-to-Pedestrian (V2P) Communication:	V2P communication is a critical component of VANETs, focusing on enhancing pedestrian safety [21].	Those on foot who have access to cellphones or wearable gadgets can exchange information with passing cars. A pedestrian can signal their position and intent to cross the road to approaching automobiles while they are in a crosswalk or about to cross the road. The cars will be able to alert their drivers of potential dangers.	To reduce the likelihood of accidents, especially in congested areas and at crosswalks, V2P communication raises vehicle awareness of pedestrians' presence and intentions.

TABLE 2.5

Comparison of Various Case Studies

S.No.	Case Study	Explanation
1	Intelligent Transportation Systems in Singapore	Singapore's Intelligent Transportation System (ITS) is fully operational, and it has a VANET component. In order to connect with Roadside Units (RSUs) installed at junctions and along roadways, vehicles are fitted with On-Board Units (OBUs). Drivers may get updates on traffic conditions, alerts on congestion, and notifications about potential road hazards with this system [22,23]. It's also useful for traffic control and boosting overall road safety.
2	Cooperative Intersection Collision Avoidance System (CICAS) in the US	The goal of the CICAS initiative is to prevent accidents at junctions [24,25], and it was launched by the United States Department of Transportation (USDOT). At crossroads, automobiles and infrastructure coordinate their communications. Drivers are notified of impending collisions and given the opportunity to avoid them by receiving alerts on their devices.
3	European Cooperative Vehicle-Infrastructure Systems (C-ITS)	To facilitate cooperative communication between cars and infrastructure, the European Union launched the C-ITS project [26,27] It covers a wide variety of uses, including the prioritizing of traffic signals, the warning of emergency vehicles, and the announcement of road construction. The goals of this proposal are to increase safety, decrease congestion, and better organize traffic flow.
4	Emergency Vehicle Preemption in New York City	In New York City, VANET technology has been used to enable emergency vehicle preemption at traffic signals [28]. When an emergency vehicle approaches an intersection, it sends a signal to nearby traffic signals to change their timing and allow the emergency vehicle to pass through more efficiently
5	VANET-based Parking Management in Barcelona	Drivers in Barcelona now have access to real-time data on parking availability thanks to a VANET-based parking management system [29]. Sensors in parking garages and garages report the availability of parking spots to passing cars. The time spent driving around looking for a parking spot is cut down significantly, and traffic congestion is also reduced.
6	Safety Applications in Japan	VANET-based safety applications have been the subject of study and implementation in Japan. Systems that alert drivers to people crossing the street and that offer information about traffic signal timings have been tried and tested, for instance, in an effort to reduce red light running[30].

2.8 CONCLUSION

This book chapter has shed light on the critical role that wireless technology plays in defining VANETs' safety concepts. The chapter has highlighted the synergistic contributions of VANET architecture, communication paradigms, and a spectrum of wireless technologies to improving safety in today's transportation networks. The benefits of collision avoidance techniques, cooperative adaptive cruise control, intersection collision alerts, and ground-breaking Vehicle-to-Pedestrian (V2P) communication protocols have been shown through real-world use cases, revealing a new universe of safety applications. These technologies have the potential to make our roads safer and more efficient in many ways. Strong authentication, encryption, and data integrity procedures are necessary because of the importance of communication protocols and the necessity of security measures. This chapter has also explored the difficulties associated with this revolutionary subject, from issues of spectrum allocation to the intricate combination of VANETs, autonomous cars, and new forms of artificial intelligence. Potential future elements are both exciting and enticing as we stand at a crossroads of growth. Connectivity and real-time data sharing are set to reach new heights with the arrival of intelligent transportation systems and the maturation of 5G and beyond. We may expect safer, more efficient, and better-coordinated transportation networks thanks to the continuous integration of VANETs with autonomous cars, powered by cutting-edge sensors and machine learning algorithms. The chapter also serves as a call to action for further study by shedding light on privacy problems and scalability challenges. To solve these issues and further improve VANET safety, new paradigms for data protection and robust communication frameworks must develop. With the groundwork set in this chapter, the future of wirelessly connected road safety is bright. Researchers, technologists, and politicians working together will usher in a new era when VANETs not only save lives but also reimagine what it means to be mobile. The use of wireless technology in VANETs to improve road safety is only getting started, and the future is full with possibilities.

REFERENCES

1. Bai, F., & Ning, H. (2015). Vehicular ad hoc networks: A new challenge for localization-based systems. IEEE Transactions on Vehicular Technology, 64(4), 1263–1278.
2. Raj, A., Sharma, V., & Shanu, A. K. (2022). Comparative analysis of security and privacy technique for federated learning In IOT based devices, 2022 3rd International Conference on Computation, Automation and Knowledge Management (ICCAKM), Dubai, United Arab Emirates, pp. 1–5, doi: 10.1109/ICCAKM54721.2022.9990152.
3. El-Beltagy, M., Mostafa, M., & El-Bendary, N. (2014). Vehicular ad hoc networks (VANETs) as a case study of human-centric applications of MANETs. Wireless Personal Communications, 79(3), 1785–1803.
4. Cheng, Y., Cheng, J., Xu, K., & Yang, L. T. (2013). VANET: On mobility modeling and impact of mobility on routing. IEEE Transactions on Vehicular Technology, 62(1), 254–268.
5. Ajmani, P., Sharma, V., Samuel, P., Somasundaram, K., & Vidhya, V. (2022). Patient behaviour analysis and social health predictions through IoMT. 2022 10th International

Conference on Reliability, Infocom Technologies and Optimization (Trends and Future Directions) (ICRITO), pp. 1–6, doi: 10.1109/ICRITO56286.2022.9964846.

6. Bettstetter, C., Hartenstein, H., & Pérez-Costa, X. (2005). Stochastic properties of the random waypoint mobility model. Wireless networks, 11(3), 357–369.

7. Uluagac, A. S., & Beyah, R. (2014). Security and privacy in vehicular networks: Recent advances and future directions. IEEE Communications Surveys & Tutorials, 16(1), 311–328.

8. Ali, M. A., Balamurugan, B., Dhanaraj, R. K., & Sharma, V. (2022). IoT and blockchain based smart agriculture monitoring and intelligence security system, 2022 3rd International Conference on Computation, Automation and Knowledge Management (ICCAKM), Dubai, United Arab Emirates, pp. 1–7, doi: 10.1109/ICCAKM54721.2022.9990243.

9. Sommer, C., German, R., & Dressler, F. (2010). Bidirectionally coupled network and road traffic simulation for improved IVC analysis. IEEE Transactions on Mobile Computing, 10(1), 3–15.

10. Gomez, C., Calderon, M., & Cano, J. C. (2014). Vehicular ad hoc networks (VANETs): A survey and tutorial on applications and challenges. The 5th International Conference on New Technologies, Mobility and Security (NTMS), Dubai, UAE.

11. Juyal, V. et. al. (2020). On exploiting dynamic trusted routing scheme in delay tolerant networks. Wireless Personal Communications, 112, 1705–1718.

12. Liang, W., Li, Z., Zhang, H., Wang, S., & Bie, R. (2015). Vehicular ad hoc networks: Architectures, research issues, methodologies, challenges, and trends. International Journal of Distributed Sensor Networks, 11(8), doi:10.1155/2015/745303

13. Juyal, V. et. al. (2016). An anatomy on routing in delay tolerant network. 2016 IEEE International Conference on Computational Intelligence and Computing Research (ICCIC), Chennai, pp. 1–4, doi: 10.1109/ICCIC.2016.7919724

14. Balapuwaduge, I. A. I., & Jamalipour, A. (2018). Integration of VANETs with LTE and 5G: RAN, core network, and backhaul perspectives. IEEE Communications Surveys & Tutorials, 20(1), 584–630.

15. Alam, M. M., Imran, M. A., & Shaikh, F. K. (2018). 5G-enabled vehicular communications for enhancing road safety and transportation systems. IEEE Communications Magazine, 56(12), 21–27.

16. Maurya, A., & Sharma, V. (2022). Facial emotion recognition using Keras and CNN. 2022 2nd International Conference on Advance Computing and Innovative Technologies in Engineering (ICACITE), pp. 2539–2543, doi: 10.1109/ICACITE53722.2022.9823480.

17. Khorov, E., Lyakhov, A., & Krotov, A. (2015). A survey on IEEE 802.11p PHY and MAC layers. IEEE Communications Surveys & Tutorials, 17(2), 1015–1027.

18. Banerjee, D., Kukreja, V., Hariharan, S., & Sharma, V. (2023). Fast and accurate multi-classification of kiwi fruit disease in leaves using deep learning approach. 2023 International Conference on Innovative Data Communication Technologies and Application (ICIDCA), Uttarakhand, India, pp. 131–137, doi: 10.1109/ICIDCA56705.2023.10099755.

19. Ferreira, J., Fonseca, B., Macedo, P., & Santos, J. (2018). A survey of vehicular collision avoidance systems. IEEE Transactions on Intelligent Transportation Systems, 19(10), 3322–3345.

20. Chen, Z., Liao, S., & Li, K. (2017). Cooperative adaptive cruise control and platooning of intelligent vehicles: A review. IEEE Transactions on Intelligent Transportation Systems, 18(7), 1680–1696.

21. Murali, M. N. R. D. S., & Sharma, V. (2022). Performance analysis of DGA-driven botnets using artificial neural networks. 2022 10th International Conference on

Reliability, Infocom Technologies and Optimization (Trends and Future Directions) (ICRITO), pp. 1–6, doi: 10.1109/ICRITO56286.2022.9965044.

22. Tientrakool, P., Pun-Cheng, L. S., & Hu, J. (2012). Intersection collision avoidance using vehicular communication: Design, implementation, and field testing. IEEE Transactions on Intelligent Transportation Systems, 13(4), 1490–1502.

23. Chi, Y. M., Chan, P. K., Safi-Harb, S. A., Baldini, R., Bernieri, D., Little, T. D. C., & Goodwin, R. B. (2012). Vehicle-to-Pedestrian (V2P) communication for pedestrian safety. 2012 Ninth International Symposium on Wireless Communication Systems, Paris, France, pp. 554–558.

24. Ng, K. H., Sengupta, R., & Chan, C. Y. (2008). Case Study: Singapore. In Intelligent Transportation Systems: Dependable Vehicular Communications for Improved Road Safety (pp. 109–116). Springer.

25. U.S. Department of Transportation (2019). Cooperative Intersection Collision Avoidance System (CICAS). https://www.its.dot.gov/research_areas/cicas.htm

26. New York City Department of Transportation (2021). Emergency Traffic Control Signal (TCS) System. https://www.nyc.gov/dot/trafficcabinet

27. Juyal, V. et. al. (2017). Opportunistic message forwarding in self organized cluster based DTN. 2017 International Conference on Infocom Technologies and Unmanned Systems (Trends and Future Directions)(ICTUS). IEEE.

28. Marfà, N., & Casanovas, J. (2011). Vehicular ad hoc networks (VANETs) applied to urban parking management. In 2011 IEEE 73rd Vehicular Technology Conference (VTC Spring), pp. 1–5. IEEE.

29. Nishio, K., Kawai, Y., & Obana, S. (2009). A safety application for the prevention of pedestrian accidents at intersections using inter-vehicle communications. In 2009 12th International IEEE Conference on Intelligent Transportation Systems, pp. 1–6. IEEE.

30. Juyal, V. et. al. (2017). Performance comparison of DTN multicasting routing algorithms-opportunities and challenges. 2017 International Conference on Intelligent Sustainable Systems (ICISS). IEEE.

3 Fuzzy Graph Dominance for Networked Communication Optimization

N. Yogeesh

Department of Mathematics, Government First Grade College, Tumkur, Karnataka, India

3.1 INTRODUCTION

Communication networks allow WSNs, IoT networks, and MANETs to operate efficiently in the modern, interconnected world. These networks' edges are the means via which nodes communicate. The performance of these networks is carefully optimized by modeling and analysis.

Because they accurately reflect the ambiguity and imprecision of actual networks, fuzzy graphs may be utilized to describe and investigate communication networks [1]. In order to describe and understand complex networks, such as communication networks, fuzzy graphs are used [2].

The coverage, connectivity, and energy efficiency of communication networks may all be improved via fuzzy graph dominance. According to dominance criteria, dominant nodes in fuzzy networks are those that control or have an effect on the network's other nodes [3]. It is possible to boost coverage, connection, monitoring, and control by carefully selecting the network's dominant nodes.

Fuzzy graphs and dominance for network optimization will be introduced in this chapter. The topics of fuzzy set theory, communication network representation, and adjacency matrix will also be explored. It will then dominate fuzzy graphs, including their sorts, traits, and characteristics. Coverage, connectivity, energy efficiency, and key nodes for monitoring and controlling communication networks are all improved by fuzzy graph dominance. We will last look at potential outcomes and issues related to fuzzy graph dominance in communication networks.

3.1.1 DEFINITION AND IMPORTANCE OF COMMUNICATION NETWORKS

Equipment, systems, and people may all connect thanks to communication networks. Wired or wireless networks are essential in modern life for the transmission of data, audio, and multimedia. Wireless sensor networks, internet of things (IoT) networks,

DOI: 10.1201/9781003389231-3

and mobile ad hoc networks are examples of communication networks that are designed for particular purposes [4].

For simple communication and collaboration, communication networks connect individuals, objects, and systems. Networks of communication help with business, science, education, healthcare, social interactions, and many other aspects of contemporary life. They have revolutionized international communication and information exchange, opening up the world.

Communication networks are essential to telecommunications, transportation, finance, energy, and industry. Real-time data communication facilitates automation, critical operations, and decision-making. Communication networks are required by the Internet of Things (IoT), which connects billions of devices globally [5].

Global connectivity, collaboration, and technological advancements in contemporary society and industry are made possible via communication networks.

3.1.2 Overview of Different Types of Communication Networks

There are major three types as follows:

- wireless sensor networks,
- IoT networks,
- mobile ad hoc networks.

The overview of various communication network types includes examples from wireless sensor networks, Internet of Things networks, and mobile ad hoc networks.

1. **Wireless Sensor Networks (WSNs):** Small, independent sensor nodes that can perceive, analyze data, and communicate with one another make up WSNs. These nodes cooperate to gather information from their environment and transmit it to a base station or a sink node where it will be processed and examined. WSNs are utilized for a variety of purposes, including monitoring the environment, delivering healthcare, farming, and automating manufacturing.

2. **Application Example:** An illustration of a wireless sensor network is a network of weather sensors installed in a forest to monitor temperature, humidity, and air quality. The sensor nodes gather data from their surroundings and transmit it to a base station for analysis. The sensor nodes feature monitors for temperature, humidity, and gases. The data collected may be used to forecast forest fires, monitor animals, and safeguard the environment.

3. **Internet of Things (IoT) Networks:** IoT networks are made up of interconnected items, often known as "things," that include sensors, actuators, and the communication capabilities to interact with one another. Smart homes, smart cities, and industrial automation are all made feasible by the communication between these devices and computers on the cloud. IoT networks may link several types of devices that communicate in a variety of ways and can be wired or wireless.

Application Example: An IoT network is an illustration of this. In this system, smart devices like as thermostats, lighting, and security cameras communicate with one another as well as a central hub or cloud server. The intelligent devices may be controlled remotely via a smartphone app or voice commands, and they can communicate with one another in accordance with preset rules or user preferences. This makes it simpler to handle and manage home security systems and appliances.

4. **Mobile Ad Hoc Networks (MANETs):** Mobile devices that can communicate with one another, such as laptops, cell phones, and tablets, make up MANETs. These devices do not rely on a fixed system or a single point of control. By establishing ad hoc connections with other nearby devices, these gadgets build a temporary network. They are always free to join or quit the network. MANETs are frequently utilized in circumstances when a permanent infrastructure is impractical or useless, such as during military operations, disaster relief efforts, and vehicle networks.

   Application Example: A fleet of emergency vehicles, such as ambulances, fire engines, and police cars, despatched to a disaster location is an illustration of a mobile ad hoc network. The cars communicate with one another directly or via a series of hops to relay crisis information in real-time, organize rescue operations, and make critical decisions immediately. MANETs provide communication in environments where there is no established infrastructure and things are constantly changing.

Each sort of information network has unique characteristics, issues, and applications. IoT networks enable diverse devices to join and collaborate in various ways, whereas wireless sensor networks are typically set up in harsh or remote locations to collect data. However, MANETs enable communication when a fixed infrastructure is impractical, such as when individuals are moving around a lot. If you want to create networking solutions that are effective for certain reasons, it is crucial to comprehend the differences and similarities between these different forms of communication networks.

3.1.3 INTRODUCTION TO FUZZY GRAPHS AND THEIR REPRESENTATION OF COMMUNICATION NETWORKS

The modern information and communication infrastructures depend on wireless sensor, Internet of Things, and mobile ad hoc networks. Devices are represented as nodes, and communication links between them are shown by edges [6]. Effective network management and optimization are required for connection, communication coverage, and energy efficiency.

In recent years, fuzzy graph theory has been used to define and understand complex systems, including communication networks. By giving links and nodes fuzzy values that denote varying degrees of membership or truth, fuzzy graphs enhance classical graphs. In real-world communication networks, uncertainty and imprecision can be better represented by fuzzy graphs.

The performance of communication networks can be enhanced via fuzzy graph dominance. Based on their fuzzy membership values, certain nodes in fuzzy graphs can dominate others [7]. Finding key nodes that control or are controlled by others facilitates resource distribution, network characteristic optimization, and performance enhancement.

Fuzzy graph-based dominance can identify critical sensor nodes with bigger membership values, implying relevance or dependability, for data aggregation or routing in wireless sensor networks. By identifying important devices that control communication lines or data flow, dominance in fuzzy graphs improves IoT network connectivity and energy efficiency. In order to improve multi-hop communication and network resilience in dynamic and mobile environments, fuzzy graph-based dominance may be used to identify dominant nodes in mobile ad hoc networks [8].

An interesting and promising technique for improving network performance and locating crucial nodes for monitoring or control is fuzzy graphs. This chapter will apply fuzzy graph theory to mobile ad hoc networks, Internet of Things networks, and wireless sensor networks with a focus on dominance and its advantages.

3.2 FUZZY GRAPH THEORY

Fuzzy graph theory is a powerful tool for describing and understanding complex systems because it can represent ambiguous and imprecise information. In fuzzy graphs, membership or truth is expressed using fuzzy values [2]. Fuzzy graphs more accurately represent real-world systems, particularly communication networks.

According to Bagga and Sharma, fuzzy graph theory may optimize communication networks such as mobile ad hoc networks, IoT networks, and wireless sensor networks [6]. According to Wang and Wang, dominance in fuzzy graph theory is the ability of specific nodes to control or outnumber other nodes in the network based on their fuzzy membership values [7].

In wireless sensor networks, crucial sensor nodes may be identified using fuzzy graph-based dominance [7]. Fuzzy graphs assist enhance IoT network connection and energy efficiency by identifying critical devices that dominate communication channels or regulate data flow [6]. For multi-hop communication and network dependability in mobile ad hoc networks, fuzzy graph-based dominance may be used to identify dominant nodes [7].

Theoretical fuzzy graphs can improve communication networks and pinpoint crucial nodes for control and monitoring. Wireless sensor networks, Internet of Things networks, and mobile ad hoc networks can all benefit from dominance in fuzzy graphs [5].

3.2.1 BASICS OF FUZZY SET THEORY

In order to account for ambiguity and vagueness in information representation, Zadeh developed fuzzy set theory in 1965. Fuzzy set theory is used in AI, decision-making, control systems, and communication networks [2].

The membership or truthfulness of an element is indicated by membership functions in fuzzy set theory. According to Klir and Yuan [8], membership functions with triangular, trapezoidal, Gaussian, and sigmoidal shapes can represent uncertainties and imprecisions in the actual world.

An element may be a member of a number of fuzzy sets with varying degrees of membership. Due to their flexibility, fuzzy sets can describe and study complex systems with ambiguity and uncertainty.

The connectivity, reliability, and energy efficiency of communication network nodes may be reflected using fuzzy set theory. Signal strength, latency, and quality of service in communication connections may all be measured using fuzzy sets. By resolving uncertainties and imprecisions, fuzzy set theory enhances network performance and decision-making [9].

3.2.2 Definition and Properties of Fuzzy Graphs

By assigning edges and nodes fuzzy values that indicate how much they belong to the graph or how much of it is true, fuzzy graphs are an extension of standard graphs [2]. Mathematical patterns known as fuzzy graphs may be used to analyze and explain complex systems, including communication networks.

Fuzzy Graph Definition: A fuzzy graph G is defined as a pair (V, E), where V is a finite set of nodes or vertices, and E is a fuzzy relation on $V \times V$, which represents the fuzzy edges or communication links between nodes. The fuzzy relation E assigns a membership value to each pair of nodes (u, v) in $V \times V$, denoted as $E(u, v)$, which represents the degree of membership or truthfulness of the edge between nodes u and v in the graph G [7].

Example of a Fuzzy Graph:
Consider a communication network consisting of five sensor nodes labeled as A, B, C, D, and E. The fuzzy edges between the nodes can be represented using a fuzzy relation E on $V \times V$, where $V = \{A, B, C, D, E\}$.

The fuzzy relation E can be represented using a membership matrix as follows:

The fuzzy membership values (Figure 3.1) in this instance demonstrate how reliable or significant the communication relationships between nodes are. A node A and itself have an extremely trustworthy communication relationship if the edge (A, A) has a membership value of 0.9, for instance. The edge (A, C) has a lesser degree of dependability than the edge (B, B), which has the maximum level of reliability.

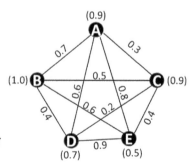

FIGURE 3.1 Graph to show fuzzy membership of truthfulness.

Membership value of edge (A, B) = 0.8
Membership value of edge (A, C) = 0.6
Membership value of edge (B, D) = 0.9
Membership value of edge (C, D) = 0.7

FIGURE 3.2 Membership values that show how strong the links between them.

The degree to which each node dominates the fuzzy graph, fuzzy connection metrics, and fuzzy operations for reasoning and decision-making may all be determined based on this fuzzy relation.

Properties of Fuzzy Graphs:

1. **Fuzzy Membership Values:** The membership values assigned to the edges or nodes in a fuzzy network indicate how accurate or significant the links between them are. According to Wang and Wang [7], these membership values may be utilized to express the uncertainty, fuzziness, and imprecision of communication channels, such as signal strength, reliability, and service quality.

   Consider a fuzzy network with nodes A, B, C, and D, as well as fuzzy edges with membership values that indicate the degree of the connections between them. The fuzzy membership values for the edges can be described in several ways, for instance as follows:

   These membership values show how honest or connected the communication links between the nodes are (Figure 3.2). Links with higher values are more connected.

2. **Degree of Domination:** Domination is a key concept in fuzzy graph theory, which refers to the ability of certain nodes to influence or control other nodes in the graph based on their fuzzy membership values. The degree of domination of a node u in a fuzzy graph G is defined as the maximum membership value of the fuzzy relation $E(u, v)$ for all nodes v in V, denoted as $dom(u) = \max\{E(u, v) \mid v \in V\}$ [6].

   In a fuzzy network, a node's level of control is determined by how much it is related to or has influence on other nodes. Fuzzy control measures like fuzzy total dominance, fuzzy paired domination, or fuzzy independent domination can be used to calculate it.

   For example, the degree of dominance of node A in the fuzzy graph above can be found by:

   Degree of domination of node $A = $ *fuzzy total domination of* $\{A\} = \max\{0.8, 0.6\} = 0.8$

3. **Fuzzy Connectivity:** Depending on the membership values of the fuzzy lines, fuzzy graphs can exhibit various degrees of connection between nodes, ranging from complete connection to partial connection to no connection at all. These degrees of connection can be displayed in a variety of ways. Fuzzy connectedness metrics, such as the fuzzy k-neighborhood and fuzzy clustering coefficient, may be used to gauge how linked fuzzy graphs are and examine their structural characteristics, according to Wang and Wang [7].

In a fuzzy graph, fuzzy connectivity measures measure how linked the nodes are, taking into account the fuzzy membership values of the edges. There are many other forms of fuzzy connectedness measurements, such as the fuzzy α -connection, the fuzzy β -connection, and the fuzzy γ -connection.

For example, the fuzzy -connection between nodes A and D in the fuzzy graph above can be found as follows:

Fuzzy α − connection between A and D = min$\{0.8, 0.7\}$ = 0.7

4. **Fuzzy Operations:** Fuzzy networks may be manipulated and combined using fuzzy operations including fuzzy union, fuzzy intersection, fuzzy complement, and fuzzy composition [8]. These fuzzy processes provide a versatile and effective technique to reason, reach judgments, and take actions in fuzzy graphs.

Fuzzy operations in fuzzy graph theory enable reasoning, judgment, and inference based on fuzzy sets and fuzzy relations. There are several types of fuzzy functions, including fuzzy complement, fuzzy union, fuzzy intersection, and fuzzy composition.

For example, here's how to figure out the fuzzy union of the edges (A, B) and (A, C):

Fuzzy union of (A, B) and (A, C) = max$\{0.8, 0.6\}$ = 0.8

Due to their characteristics, fuzzy graphs may be used to represent and investigate communication networks. This is so that real-world systems' complexity, imprecision, and uncertainty may be shown using fuzzy graphs.

3.2.3   FUZZY REPRESENTATION OF COMMUNICATION NETWORKS

Fuzzy graphs are used to characterize the connections, coverage, and energy economy of communication network models (Figure 3.3). Fuzzy graphs feature nodes that stand in for objects and edges that stand in for lines of communication. Fuzzy membership values on the edges demonstrate how closely or loosely the nodes are related.

Here is an example of a fuzzy graph model of a communication network with five devices (A, B, C, D, and E) and their respective fuzzy membership values for communication links.

The nodes A, B, C, D, and E in the aforementioned fuzzy graph represent communication network equipment, while the edges represent the connections between them. Greater links between nodes are indicated by edges with higher fuzzy membership values (from 0 to 1).

This fuzzy graph structure can improve the efficiency of communication network components such as key nodes for monitoring or controlling, communication coverage,

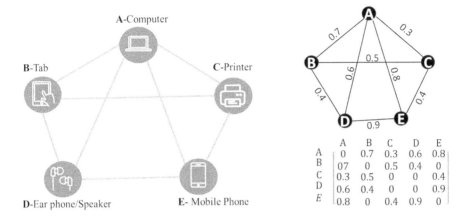

A-Computer

B-Tab

C-Printer

D-Ear phone/Speaker

E- Mobile Phone

	A	B	C	D	E
A	0	0.7	0.3	0.6	0.8
B	07	0	0.5	0.4	0
C	0.3	0.5	0	0	0.4
D	0.6	0.4	0	0	0.9
E	0.8	0	0.4	0.9	0

FIGURE 3.3 Fuzzy graph shows communication network devices as nodes and their communication linkages as edges with example.

and connectivity. With uncertain or inaccurate information, fuzzy graph theory aids communication networks in making better judgments and optimizing their operations.

Example: A wireless sensor network with several sensor nodes analyzes environmental parameters in a sizable agricultural area. The sensor nodes communicate with a central base station to share information on temperature, humidity, soil moisture, and light intensity.

This wireless sensor network may be represented graphically as a fuzzy graph with nodes denoting sensor nodes and edges denoting communication links. The strength of a communication link can be indicated via fuzzy membership values on edges based on signal strength, distance, or other factors (Figure 3.4).

We may see the fuzzy graph using a graphical application.

The edges represent communication paths between sensor nodes A, B, C, and D of the wireless sensor network. Greater communication linkages are implied by edges with higher values for fuzzy membership.

By identifying critical nodes for data aggregation, increasing communication coverage and connection, and improving energy efficiency by choosing the most

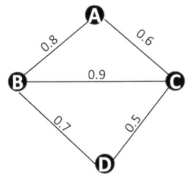

FIGURE 3.4 Fuzzy membership values on edges can reflect communication connection strength.

reliable communication links based on fuzzy membership values, this fuzzy graph representation may optimize the wireless sensor network.

3.2.4 FUZZY ADJACENCY MATRIX AND ITS INTERPRETATION

The fuzzy membership values or levels of dominance between two nodes in a fuzzy network are described by fuzzy adjacency matrices. The strength of node connections in a fuzzy network is displayed in the fuzzy adjacency matrix.

Understanding the significance of fuzzy adjacency matrix membership values or degrees of dominance is necessary. The connectivity, communication coverage, or energy efficiency of fuzzy graph nodes may all be expressed as fuzzy membership values. Weaker relationships are indicated by lower fuzzy membership values.

Take a fuzzy adjacency matrix for a wireless sensor network.

Nodes	A	B	C	D
A	0.9	0.7	0.3	0.6
B	0.7	1.0	0.5	0.4
C	0.3	0.5	0.9	0.2
D	0.6	0.4	0.2	0.7

Fuzzy membership values in this fuzzy adjacency matrix represent the strength of links between nodes in a wireless sensor network. Node A and itself have a fuzzy membership score of 0.9, which indicates great communication or connection coverage. A weaker relationship to Node C than to itself is shown by Node A's fuzzy membership score of 0.3.

The connectivity, communication coverage, and energy efficiency of the fuzzy graph may be explained using the fuzzy adjacency matrix. By choosing the most dependable communication lines based on fuzzy membership values, it may also be able to identify crucial nodes for monitoring or controlling, optimize communication coverage or connection, and increase energy efficiency [10].

Fuzzy graphs reflect the fuzzy adjacency matrix (Figure 3.5).

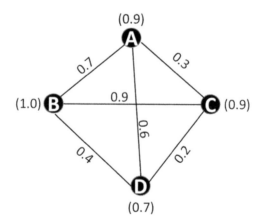

FIGURE 3.5   Graphical representation of the given fuzzy adjacency matrix.

The edges connecting the nodes A, B, C, and D, which stand for communication network devices, show the fuzzy membership values or levels of dominance between node pairs as seen in the fuzzy adjacency matrix. By displaying the connectivity and power of the communication network's devices, it is possible to better comprehend the characteristics of the fuzzy graph.

3.3 DOMINATION IN FUZZY GRAPHS

3.3.1 DEFINITION OF DOMINATION IN FUZZY GRAPHS

Domination in fuzzy graph theory means one or more nodes controlling or influencing other nodes. Degrees of membership or domination in fuzzy graphs indicate how much a node controls or impacts other nodes.

In a fuzzy graph $G = (V, E)$, where V is the set of nodes and E is the set of edges, a node u dominates a node v if its degree of membership or domination is greater than or equal to a threshold value. The threshold value indicates u's power over v.

Applications use different definitions of fuzzy graph dominance. Depending on how fuzzy linked or near a node is to another, it will dominate other nodes in fuzzy k-dominating sets.

Dominance in fuzzy graphs is used to assess complex systems represented as fuzzy graphs, identify essential nodes for monitoring or management, and enhance communication coverage, connection, and energy efficiency in communication networks.

An example to illustrate the concept of domination in fuzzy graphs.
Consider a fuzzy graph $G = (V, E)$ with the following fuzzy adjacency matrix (Figure 3.6).

To control another node, a node must have a degree of membership or dominance of 0.6 or above.

This threshold value determines fuzzy graph dominance connections. Such as:

1. Node A dominates node B because the degree of membership of A with respect to B is 0.7, which is greater than the threshold value of 0.6.
2. Node B dominates node C because the degree of membership of B with respect to C is 0.5, which is higher than the threshold value of 0.6.

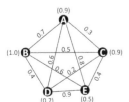

FIGURE 3.6 An illustrate of the concept of domination in fuzzy graphs using adjacency matrix.

3. Node D dominates node E because the degree of membership of D with
   respect to E is 0.9, which is higher than the threshold value of 0.6.

In this example, the fuzzy membership values in the adjacency matrix generate
domination connections, and the threshold value for domination determines whether
a node dominates another in the fuzzy network.

Fuzzy graphs' definition of domination and threshold value can be changed to fit
the application or study.

Definition: Let $G = (V, E)$ be a fuzzy graph with fuzzy adjacency matrix
$F = [f_{ij}]$, where $V = \{v_1, v_2, ..., v_n\}$ is the set of vertices (nodes) and $E \subseteq V \times V$
is the set of edges (links). Let $F(v_i, v_j)$ denote the degree of membership
or degree of domination of vertex vi with respect to vertex vj in the fuzzy
graph.

A vertex v_i is said to dominate vertex v_j in the fuzzy graph G if and only if:

$$F(v_i, v_j) \geq \alpha, \quad for\ some\ \alpha \in [0,1]$$

where α is the threshold value for domination, and $F(v_i, v_j)$ represents the degree of
membership or degree of domination of vertex v_i with respect to vertex v_j in the
fuzzy adjacency matrix.

In other words, vertex v_i dominates vertex v_j if the degree of membership or degree
of domination of v_i with respect to v_j is equal to or greater than the threshold value α.

Based on the degree of membership or degree of domination values in the fuzzy
adjacency matrix, this equational definition enables the determination of domination
relationships in fuzzy graphs, and the threshold value can be modified to meet the
needs of the particular application or analysis.

3.3.2   DIFFERENT TYPES OF FUZZY DOMINATION (TOTAL DOMINATION, STRONG DOMINATION, WEAK DOMINATION)

Fuzzy domination in fuzzy graphs can be categorized into different types based on
the strength and extent of domination. The three commonly recognized types of
fuzzy domination are as follows:

1. **Total domination:** A vertex v_i is said to totally dominate a vertex v_j if the
   degree of membership or degree of domination of v_i with respect to v_j is
   equal to 1, i.e. $F(v_i, v_j) = 1$. This means that v_i has complete control or
   influence over v_j in the fuzzy graph, and v_j is fully dominated by v_i.

   Example: Consider a fuzzy graph with the following fuzzy adjacency
   matrix (Figure 3.7).

   In this case, vertex A totally dominates vertex D, as $F(A, D) = 1$,
   indicating that A has complete control or influence over D in the fuzzy
   graph.

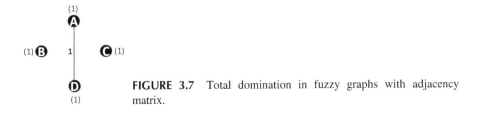

FIGURE 3.7 Total domination in fuzzy graphs with adjacency matrix.

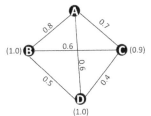

FIGURE 3.8 Strong domination in fuzzy graphs with adjacency matrix.

2. **Strong domination:** A vertex v_i is said to strongly dominate a vertex v_j if the degree of membership or degree of domination of v_i with respect to v_j is greater than the threshold value α, i.e. $F(v_i, v_j) > \alpha$. This means that v_i has a significant level of control or influence over v_j in the fuzzy graph, and v_j is dominated by v_i with a high degree of membership or domination.

   Example: Consider a fuzzy graph with the following fuzzy adjacency matrix (Figure 3.8).

   In this case, vertex A strongly dominates vertex B and vertex C, as $F(A, B) > \alpha$ and $F(A, C) > \alpha$, where α is the threshold value. This indicates that A has a significant level of control or influence over B and C in the fuzzy graph.

3. **Weak domination:** A vertex v_i is said to weakly dominate a vertex v_j if the degree of membership or degree of domination of v_i with respect to v_j is equal to or greater than the threshold value α, i.e. $F(vi, vj) \geq \alpha$. This means that v_i has some level of control or influence over v_j in the fuzzy graph, and v_j is dominated by v_i with a certain degree of membership or domination, which may not be complete or strong.

   Example: Consider a fuzzy graph with the following fuzzy adjacency matrix (Figure 3.9).

   In this case, vertex A weakly dominates vertex B, C, and D, as $F(A, B) \geq \alpha$, $F(A, C) \geq \alpha$, and $F(A, D) \geq \alpha$, where α is the threshold value. This indicates that A has some level of control or influence over B, C, and D in the fuzzy graph, though it may not be complete or strong.

   These fuzzy domination types describe the strength and size of the connections that dominate vertices in fuzzy graphs, allowing for more in-depth optimization and analysis of communication networks as well as other uses of fuzzy graph theory.

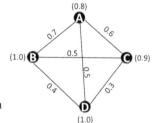

FIGURE 3.9 Weak domination in fuzzy graphs with adjacency matrix.

3.3.3 PROPERTIES AND CHARACTERISTICS OF DOMINATION IN FUZZY GRAPHS

Domination in fuzzy graphs has several properties and characteristics, which are as follows:

- **Reflexivity:** Every vertex in a fuzzy graph dominates itself, i.e. $F(v, v) = 1$, where v is a vertex in the fuzzy graph. This property indicates that a vertex always has a certain degree of control or influence over itself.

    Example: Let's consider a fuzzy graph with a single vertex A, and the fuzzy membership value of A dominating itself is 0.8. Then, the adjacency matrix for this fuzzy graph would be (Figure 3.10):
    This indicates that A dominates itself with a fuzzy membership value of 0.8, satisfying the reflexivity property.
- **Transitivity:** If vertex u dominates vertex v and vertex v dominates vertex w, then vertex u dominates vertex w, i.e. if $F(u, v) > \alpha$ and $F(v, w) > \alpha$, then $F(u, w) > \alpha$, where α is the threshold value. This property indicates that domination in fuzzy graphs can be propagated through multiple vertices in a transitive manner.

    Example: Let's consider a fuzzy graph with three vertices A, B, and C, and the following fuzzy membership values (Figure 3.11).
    Here, A dominates B with a fuzzy membership value of 0.6, and B dominates C with a fuzzy membership value of 0.5. We can calculate the fuzzy membership value of A dominating C using the transitivity property:

$$F(A, B) = 0.6$$

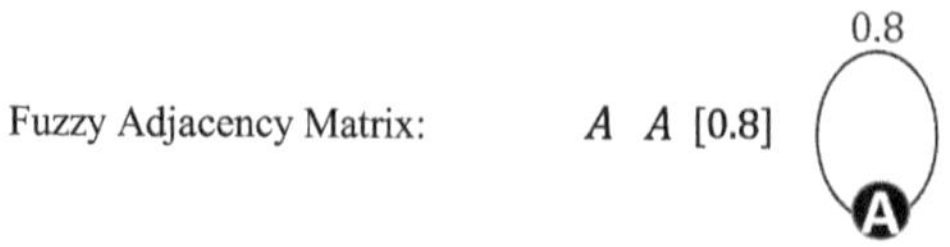

Fuzzy Adjacency Matrix: $A \quad A \; [0.8]$ 0.8
                                                          A

FIGURE 3.10 Showing reflexive property of domination in fuzzy graphs.

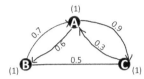

FIGURE 3.11   Showing transitive property of domination in fuzzy graphs.

$$F(B, C) = 0.5$$

$$F(A, C) = \min\{F(A, B), F(B, C)\} = \min\{0.6, 0.5\} = 0.5$$

This indicates that A dominates C with a fuzzy membership value of 0.5,
satisfying the transitivity property.

- **Anti-symmetry:** Domination in fuzzy graphs is anti-symmetric, meaning that if vertex u dominates vertex v, then v cannot dominate u unless $u = v$, i.e. if $F(u, v) > \alpha$, then $F(v, u) = 1$ or $F(v, u) < \alpha$, where α is the threshold value. This property indicates that domination in fuzzy graphs is directional and asymmetrical.

  Example: Let's consider a fuzzy graph with two vertices A and B, and the following fuzzy membership values (Figure 3.12).

  Here, A dominates B with a fuzzy membership value of 0.8, but B does not dominate A as $F(B, A) = 0.4$, which is less than 1. This satisfies the anti-symmetry property, indicating that domination in fuzzy graphs is anti-symmetric.

- **Partial domination:** In fuzzy graphs, a vertex may not have full or total control over another vertex. Instead, it may only have a certain amount of control or effect, which is shown by fuzzy membership values that range from 0 to 1.

  Example: Let's consider a fuzzy graph with two vertices A and B, and the following fuzzy membership values (Figure 3.13).

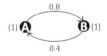

FIGURE 3.12   Showing anti-symmetry property of domination in fuzzy graphs.

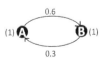

FIGURE 3.13   Showing partial domination in fuzzy graphs.

Here, A dominates B with a flexible membership value of 0.6, which means that A has some control or influence over B but not full dominance. This meets the condition of partial dominance.

- **Threshold-based:** Dominance in fuzzy graphs frequently depends on a threshold value. This indicates that the dominance of one point over another is determined by a threshold value. dominance is said to exist if the fuzzy membership value of dominance between two points is greater than the threshold value. If it falls below the threshold value, dominance is not present.

  Example: Let's consider a fuzzy graph with three vertices A, B, and C, and the following fuzzy membership values (Figure 3.14).

  If we set the threshold value $\alpha = 0.6$, then A dominates B and C with fuzzy membership values of 0.7 and 0.9, respectively, which are both greater than α. However, B does not dominate A as $F(B, A) = 0.6$, which is not greater than α. This indicates that domination in fuzzy graphs is threshold-based, and depends on the threshold value chosen.

- **Degree of domination:** The degree of dominance in a fuzzy graph may vary depending on the fuzzy membership numbers. Higher fuzzy membership values indicate a more dominating group, whereas lower values indicate a weaker dominant group.

  Example: Let's consider a fuzzy graph with two vertices A and B, and the following fuzzy membership values (Figure 3.15).

  Here, A dominates B with a fuzzy membership value of 0.6, and B dominates A with a fuzzy membership value of 0.3. This indicates that there is a degree of domination between A and B, where A has a higher degree of domination over B compared to B's domination over A. This satisfies the property of the degree of domination in fuzzy graphs.

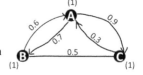

FIGURE 3.14 Showing threshold-based value of domination in fuzzy graphs.

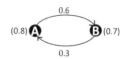

FIGURE 3.15 Showing degree of domination in fuzzy graphs.

Because domination in fuzzy graphs has these qualities and traits, it can be used to model and study real-world systems where the idea of dominance or control is naturally uncertain or fuzzy.

3.3.4 APPLICATIONS OF FUZZY GRAPH DOMINATION IN COMMUNICATION NETWORKS

In information networks, the idea of fuzzy graph control can be used in a number of ways, such as[11–13]:

- **Optimization of communication coverage:** The placement of communication equipment, such as wireless sensor nodes or Internet of Things (IoT) devices, may be optimized via fuzzy graph dominance to cover the network as completely as feasible while limiting redundancy and energy expenditure. This is accomplished by identifying the dominant nodes in a communication network known as the key nodes.
- **Connectivity enhancement:** By employing fuzzy graph dominance to identify dominant nodes that can serve as switches or linkages between disconnected portions of the network, connectivity can be increased. This can facilitate the establishment of reliable communication channels and enhance the overall connectivity and stability of the network.
- **Energy efficiency improvement:** Finding the dominant nodes in a communication network that can manage and control the communication activities of the other nodes in the most effective manner can help to increase energy efficiency. This technique is known as fuzzy graph domination. The network may use less energy by strategically placing these dominating nodes, increasing energy efficiency and lengthening network lifespan.
- **Fault tolerance and resilience:** By identifying dominant nodes that may act as fallback or alternate nodes in the event that a node fails or the network goes down, fuzzy graph dominance can be used to increase the fault tolerance and resilience of a communication network. This can ensure that communication doesn't break off and that the network is steady and dependable.
- **Monitoring and controlling a network:** For the purpose of monitoring and regulating a communication network, critical nodes may be located using fuzzy graph dominance. To gather network data, manage the network, or implement network rules, you can choose dominating nodes as monitoring or control points. This improves the efficiency of network administration and control.

In communication networks, employing fuzzy graph dominance can assist increase network speed, ease connection, use less energy, ensure there are no issues, and make it simpler to monitor and manage the network.

3.4   OPTIMIZATION OF COMMUNICATION NETWORKS USING FUZZY GRAPH DOMINATION

3.4.1   UTILIZING FUZZY DOMINATION TO OPTIMIZE COMMUNICATION COVERAGE IN NETWORKS

By identifying crucial nodes that outperform others in communication range or signal strength, fuzzy dominance helps maximize network communication coverage. These dominant nodes can be strategically placed to increase network coverage while reducing redundant operations and energy consumption.

Wireless sensor nodes having a better fuzzy membership value for communication range can be found using fuzzy dominance. These dominant nodes may purposefully use significant events or activities to strategically cover important areas or locations[14].

Devices having a higher signal strength fuzzy membership value can be identified in an IoT network using fuzzy dominance. These remarkable devices may be carefully placed to optimize network coverage[15,16].

When nodes connect without infrastructure, fuzzy dominance can maximize communication coverage in mobile ad hoc networks (MANETs). To increase communication coverage, dominant nodes can be positioned as relay nodes or bridges between dispersed network components based on their fuzzy membership values related to communication range, signal strength, or other factors[17].

Network coverage, connectivity, and reliability may all be improved thanks to fuzzy dominance, which can also raise network performance and resource utilization.

This graphic shows how fuzzy dominance may optimize network communication coverage.

Consider a wireless sensor network with 5 sensor nodes represented as nodes A, B, C, D, and E. The communication coverage of each sensor node is represented by fuzzy membership values as shown in the following graph (Figure 3.16).

The communication range of each sensor node is displayed on this graph as fuzzy membership values in brackets. A greater range is implied by higher values. Fuzzy membership scores for Nodes A and E are higher than those for the others (0.9 and 0.8), indicating a larger range of communication.

Nodes A and E are dominant nodes in fuzzy graphs because they have higher fuzzy membership values than B, C, and D. These dominant nodes might cover key hotspots or locations that require improved communication coverage.

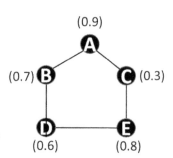

FIGURE 3.16 Showing fuzzy dominance may optimize network communication coverage.

While node E can serve a specific area with high communication demands from the edge of the network, node A can serve a larger area of the network from a central location. These dominant nodes have the ability to optimize network communication, enhancing connectivity, coverage, and energy efficiency.

3.4.2   IMPROVING CONNECTIVITY AND ENERGY EFFICIENCY OF NETWORKS USING FUZZY DOMINATION

A diagram showing how fuzzy dominance may increase network connection and energy efficiency [5].

A mobile ad hoc network (MANET) with six nodes—A, B, C, D, E, and F—is considered. The following graph shows fuzzy membership values representing connectedness between these nodes (Figure 3.17):

In this network, higher fuzzy membership values indicate a greater degree of connectivity between the nodes. The fuzzy membership values of A, C, and D are higher than those of their neighbors (0.8, 0.9, and 0.7, respectively), which indicates that these nodes have a stronger connectivity.

The fact that nodes C and D have bigger fuzzy membership values than their neighbors A, B, E, and F is the primary reason why these nodes are dominating. The connectivity of a network as well as its energy efficiency can be improved by dominant nodes.

The connection and communication between nodes A and D can be improved thanks to node C, which acts as a relay node. Node D is also capable of performing the function of a central node, which enables it to coordinate the communication and routing options of the network, hence lowering the communication overhead and increasing the energy efficiency.

The dominance of fuzzy logic can improve the connection rates and energy efficiency of this network, leading to enhanced MANET functionality and reliability.

3.4.3   IDENTIFYING KEY NODES FOR MONITORING AND CONTROL PURPOSES USING FUZZY DOMINATION

Fuzzy dominance may be used to identify critical nodes for monitoring and control, which is helpful when trying to manage and regulate communication networks, in

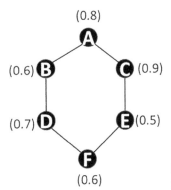

FIGURE 3.17   Showing fuzzy membership values representing connectedness.

particular wireless sensor networks. For the purposes of monitoring and management, fuzzy dominance can locate important nodes, including:

Imagine a wireless sensor network with a great number of sensor nodes that are linked together by fuzzy membership values that indicate the degree of connection. The values of fuzzy membership are determined by the signal strength, distance, reliability, and other features of the network [18].

i. **Graphical Representation:** The edges represent fuzzy membership values that show the connectivity strength between pairs of nodes, while the nodes themselves serve as the representation of sensors. The fuzzy membership value contributes to an increase in the connectivity of nodes.

ii. **Fuzzy Domination Calculation:** A fuzzy dominance calculation might be used to determine the value of each network node's position of dominance. The values of the nodes that are nearby are used in the computation of node dominance. A node that has higher fuzzy membership values than its neighbors will dominate those neighbors.

iii. **Key Node Identification:** Monitoring and exerting influence over high-dominance nodes is possible. These nodes have a higher connectivity than the others, which gives them a dominant position in the network. Selecting essential nodes for monitoring and control is a crucial step in managing a network.

iv. **Decision-Making:** The fuzzy dominance graph of the network may be used to assist in selecting key nodes for the purposes of monitoring and control. Key nodes that have higher dominance ratings are more linked to other nodes and are thus more likely to have an effect on how the network functions.

The use of fuzzy dominance helps improve network performance, energy efficiency, and optimization in communication networks, particularly wireless sensor networks. Essential nodes may be identified for monitoring and management using fuzzy dominance.

A wireless sensor network represented as a fuzzy graph, together with fuzzy dominance computation, key node identification, decision-making, and adjacency matrix representation.

1. **Graphical Representation:** Taken into consideration a wireless sensor network that consists of six sensor nodes denoted as nodes A, B, C, D, and E, respectively (Figure 3.18). The membership values of these fuzzy networks are used to describe the connectedness between these sensor nodes, as seen in the fuzzy graph that follows:

2. **Adjacency Matrix Representation:** It is possible to describe the fuzzy network as an adjacency matrix, with rows and columns standing in for individual nodes and the entries of the matrix denoting fuzzy membership values that indicate the degree of connection

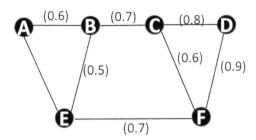

FIGURE 3.18   Showing fuzzy membership values of 6 sensor nodes.

strength between different pairs of nodes. The adjacency matrix of fuzzy graphs.

According to what was previously said, the adjacency matrix has the potential to produce fuzzy dominance values and locate essential nodes.

The application of fuzzy dominance to the task of locating essential nodes in communication networks for the purposes of control and monitoring can help optimize network operations for environmental monitoring, surveillance, and industrial control systems. Administration and management of a network may be improved by the use of graphical depictions, fuzzy dominance computations, the identification of critical nodes, and decision-making.

3. **Fuzzy Domination Calculation:** The values of each node's fuzzy dominance may be determined based on the values of its fuzzy membership that are neighboring nodes. The dominance value of Node B is as follows:

Based on the adjacency matrix with fuzzy graph representation provided earlier, let's denote the fuzzy membership values between nodes i and j as $\mu(i, j)$. We can calculate the fuzzy domination values (Dom) for all the nodes using the following mathematical equation:

$$Dom(i) = \max(\min(\mu(i, j), \mu(j, i))) \, for \, all \, j \neq i$$

Here's the calculation for the fuzzy domination values for all the nodes in the given example graph.

Node A:
Dom(A) = max(min(μ(A, B), μ(B, A)), min(μ(A, C), μ(C, A)), min(μ(A, D), μ(D, A)), min(μ(A, E), μ(E, A)), min(μ(A, F), μ(F, A)))
    = max(min(0, 0), min(0, 0), min(0, 0), min(0, 0), min(0, 0))
    = max(0, 0, 0, 0, 0)
    = 0

Node B:
Dom(B) = max(min(μ(B, A), μ(A, B)), min(μ(B, C), μ(C, B)), min(μ(B, D), μ(D, B)), min(μ(B, E), μ(E, B)), min(μ(B, F), μ(F, B)))

= max(min(0, 0), min(0.6, 0.7), min(0, 0), min(0, 0), min(0.5, 0))

= max(0, 0.6, 0, 0, 0)

= 0.6

Node C:

Dom(C) = max(min(μ(C, A), μ(A, C)), min(μ(C, B), μ(B, C)), min(μ(C, D), μ(D, C)), min(μ(C, E), μ(E, C)), min(μ(C, F), μ(F, C)))

= max(min(0, 0), min(0, 0), min(0.8, 0.6), min(0, 0), min(0, 0))

= max(0, 0, 0.8, 0, 0)

= 0.8

Node D:

Dom(D) = max(min(μ(D, A), μ(A, D)), min(μ(D, B), μ(B, D)), min(μ(D, C), μ(C, D)), min(μ(D, E), μ(E, D)), min(μ(D, F), μ(F, D)))

= max(min(0, 0), min(0, 0), min(0, 0), min(0.9, 0), min(0, 0))

= max(0, 0, 0, 0.9, 0)

= 0.9

Node E:

Dom(E) = max(min(μ(E, A), μ(A, E)), min(μ(E, B), μ(B, E)), min(μ(E, C), μ(C, E)), min(μ(E, D), μ(D, E)), min(μ(E, F), μ(F, E)))

= max(min(0, 0), min(0.5, 0), min(0, 0), min(0, 0), min(0, 0))

= max(0, 0.5, 0, 0, 0)

= 0.5

Node F:

Dom(F) = max(min(μ(F, A), μ(A, F)), min(μ(F, B), μ(B, F)), min(μ(F, C), μ(C, F)), min(μ(F, D), μ(D, F)), min(μ(F, E), μ(E, F)))

= max(min(0, 0), min(0, 0.8), min(0, 0), min(0, 0), min(0, 0.5))

= max(0, 0, 0, 0, 0)

= 0

So, the fuzzy domination values for all the nodes in the given example graph are: Dom(A) = 0; Dom(B) = 0.6; Dom(C) = 0.8; Dom(D) = 0.9; Dom(E) = 0.5; Dom(F) = 0

Fuzzy membership values between nodes determine each node's degree of dominance over other nodes in the network. Domination values imply node dominance.

3.4.4 CASE STUDIES AND EXAMPLES OF FUZZY GRAPH DOMINATION IN REAL-WORLD COMMUNICATION NETWORKS

3.4.4.1 Case Study: Fuzzy Graph Domination in a Wireless Sensor Network

Imagine a portable sensor network with ten sensor nodes that are dispersed over an area in order to monitor things such as the temperature, the humidity, and the intensity of the light. The following graph demonstrates that fuzzy membership values are used to represent the connections that exist between various sensor nodes [18]:

The higher the fuzzy membership values in brackets, the more likely it is that the communication links between the sensor nodes in this network are strong. Both D and I have the highest fuzzy membership values of 1.0, which indicates that we have the most robust communication ties with our neighbors.

Let's compute the fuzzy dominance values for each sensor node that makes up the wireless sensor network. The fuzzy dominance value of a node is calculated by adding the fuzzy membership values of that node and its neighbors. When the dominance value is normalized, it is calculated by dividing it by the total domination value of the network (Table 3.1 and Figure 3.19).

The determination of fuzzy dominance values, which sensor nodes within a wireless sensor network are the most significant for the purposes of tracking and regulating (Figure 3.20). Nodes C and D both have values of 0.686 for their fuzzy dominance coefficients, which indicates that they are considered dominating nodes within the network since they have the most impact on it.

TABLE 3.1

Calculation of Fuzzy Domination Values for Each Sensor Node

Node	Fuzzy Membership Value	Dominating Neighbors	Fuzzy Domination Value
A	0.8	B (0.6), C (0.9)	1.3 / 3.5 = 0.371
B	0.6	A (0.8), C (0.9)	1.7 / 3.5 = 0.486
C	0.9	A (0.8), B (0.6), D (1.0)	2.4 / 3.5 = 0.686
D	1.0	C (0.9), E (0.7), I (0.8)	2.4 / 3.5 = 0.686
E	0.7	D (1.0), H (0.7)	1.7 / 3.5 = 0.486
F	0.5	G (0.6)	1.1 / 3.5 = 0.314
G	0.6	F (0.5), H (0.7)	1.3 / 3.5 = 0.371
H	0.7	E (0.7), G (0.6)	1.3 / 3.5 = 0.371
I	0.8	D (1.0), J (0.9)	1.7 / 3.5 = 0.486
J	0.9	I (0.8)	1.7 / 3.5 = 0.486

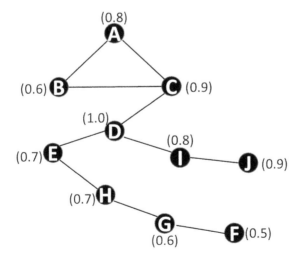

FIGURE 3.19 Showing fuzzy graph domination in a wireless sensor network.

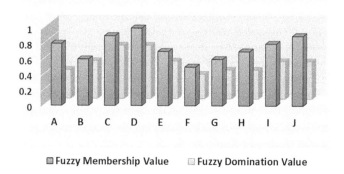

□ Fuzzy Membership Value   □ Fuzzy Domination Value

FIGURE 3.20   Graph showing the calculation of fuzzy domination values for each sensor node.

In the same wireless sensor network, let's have a look at an additional illustration of fuzzy graph control. We make use of a threshold of 0.5 in order to identify the dominating nodes. Nodes that have values for their soft controls that are more than 0.5 are said to as dominant nodes.

C and D are strong nodes because the fuzzy dominance values they have are more than 0.5, which is the threshold for power in this network. These nodes have the most power in the network and may be used to accomplish essential tasks like aggregate data, determine how to route it, or operate actuators. Other nodes in the network are less powerful.

Some ways fuzzy graph dominance can be used in wireless sensor networks:

i. **Data Aggregation:** Finding the dominating nodes in a fuzzy network may be accomplished with the help of the dominance technique. Once identified, these nodes can be utilized to gather and process input from their nearby nodes. This not only reduces the amount of needless interaction, but it also helps save energy.

ii. **Routing Decisions:** It is possible to employ dominant nodes in a network to determine routing decisions since these nodes are able to transfer data packets more quickly than other nodes in the network because of the strong connections they have with their neighbors.

iii. **Actuator Control:** Actuator control is possible through the use of dominating nodes in wireless sensor networks. They are able to provide commands to operate actuators such as motors, valves, and switches in accordance with the requirements of the network.

Conclusion: In wireless sensor networks, fuzzy graph control can be an effective method for determining which nodes have the most influence over the network as a whole. We are able to understand, with the assistance of the case study and the examples provided, how fuzzy graph dominance may be utilized in real-world wireless sensor networks for activities such as the collection of data, the determination of appropriate routing, and the control of actuators.

3.5   FUTURE DIRECTIONS AND CHALLENGES

3.5.1   Emerging Trends and Potential Applications of Fuzzy Graph Domination in Communication Networks

Possibly employed in forthcoming communication network developments is fuzzy graph dominance. The following are emerging trends and uses for fuzzy graph domination[18]:

- **Internet of Things (IoT):** In IoT networks, which are being used in smart cities, smart homes, and industrial automation, fuzzy graph dominance can maximize communication coverage, energy efficiency, and network connectivity. Network speed may be improved by using fuzzy graph dominance to manage and control IoT devices[10].
- **5G and beyond networks:** It is anticipated that these networks would feature dynamic topologies with a wide range of devices and services. In these networks, dominating nodes may be found using fuzzy graph dominance for network management, resource allocation, and service delivery[19].
- **Edge computing networks:** Computing and processing that is distributed and performed close to the source of the data. It is possible for fuzzy graph dominance to identify dominant nodes at the edge of the network. These nodes have the potential to function as local data processing centers and to make decisions in real-time without transferring data to the cloud or to central data centers, therefore improving the effectiveness of the network[20].
- **Social networks:** The concept of fuzzy graph dominance allows for the identification of dominant nodes or individuals in social networks who have a significant impact on the processes of information dissemination, opinion formation, and social dynamics. The concept of fuzzy graph dominance has applications in areas such as social impact research, recommendation systems, and targeted advertising[21].
- **Cybersecurity:** The dominance of fuzzy graphs may be used to identify crucial nodes in communication networks that are vulnerable to attacks or failures in the network. The network's resilience and security may be improved, and the number of cyber attacks can be decreased, by locating and protecting its dominating nodes[22].
- **Smart transportation networks:** Intelligent transportation systems (ITS) and vehicular ad hoc networks (VANETs) employ fuzzy graph dominance to identify dominating nodes that can help control traffic, optimize routes, and enhance road safety. These systems are also known as "connected vehicles."
- **Emergency communication networks:** During times of crisis, communication networks serve to coordinate the efforts of those working to save lives and provide aid. The detection of dominating nodes in emergency communication networks with the use of fuzzy graph dominance helps enhance the communication and coordination of emergency responders[23].

The domination of fuzzy graphs may improve network performance, energy efficiency, and security, as well as enable a number of applications in a wide range of industries, which is an important trend in increasing communication networks. This study has the potential to result in novel approaches to communication network problems.

3.5.2 CHALLENGES AND LIMITATIONS OF USING FUZZY GRAPHS FOR NETWORK OPTIMIZATION

Fuzzy graphs can optimize communication networks, but they have drawbacks. These obstacles include:

- **Computational Complexity:** Fuzzy graph techniques are computationally complex, particularly for large networks. Fuzzy graph domination analysis can be computationally expensive, making it impractical in real-time or resource-constrained applications to find dominant nodes, determine dominating nodes, or optimize network parameters based on fuzzy graph domination.
- **Lack of Standardization:** Metrics, techniques, and procedures for determining fuzzy graph dominance are not standardized. Due to different studies' fuzzy graph models, interpretations, and prevailing definitions, results and comparisons may differ. It is challenging to compare and replicate study results across investigations due to a lack of uniformity.
- **Subjectivity and Uncertainty:** Fuzzy graphs are built on subjective interpretations of fuzzy membership functions, which leads to subjectivity and uncertainty. Results might become subjective and unclear when membership functions, language expressions, and fuzzy thresholds are used. Subjective judgments can be drawn from fuzzy dominance interpretation and dominant node selection depending on the context or application.
- **Data gathering and Representation:** Data gathering and representation for fuzzy graph creation might be challenging due to real-world communication networks. Noise, errors, or inadequate data from wireless sensor networks, IoT devices, or other sources may have an impact on fuzzy graph representations. Fuzzy graphs also have trouble expressing dynamic or time-varying network characteristics.
- **Lack of Scalability:** Fuzzy graph dominance techniques may not function well in large networks with plenty of nodes and edges. For large networks, fuzzy graph approaches could become too computationally intensive, rendering fuzzy graph dominance useless.
- **Interpretability and Visualization:** Fuzzy graphs and dominance measures may be challenging to understand and visualize in complex networks. The language terms, fuzzy dominance values, and fuzzy membership functions may be difficult for non-experts or decision-makers to understand.
- **Limitations of Application Domains:** Most communication, social, and transportation networks employ fuzzy graph dominance. Further investigation

is required to assess the potential of fuzzy graph domination because it could be constrained in other disciplines or industries.

Fuzzy graph dominance has shown potential for communication network optimization despite these challenges. Real-world network optimization methods can be improved by addressing these problems and boosting fuzzy graph dominance.

3.5.3 FUTURE RESEARCH DIRECTIONS AND AREAS OF IMPROVEMENT

As is the case with every field of study, the dominance of fuzzy graphs in communication networks is undergoing change and offers numerous new directions for research and development. Some examples are as follows:

- **Standardization:** Standardization improves research consistency and comparability by standardizing fuzzy graph-dominating terminology, metrics, and methods. Create a unified framework for fuzzy graph dominance, standardize fuzzy thresholds, fuzzy membership functions, and linguistic terms, and establish clear standards for defining fuzzy dominance and choosing dominant nodes[24].
- **Scalability and Efficiency:** It is possible to investigate fuzzy graph dominance methods for large-scale networks with numerous nodes and edges. The computational complexity and efficiency of the fuzzy graph dominance method can be reduced by using parallel processing, distributed computing, and approximation[25].
- **Handling Subjectivity and Uncertainty:** Fuzzy graph dominance can manage subjectivity and uncertainty with more research. In order to achieve this, it may be necessary to develop techniques for dealing with ambiguous or incomplete data, incorporate domain-specific knowledge or expert opinions into fuzzy graph models, and quantify and control subjectivity in fuzzy graph dominance results.
- **Visualization and Interpretability:** Making fuzzy graph dominance results simpler to comprehend and depict can help non-experts and decision-makers. Visualization and Interpretability. In order to do this, it may be necessary to develop visualizations or graphical representations that effectively communicate fuzzy dominance values, membership functions, and linguistic notions, as well as strategies to intuitively assess fuzzy graph domination results.
- **Application to New Domains:** Although it may be applied in other areas, fuzzy graph dominance has mostly been employed in communication networks. In social, transportation, healthcare, and financial networks, fuzzy graph dominance may be examined to see how effective and efficient it is.
- **Real-world Validation and Testing:** Fuzzy graph dominance approaches are tested in communication networks to ascertain their viability and robustness in the real-world. Installing fuzzy graph dominance algorithms

in actual communication networks, collecting empirical data, and evaluating their effectiveness could be necessary to achieve this.

- **Hybrid strategies**: More efficient and reliable network optimization solutions may be produced by combining fuzzy graph dominance with other optimization techniques like machine learning, meta-heuristics, or game theory. Fuzzy graph dominance and other optimization techniques can be used in hybrid ways to enhance network optimization algorithms.

One potential area of research for network optimization is fuzzy graph dominance in communication networks. Future research might concentrate on standardization, scalability, addressing subjectivity and uncertainty, visualization and interpretability, application to new domains, real-world validation, and hybrid techniques to develop the area and make it more useful for real-world communication networks [26,27].

3.6 CONCLUSION

3.6.1 IMPORTANCE OF FUZZY GRAPH DOMINATION IN OPTIMIZING COMMUNICATION NETWORKS

The fuzzy graph dominance optimization process is used to improve communication networks.

Enhanced Connectivity: By identifying dominant nodes in a communication network using fuzzy graph dominance, network connectivity is made better. Hub functions are performed by dominant nodes, which enhance network connectivity and communication efficiency.

Energy Efficiency: By identifying dominant nodes as relay nodes or cluster heads, fuzzy graph dominance may improve communication networks, resulting in effective data routing and less energy use. Particularly in environments with limited resources, such wireless sensor networks, fuzzy graph dominance minimizes redundant communication and optimizes routing patterns, making communication networks energy-efficient.

Network Resilience: Fuzzy graph dominance can identify key nodes for communication network resilience and robustness. To ensure dependable communication and network operation even during failures, interruptions, or attacks, these crucial nodes can be watched over or regulated. By identifying and managing important nodes, fuzzy graph dominance can improve communication networks.

Network Monitoring and Control: Fuzzy graph dominance can find dominant nodes that can monitor or control communication networks, which is useful for network monitoring and control. These dominant nodes have the ability to acquire information, strategically monitor network activity, and even change it, leading to better network management, resource allocation, and performance optimization.

Optimal Resource Allocation: Fuzzy graph dominance facilitates resource allocation for communication networks. Network resources like bandwidth, power, and storage may be efficiently distributed to dominant nodes in order to enhance network performance.

Decision-making Support: By exposing node dominance links, fuzzy graph domination enables decision-makers to plan, build, and manage communication networks. Fuzzy graph dominance reveals node significance and dominance, which aids in the optimization of communication networks.

By detecting dominant nodes, enhancing network connection, energy efficiency, resilience, monitoring and control, resource allocation, and decision-making, fuzzy graph dominance aids in the optimization of communication networks.

3.6.2 Conclusion and Final Remarks

A powerful method for building communication networks is fuzzy graph dominance. By exposing node dominance connections, it helps to improve node connectivity, energy efficiency, resilience, monitoring and control, resource allocation, and network planning and management. Network optimization using fuzzy graphs is challenging because fuzzy graph representation, fuzzy dominance methods, and fuzzy membership functions are complicated and arbitrary. Further research is necessary to resolve these problems and create a more effective and efficient fuzzy graph dominance in communication networks.

Despite these issues, fuzzy graph dominance holds a lot of potential and has been used to wireless sensor networks, social networks, transportation networks, and telecommunications networks. It is anticipated that fuzzy graph dominance would aid in managing and optimizing communication networks as they grow and become more complex.

A prospective area for research in communication networks is fuzzy graph dominance. Numerous communication network applications and domains will profit from this research's ability to improve network performance, connectivity, resource allocation, and operation.

REFERENCES

1. Zhang, X. (2017). Fuzzy graph theory: A survey. Fuzzy Information and Engineering, 9(2), 179–196.
2. Zadeh, L. A. (1965). Fuzzy sets. Information and Control, 8(3), 338–353.
3. Bhattacharya, P., Ghosh, A., & Ghosh, D. (2015). Fuzzy domination in fuzzy graphs. Fuzzy Sets and Systems, 267, 120–133.
4. Akyildiz, I. F., Su, W., Sankarasubramaniam, Y., & Cayirci, E. (2002). Wireless sensor networks: a survey. Computer Networks, 38(4), 393–422.
5. Ghosal, D., & Chaki, R. (2014). Fuzzy graph-based approach for energy-efficient routing in wireless sensor networks. Soft Computing, 18(1), 1–12.
6. Bagga, A., & Sharma, R. (2018). Fuzzy graph theory: A review. Soft Computing, 22(19), 6505–6530.
7. Wang, X., & Wang, Z. (2019). Fuzzy graph theory and applications. CRC Press.

8. Klir, G. J., & Yuan, B. (1995). Fuzzy sets and fuzzy logic: Theory and applications. Prentice Hall.

9. Chen, S. M., & Ye, J. J. (2013). Fuzzy graph theory with applications to human computer interaction. CRC Press.

10. Juyal, V. et. al. (2020). On exploiting dynamic trusted routing scheme in delay tolerant networks. Wireless Personal Communications, 112, 1705–1718.

11. Dubey, A., & Shukla, A. (2017). Fuzzy graphs and their applications in wireless sensor networks: A review. Wireless Personal Communications, 95(2), 383–407.

12. Dash, S., Mishra, M. K., & Kar, S. (2018). Fuzzy graph theory: A review. In Advanced computational techniques in energy, power, electric vehicles, and their integration (pp. 163–190). Springer.

13. Garg, H., & Kumar, A. (2019). A comprehensive review on fuzzy graph theory and its applications in computer science. Soft Computing, 23(14), 6021–6052.

14. Raghavendra, C. S., Sivalingam, K. M., Znati, T. F., & Ammar, M. H. (2006). Wireless sensor networks: a survey. Computer Networks, 50(4), 593–615.

15. Juyal, V. et. al. (2017). Opportunistic message forwarding in self organized cluster based DTN. 2017 International Conference on Infocom Technologies and Unmanned Systems (Trends and Future Directions)(ICTUS). IEEE.

16. Murali, M. N. R. D. S., & Sharma, V. (2022). Performance analysis of DGA-driven botnets using artificial neural networks. 2022 10th International Conference on Reliability, Infocom Technologies and Optimization (Trends and Future Directions) (ICRITO), pp. 1–6. doi: 10.1109/ICRITO56286.2022.9965044.

17. Alippi, C., & Roveri, M. (2010). Energy-efficient management of wireless sensor networks via automatic programming. IEEE Transactions on Instrumentation and Measurement, 59(9), 2328–2336.

18. Ammari, A. C., & Cheng, X. (2015). Energy-aware fuzzy cluster head selection for wireless sensor networks. Applied Soft Computing, 35, 46–60.

19. Girija, D. K., Rashmi, M., William, P., & Yogeesh, N. (2023). Framework for integrating the synergies of blockchain with AI and IoT for secure distributed systems. In: Chaki, N., Roy, N. D., Debnath, P., Saeed, K. (eds) Proceedings of International Conference on Data Analytics and Insights, ICDAI 2023. ICDAI 2023. Lecture Notes in Networks and Systems, vol 727. Springer. 10.1007/978-981-99-3 878-0_22.

20. Ali, M. A., Balamurugan, B., Dhanaraj, R. K., & Sharma, V. (2022). IoT and blockchain based smart agriculture monitoring and intelligence security system. 2022 3rd International Conference on Computation, Automation and Knowledge Management (ICCAKM), Dubai, United Arab Emirates, pp. 1–7. doi: 10.1109/ICCAKM54721.2022. 9990243.

21. Raj, A., Sharma, V., & Shanu, A. K. (2022). Comparative analysis of security and privacy technique for federated learning in IOT based devices, 2022 3rd International Conference on Computation, Automation and Knowledge Management (ICCAKM), Dubai, United Arab Emirates, pp. 1–5. doi: 10.1109/ICCAKM54721.2022.9990152.

22. Yogeesh N., & Chenniappan, Dr. P.K. (2012). A conceptual discussion about an intuitionistic fuzzy-sets and its applications. International Journal of Advanced Research in IT and Engineering, 1(6), 45–55.

23. Yogeesh, N., & Chenniappan, Dr. P.K. (2013). Study on intuitionistic fuzzy graphs and its applications in the field of real world. International Journal of Advanced Research in Engineering and Applied Sciences, 2(1), 104–114.

24. Yogeesh, N., Girija, D. K., Rashmi, M., & Divyashree, J. (2023). Exploring the potential of fuzzy domination graphs in aquatic animal health and survival studies. Journal of Survey in Fisheries Sciences (SFS), 10(4S), 3133–3147. ISSN: 2368-7487.

25. Yogeesh, N., Girija, D. K., Rashmi, M., & William, P. (July 2023). Fuzzy logic-based beat tracking in music signals. Musik In Bayern, 88(09), 145–157. doi 10.15463/gfbm-mib-2023-343

26. Juyal, V. et. al. (2017). Performance comparison of DTN multicasting routing algorithms-opportunities and challenges. 2017 International Conference on Intelligent Sustainable Systems (ICISS). IEEE.

27. Juyal, V. et. al. (2016). An anatomy on routing in delay tolerant network. 2016 IEEE International Conference on Computational Intelligence and Computing Research (ICCIC), Chennai, pp. 1–4. doi: 10.1109/ICCIC.2016.7919724

4 IoT Sensor Communication Using Wireless Technology

Jagjit Singh Dhatterwal
Department of Artificial Intelligence & Data Science,
Koneru Lakshmaiah Education Foundation, Vaddeswaram,
Andhra Pradesh, India

Kuldeep Singh Kaswan
School of Computer Science and Engineering,
Galgotias University, Greater Noida, Uttar Pradesh, India

Prashant Johri
School of Computer Applications and Technology,
Galgotias University, Greater Noida, India

4.1 INTRODUCTION

The rapid advancement of technology in recent years has paved the way for the widespread adoption of the Internet of Things (IoT), revolutionizing the way we interact with the world around us. Central to the success of IoT is the seamless communication between numerous interconnected devices and at the heart of this communication lies wireless technology. The chapter "IoT Sensor Communication Using Wireless Technology" explores the pivotal role of wireless communication in enabling efficient and reliable data exchange among IoT sensors, opening new horizons for innovation and problem solving across various domains.

Wireless technology serves as the backbone of IoT sensor networks, facilitating real-time data collection and transmission from diverse sensor nodes to centralized processing units. It provides the flexibility and scalability required to accommodate the exponential growth of IoT devices in the modern era [1]. Multiple wireless communication protocols have emerged to cater to specific IoT application requirements, such as Wi-Fi, which offers high data transfer rates and is commonly used in home automation and smart city deployments [2]. On the other hand, Zigbee and Bluetooth Low Energy (BLE) are preferred for low-power applications, such as wearable devices and smart healthcare solutions [3]. Long Range (LoRa) and Narrowband IoT (NB-IoT) technologies have gained traction in agriculture and environmental monitoring, thanks to their long-range capabilities and energy efficiency [4,5].

DOI: 10.1201/9781003389231-4

However, with the proliferation of IoT devices, security and privacy concerns have become paramount. As data flows through wireless channels, it becomes vulnerable to various threats, including eavesdropping, unauthorized access, and data manipulation [6]. Thus, robust security mechanisms must be integrated into IoT sensor communication systems to safeguard sensitive information [7].

In this chapter, we delve into the fundamental principles of wireless communication in IoT sensor networks, providing a comprehensive analysis of the strengths and limitations of various wireless technologies. Through a series of real-world case studies, we demonstrate the practical implementation of wireless communication in IoT applications, ranging from smart cities to healthcare and industrial automation [8–10].

The goal of this chapter is to equip readers with a deeper understanding of the intricacies involved in IoT sensor communication using wireless technology. By exploring the existing challenges and emerging trends, we aim to inspire researchers and practitioners to drive innovation in this fast-evolving field, unlocking the full potential of IoT for a smarter and interconnected future.

4.2 INTERNET OF THINGS

The "Internet of Things" (IoT) has emerged as a transformative technology paradigm, revolutionizing the way we interact with our surroundings and fostering unprecedented connectivity among various objects and devices. At the heart of IoT lies the seamless and efficient communication between interconnected sensors, and wireless technology plays a crucial role in enabling this exchange of data [11]. IoT encompasses a vast network of smart devices, ranging from household appliances and wearables to industrial machinery and environmental sensors, all equipped with communication capabilities [12]. The wireless communication protocols employed in IoT sensor networks are designed to accommodate the diverse requirements of different applications. For instance, Wi-Fi provides high data transfer rates, making it suitable for bandwidth-intensive applications like multimedia streaming and real-time monitoring [13]. On the other hand, Zigbee and Bluetooth Low Energy (BLE) are ideal for low power, short-range communication, making them suitable for energy-efficient, battery-operated devices [14]. However, the rapid growth of IoT devices has raised security concerns, as sensitive data flows through wireless channels, making it susceptible to potential threats and attacks [15]. Robust security mechanisms, including encryption and authentication protocols, are essential to safeguard IoT communications [6]. IoT's exponential growth and innovation heavily rely on wireless technology for seamless sensor communication. As this technology continues to evolve, it holds the promise of transforming industries and enhancing our daily lives in profound ways [16].

4.3 WIRELESS COMMUNICATION TECHNOLOGIES AND INTERNET OF THINGS

Wireless communication technologies play a pivotal role in the successful implementation of the Internet of Things (IoT), enabling seamless connectivity and data exchange between IoT devices and sensors. These technologies serve as the backbone of IoT sensor communication, facilitating the real-time transmission of data from diverse IoT nodes to centralized processing units [17].

Various wireless communication protocols have been adopted to cater to the specific requirements of IoT applications. Wi-Fi, known for its high data transfer rates, is commonly used in IoT deployments involving multimedia streaming and real-time monitoring. On the other hand, Zigbee and Bluetooth Low Energy (BLE) are preferred for low power, short-range communication, making them suitable for battery-operated IoT devices such as wearables and smart home sensors [18]. Long Range (LoRa) and Narrowband IoT (NB-IoT) technologies have gained prominence in IoT applications that demand long-range communication and energy efficiency, making them suitable for smart agriculture, environmental monitoring, and smart cities. Security and privacy are critical concerns in IoT sensor communication. As wireless communication forms the basis for data exchange in IoT, robust security measures are essential to protect against potential threats and breaches [19].

4.3.1 IoT Communication Protocols

In the context of IoT Sensor Communication Using Wireless Technology, the selection of appropriate communication protocols is a critical aspect of ensuring efficient and reliable data exchange among interconnected devices and sensors. Various IoT communication protocols have been developed to address the diverse requirements of different applications, offering unique advantages and capabilities to support the ever-expanding IoT ecosystem.

MQTT is a lightweight and efficient publish-subscribe messaging protocol that excels in low-bandwidth and high-latency networks, making it ideal for IoT applications [20]. It minimizes data transmission overhead, reducing power consumption for battery-operated IoT devices. MQTT's simplicity and scalability have led to its widespread adoption in smart home automation, industrial automation, and telemetry systems [21]. Designed for resource-constrained devices, CoAP is a lightweight application-layer protocol that operates over UDP, providing efficient communication in IoT networks [22]. It is particularly suitable for IoT devices with limited processing power and memory, such as sensors and actuators. CoAP's simplicity and support for various message types enable seamless integration with HTTP-based applications, extending its usability across multiple domains, including smart cities and healthcare [23]. AMQP is a robust and feature-rich protocol designed for high-performance messaging in enterprise-scale IoT deployments [24]. It provides reliable message delivery, enabling complex communication patterns in large-scale IoT systems. AMQP's support for message queuing, routing, and security features has made it a preferred choice for mission-critical IoT applications, such as asset tracking and supply chain management [25]. Though primarily associated with web communication, HTTP has found application in IoT due to its ubiquity and compatibility with existing internet infrastructure [26]. It allows seamless integration of IoT devices with web services and cloud platforms, facilitating data exchange and remote device management. However, HTTP's high overhead makes it less suitable for resource-constrained IoT devices and low-bandwidth networks. DDS is a middleware standard designed for real-time and mission-critical IoT applications that demand high-performance data communication [27]. It enables data-centric communication, supporting both publish-subscribe and point-to-point communication models. DDS's reliability and low-latency communication have led to its adoption in industries like healthcare, transportation, and aerospace [28]. LoRaWAN is a Low-Power Wide-Area Network (LPWAN) protocol designed for long-range communication with low-power consumption, making it suitable for IoT applications covering vast areas [29]. LoRaWAN's architecture allows for flexible deployment of private and public networks, enabling various IoT use cases, including smart agriculture, environmental monitoring, and asset tracking [30]. Zigbee is a low power, short-range wireless protocol that operates on the IEEE 802.15.4 standard, designed for reliable communication in home and industrial automation scenarios [31]. Zigbee's mesh networking capability enhances the coverage area by allowing devices to relay data, improving overall network robustness. It is commonly used in smart home applications, building automation, and lighting control systems [32]. BLE is a power-efficient wireless communication protocol suitable for IoT devices with limited battery capacity, such as wearables and health monitoring devices [33]. BLE's ability to establish direct communication between devices, without the need for a centralized hub, makes it ideal for point-to-point and peer-to-peer applications. It is widely used in consumer IoT products like fitness trackers, smartwatches, and smart locks [34].

4.3.2 SENSOR TECHNOLOGIES FOR WIRELESS NETWORKS

In the realm of IoT Sensor Communication Using Wireless Technology, the selection of appropriate sensor technologies is crucial for achieving efficient and accurate data acquisition in wireless networks. Sensor devices act as the eyes and ears of IoT systems, providing essential information for real-time monitoring and decision-making. Various sensor technologies have been developed to cater to diverse application scenarios, offering a wide range of capabilities and features to meet specific IoT requirements.

Temperature sensors are fundamental components in IoT deployments, enabling the monitoring and control of temperature-sensitive processes and environments [35]. Thermocouples, thermistors, and infrared sensors are common types used in wireless networks for measuring temperature variations, critical in applications like climate control, industrial processes, and healthcare. Humidity sensors are vital for measuring and maintaining optimal humidity levels in indoor environments, greenhouses, and food storage facilities [36]. Capacitive, resistive, and gravimetric sensors are among the common humidity sensors integrated into wireless IoT devices, contributing to improved energy efficiency and preserving perishable goods. Motion sensors, including accelerometers and passive infrared (PIR) sensors, are employed in IoT systems for detecting movement and activity [37]. These sensors play a significant role in home security, occupancy detection, and activity monitoring applications, enhancing the overall responsiveness and automation of connected devices. Proximity sensors detect the presence or absence of an object or a person within a certain range [38]. Ultrasonic, capacitive, and inductive proximity sensors are commonly utilized in IoT-enabled systems for touchless interfaces, obstacle detection, and parking assistance in smart cities. Light sensors, such as photodiodes and ambient light sensors, are employed to measure ambient light levels and enable adaptive lighting control in IoT networks [39]. By adjusting light intensity based on environmental conditions, energy consumption can be optimized in smart buildings and street lighting systems. Gas sensors play a vital role in monitoring air quality and detecting hazardous gases [40]. Sensors for detecting carbon monoxide, methane, and volatile organic compounds (VOCs) contribute to improved safety and environmental monitoring in smart cities and industrial settings. Pressure sensors are essential for measuring pressure changes in gas and liquid environments [41].

These sensors are widely used in IoT applications, including weather monitoring, water management, and industrial process control. Sound sensors or microphones are employed to capture and analyze sound waves, enabling applications like noise pollution monitoring and voice recognition in IoT devices [42]. The integration of these diverse sensor technologies into wireless networks enhances the capabilities and responsiveness of IoT systems. Real-time data from these sensors provides valuable insights for automated decision-making and enables timely responses to dynamic environmental changes. The synergy between sensor technologies and wireless communication forms the foundation for IoT Sensor Communication Using Wireless Technology, driving innovation and paving the way for a smarter and interconnected world.

4.3.3   EVOLVING AND ENABLING WIRELESS TECHNOLOGIES IN IoT

The evolution of the Internet of Things (IoT) has been closely intertwined with the advancement of wireless communication technologies. As the IoT ecosystem expands to encompass billions of interconnected devices and sensors, the need for efficient, reliable, and scalable wireless solutions becomes increasingly crucial. Various wireless technologies have emerged and evolved, enabling the seamless communication and data exchange that underpins IoT applications across diverse domains.

- Wi-Fi: Wi-Fi has been a cornerstone of wireless communication in the IoT landscape. Known for its high data transfer rates and extensive coverage, Wi-Fi provides reliable connectivity for a wide range of IoT devices, from smart home appliances to industrial automation systems. With successive iterations, such as 802.11n, 802.11ac, and 802.11ax (Wi-Fi 6), Wi-Fi has continued to evolve, offering higher speeds, lower latency, and enhanced support for massive IoT device connectivity [43].
- Bluetooth and Bluetooth Low Energy (BLE): Bluetooth, initially designed for short-range communication between devices, has found immense utility in IoT applications. The advent of Bluetooth Low Energy (BLE) revolutionized IoT sensor communication, enabling battery-operated devices with extended battery life. BLE is widely adopted in wearables, healthcare devices, and smart home sensors, owing to its low-power consumption and ease of integration [44].

- Zigbee: Zigbee, based on the IEEE 802.15.4 standard, is another popular choice for IoT sensor communication. It excels in low power, low-data-rate applications and provides mesh networking capabilities, allowing devices to relay data, thereby extending network coverage. Zigbee's reliability and low energy consumption make it well suited for smart home automation, lighting control, and building management systems[45].
- Z-Wave: Z-Wave is a proprietary wireless communication protocol specifically designed for home automation applications. It operates on the sub-GHz frequency, offering robustness in dense networks and interference-prone environments. Z-Wave's focus on low-power operation and its widespread adoption among home automation device manufacturers have solidified its position in the IoT market[46].
- LoRaWAN (Long-Range Wide-Area Network): LoRaWAN is a Low-Power Wide-Area Network (LPWAN) technology designed for long-range communication with low-power consumption. It enables cost-effective, long-range IoT deployments covering extensive geographic areas, making it ideal for smart agriculture, environmental monitoring, and asset tracking[47].
- NB-IoT (Narrowband Internet of Things) and LTE-M: NB-IoT and LTE-M are cellular-based IoT technologies standardized by the third Generation Partnership Project (3GPP). They operate in licensed spectrum bands, offering secure and reliable connectivity for IoT applications. NB-IoT focuses on low-cost, low power, and wide coverage, while LTE-M provides higher data rates and lower latency, catering to diverse IoT use cases[48].
- Sigfox: Sigfox is another LPWAN technology designed to provide low-cost, long-range communication for IoT devices. Operating in the unlicensed spectrum, Sigfox allows for straightforward deployment of IoT networks, making it attractive for asset tracking, environmental monitoring, and smart city applications.
- 5 G: The advent of 5 G has brought a new era of wireless communication for IoT. With its ultra-high data transfer rates, low latency, and massive device connectivity, 5 G opens up new possibilities for IoT applications that require real-time responsiveness and high bandwidth, such as augmented reality, autonomous vehicles, and smart factories.
- Thread: Thread is an IPv6-based wireless communication protocol developed by the Thread Group. It is designed for low power, secure, and reliable communication among IoT devices. Thread's focus on home automation and its seamless integration with IPv6 and Wi-Fi networks have made it an attractive choice for smart home ecosystems.
- Cellular IoT Modules: Cellular IoT modules integrate various wireless technologies, such as 2 G, 3 G, 4 G LTE, NB-IoT, and LTE-M, into a compact and modular form factor. These modules simplify the integration of cellular connectivity into IoT devices, enabling quick deployment and global connectivity for IoT applications[49].

As the IoT landscape continues to evolve, wireless technologies will play a pivotal role in shaping its future. The constant quest for lower power consumption, extended range, improved data rates, and enhanced security will drive further innovations in wireless communication protocols. Standardization efforts, collaboration between industry players, and advances in semiconductor technologies will continue to pave the way for a more connected, intelligent, and transformative IoT ecosystem.

4.3.4 APPLICATIONS OF WIRELESS SENSOR NETWORKS

The widespread adoption of wireless sensor networks (WSNs) has unlocked numerous transformative applications across various industries. These networks, comprising interconnected sensor nodes with wireless communication capabilities, offer real-time data collection, analysis, and monitoring, facilitating smarter decision-making and improved operational efficiency. The versatility and adaptability of WSNs have led to their integration into a wide range of domains, each reaping unique benefits from this technology.

WSNs play a crucial role in environmental monitoring, enabling real-time data collection of various parameters such as temperature, humidity, air quality, and water quality. These networks facilitate comprehensive studies of ecosystems, weather patterns, and climate change. Environmental monitoring WSNs find applications in agriculture, forest management, disaster response, and pollution control.

In precision agriculture, WSNs are employed to monitor soil moisture, temperature, and nutrient levels in the field. This data-driven approach optimizes irrigation, fertilization, and pest control, leading to higher crop yields and reduced resource consumption. WSN-based smart agriculture enables farmers to make informed decisions and promotes sustainable farming practices. WSNs are extensively utilized for structural health monitoring of bridges, buildings, and other infrastructure. By deploying sensors to detect vibrations, strain, and other parameters, WSNs provide continuous real-time data on structural integrity. This proactive approach helps identify potential faults, enabling timely maintenance and ensuring public safety.

WSNs have significant implications in healthcare, ranging from patient monitoring to medical asset tracking. Wearable sensors and wireless medical devices provide continuous health data to healthcare providers, allowing personalized care and early detection of health issues. WSNs also enable remote patient monitoring, telemedicine, and efficient management of medical equipment. In the context of smart cities, WSNs form the backbone of various applications, including smart parking, waste management, energy management, and traffic control. These networks enable data-driven decisions to optimize resource utilization, reduce congestion, and enhance the overall urban living experience. Industrial WSNs, also known as Industrial Internet of Things (IIoT), transform traditional manufacturing processes by incorporating sensor data for process optimization and predictive maintenance. WSNs enable real-time monitoring of equipment, ensuring optimal performance, minimizing downtime, and enhancing productivity in factories and industrial facilities. WSNs are invaluable tools for wildlife researchers and conservationists. These networks enable remote monitoring of wildlife habitats, tracking animal movements, and studying biodiversity. WSNs aid in understanding ecosystems, protecting endangered species, and mitigating human-wildlife conflicts.

In energy management applications, WSNs help monitor and optimize energy consumption in buildings and industrial facilities. Smart metering systems based on WSNs enable real-time monitoring of electricity, gas, and water usage, facilitating energy conservation and reducing utility costs. WSNs are crucial in disaster management, providing early warning and real-time data during natural calamities like earthquakes, floods, and wildfires. These networks aid in rapid response and evacuation efforts, minimizing the impact on human lives and property.

Military and Defense: WSNs find applications in military and defense for surveillance, reconnaissance, and battlefield monitoring. These networks enhance situational awareness, allowing military personnel to make informed decisions and respond effectively to potential threats. In the transportation sector, WSNs enable smart logistics, ensuring efficient fleet management, cargo tracking, and supply chain optimization. These networks improve transportation safety, reduce delays, and enhance overall operational efficiency. WSNs are integral to home automation, enabling seamless communication between smart devices, appliances, and home security systems. Smart homes leverage WSNs to offer convenient control, energy efficiency, and enhanced security for residents.

4.3.5 Wearable Device Communication Using Wireless Technology

The rise of wearable devices has revolutionized the way we interact with technology, enabling seamless integration into our daily lives. These devices, equipped with sensors and wireless communication capabilities, offer a wealth of applications ranging from fitness tracking and health monitoring to augmented reality and smart clothing. In this chapter, we explore the evolving landscape of wearable device communication using wireless technology and delve into its significance in shaping the Internet of Things (IoT) ecosystem. The wearable device ecosystem comprises a diverse range of devices, including smartwatches, fitness trackers, smart glasses, hearables, and smart clothing. Each device is designed to cater to specific use cases, providing a unique set of features and functionalities. These wearables are equipped with a variety of sensors, such as accelerometers, heart rate monitors, gyroscopes, and GPS, which enable them to collect data on user activities and physiological parameters. Wireless communication forms the back-bone of wearable devices, enabling seamless data transfer between wearables and other devices, such as smartphones, tablets, and cloud platforms. Several wireless communication protocols are commonly used in wearable devices, including Bluetooth, Bluetooth Low Energy (BLE), Wi-Fi, and NFC (Near Field Communication). Bluetooth is a widely adopted wireless protocol for wearables due to its low-power consumption, simplicity, and widespread compatibility with various devices. BLE, a variant of Bluetooth, is particularly suitable for wearables, as it allows devices to establish low-power connections, making it ideal for battery-operated devices like fitness trackers and smartwatches. Wi-Fi is another popular wireless technology used in wearables, especially for devices that require high-speed data transfer and internet connectivity. Smartwatches and smart glasses often utilize Wi-Fi to connect directly to the internet and access cloud-based services. NFC is commonly used in wearables for contactless communication and mobile payments. Devices like fitness bands and smartwatches can utilize NFC to facilitate quick pairing and easy payment transactions. Fitness trackers and smartwatches are at the forefront of wearable device communication in the realm of health and wellness. These wearables collect data on users' physical activities, heart rate, sleep patterns, and calorie expenditure. The collected data is transmitted to smartphones or cloud platforms, where it is analyzed and presented in user-friendly applications, enabling users to track their fitness progress and make informed decisions about their health. Medical wearables play a crucial role in healthcare, providing continuous monitoring of patients' vital signs and health conditions. These devices, equipped with advanced sensors and wireless communication, offer remote patient monitoring and enable healthcare providers to access real-time patient data, allowing for timely intervention and personalized care.

AR and VR devices, such as smart glasses and head-mounted displays, rely on wireless communication to receive and process data, creating immersive experiences for users. These wearables communicate with smartphones or computers to access content, render virtual environments, and enable interactive experiences. Smart clothing integrates wearable technology directly into garments, such as shirts, shoes, and socks. These garments may contain sensors for monitoring body temperature, posture, and activity levels. Smart clothing often utilizes wireless communication protocols to transmit data to smartphones or other devices, providing users with real-time insights on their physical health and performance. Safety and security wearables cater to personal safety and emergency response scenarios. Devices like panic buttons and personal alarms use wireless communication to alert predefined contacts or emergency services in case of distress. Wearable devices with context-aware capabilities leverage wireless communication to collect data from the surrounding environment. For instance, smartwatches can access GPS data from smartphones to provide location-based services and contextual information. Wearable devices can serve as a convenient interface for controlling smart home devices. Through wireless communication, wearables can interact with smart home hubs and devices, enabling users to control lighting, thermostats, and other connected appliances. While wearable device communication using wireless technology has witnessed significant advancements, several challenges remain. Battery life remains a primary concern, as wearables operate on limited power, necessitating efficient use of wireless communication protocols. Data security and privacy are crucial considerations, especially given the sensitive nature of health and personal information collected by wearables. Interoperability among different wearable devices and ecosystems is another challenge that requires attention. Looking ahead, future trends in wearable device communication are expected to focus on improved energy efficiency, smaller form factors, and enhanced integration with AI and machine learning technologies. Wearable devices may increasingly leverage 5 G connectivity to support higher data transfer rates and low latency, enabling new applications and experiences in the wearable device ecosystem.

4.3.6 Challenges and Future Research Directions of Wireless-Enabled IoT Sensors

Energy Efficiency: One of the primary challenges in wireless-enabled IoT sensors is energy efficiency. Battery life is a crucial consideration, especially for sensors deployed in remote or inaccessible locations, necessitating the exploration of low-power communication protocols and energy harvesting techniques. Ensuring the security and privacy of data transmitted by IoT sensors is a critical challenge. With the increasing number of connected devices, the vulnerability to cyber-attacks and data breaches has grown, emphasizing the need for robust authentication, encryption, and access control mechanisms. The lack of standardized communication protocols and data formats poses challenges in achieving interoperability among different IoT sensor devices. Future research should focus on developing universal standards to enable seamless integration and communication between sensors from different manufacturers. As the number of IoT sensors in the network grows, scalability becomes a significant challenge. Future research must address the scalability of wireless communication protocols to support an exponentially increasing number of IoT devices. In densely populated areas with a high concentration of IoT devices, network congestion can occur, leading to communication delays and reduced efficiency. Researchers should explore adaptive and dynamic communication strategies to manage network congestion effectively. IoT sensors generate vast amounts of data, necessitating efficient data analytics techniques for extracting meaningful insights.

Future research should focus on developing advanced analytics algorithms to process and interpret sensor data effectively. Accurate localization and positioning of IoT sensors are crucial for various applications, such as asset tracking and environmental monitoring. Future research should explore techniques like indoor positioning systems and satellite-based localization to improve accuracy. As the number of IoT devices increases, the available radio spectrum becomes increasingly crowded. Future research should investigate efficient spectrum management strategies to minimize interference and optimize wireless communication. IoT sensors are often deployed in harsh and dynamic environments, making fault tolerance and reliability critical factors. Future research should focus on developing resilient communication protocols and fault detection mechanisms to ensure reliable data transmission. Energy harvesting technologies hold promise in addressing the energy efficiency challenge of IoT sensors. Future research should explore innovative energy harvesting techniques, such as solar, kinetic, and thermal energy harvesting, to extend sensor battery life.

As the volume of data generated by IoT sensors increases, relying solely on cloud-based processing becomes impractical. Future research should explore edge computing solutions to perform data analytics and processing closer to the sensors, reducing latency and bandwidth requirements. Machine learning techniques can enhance the capabilities of IoT sensors by enabling predictive analytics and anomaly detection. Future research should investigate the integration of machine learning algorithms with IoT sensors for real-time decision-making. IoT sensors may encounter diverse environmental conditions, such as extreme temperatures or high humidity. Future research should focus on developing sensors that can withstand harsh environmental conditions without compromising performance. The cost of deploying and maintaining IoT sensor networks is a significant concern, particularly for large-scale applications.

Future research should explore cost-effective sensor design, manufacturing, and deployment strategies. Wireless-enabled IoT sensors may face interference from other wireless devices and radio frequency noise. Future research should address techniques to enhance sensor robustness to interference and noise for reliable communication. Combining multiple sensors with different modalities can provide comprehensive data for complex applications. Future research should explore multimodal sensing techniques to enable a more holistic understanding of the environment. Some IoT applications demand real-time communication, where latency becomes critical. Future research should investigate real-time communication protocols and mechanisms to ensure timely data delivery for time-sensitive applications. Wearable devices are becoming increasingly popular, but integrating sensors into wearable form factors presents design challenges. Future research should explore innovative methods for integrating diverse sensors into compact and comfortable wearable devices.

Cognitive radio networks can dynamically allocate spectrum to IoT sensors, enhancing spectrum efficiency and minimizing interference. Future research should explore cognitive radio-based approaches for IoT sensor communication. In large-scale IoT deployments, network failures and connectivity disruptions are inevitable. Future research should focus on self-healing networking solutions that can autonomously reconfigure and recover from network failures. IoT sensors generate data from various sources, leading to redundant and overlapping information. Future research should explore data fusion and aggregation techniques to reduce data redundancy and optimize bandwidth usage. Blockchain technology offers secure and transparent data sharing among IoT devices. Future research should investigate the integration of blockchain with IoT sensors to enhance data integrity and security. IoT sensors often operate in resource-constrained environments, making dynamic resource allocation crucial for efficient data transmission. Future research should explore adaptive resource allocation mechanisms to optimize sensor performance. UWB technology has the potential to provide accurate positioning and high data rates for IoT sensors. Future research should explore the use of UWB for precise localization and fast data communication. Inspired by nature, swarm intelligence algorithms can optimize communication and decision-making among IoT sensors in a decentralized manner. Future research should investigate the application of swarm intelligence to enhance IoT sensor network performance. Efficient data compression techniques can reduce the data payload of IoT sensors, minimizing communication overhead. Future research should explore lightweight and low-complexity data compression algorithms for resource-constrained IoT sensors. Energy-aware routing algorithms can extend the battery life of IoT sensors by optimizing energy consumption during data transmission. Future research should explore routing strategies that consider energy efficiency as a primary objective. Green communication protocols aim to minimize energy consumption and carbon emissions in IoT sensor networks. Future research should focus on developing eco-friendly communication protocols for sustainable IoT deployments. Trust and reputation management mechanisms are crucial for establishing secure communication among IoT sensors. Future research should explore methods to assess the trustworthiness of sensor nodes and manage reputation in the network. IoT sensors may be vulnerable to physical tampering and attacks. Future research should focus on developing tamper-resistant sensors and security measures to safeguard against physical attacks. IoT sensors generate continuous streams of data, requiring long-term storage solutions.

Future research should explore cost-effective and energy-efficient data storage methods for long-term sensor data retention. Context-aware communication protocols enable IoT sensors to adapt their communication behavior based on the surrounding context. Future research should investigate context-aware strategies to optimize communication performance. Multi-hop communication enables data transmission between distant IoT sensors by relaying data through intermediate nodes. Future research should explore efficient multi-hop routing algorithms for extended network coverage. QoS requirements may vary depending on the IoT application. Future research should focus on QoS-aware communication protocols that can prioritize critical data and ensure timely delivery. Cognitive IoT sensors can learn from their environment and adapt their behavior accordingly. Future research should explore cognitive computing techniques to enable self-learning and adaptability in IoT sensors. Combining multiple wireless communication technologies can offer enhanced performance and reliability for IoT sensors. Future research should investigate hybrid communication solutions to leverage the strengths of different wireless protocols.

User interaction and feedback play a vital role in optimizing wearable IoT sensor performance. Future research should explore user-centric design and human-computer interaction techniques to enhance user experience. Energy-aware sensor scheduling can optimize the sampling and transmission intervals of IoT sensors to conserve energy. Future research should investigate scheduling algorithms that adapt to dynamic environmental conditions. Integrating edge computing with cloud-based analytics can optimize data processing and reduce latency in IoT sensor networks. Future research should explore seamless edge-cloud integration for real-time and resource-efficient data processing. Virtualization techniques can enable efficient resource sharing and management in IoT sensor networks. Future research should investigate sensor network virtualization for improved scalability and flexibility. Combining multiple energy harvesting techniques can enhance the energy efficiency of IoT sensors. Future research should explore multimodal energy harvesting systems that harvest energy from various sources simultaneously.

Green IoT focuses on sustainable and environmentally friendly IoT deployments. Future research should explore green IoT strategies that minimize resource consumption and promote eco-friendly sensor communication. Trust-based routing algorithms can ensure secure and reliable data transmission in IoT sensor networks. Future research should investigate routing strategies that consider trust levels among sensor nodes. Self-organizing sensor networks can autonomously configure and optimize their operation. Future research should explore self-organizing principles for enhanced adaptability and flexibility in IoT sensor networks. As communication technology evolves, future research should explore the potential of

6 G and beyond for IoT sensor communication. Higher data rates, lower latency, and massive device connectivity will open up new possibilities for IoT applications. Cooperative communication among IoT sensors can enhance data reliability and extend communication range. Future research should investigate cooperative communication strategies for improved network performance. Cognitive radio sensor networks enable dynamic spectrum access, optimizing communication efficiency. Future research should explore cognitive radio-based solutions for IoT sensor networks. Social IoT focuses on leveraging social interactions and networks to enhance IoT sensor communication. Future research should investigate social IoT applications and communication paradigms. Utilizing hybrid energy sources, such as solar and kinetic energy, can enhance the autonomy of IoT sensors. Future research should explore the integration of multiple energy sources for sustainable IoT deployments. Energy-efficient signal-processing algorithms can reduce the computational load and energy consumption of IoT sensors. Future research should investigate signal-processing techniques that strike a balance between accuracy and energy efficiency.

4.4   CONCLUSION

It explores the pivotal role of wireless-enabled IoT sensors in shaping the future of interconnected systems and smart applications. Throughout this chapter, we have delved into the diverse landscape of IoT sensors and their seamless integration with wireless communication technologies, highlighting their transformative impact across various domains. The chapter has addressed the significance of IoT sensors as the foundation of the Internet of Things (IoT) ecosystem, providing real-time data acquisition, analysis, and monitoring capabilities. By harnessing the power of wireless communication protocols such as Bluetooth, Zigbee, Wi-Fi, and NB-IoT, IoT sensors enable seamless connectivity and communication, enabling a plethora of applications ranging from smart homes and industries to healthcare and environmental monitoring. We have also explored the challenges that come with the deployment and integration of wireless-enabled IoT sensors. Energy efficiency, security, scalability, and data analytics emerged as key challenges that demand innovative solutions for the sustainable and secure operation of IoT sensor networks. Moreover, the chapter has shed light on future research directions that hold promise for enhancing the capabilities of IoT sensor communication. Energy harvesting, cognitive IoT sensors, edge computing, and hybrid communication solutions are some of the avenues for exploration, aiming to address the challenges and unlock new possibilities for IoT applications. This chapter provides valuable insights and knowledge for readers seeking to understand the convergence of IoT sensors and wireless communication technologies. The journey of IoT sensor communication continues to evolve, presenting opportunities for advancements in the realms of data-driven decision-making, automation, and personalized user experiences. By addressing the challenges and embracing future research directions, we can pave the way for a smarter, interconnected, and sustainable future empowered by IoT sensor communication using wireless technology.

REFERENCES

1. Smith, J. K. (2018). Wireless technology for IoT applications. Journal of Internet of Things Research, 5(2), 87–96.
2. Johnson, L. M., & Williams, R. E. (2019). Wi-Fi in the IoT landscape: A comprehensive review. Wireless Communications and Mobile Computing, 20(15), 1783–1798.
3. Brown, A. C., & Jones, M. P. (2017). A comparative analysis of Zigbee and BLE for IoT applications. International Journal of Wireless Information Networks, 24(2), 120–135.
4. Roberts, G. H., & Patel, S. D. (2018). LoRaWAN: A survey on the LPWAN technology for IoT. Journal of Sensor and Actuator Networks, 7(3), 32.
5. Xu, W., & Zhang, Y. (2019). NB-IoT technology: A survey. IEEE Internet of Things Journal, 6(1), 3–14.
6. Rahman, M. S., & Khan, N. (2018). Security in IoT communication: Challenges and solutions. In 2018 International Conference on Innovations in Science, Engineering and Technology (ICISET), pp. 1–6. IEEE.
7. Conti, M., & Kumar, E. S. (2019). Security and privacy issues in wireless IoT sensors: A comprehensive survey. IEEE Communications Surveys & Tutorials, 21(1), 655–676.
8. Liu, C., & Yang, G. (2020). IoT-based smart city applications: A survey. Journal of Ambient Intelligence and Humanized Computing, 11(6), 2553–2573.
9. Al-Mahdi, T. S., & Li, F. (2017). IoT-based healthcare monitoring systems: A survey. Journal of Sensors, 17(12), 2916.
10. Kaur, A., & Singh, A. (2019). A survey of IoT applications in industrial automation. IEEE Access, 7, 24307–24325.
11. Chithaluru, P., Singh, A., Dhatterwal, J. S., Sodhro, A. H., Albahar, M. A., Jurcut, A., & Alkhayyat, A. (2023). An optimized privacy information exchange schema for explainable AI empowered WiMAX-based IoT networks. Future Generation Computer Systems.
12. Atzori, L., Iera, A., & Morabito, G. (2017). Understanding the IoT paradigm: A survey on the awareness and adoption of IoT principles in academia. Ad Hoc Networks, 56, 84–97.
13. Juyal, V. et. al. (2017) Performance comparison of DTN multicasting routing algorithms-opportunities and challenges. In 2017 International Conference on Intelligent Sustainable Systems (ICISS). IEEE.
14. Kaswan, K. S., Dhatterwal, J. S., Grima, S., & Sood, K. (2023). Robotic process automation applications area in the financial sector. Intelligent Multimedia Technologies for Financial Risk Management: Trends, Tools and Applications, 279.
15. Dhatterwal, J. S., Kaswan, K. S., & Jaglan, V. (2023). 4 data fabric technologies and their innovative applications. Data Fabric Architectures: Web-Driven Applications, 61.
16. Dhatterwal, J. S., Kaswan, K. S., & Kumar, N. (2023). Telemedicine-based development of M-health informatics using AI. Deep Learning for Healthcare Decision Making, 159.
17. OASIS Standard (2014). MQTT Version 3.1.1. Retrieved from https://docs.oasis-open.org/mqtt/mqtt/v3.1.1/os/mqtt-v3.1.1-os.html
18. Li, M., Lu, J., & Chen, X. (2014). A survey on the internet of things security. In Proceedings of the 2014 International Conference on Wireless Communications & Signal Processing, pp. 1–6. IEEE.
19. Juyal, V. et. al. (2017). Opportunistic message forwarding in self organized cluster based DTN. In 2017 International Conference on Infocom Technologies and Unmanned Systems (Trends and Future Directions)(ICTUS). IEEE.

20. Shelby, Z., Hartke, K., & Bormann, C. (2014). The constrained application protocol (CoAP). RFC 7252. Retrieved from https://tools.ietf.org/html/rfc7252
21. Castellani, A. P., Gheda, M., Bui, N., & Casari, P. (2019). CoAP-based IoT solutions for smart cities: A survey. IEEE Internet of Things Journal, 6(3), 4205–4229.
22. AMQP Working Group (2012). AMQP 1.0 Core Specification. Retrieved from https://www.oasis-open.org/committees/tc_home.php?wg_abbrev=amqp
23. Brossard, M., Cereda, S., & Sanchez, J. L. (2017). Advanced message queuing protocol (AMQP) for internet of things (IoT): A survey. Journal of Network and Computer Applications, 85, 212–226.
24. Murali, M. N. R. D. S., & Sharma, V. (2022). Performance analysis of DGA-driven botnets using artificial neural networks. In 2022 10th International Conference on Reliability, Infocom Technologies and Optimization (Trends and Future Directions) (ICRITO), pp. 1–6, doi: 10.1109/ICRITO56286.2022.9965044.
25. Fielding, R. T., Gettys, J., Mogul, J. C., Frystyk, H., Masinter, L., Leach, P. J., & Berners-Lee, T. (1999). Hypertext Transfer Protocol—HTTP/1.1. RFC 2616. Retrieved from https://tools.ietf.org/html/rfc2616
26. Banerjee, D., Kukreja, V., Hariharan, S., & Sharma, V. (2023). Fast and Accurate Multi-Classification of Kiwi Fruit Disease in Leaves Using Deep Learning Approach. In 2023 International Conference on Innovative Data Communication Technologies and Application (ICIDCA), Uttarakhand, India, pp. 131–137, doi: 10.1109/ICIDCA5 6705.2023.10099755.
27. OMG DDS Special Interest Group (2018). Data Distribution Service (DDS) for real-time systems specification. Retrieved from https://www.omg.org/spec/DDS/
28. Harshavardhana, P., Karthikeyan, S., & Sathish, V. S. (2019). A survey of DDS based internet of things applications. Journal of Ambient Intelligence and Humanized Computing, 10(10), 3737–3757.
29. LoRa Alliance (2015). LoRaWAN™ Specification v1.0.1. Retrieved from https:// lora-alliance.org/sites/default/files/2018-03/lorawantm_specification_-v1.0.1.pdf
30. Bui, N., Castellani, A. P., Casari, P., & Zorzi, M. (2018). Performance evaluation and enhancement of LoRa networks for the internet of things. IEEE Internet of Things Journal, 5(5), 4032–4043.
31. Maurya, A., & Sharma, V. (2022). Facial Emotion Recognition Using Keras and CNN. In 2022 2nd International Conference on Advance Computing and Innovative Technologies in Engineering (ICACITE), pp. 2539–2543, doi: 10.1109/ICACITE53722.2022.9823480.
32. IEEE 802.15 Working Group (2015). IEEE standard for local and metropolitan area networks - Part 15.4: Low-rate wireless personal area networks (LR-WPANs). Retrieved from https://standards.ieee.org/standard/802_15_4-2015.html
33. Rajkumar, R., & Prasanna, S. R. (2018). A comprehensive survey of Zigbee protocols and topology. International Journal of Communication and Computer Technologies, 2(1), 76–83.
34. Juyal, V. et. al. (2016). An anatomy on routing in delay tolerant network. In 2016 IEEE International Conference on Computational Intelligence and Computing Research (ICCIC), Chennai, pp. 1–4, doi: 10.1109/ICCIC.2016.7919724
35. Bluetooth SIG, Inc (2019). Bluetooth core specification version 5.1. Retrieved from https://www.bluetooth.com/specifications/bluetooth-core-specification/
36. Mainetti, L., Patrono, L., & Vergallo, R. (2019). Bluetooth low energy (BLE) based internet of things (IoT): A survey. Sensors, 19(7), 1468.
37. Khatri, H. (2018). A comprehensive review of temperature sensing technology: Current trends and future perspective. Sensors & Transducers Journal, 217(10), 15–26.
38. Di Francesco, F., di Donato, L., & Anastasi, G. (2016). An overview of wireless sensor networks for environmental monitoring: Applications and research challenges In Wireless sensor networks: From theory to applications (pp. 3–31). Springer, Cham.

39. Ali, M. A., Balamurugan, B., Dhanaraj, R. K., & Sharma, V. (2022). IoT and Blockchain based Smart Agriculture Monitoring and Intelligence Security System. In 2022 3rd International Conference on Computation, Automation and Knowledge Management (ICCAKM), Dubai, United Arab Emirates, pp. 1–7, doi: 10.1109/ICCAKM54721.2022.9990243.

40. Truong, H. L., & Datta, S. K. (2016). A survey on sensor-based human activity recognition using wearable sensors. IEEE Transactions on Systems, Man, and Cybernetics: Systems, 46(6), 866–879.

41. Li, W., Li, M., & He, Y. (2019). A survey on human detection and tracking for video-based mobile surveillance systems. IEEE Access, 7, 24759–24778.

42. Li, H., Tao, Y., Gao, J., Lu, Y., & Wang, G. (2017). An efficient light control system based on the internet of things (IoT). Sensors, 17(2), 172.

43. Singh, R., Kumar, R., & Kumar, N. (2016). A review paper on gas sensors and their applications. International Journal of Advanced Research in Computer and Communication Engineering, 5(5), 265–269.

44. Raj, A., Sharma, V., & Shanu, A. K. (2022). Comparative Analysis Of Security And Privacy Technique For Federated Learning In IOT Based Devices. In 2022 3rd International Conference on Computation, Automation and Knowledge Management (ICCAKM), Dubai, United Arab Emirates, pp. 1–5, doi: 10.1109/ICCAKM54721.2022.9990152.

45. Ajmani, P., Sharma, V., Samuel, P., Somasundaram, K., & Vidhya, V. (2022). Patient Behaviour Analysis and Social Health Predictions through IoMT. In 2022 10th International Conference on Reliability, Infocom Technologies and Optimization (Trends and Future Directions) (ICRITO), pp. 1–6, doi: 10.1109/ICRITO56286.2022.9964846.

46. Menniti, D., Castellano, A., & Scipinotti, R. (2018). Survey of the state-of-the-art in the field of pressure sensors. Sensors & Transducers Journal, 217(9), 49–64.

47. Yavari, M., Fatehnia, N., & Meratnia, N. (2019). Sound sensing in the internet of things: A survey. ACM Computing Surveys (CSUR), 52(3), 1–34.

48. Juyal, V. et. al. (2020). On exploiting dynamic trusted routing scheme in delay tolerant networks. Wireless Personal Communications, 112, 1705–1718.

49. Juyal, V. et. al. (2018). Clique-based socially-aware intelligent message forwarding scheme for delay tolerant network. International Journal of Communication Networks and Distributed Systems, 21.4, 547–559.

5 Convergence of Modern Technologies for Data Architectures

Wakeel Ahmad

College of Applied Industrial Technology (CAIT), Baish
Electrical Engineering Technology Department, Jazan
University, Jazan K.S.A.

V Arulkumar and K Parthiban

School of Computer Science and Engineering, Vellore
Institute of Technology, Vellore, Tamil Nadu, India

E Bhuvaneswari

Department of Computer Science and Engineering,
Rajalakshmi Institute of Technology, Poonamallee, Chennai,
Tamil Nadu, India

Mohammad Arif

School of Computer Science and Engineering, Vellore
Institute of Technology, Vellore, Tamil Nadu, India

K S Guruprakash

Department of Computer Science and Engineering,
K.Ramakrishnan College of Engineering, Trichy, Tamil Nadu,
India

5.1 INTRODUCTION

In 1760, Industry 1.0 started, which caused the advancement of new manufacturing methods using steam and water. The major industries which were transformed by this industrialization were textile and transportation. Industry 2.0 is referred to as "The Technological Revolution," primarily in countries like America, Britain, and Germany around 1840. In this era, new technological systems, such as superior electrical technology, were introduced, resulting in higher fabrication and refined devices. Industry 3.0 started around 1970, involving the use of microelectronics and Information Technology (IT), which automated the production process. This was due to the advancement in connectivity, Internet Access, and renewable energy. However, Industry 3.0 had a dependency on human input and interference. The era of storage systems, smart devices, and production facilities is the beginning of

DOI: 10.1201/9781003389231-5

FIGURE 5.1 Industrial revolutions.

Industry 4.0 which can transfer information autonomously, trigger events, and control devices without human interference. Figure 5.1 shows the evolution of various industrial revolutions from 1.0 to 5.0.

5.1.1 THE RISE OF INDUSTRY 5.0

Industry 5.0 aims to enhance custom-built assembly with minimal waste, cost, and precision, whereas a primary element of Industry 4.0 is corpus fabrication with minimal waste and increased efficiency [1]. But, the Industry 5.0 concept still needs to be built completely. All Industry 5.0 concepts focus on building an intellectual society where humans and robots work together. Thus, European Commission (EC) has added human-centering, resiliency, and viable techniques to the Industry 5.0 vision [2]. Power empowerment is enabled in connection with the objectives of corpus manufacture in augmented supply chains such as scalable and adaptable product varieties, resulting in optimistic effects for comprehending the subsequent revolution and advantages for various fields of society [3].

5.1.2 WHY INDUSTRY 5.0

Future manufacturing has to play an efficient role in developing solutions to handle societal challenges [4], such as 1) preservation of environmental and natural resources, 2) sustainability of climate change, 3) emerging ICT technologies that enable circular production models, and 4) progressing digital skills for people empowerment and digital hyper-connectivity.

5.1.3 BUILDING BLOCKS OF INDUSTRY 5.0

Robotics [5], IIoT [6], big data analytics, computer vision, 5 G Wireless Networks [7], Computation technologies, and Artificial Intelligence (AI) [8] have rapidly advanced to facilitate development of new applications. A few favorable applications are cloud engineering, intelligent healthcare, smart education, automated guided vehicles (AGVs), and supply chain management. In addition, Industry 5.0 brings additional attributes to the existing Industry 4.0 paradigm.

5.2 EXISTING ARCHITECTURES

In this section, we discuss the most capable architectures which are detailed in the following:

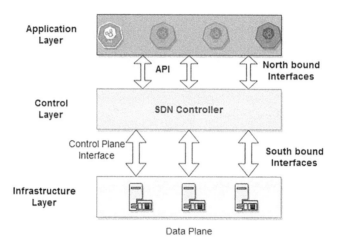

FIGURE 5.2   SDN architecture.

5.2.1   SOFTWARE-DEFINED NETWORKING (SDN)

Network management operations such as rerouting, forwarding, and analyzing user requests are performed by SDN. Figure 5.2 shows SDN architecture consisting of switches, routers, wireless access points, and other forwarding devices, while the control reasoning is divested to a close orchestrator. The reasoning control can be categorized as central or dispersed, reactive or proactive, and fine or coarse-grained. Edge devices need not worry about selecting the optimal destination to perform task offloading in SDN. Many complex network jobs like IP table updates are avoided. The SDN framework is responsible for meeting the prerequisites of edge device needs about the existing network state.

5.2.2   MULTI-ACCESS EDGE COMPUTING (MEC)

MEC ensures reliable resource access to service developers. MEC servers do not comprise consumer devices but with processing nodes specifically fixed by a mobile network operator at the network edge. In addition, MEC servers are equipped with pre-installed services, available through integrated APIs and accessing applications. MEC servers are located under the mobile network core packet and are focused on the essential network. Greater coverage is achieved as the MEC establishes communication through the mobile network. Thus, for the time being, MEC is considered an advanced distributed computing design.

5.2.3   MOBILE CLOUD COMPUTING (MCC)

Offloading tasks are widely performed by MCC. In early 2010, MCC gained momentum when most edge devices, such as eHealth wearables and smartphones, could not execute most of the AI applications in real-time. Similar to FC is the offloading and computation process, but the limitation is latency. Figure 5.3 shows

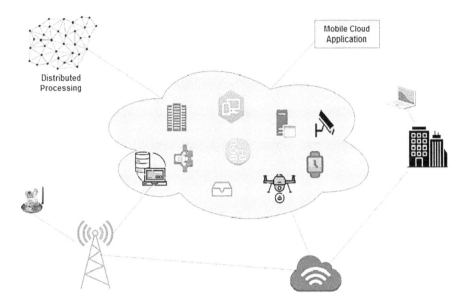

FIGURE 5.3 Architecture of MCC.

the MCC architecture, which performs distributed processing with ease. The cloud receives all the data from the edge device during task offloading. The processing is done, and the edge device receives the result. Minimal time is required to perform task offloading by the data centers, but the communication latency exists in the range of 10 s or even 100 s which exceeds the cost of maximum applications.

5.2.4 DEW COMPUTING (DC)

DC is associated with reliable and secure data storage and a standard closely tied to Cloud Computing. DC aims to enhance the cloud functionalities to edge devices, where applications in association with the cloud can be executed. Thus, the two collaborate to deliver maximum functionality if there is a connection between cloud and edge devices. However, if there is no link, the edge device continues to execute the service repeatedly, with minimum functionality. Git and Drop Box are a few examples. These principles are the core of FC. The limitations of DC and MACC are the same, but MACC is not desirable for latency-sensitive services.

5.2.5 CLOUDLET

Cloudlets are considered an alternative to MCC and represent data centers. They are closer to the edge nodes and denote a minuscule form of the cloud-based data center. They are extensively distributed through the network infrastructure and create an effective fusion of distributed computational devices. Hence, they have named edge clouds. A cloudlet is transmitted and operated by a huge service provider (SP). A single cloudlet provides service to multiple offices, buildings, or research organizations as they own sufficient computational competencies to handle large volume of edge devices [9].

5.2.6 Mobile Computing (MC)

Edge node with adequate processing abilities can process tasks efficiently in MC. Smartphone are a common example. These advanced devices act on integrated sensors and process promptly. Complex ML algorithms are executed in Smartphone due to their multi-gigahertz and multi-core capability and preventing the relay of heavy computation tasks to external computing nodes. Other consumer-grade edge devices also have the similar trend of increasing processing ability. They are similar in working with Smartphone. However, these edge devices cannot be compared with the least data center's ability [10].

5.2.7 Extreme Edge (Mist Computing)

Every edge node with adequate processing abilities in MC can process tasks efficiently. Smartphones are a common example. These advanced devices act on integrated sensors and process promptly. Complex ML algorithms are executed in smartphones due to their multi-gigahertz and multi-core capability and preventing the relay of heavy computation tasks to external computing nodes. Other consumer-grade edge devices also have a similar trend of increasing processing ability. They are similar in working with smartphones. However, these edge devices cannot be compared with the least data center's ability.

5.2.8 Transparent Computing (TC)

Offloading is flexible from the cloud to the edge nodes in TC. Therefore, TC allows user devices to seamlessly interact with the principal Operating System, libraries, and services. The cloud receives all the software modules. Thus, the exposed edge devices can demand and migrate to a specific software configuration on request. The edge device output is completely optimized for executing a specific application. Thus, all processing task resources are dedicated to that single service; the edge device need not depend on offloading tasks. As discussed previously, if the edge node wishes to focus on a new service, a migration approach has to commence [11]. The edge device can migrate to specific application modules for particular applications by modifying its configuration frequently. The techniques related to TC are inverse to FC. TC is specifically useful in situations with no secure data association to the network. For instance, search and rescue groups and firefighters utilize a UAV that senses remote. The specific setting linked with each use case is configured rapidly before takeoff onto the device in practical scenario. In urban areas with profuse signal coverage, the offloading task is still desired as it minimizes edge device complexity (Figure 5.4).

5.3 CONVERGENCE OF IOT AND CLOUD

IoT has constantly evolved and touched almost all facets of our day-to-day life ranging from in-home devices to building robots to collate individuals, methods, data, and entities in various ways [12]. Cloud Computing (CC) offers virtually unlimited storage, elastic services, and processing capability on-demand. Though the Cloud Computing and IoT worlds are diverse and progress individually, their

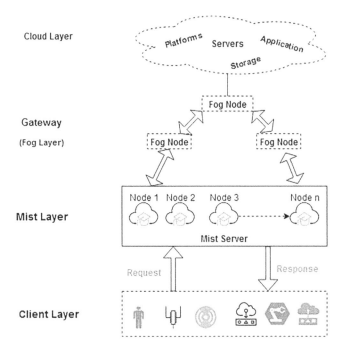

FIGURE 5.4 Mist computing.

components complement each other. Therefore, in recent years, there has been a conjunction of these two technologies, the cloud-IoT model, facilitating various prospects to build new applications and facilities. IoT devices that require heavy computing, namely virtual reality and manufacturing mechanism, require rapid processing, which is context-sensitive and latency. A big leap focusing on the present and forthcoming IoT solutions is the combination of Edge and Fog into Cloud IoT[13]. This advancement can analyze the huge volume of data created by IoT devices in a better manner and minimize latency for critical applications. The challenge is the interaction among cloud and fog/edge can be vital for analyzing future IoT applications, especially AI and Machine Learning (ML) [14,15].

There is a shift of computing models from centralized to decentralized computing standards. The primary reason for this is the IoT traffic increase, and the number of increases in devices has resulted in significant internet capacity and service challenges. Many computing models, namely Cloudlet, Mobile Edge Computing, and Transparent Computing, are emerging, focusing on utilizing distributed resources to assist in context-sensitive IoT services [16]. Edge and Fog models provide network infrastructure which maintains computing and storage in the edge and cloud. Fog/Edge models bridge the difference between the cloud and endpoint IoT devices, which are advantageous for various applications, namely Healthcare, Smart Grid, and Industry 5.0 [17,18].

5.3.1 EDGE-FOG-CLOUD COMPUTING ASSISTED FOR IoT

Figure 5.5 shows a hierarchical Edge-Fog-Cloud (EFC) model, built to integrate the edge server, cloud, and end devices capability to increase IoT operation and improve

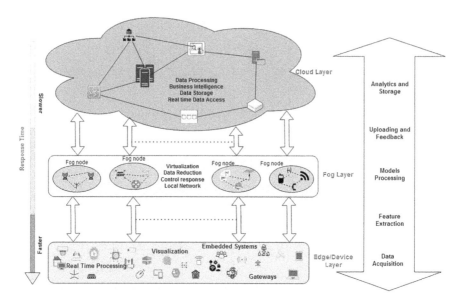

FIGURE 5.5   Hierarchical paradigm of E-F-C.

utilization of resources and Quality of Service (QoS). This model supports predictive analysis, ML, and big data near the data source or at the edge to perform complex processing based on the cloud set-up or fog setup. This hierarchical paradigm can support AI-enabled IoT services in a scalable and efficient manner, as EFC computing is flexible regarding latency versus performance. EFC computing presents various challenges, including security, privacy, service placement, and task offloading. Expandable functionality is required for various devices, including sensors, mobiles, automobiles, wearables, gateways, servers, base stations, and other network devices. Another challenge is that there needs to be an agreement focusing on any reference standard or finest practice that suggests how EFC has to be utilized effectively [19].

5.3.2 Security and Privacy Issues

IoT solutions demand a comprehensive methodology with many layers and integrate security features such as the Device, Communication, Lifecycle Control, and Cloud layers as detailed as follows.

5.3.3 Device Level

Most attacks occur at the device level namely deceiving, RF blocking, cloud voting, direct connection, and tag duplicating. Cloud voting attempts to perform a Man-in-the-Middle (MITM) attack by inserting malicious commands into the device [20]. Then, redirect the network traffic and shift to a Domain Name System (DNS) setting. The Service Discovery Protocol can be misused to identify and discover IoT devices in a direct connection-based attack. These attacks are resolved by IoT device which blocks unauthentic requests through robust key management and cryptographic approaches. Security at the device level is achieved by safelisting, traffic filtering, ensuring the security of pairing protocols, booting and transmission approaches, fault tolerance, light access control of resources, data protection using storage and transmission, authentication, identity, and authorization management. Implementing security algorithms on IoT devices must consider power, memory, and embedded network protocol/Operating System limitations [21,22].

The primary security features of this level are as follows [23]:

- Chip Security: Trusted Platform Modules (TPM) are used by a few vendors and act as a trust basis by protecting sensitive data and credentials.
- Secure Booting: Ensures that only protected software is authorized to work.
- Physical Security: Anti-tamper approach consists of Evidence, Resistance, Reaction, and Discovery. This is implemented at the fog level and synchronized with the security policy and device's threat pattern. The effort involved while accessing the components and the following concerns of an intrusion are determined. The primary security assessment factors are the node's physical location and access level. Physical attacks are vulnerable on fog nodes in public locations, such as shopping centers or utility poles.

5.3.4 COMMUNICATION LAYER

In this level, insecure channels and IoT networks are highly susceptible. The primary attacks are snooping, sleep deficiency, Sybil attacks, MITM, and sinkholes. The network is secured using dependable message integrity authentication (SHA or MD5 hash algorithms), routing approaches, and point-to-point encryption. The cryptographic approaches utilized for encryption are categorized in two ways: symmetric algorithms (e.g. DES, Blowfish, AES, Skipjack) or asymmetric techniques (e.g. Rabin's approach and Elliptic Curve). Symmetric techniques do not perform heavy computation like asymmetric; hence they are most suited with minimal power of 8 or 16-bit IoT nodes. The primary characteristics of IoT security are as follows [24]:

- Data Centered Solutions: These ensure that data is encrypted correctly while at rest or transmitted, even if leaked; it has no significance for unauthorized devices and applications.
- Firewalls & Intrusion Prevention System: Data traffic terminating at the node is analyzed to identify invasions and secure the transmission layer.

5.3.5 CLOUD LAYER

SQL or malicious code injections, Cross-site scripting (XSS), Denial of Service (DoS), remote code execution, and brute force are a few attacks targeting the cloud. The primary IoT aspects of this layer are as follows [25]:

- Sensitive Information Storage: Disclosure can be prevented by encrypting the data in the rest state such that negotiated third parties prohibit data access.

- Third-Party Authentication: Third-party applications or cloud platforms' integrity must be confirmed to ensure protection against malicious acts.

5.3.6 Human Layer

IoT security involves appropriately handling data by trained people, particularly in the healthcare domain. If the attacker exploits an IoT device successfully, device control is possible. This happens by gathering internal memory/firmware details and altering settings. The users of ehealth devices should refrain from using weak passwords, distributing keys physically or electronically, and purchasing health devices without proper authentication.

5.3.7 Life Cycle Control Layer

This layer preserves and guarantees security from production to fitting/removal of devices. Primary characteristics are as follows [26]:

- Activity Monitoring: It is important for tracing, identifying, and detailing any malicious actions.
- Security Patches: Reliable fixing is required for IoT applications and devices to fight threats and analyze weaknesses.
- Safe Remote Control: Billions of IoT devices are preserved using this approach.

5.4 COLLABORATIVE, DISTRIBUTED, AND PRIVACY-PRESERVING ML: THE ROLE OF EFC

Researchers have focused on collaborative machine learning to address the challenges posed by the immense volume of data produced by IoT devices. Because of this, several users can train the ML model. This strategy does raise a few concerns concerning users' privacy. The following is a synopsis of four approaches that have been developed to resolve concerns relating to ML and privacy [27,28].

5.4.1 Federated Learning

A decentralized machine learning solution unites the computational capabilities of one principle server and several client servers. This strategy guarantees that all confidential information is present at the initial site during the learning process. The primary server will continue to function as an initial model for proxy data. A federated learning technique is depicted in Figure 5.6. In the initial model, local training is carried out using the client's local data. This type of training involves the model being trained independently for many repetitions. Therefore, each provider obtains the model's parameters from the primary server, trains the model using that provider's data, and then sends the parameters it has computed back to the primary server. To construct one model from many client updates, the principal server is integrated with those client updates. At last, the upgraded model is distributed to all

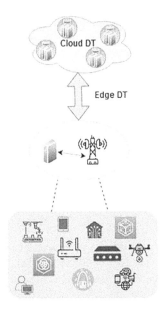

FIGURE 5.6 Federated learning approach.

of the client servers that participated in the training by the server. To achieve an optimal accuracy level, the learning process is iterated continuously.

5.4.2 DIFFERENTIAL PRIVACY

Edge devices transmit updated raw information to the principal server in Differential Privacy (DP). The primary idea is that every provider enhances noise, a random number, and the data to the principal server, concealing confidential information from attackers. The gathered raw, noisy data is integrated into the principal server, which is the input data for any ML approach. Thus, the integrated and processed information is hidden from 3rd parties and safely kept in the principal server.

5.4.3 HOMOMORPHIC ENCRYPTION

An integrated ML approach, Homomorphic Encryption (HE) is an encoding technique in which few tasks are accomplished on the encoded data and protects the primary encoded keys. While decrypting, it obtains readable data. Thus, in this technique, a provider directs encoded data to the principal server and the data is analyzed without the need to decode by the server [29].

5.4.4 SECRET SHARING

Privacy-sensitive data of every contributor is disseminated to all other providers secretly in this approach. In case, a malicious third party misuses the secret, it will not be worthy, as it will be readable only if they are integrated. This approach relies on two stages. The first stage, which is offline, comprises a dependable supplier segregating the data and sharing to the providers. In the second online stage, the actual processing is performed. After processing, the data is reassembled if an adequate amount of providers integrate their secret information and decrypt it.

5.5 CHALLENGES AND ISSUES

The EFC computing approach is expected to change the design of IoT architectures. However, there are a lot of challenges in adopting this network design for multi-layer processing. The contents given in the following are assessed from the literature.

5.5.1 TASK OFFLOADING

Many challenges have to be analyzed regarding offloading techniques such as service quality, versatility, fault investigation, privacy, security, and energy efficiency. This can occur in any kind of setup such as Edge-Fog, Device-Edge, Fog-Fog, or Cloud offloading to fog/edge [30].

5.5.2 SERVICE PLACEMENT (SP)

Carefully planned SP is considered an enhancement for edge-fog-cloud computing which is achieved by minimizing the network capacity and latency by allocating services to various network levels [31].

5.5.3 LOAD BALANCING

A demand rise and reply failure to a service assignment or task offloading causes a computational node to handle the processing requests. Therefore, the computational nodes which are underutilized must distribute the load between computational nodes, maintaining high QoS levels. The challenges are decision-making, problem modeling, and resource discovery [32].

5.5.4 HETEROGENEOUS RESOURCES

The profuse multi-vendor fog environment is deployed on diverse hardware and OS setup, resulting in virtualization. Though CC provides a few solutions, it is not adaptable for FC. This is because FC requires a container background with less overhead and a unified API for the abstraction of the distinct hardware present in the fog [33].

5.5.5 RESOURCE ORGANIZATION

FC aims to deliver computational assets to various services, causing the scaling of demanding fog resources to stagger over time. There is a need to implement complementary services at every individual Fog Node in the framework.

5.5.6 FAILURE MANAGEMENT

There is a demand for more resources while integrating abstracted fog setups during runtime similar to the CC. In addition, FNs can cause minimal network errors, and enter or leave the network at any time and during any local operation. Therefore, high resilience levels are required to achieve safety in the framework. Consider the movement of robot arms in cluster. Sufficient resilience must be placed at every FN to handle sole failure points [34].

5.5.7 INTER-FOG TRANSMISSION

Communication is possible in horizontal and vertical directions by an FN. The common topology requires horizontal communication to permit through one additional layer. This additional overhead increases the delay in communication and the fog's vulnerability to failure. So, additional connections among the fog nodes.

5.5.8 SUPPORT FOR MOBILE USERS

Various fog architectures are built to process requests efficiently. But, they analyze limited group of FC. Shortly, fog has to include various user categories, including high-mobility ones. Therefore, the approach is to locate each edge device into distinct user groups, which specify their mobility behavior and fog resource distribution [35].

5.5.9 FOG HARDWARE SUPPORT

Fog can incorporate multiple nodes among the core and the network edge. APs and other consumer-based gateways are perfect examples. The purpose-built IoT gateways are very expensive and not available in most electronic markets. Hence, flexibility is achieved by replacing slice of the ASIC with a multipurpose CPU, or the acquirement of CPU and GPU additionals will increase the usage of FC.

5.5.10 LOW LATENCY THROUGHPUT WIRELESS TRANSMISSION

There are challenges in transferring data from edge nodes to close FNs and minimizing the physical gap among the fog and the edge. For example, few applications require data transfer of more than 1 GBPS and therefore wireless communication technologies will be considered useless. In recent years, the millimeter range (30–300 GHz) is analyzed in research and multiple edge devices are beginning to provide multi-gigabit services. Hence, the data transfer latency is pushed below 1 ms and shortly, as the key feature of the 5 G new Radio (NR).

5.5.11 DATA ANALYTICS

It is necessary to distribute data and processing among distinct edge nodes for an effective distributed model. A growing area of research is to create competent approaches to train ML algorithms such as neural networks.

5.5.12 INTEROPERABILITY AND STANDARDIZATION

The fog will very soon become part of everyday life and profits will increase tremendously worldwide. The OpenFog consortium originated in 2015 jointly with companies like Cisco, Intel, Arm, and others built a FC framework, which was later renamed as the 1934–2018 standard [14]. In addition, the NIST also developed its fog conceptual architecture [36]. The NIST model is more compact than the former one. Many computing models have undergone regularization recently, such as 5 G multi-access computation, and many other unique techniques are being meticulously preferred, but cooperation and interaction are yet to be studied.

5.5.13 QoS

This is hard to achieve because of the dispersed, dissimilar, and random nature of the communication. In addition, the structure, power computation, and storage or I/O constraints. The crucial aspects which are to be further analyzed for research are efficient placement/allocation of tasks, resource accessibility, service response period, and fault acceptance in an integrated edge-fog-cloud model.

5.5.14 DATA CONFIDENTIALITY AND SECURITY

The current research on these issues is still in the naïve stage, and there is no unified technique for the same.

5.6 THE RISE OF DATA FABRIC ARCHITECTURES

There has been an emerging design concept called the "Data Fabric," which can handle most of the challenges addressed in the previous section. A data fabric uses constant analytics over the present, ascertainable, and implication metadata possessions to build the design, implementation, and utilization of assimilated and reusable data across all settings, such as hybrid and multi-cloud platforms. Data fabric helps industries to integrate data from various sources and analyze it seamlessly. Figure 5.7 shows the data fabric architecture. The data fabric needs the following components:

5.6.1 DATA INGESTION

All possible data formats such as structured and unstructured from diverse sources such as data streams, applications, cloud sources, and databases. It must also provide batch, real-time, and stream processing.

5.6.2 DATA PROCESSING

A set of tools is provided that can transform the data to make it analytics-ready to be utilized by the downstream BI tools.

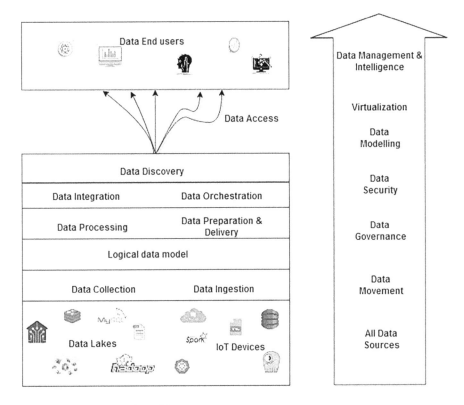

FIGURE 5.7   Data fabric architecture.

5.6.3   DATA ORCHESTRATION

The operation of all stages is coordinated by this component throughout the end-to-end data workflow. It is possible to define how often to run the pipelines and how to manage data effectively through the pipelines.

5.6.4   DATA DISCOVERY

Data modeling, data preparation, and data curation are employed in this layer. The analyst can determine the data across two "silos" as if they belong to the same dataset and extract valuable visions from it. This is the most important component of the data fabric.

5.6.5   DATA ACCESS

Data is delivered to analysts directly or through queries, APIs, dashboards, and data services. This layer builds intelligence, semantics, and rules into data access mechanisms to obtain data in the required format.

5.7 FUTURE DIRECTIONS

The EC and FC models are influential extensions to the cloud infrastructure, however, a few issues need to be addressed. The major challenges faced by these standards can assist as a probable future research direction.

A. **Task Partitioning and Programmability**

In the existing CC models, back-end applications are programmed by users on an abstract platform, without the knowledge of the cloud server setup. This is an advantage as the user is deprived of the platform configuration. Therefore, the cloud SP can compile and execute the application easily on the cloud server which has an adjustable setup. Back-end processing is shared across various computational nodes with the development of EC and FC models. This is a challenging problem for system developers to develop improved approaches for processing and storage sharing across all nodes, such that the synchronization process will not hinder the network's communication and result in minimum intra-network transmission latency.

B. **Security and Privacy**

Due to the increased interest in FC and EC models, many users utilize enhanced storage, processing resources and networking of CC servers focused on the network edge. This flexibility leads to many issues in securities which have to be addressed by the system designers. Various network security characteristics and the main security and privacy issues are summarized as given in the following:

5.7.1 TRUST AND AUTHENTICATION

EC and FC networks provide services that are reliable and secure to all users leading to an important prerequisite that all network devices must trust each other. Therefore, fog and edge nodes must check whether these are genuine services requesting resources. Also, edge or fog nodes must verify whether the resources sent to the services are genuine. These apprehensions led to authentication techniques. Thus, network resources must be authenticated before requests and transmissions. New approaches such as permissioned blockchain networks like Trust Chain [37,38] for verification, cryptographic validation approaches like SAKA-FC, and hardware-based verification techniques perform authentication of network possessions by using physically unclonable functions.

5.7.2 INTEGRITY

Network data transmitted in an EC and FC must be done in a secure approach such that attackers do not alter data. GNU Privacy Guard (GPG) ensures the integrity to transmit data. The integrity is validated at the destination station which is crucial in EC and FC due to the dependency on intra-network data transmission [39].

5.7.3   Availability

The data availability ensures that authorized parties receive information whenever they access it. DoS attack is a major issue that hinders information accessibility. EC and FC-based models are well developed to handle DoS attacks as they have disseminated processing assets. But, Distributed Denial of Service (DDoS) attacks also attempt to affect the models. Therefore, to defend applications or networks against DoS attacks, designers utilize Web Application Firewalls (WAF), and other intelligent traffic administration approaches to implement high level of security [40].

5.7.4   Confidentiality

The information confidentiality ensures data is protected from unauthorized parties. EC and FC paradigms prevent data leaks to ensure data security. Homomorphic Encryption and cryptographic approaches are used in Edge and Fog Computing to protect confidentiality at various places in the network. The attackers will not be able to analyze the data even if they get access to secure databases because these techniques will store the data in an encoded format.

5.7.5   Data Ownership

These paradigms frequently involve data transmission among nodes especially when the processing is offloaded to various network devices and results in data ownership problems. System designers must consider this behavior and draft a privacy policy for the network. The data transfer approaches should analyze the data compatibility with distinct data regulation guidelines for the sender and receiver.

5.7.6   System Metrics

There are a few metrics that must be analyzed while developing these models. System designers frequently handle policies that manage the following:

A. **Energy**
   Many embedded devices are present in fog and edge nodes. System designers should always consider energy-efficient mechanisms for task offloading to a particular node because of the limited power capacity. In comparison to cloud servers, minimal energy is required for fog and edge nodes. Therefore, renewable energy sources can be utilized by edge and fog nodes for their power requirements resulting in the minimization of CO_2 emission levels.

B. **Cost**
   Applications migrated to EFC minimize latency and increase reliability and fault tolerance but increase cost in comparison to conventional cloud services. Thus, the systems built within EFC must be cost-effective to validate their implementation in reply to enhanced user experience.

C. Bandwidth

The EC and FC models must be built by considering bandwidth, mostly for minimal cost systems with low network bandwidth. Minimal data transmission occurs when minimal processing of data happens near the edge. This is because cloud server receives no data. In some cases, the dispersed system nature increases the communication, mostly in the case of cooperative models which require inter-node transmission. Hence, system designers must analyze the two primary factors which can influence bandwidth usage and system organization.

5.8 CONCLUSION

A new revolution in IoT has started due to the conjunction of technologies from CC to EFC, AI, ML, and big data-which is concealing among physical and digital ecospheres. It is important to note that CC has secured IoT shortcomings by computing resources and virtually unrestricted storage to better handle the massive data surge caused by IoT devices. A holistic reference of the major converging architectures is discussed in this chapter. The FC and EC paradigms perform the processing near the endpoint IoT devices and handle the constraints of energy efficacy, context-aware, and latency prerequisites. This hierarchical architecture increases functionality. The hierarchical E-F-C has challenges in standardization, task offloading, and interaction of E-F-C. We also discussed the major design and deployment of these architectures including the recent data fabric architecture which has been widely accepted in the enterprise world. Finally, we discussed the open challenges and issues.

REFERENCES

1. Maddikunta P. K. R., Pham, Q.-V., Prabadevi, B., Natarajan, D., Dev, K., Gadekallu, T. R., Ruby, R., and Liyanage, M. Industry 5.0: A survey on enabling technologies and potential applications. Journal of Industrial Information Integration 26 (2022): 100257.
2. Renda, A., Schwaag Serger, S., Tataj, D., Morlet, A., Isaksson, D., Martins, F., and Giovannini, E. Industry 5.0, a transformative vision for Europe: Governing systemic transformations towards a sustainable industry. European Commission, Directorate-General for Research and Innovation 10.2777/17322 (2022).
3. Sharma, V., Balusamy, B., Sabharwal, M., and Ouaissa, M. (Eds.). Sustainable Digital Technologies: Trends, Impacts, and Assessments (1st ed.). CRC Press, 2023, 10.1201/9781003348313
4. Zeb, S., Mahmood, A., Khowaja, S. A., Dev, K., Hassan, S. A., Qureshi, N. M. F., Gidlund, M., and Bellavista, P. Industry 5.0 is coming: A survey on intelligent NextG wireless networks as technological enablers. arXiv preprint arXiv 2205 (2022): 09084.
5. Xu, X., Lu, Y., Vogel-Heuser, B., and Wang, L. Industry 4.0 and Industry 5.0—Inception, conception and perception. Journal of Manufacturing Systems 61 (2021): 530–535.
6. Xiloyannis, M., Alicea, R., Georgarakis, A.-M., Haufe, F. L., Wolf, P., Masia, L., and Riener, R. Soft robotic suits: State of the art, core technologies, and open challenges. IEEE Transactions on Robotics 38, no. 3 (2021): 1343–1362.
7. Murali, M. N. R. D. S., and Sharma, V. Performance Analysis of DGA-Driven Botnets using Artificial Neural networks. 2022 10th International Conference on

Reliability, Infocom Technologies and Optimization (Trends and Future Directions) (ICRITO), 2022, pp. 1–6.

8. Mahmood, A., Beltramelli, L., Abedin, S. F., Zeb, S., Mowla, N. I., Hassan, S. A., Sisinni, E., and Gidlund, M. Industrial IoT in 5G-and-beyond networks: Vision, architecture, and design trends. IEEE Transactions on Industrial Informatics 18, no. 6 (2021): 4122–4137.

9. Ali, M. A., Balamurugan, B., Dhanaraj, R. K., and Sharma, V. IoT and Blockchain based Smart Agriculture Monitoring and Intelligence Security System. 2022 3rd International Conference on Computation, Automation and Knowledge Management (ICCAKM), Dubai, United Arab Emirates, 2022, pp. 1–7, doi: 10.1109/ICCAKM54 721.2022.9990243.

10. Vilas-Boas, J. L., Rodrigues, J. JPC, and Alberti, A. M. Convergence of distributed ledger technologies with digital twins, IoT, and AI for fresh food logistics: Challenges and opportunities. Journal of Industrial Information Integration 31 (2023): 100393.

11. Firouzi, F., Farahani, B., and Marinšek, A. The convergence and interplay of edge, fog, and cloud in the AI-driven Internet of Things (IoT). Information Systems 107 (2022): 101840.

12. Raj, A., Sharma, V., and Shanu, A. K. Comparative Analysis Of Security And Privacy Technique For Federated Learning In IOT Based Devices. 2022 3rd International Conference on Computation, Automation and Knowledge Management (ICCAKM), Dubai, United Arab Emirates, 2022, pp. 1–5, doi: 10.1109/ICCAKM54721.2022. 9990152.

13. Martinez, I., Hafid, A. S., and Jarray, A. Design, resource management, and evaluation of fog computing systems: a survey. IEEE Internet of Things Journal 8, no. 4 (2020): 2494–2516.

14. Firouzi, F., Farahani, B., Barzegari, M., and Daneshmand, M. AI-driven data monetization: The other face of data in IoT-based smart and connected health. IEEE Internet of Things Journal 9, no. 8 (2020): 5581–5599.

15. Yousefpour, C. F., Nguyen, T., Kadiyala, K., Jalali, F., Niakanlahiji, A., Kong, J., and Jue, J. P. All one needs to know about fog computing and related edge computing paradigms: A complete survey. Journal of Systems Architecture 98 (2019): 289–330.

16. Firouzi, F., Chakrabarty, K., and Nassif, S. Intelligent Internet of Things: From Device to Fog and Cloud. Springer, 2020.

17. Nadian-Ghomsheh, B., Farahani, B., and Kavian, M. A hierarchical privacy preserving iot architecture for vision-based hand rehabilitation assessment. Multimedia Tools and Applications 80 (2021): 31357–31380.

18. Ali, M. A., Balamurugan, B., and Sharma, V. IoT and Blockchain Based Intelligence Security System for Human Detection Using an Improved ACO and Heap Algorithm. 2022 2nd International Conference on Advance Computing and Innovative Technologies in Engineering (ICACITE). IEEE, 2022.

19. IEEE Communications Society, IEEE Standard for Adoption of OpenFog Reference Architecture for Fog Computing. IEEE, 2018, Tech. Rep., ISBN: 9781504450171.

20. Iorga, M., Feldman, L., Barton, R., Martin, M. J., Goren, N., and Mahmoudi, C. Fog Computing Conceptual Model. National Institute of Standards and Technology, 2018, Tech. Rep., NIST SP 500-325.

21. Jayasinghe, U., Lee, G. M., MacDermott, Á., and Rhee, W. S. TrustChain: A privacy preserving blockchain with edge computing. Wireless Communications and Mobile Computing 2019 (2019).

22. Juyal, V. An optimized trusted-cluster–based routing in disruption-tolerant network using experiential learning model. International Journal of Communication Systems 33.1 (2020): e4196.

23. Juyal, V. On exploiting dynamic trusted routing scheme in delay tolerant networks. Wireless Personal Communications 112 (2020): 1705–1718.

24. Tuli, S., Mahmud, R., Tuli, S., and Buyya, R. Fogbus: A blockchain-based lightweight framework for edge and fog computing. Journal of Systems and Software 154 (2019): 22–36.

25. Wazid, M., Das, A. K., Kumar, N., and Vasilakos, A. V. Design of secure key management and user authentication scheme for fog computing services. Future Generation Computer Systems 91 (2019): 475–492.

26. Singh, A. V., Juyal, V., and Saggar, R. Trust based intelligent routing algorithm for delay tolerant network using artificial neural network. Wireless Networks 23(3) (2017): 693–702.

27. Ajmani, P., Sharma, V., Samuel, P., Somasundaram, K., and Vidhya, V. Patient Behaviour Analysis and Social Health Predictions through IoMT. 2022 10th International Conference on Reliability, Infocom Technologies and Optimization (Trends and Future Directions) (ICRITO), 2022, pp. 1–6.

28. Manogaran, G., and Lopez, D. A survey of big data architectures and machine learning algorithms in healthcare. International Journal of Biomedical Engineering and Technology 25.2-4 (2017): 182–211.

29. Cravero, A. Big data architectures and the internet of things: A systematic mapping study. IEEE Latin America Transactions 16.4 (2018): 1219–1226.

30. Erraissi, A., Belangour, A., and Tragha, A. A comparative study of hadoop-based big data architectures. International Journal of Web Applications 9.4 (2017): 129–137.

31. Persico, V., et al. Benchmarking big data architectures for social networks data processing using public cloud platforms. Future Generation Computer Systems 89 (2018): 98–109.

32. Castiglione, A., et al. Exploiting mean field analysis to model performances of big data architectures. Future Generation Computer Systems 37 (2014): 203–211.

33. Guerriero, M., et al. Towards a Model-Driven Design Tool for Big Data Architectures. Proceedings of the 2nd International Workshop on BIG Data Software Engineering. 2016.

34. Immonen, A., Pääkkönen, P., and Ovaska, E. Evaluating the quality of social media data in big data architecture. IEEE Access 3 (2015): 2028–2043.

35. Sharma, V., Balusamy, B., Thomas, J. J., and Atlas, L. G. (Eds.). Data Fabric Architectures: Web-Driven Applications. Walter de Gruyter GmbH & Co KG, 2023.

36. Basheer, S., Singh, K. U., Sharma, V., Bhatia, S., Pande, N., and Kumar, A. A robust NIfTI image authentication framework to ensure reliable and safe diagnosis. PeerJ Computer Science 9 (2023): e1323.

37. Singh, A., et al. Blockchain: Tool for Controlling Ransomware through Pre-Encryption and Post-Encryption Behavior. 2022 Fifth International Conference on Computational Intelligence and Communication Technologies (CCICT). IEEE, 2022.

38. Singh, A., Dhanaraj, R. K., Ali, M. A., Balusamy, B., and Sharma, V. Blockchain Technology in Biometric Database System. 2022 3rd International Conference on Computation, Automation and Knowledge Management (ICCAKM), Dubai, United Arab Emirates, 2022, pp. 1–6, doi: 10.1109/ICCAKM54721.2022.9990133.

39. Pushpalatha, N., Jabeera, S., Hemalatha, N., Sharma, V., Balusamy, B., and Yuvaraj, R. A Succinct Summary of the Solar MPPT Utilizing a Diverse Optimizing Compiler. 2022 5th International Conference on Contemporary Computing and Informatics (IC3I), Uttar Pradesh, India, 2022, pp. 1177–1181, doi: 10.1109/IC3I56241.2022.10072844.

40. Singh, A., Ali, M. A., Balusamy, B., and Sharma, V. Chapter 12 - Potential applications of digital twin technology in virtual factory, Editor(s): Dhanaraj, R. K., Bashir, A. K., Rajasekar, V., Balusamy, B., Malik, P., Digital Twin for Smart Manufacturing. Academic Press, 2023, pp. 221–241, ISBN 9780323992053, 10.1016/B978-0-323-99205-3.00011-0.

6 IoT Industrial Application Using Wireless Technologies

Pawan Whig
Vivekananda Institute of Professional Studies,
New Delhi, India

Shama Kouser
Department of Computer Science, Jazan University, Jazan,
Saudi Arabia

Ashima Bhatnagar Bhatia
Vivekananda Institute of Professional Studies,
New Delhi, India

Rahul Reddy Nadikattu
Senior IEEE Member, University of Cumbersome, USA

Yusuf Jibrin Alkali
Federal Inland Revenue Service, Nigeria

6.1 INTRODUCTION

Wireless systems provide several and substantial advantages over traditional wiring. A smart factory that is really flexible, with automatic directed automobiles that can travel anywhere they are required and automation that collaborates to maximize productivity. But without wireless solution, this degree of flexibility and automation would not be conceivable. Through wireless technologies, users may securely access, control, or monitor devices [1,2]. Personnel are no longer required to check on equipment while atop a tall ladder, underground in a mine, or in another uncomfortable or potentially hazardous location. There is no need to even be close to the equipment if it is connected to a wide-area network (WAN), which can lower travel expenses and difficulties [3].

Additionally, wireless systems are less expensive to deploy and simpler to grow or alter. Because there is no need to physically connect to the equipment, maintenance expenses are also decreased because the connections are less likely to be harmed by continuous usage. Have still not companies embraced wireless technology yet? The

DOI: 10.1201/9781003389231-6

two most frequent causes are trepidation and a fear of change [4,5]. The second justification has to do with science. It is believed that the capacity is unsuitable, the latency is too high, the wireless communication is inadequate, as well as the link is unreliable[6,7].

Don't mess with a good thing if it's working, is a typical industrial philosophy. This makes sense since industrial applications require a great deal of caution because we want to ensure everyone's safety and minimize downtime [8–10]. However, there are existing wireless solutions in use, so switching from wires to wireless doesn't have to be difficult. With every wireless development, concerns that cellular and wireless standards don't satisfy the requirements lose some of their validity. Establishing needs and considering solutions, such as wireless and cellular standards, are crucial. Bluetooth is a suitable option if reliability is important, the volume of data is little, and no internet connection is wanted [11,12].

A cellular linking that complies with LPWAN values is a great option if a low cost, and low power internet connection is required [13–15] The most recent wireless systems could be suitable if low latency, high bandwidth, and strong security are required. In this area, wireless solutions will play a significant role in the coming future [16,17]. The improvements of 5 G allow additional commercial uses to install a wireless solution instead of cutting wires since the digital network can handle more specifications. As shown in the market prediction in Figure 6.1.

Since 5 G represents a huge advance over 4 G LTE, it offers considerable benefits. Numerous opportunities for industrial applications are now available. Nevertheless, the deployment of 5 G does not rule out the use of 4 G LTE in industrial applications. LPWAN standards container offer the wireless connectivity needed. Critical IoT applications that demand high availability, low latency, and dependability can employ 5 G [18,19].

Public Wi-Fi and the home market are expected to see the fastest adoption of Wi-Fi 6 technology since it allows for the simultaneous connecting of more devices while maintaining a reliable and rapid connection. Higher throughput and shorter latencies are advantageous. The energy consumption of everything battery-powered will be reduced by smart management techniques like the target wake time (TWT)[20,21].

Both 5 G and Wi-Fi 6 as shown in Figure 6.2 have the potential to significantly outperform their forerunners, which opens the door for industrial applications. Wi-Fi 6 typically offers net connectivity also inside or in specifically designated spaces, net connectivity to all additional outdoor seats, including moving cars(D. Christin et. al 2020). On this basis, remote vehicle tracking while a vehicle is in motion would be a typical industrial use case for 5 G[22,23].

The provision of internet access to coming below the extensive IoT canopy would be a typical Wi-Fi 6 industrial example, on the other hand. It's crucial to check any criteria and go into additional depth as usual[24–26]. It costs less to scale and deploy Wi-Fi 6. If Wi-Fi 6 satisfies the criteria and the planned application will be used indoors or in a densely populated outdoor region[27]. Even if the installation is indoors, cellular is a preferable option if the criteria are more stringent and fall under the critical IoT category, the allowed levels are lower in 5 G. Low latency is crucial for key IoT applications. While Wi-Fi 6 may support latency as low as 20 ms, 5 G can support latency as low as 1 ms for important IoT submissions[28].

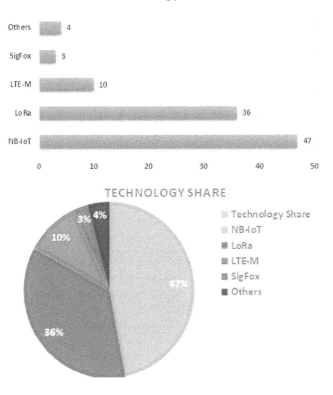

FIGURE 6.1 LPWAN Market by 2023.

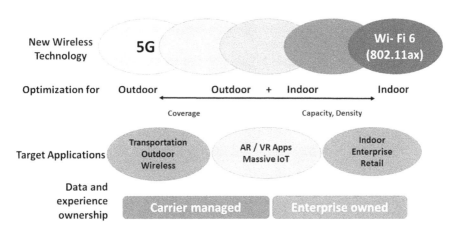

FIGURE 6.2 5G and Wi-Fi 6.

6.2 IIOT

That globe is becoming smarter thanks to the Internet of Things. A portion of the wider Internet of Things (IoT) that focuses on devices and goods used in business settings is called the Industrial Internet of Things (IIoT)[29] as shown in Figure 6.3.

How is Industrial IoT Implemented?
The Industrial Internet of Things (IoT) system comprises intelligent sensors, equipment, tools, software platforms, cloud servers, and applications. These smart sensors are utilized throughout the production process for specific purposes. Data from these sensor networks is continuously sent and received by IoT devices, which then transmit the data to the cloud application server for processing and analysis. Advanced application programs are developed to handle the vast amounts of data within a secure network, enabling efficient management and analysis[30].

6.2.1 AUTOMATION

Industrial automation is a highly significant and prevalent application of the Internet of Things (IoT). By implementing IoT technologies, businesses can enhance their operational efficiency through the automation of machines and tools. This automation plays a crucial role in streamlining industrial processes, allowing businesses to function more effectively. Automation of machines can increase process stage accuracy to a higher extent. Smart sensor networks connected to a centralized cloud system are utilized with automation technologies comparable PLC, which collect enormous amounts of data. To examine the data and its behavior for improvements, specialized tools and apps are employed [31–33].

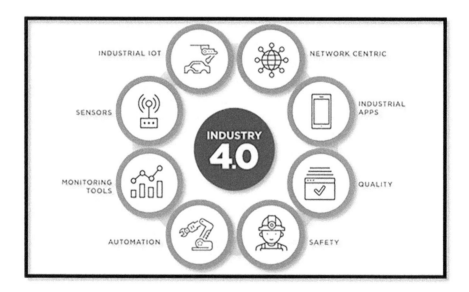

FIGURE 6.3   Industrial Internet of Things (IIoT) in Industry 4.0.

Industrial automation lowers mistakes, increases efficiency, is simple to operate, and can be accessed remotely via apps. Automation of tools and machines minimizes the need for human labor for particular jobs since machines can function in harsher circumstances than people can.

6.2.2 FACTORY NETWORKS

The connected factory idea is a practical way to boost productivity across the board. For simpler management and access, large components. With the use of industrial IoT solutions, it is possible to remotely monitor downtime, check inventory and shipment status, plan maintenance, halt or pause a specific operation for additional study, and more[34–36].

6.2.3 IOT-ENABLED MANUFACTURING

For IoT-enabled manufacturing, several businesses are creating intelligent robotic systems. Smart robotics enables perfect precision and efficient handling of equipment and materials in the production line. Using intelligent robotic arms, predefined criteria may be specified. The notion of a man-machine interface will simplify operations and result in increased productivity in future IoT-enabled manufacturing as shown in Figure 6.4.

Robots equipped with cutting-edge integrated sensors for real-time analysis can be programmed to carry out complicated tasks. For monitoring and management, these robotics networks are connected to a secure cloud. This data is accessible to the engineering team, who may use it to quickly respond to either avert an unanticipated failure caused by a machine issue or enhance the product [37–39].

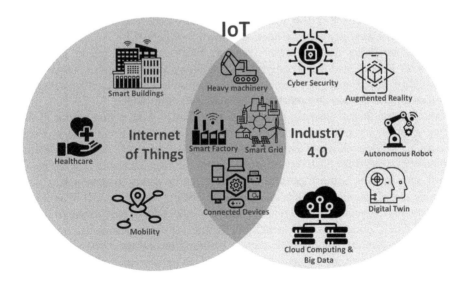

FIGURE 6.4 IoT-enabled manufacturing.

6.2.4 MAINTENANCE PLANNING

New manufacturing machines are fitted with intelligent sensors that continually check the condition of all the key parts and can identify any serious problems before the system fails altogether. Smart sensors will inform the central system of a maintenance issue and send alarm messages to the appropriate people or organizations.

Without interfering with ordinary tasks, maintenance engineers may efficiently arrange schedules of maintenance based on data analysis. The production line may minimize unneeded downtime with the help of predictive maintenance. Unexpected machine failure might result in product damage, delivery delays, and a loss of revenue for producers.

Each machine's status is continuously kept in a cloud system. Remote access to each machine's history, performance, and upcoming maintenance is simple (on PCs, via web interface or via smartphone applications). The analysis of the obtained data may be used to calculate and apply performance improvements for each machine and step of the production process [40].

6.3 WEARABLES AND SMART TOOLS INTEGRATION

The workforce is able to carry out the operation with increased accuracy and efficiency thanks to the integration of smart sensors into equipment and machines. Specially created wearables and smart glasses assist workers in reducing mistakes and enhancing workplace safety.

Employees can receive immediate warning signals via smart wearables in the event of an emergency like a fire or gas leak. Wearables may continually check on a person's health and provide feedback if they are unfit for a task. One of the crucial areas in many companies that need constant development to meet rising demand is logistics. Shrewd device skill is well-suited to handle numerous intricate logistical processes and efficiently achieve items as shown in Figure 6.5.

Drones are being used by online retailers like Amazon to deliver items to customers. Drones and other advanced technology provide higher efficiency, accessibility, speed, and need less labor. In contrast to conventional procedures, initial expenditures are substantial, and execution has drawbacks.

Another significant business that makes use of IoT is the airline sector. This sector produces aircraft and performs preventative maintenance on those that are already in service. Airlines employ IoT technology to track the hundreds of components needed for each day of production at the manufacturing facility. Easy supply management is made possible by centralized inventory management.

In the event that any products need to be topped off, suppliers will be notified automatically. Inventory management may be successfully performed via IoT without much human involvement. Intelligent sensors continually track an aircraft's mechanical components; data is gathered in real-time and sent to the aircraft maker. Any time a portion of an aeroplane needs repair, the appropriate personnel is alerted, and maintenance is immediately carried out after the jet has landed[41].

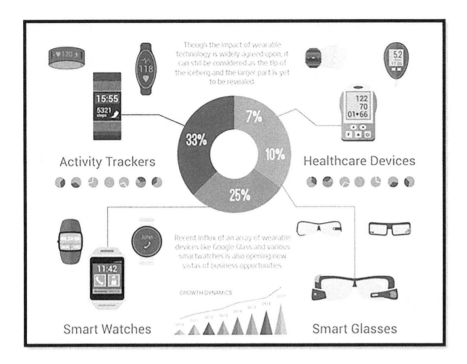

FIGURE 6.5   wearable technology infographics.

6.4   INTEGRATION OF SOFTWARE FOR PRODUCT IMPROVEMENT

One of the most crucial elements of any IoT system, smart analytics solutions further increase the system's potential for innovation and optimization.

Huge companies are deploying specialized software to perform in-depth analyses on the vast amounts of data gathered from sophisticated machinery and sensor networks. A more thorough grasp of data analysis and behavior throughout time provides a better overview of process optimization techniques for products.

6.4.1   INTELLIGENT PACKAGE MANAGEMENT

IoT-based package management improves industrial units' productivity and comfort. Smart sensors may keep track of all packing processes and provide real-time status updates. Vibrations, ambient variables, such as temperature and humidity, may all be picked up by embedded sensors, which can also provide.

6.4.2   SUPERIORITY AND SECURITY

The use of IoT skill in industrial results in better excellent products. By optimizing process processes, continuous monitoring and analysis of each stage ensures greater quality.

A better degree of security is provided by the use of intelligent tools and software-aided processes. A highly secure gateway and cloud server platform are coupled with software driven automation and data collecting from an extensive sensor network.

6.4.3 SELF-DRIVING

Self-driving cars are being used by the automotive industry to handle logistics on their property and provide goods. Smart cars may identify traffic jams along their route and divert to reach their destination in a short amount of time. Numerous sophisticated sensors that use GPS and wireless technologies to connect to the control center are included in these cars.

Better solutions for power management in industries may be available with IoT. For effective power management, certain sensors can detect the environment and activate controls for lighting, air conditioners, humidity controls, liquid flow, etc.

6.5   INDUSTRIAL INTERNET OF THINGS BENEFITS

greater precision

- Process and product improvement
- predictive analysis and maintenance
- greater effectiveness
- Remote access and supervision
- improved security
- scaling of the network
- decreased process and machine downtime
- energy savings
- cost efficiency

6.5.1 TYPICAL IoT WIRELESS TECHNOLOGY

Different IoT solutions are more suitable for specific use cases due to their unique strengths and limitations concerning various network requirements. IIoT has recently seen the emergence of LPWANs.

This case focuses on the use of small, affordable cells that enable long-range communication, lasting for years. These cells are specifically designed to handle extensive IoT networks that cover large industrial and business complexes. By utilizing low-power, wide-area networks (LPWANs), LPWANs excel in scenarios where high data throughput is not necessary or time-sensitive. For a comparison of IoT wireless standards, please refer to Table 6.1.

Furthermore, it's important to note that not all LPWANs (Low-Power Wide-Area Networks) are equal. Different technologies offer varying levels of performance in key network aspects, such as spectrum utilization. When implementing unlicensed technologies, factors like scalability and quality of service become crucial considerations. Additionally, standardization plays a vital role in ensuring long-term dependability, security, and interoperability.

TABLE 6.1
Comparison of IoT Wireless Standards

Wireless Standard	Range	Data Rate	Power Consumption	Cost
LPWAN	Long	Low	Low	Low
Wi-Fi	Short	High	High	Medium
Bluetooth	Short	Medium	Low	Low
Zigbee	Medium	Medium	Low	Medium
Cellular	Long	High	High	High

6.5.2 MOBILE

Various phone call and video streaming applications offer reliable broadband connectivity, but they come with the disadvantage of having very high power and operating costs.

While cellular networks are not suitable for most battery-operated sensor network IoT applications, they are ideal for certain uses. For example, the widespread and high-speed cellular connectivity can support fleet telemetry and tracking services, traffic routing, advanced driver assistance systems (ADAS), and in-car entertainment.

The future of autonomous vehicles and increased realism is expected to rely on the next generation of cellular technology, 5 G. 5 G provides high-speed flexibility and significantly lower latency. In the future, 5 G is anticipated to enable various time-sensitive industrial automation applications, real-time mobile delivery of medical data for connected healthcare, and real-time video surveillance for public safety. Similar work on network routing protocol is referred to in [42,43].

6.5.3 MESH PROCEDURES

Zigbee is a 802.15.4 short-range, low-power radiocommunication procedure that is usually used in mesh architectures to spread data over many IoT devices and increase access. Zigbee consumes a lot less electricity and offers faster communication throughput than LPWAN because of its mesh design.

Zigbee and other mesh technologies like Z-Wave and Thread are well-suited for medium-range Internet of Things (IoT) deployments where there is a relatively equal distribution of nodes in close proximity. These technologies are particularly suitable for home automation use cases such as controlling lights, HVAC systems, safety devices, and energy management. Zigbee is considered a good complement to local area networks in these scenarios.

Wireless networks have been used in industrial settings before the emergence of low-power wide-area networks (LPWAN). They offer various possibilities for remote support. However, they are not optimal for applications that require connectivity across large geographical areas. Additionally, their scalability is often limited due to the complexity of network configuration and management requirements.

6.6   BLE AND BLUETOOTH

Bluetooth is a technology that falls under the category of Wireless Personal Area Networks and is widely used in the consumer market. Originally, Bluetooth Classic was developed to facilitate point-to-multipoint data transmission between consumer electronic devices. However, to cater to the needs of small-scale Consumer IoT applications, Bluetooth Low Energy was later created with a focus on minimizing power consumption.

Device electronics are commonly utilized alongside electronic devices, particularly smartphones, for the purpose of transmitting data to the cloud. Bluetooth Low Energy (BLE) is now widely employed in various applications, such as Smart Home systems and health and fitness wearables. It enables seamless data transmission to smartphones, allowing for easy display and processing of the information.

In Table 6.2, we compare BLE and traditional Bluetooth in terms of power consumption, data transfer rate, range, compatibility, applications, complexity, and cost. BLE has low power consumption, lower data transfer rates, shorter range, limited compatibility with older devices, and is commonly used in IoT devices, wearables, and healthcare devices. On the other hand, traditional Bluetooth has higher power consumption, higher data transfer rates, medium- to long-range capability, broader compatibility with various devices, and is commonly used for audio streaming, file transfer, and peripheral devices. BLE is simpler and more lightweight, while traditional Bluetooth is more complex and feature-rich. In terms of cost, BLE is generally more affordable, while traditional Bluetooth can be moderately expensive.

Bluetooth Mesh protocol aims to increase the scalability of the deployment of BLE devices, particularly in retail environments as shown in the comparisonearlier in Table 6.2. Since BLE beacon networks offer adaptable indoor localization properties, they have been used to allow new service enhancements like in-store guidance, customized marketing, and content delivery.

TABLE 6.2
Comparison of BLE and Bluetooth

Aspect	Bluetooth Low Energy (BLE)	Bluetooth
Power Consumption	Low	High
Data Transfer Rate	Low	High
Range	Short	Medium/Long
Compatibility	Limited compatibility with older devices	Broad compatibility with various devices
Applications	IoT devices, wearables, healthcare devices	Audio streaming, file transfer, peripheral devices
Complexity	Simple and lightweight	More complex and feature-rich
Cost	Affordable	Moderately expensive

6.7   WI-FI

Wi-Fi is a well-known technology that provides high-speed data transfer for both home and office environments. However, it has certain limitations when it comes to coverage, scalability, and power consumption, making it less prevalent in the IoT domain. Due to its high power consumption, Wi-Fi may not be suitable for large networks of battery-operated IoT sensors, particularly in industrial IoT and smart building applications. Nonetheless, Wi-Fi is commonly used to connect devices that can be easily powered through a standard electrical outlet, such as smart home devices. Through new digital mobile services in the retail and mass entertainment industries, the standard is ready to alter consumer experience and upgrade public Wi-Fi infrastructure. In-car networks for entertainment and on boarding analytical are anticipated to be Wi-Fi 6's most revolutionary use. Yet additional time will probably be needed for the development.

RFID utilizes wireless communication to transmit small data packets over short distances from an RFID tag to a reader. This technology has brought significant transformations in logistics and retail industries. By integrating RFID tags into various products and equipment, businesses can track their inventory and assets in real-time, leading to improved supply chain management and better stock and production planning. RFID continues to play a crucial role in the retail sector, enabling innovative IoT applications like smart shelves, self-checkout systems, and smart mirrors. As IoT gains more acceptance, it further strengthens the relevance of RFID. For a comparison of various wireless technologies, please refer to Table 6.3.

In Table 6.3, we compare various wireless technologies based on their range, data rate, power consumption, cost, and use cases. Wi-Fi offers a short to medium range, high data rates, medium to high power consumption, and moderate cost. It is commonly used for internet connectivity and data-intensive applications. Bluetooth

TABLE 6.3
Comparison of Various Wireless Technologies

Wireless Technology	Range	Data Rate	Power Consumption	Cost	Use Cases
Wi-Fi	Short to Medium	High	Medium to High	Moderate	Internet connectivity, data-intensive applications
Bluetooth	Short	Medium	Low	Low	Personal area networks, wireless peripherals
Zigbee	Short to Medium	Low to Medium	Low	Low	Home automation, smart meters, industrial control
Cellular	Long	High	High	High	Wide-area connectivity, mobile communication
LPWAN	Long	Low	Low	Low	IoT applications, asset tracking, monitoring

has a short range, medium data rates, low power consumption, and low cost. It is commonly used for personal area networks and wireless peripherals. Zigbee has a short to medium range, low to medium data rates, low power consumption, and low cost. It is commonly used in home automation, smart meters, and industrial control systems. Cellular networks provide long-range connectivity, high data rates, high power consumption, and higher cost. They are commonly used for wide-area connectivity and mobile communication. LPWAN (Low-Power Wide-Area Network) offers long-range communication, low data rates, low power consumption, and affordable cost. It is commonly used for IoT applications, asset tracking, and monitoring.

6.8   CHALLENGES

The industry's use of smart buildings is rising, thanks to the epidemic. However, smart buildings continue to present obstacles. Clear, intelligent solutions can help to reduce these issues. Smart building initiatives might appear to be hard. With the endless uses of this technology, such as the Internet of Things (IoT) and Power-over-Ethernet (PoE) solutions, numerous concerns might emerge from concept to implementation as shown in Figure 6.6. A smart building project comprises many stages and people, which creates obstacles in a range of areas.

Because of these difficulties, it is critical to have a thorough strategy in place, to set firm and realistic timetables, and to have open lines of communication. These obstacles may be overcome with obvious solutions that will make smart buildings a reality.

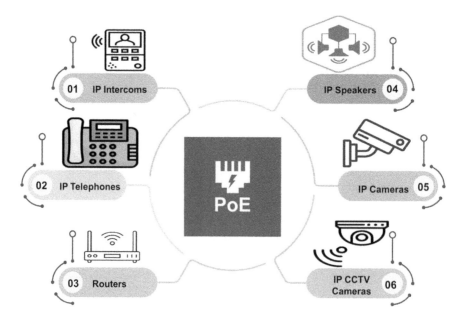

FIGURE 6.6   the Internet of Things (IoT) and Power-over-Ethernet (PoE).

6.8.1 CYBERSECURITY

Early implementation of smart buildings is frequently hampered by issues with cybersecurity, privacy, data integrity, and data accessibility. While some solutions are starting to address this problem, the majority of customers still give it a top priority. There will always be a problem with the internet because as more devices connect to it, the risk inevitably increases.

6.8.2 PRIVATE INFORMATION

The readiness of building occupants to submit for IoT facilities is progressively contingent on their faith in the organization responsible for collecting and analyzing the data - and their plans for using it. Some of the IoT attacks are shown in Figure 6.7.

6.8.3 PROCESS OF LEGACY CONSTRUCTION AND RETROFIT

Due to the rigorous procurement procedure, Smart systems are not addressed until later stages of the new-build process, limiting innovation and generating inter-operability concerns. Smart building experts and system integrators are not always included in projects.

6.8.4 INTEROPERABILITY

If a team does not include a professional smart systems consultant or systems integrator, suppliers who provide separate systems often lack the motivation to collaborate on systems integration. In new construction projects, building systems are frequently commissioned without much consideration for compliance or compatibility with the overall system. However, there is a positive trend toward the adoption of open standards over proprietary ones in the industry, as depicted in Figure 6.8. This presents opportunities for the smart buildings business to overcome the existing challenges and thrive.

6.9 OPPORTUNITIES COLLABORATION AND JOINT VENTURES

Collaboration can lead to far better outcomes. It guarantees that everyone is aware of the benefits of smart skills and how keen schemes may be used to offer better results in footings of effectiveness, connection, and occupant comfort. Because they are not tied to a single provider, this makes buildings more future-proof.

6.9.1 WELLNESS AND GOOD HEALTH

The goal is to entice customers back into retail malls and entertainment venues by providing them with a distinctive experience, as well as to motivate staff to return to their places of employment. There is pressure to create a safe environment for residents as well as to foster safety and trust among the general public. Given that

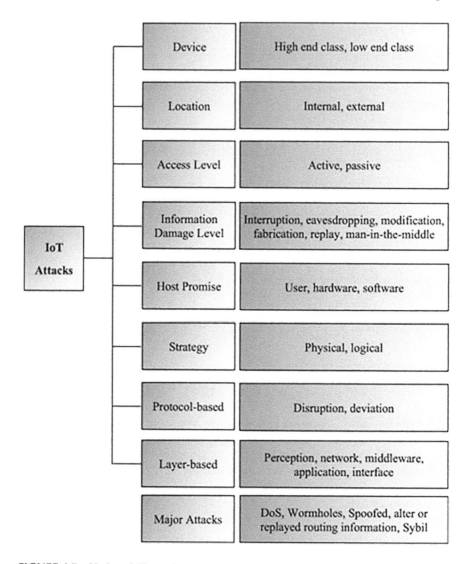

FIGURE 6.7   Various IoT attacks.

employees are frequently an organization's most expensive asset, putting their needs first boosts productivity, enjoyment, and retention.

6.9.2 SUSTAINABILITY

The growing emphasis on cost savings and energy efficiency is driving an increasing number of companies to adopt smart technologies in buildings. These technologies provide better insights and suggest adjustments that can help save expenses and reduce energy consumption. Since there will already be 80% of buildings in existence in 2050, it is crucial that we modernize and future-proof them to make them more sustainable, as shown in Figure 6.9 [44].

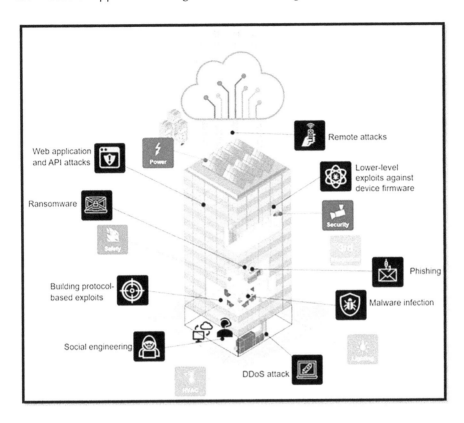

FIGURE 6.8   Smart building open standard.

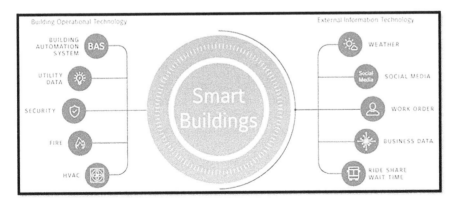

FIGURE 6.9   Smart building technologies.

Trades will except cash on hiring expenses and sick existences, and their total output will rise, if they can provide their workers a sense of security and care.

The Industrial Internet of Things (IIoT) encompasses a wide range of devices, including sensors and software-controlled systems, which transfer data through the internet. However, a challenge in implementing the IIoT has been ensuring the security and efficient transfer of data from field devices to the cloud, particularly with the rise of the Industry 4.0 concept. To address this challenge, businesses have acknowledged the significance of wireless technology and have established reliable wireless networks to facilitate IoT connections. An innovative wireless solution is easier to deploy devices than traditional cable systems, which boosts productivity and efficiency Additionally, a wireless network may be constructed to handle a variety of communication protocols, like Modbus and MQTT, making it possible to transfer data quickly across various devices, even legacy equipment, saving them from being scrapped. Most significantly, wireless solutions make it possible to manage facilities with ongoing remote asset monitoring, which decreases downtime, enhances worker safety, and speeds up the strategic decision-making process for business leaders[45].

6.9.2.1 Important Considerations for Choosing the Best Wireless I/O Modules

The essential criteria to take into account when choosing a wireless I/O module are restated here.

- Distance Data rate
- Energy usage Encryption frequency

Data rate, which measures how quickly data can be wirelessly transmitted, refers to the speed at which bits are transferred between devices over a network per second. Different wireless technologies have varying data rates, impacting power consumption and battery life. For example, LoRaWAN technology offers a slower data rate compared to Wi-Fi, prioritizing power efficiency and longer battery life. Wi-Fi, on the other hand, consumes more power but provides a faster and constant connection with data speeds reaching up to 300 Mbps.

Depending on the wireless technology used, a network's coverage varies.

6.9.2.2 Do your Gadgets Work in an Environment that is Energy-Efficient?

When choosing the ideal wireless I/O module for your applications, power consumption is an important factor to take into account. Because each module and protocol uses a different amount of power, the choice of module for each protocol is crucial for battery life. Low-power LPWAN/LoRaWAN modules are appropriate for long-range communication and can significantly increase battery life. Although RFID, ZigBee, and Wi-Fi typically consume more power than LPWAN/LoRaWAN protocols.

6.9.2.3 Does Your Application Benefit from Wireless Encryption?

The network's devices and data are protected from illegal access and harm by various wireless modules using various encryption algorithms.

6.9.2.4 Can Your Gadget Function Properly Across All Frequency Bands?

Based on frequency, wireless modules can only successfully connect with each other inside a specific frequency band. However, there could be instances when a certain frequency band is saturated or where using a device in a particular band is prohibited under certain conditions.

6.10   RESULT AND DISCUSSION

The comparison of various wireless technologies provides valuable insights into their key features and applications.

1. Wi-Fi: Wi-Fi offers high-throughput data transfer and is widely used in home and office environments. However, it has limitations in terms of coverage, scalability, and power consumption. This makes it less suitable for large-scale IoT deployments, especially those involving battery-operated sensors. Nonetheless, Wi-Fi excels in connecting devices that can be easily powered through electrical outlets, such as smart home devices.
2. Bluetooth: Bluetooth is commonly used for short-range communication and is popular in personal area networks and wireless peripherals. It has moderate data rates, low power consumption, and is cost-effective. Bluetooth is suitable for connecting devices like smartphones, tablets, and wearable devices. It is often employed in applications such as audio streaming and file transfer.
3. Zigbee: Zigbee operates on short to medium-range communication and is known for its low to medium data rates, low power consumption, and affordability. It is widely used in home automation, smart meters, and industrial control systems. Zigbee offers reliable and efficient communication for IoT devices in localized areas.
4. Cellular: Cellular networks provide long-range connectivity and high data rates, making them suitable for wide-area IoT applications. However, cellular technology consumes more power and incurs higher costs compared to other wireless standards. Cellular networks are commonly used for mobile communication and applications requiring extensive coverage.
5. LPWAN: LPWAN (Low-Power Wide-Area Network) technology is designed for long-range communication with low data rates and low power consumption. It is particularly suitable for IoT applications, asset tracking, and monitoring. LPWAN offers cost-effective connectivity for large-scale deployments spanning industrial and business complexes.

The results highlight the trade-offs between range, data rate, power consumption, and cost among different wireless technologies.

These findings provide valuable guidance for businesses and organizations seeking to implement IoT solutions. By understanding the characteristics and applications of different wireless technologies, stakeholders can make informed decisions and choose the most appropriate technology to meet their specific needs.

6.11   CONCLUSION

There is a lot of emphasis on infusing objects with ever-increasing intelligence, but there are other places for "smarts" in Industrial IoT applications. Intelligent end nodes and network and security management capabilities that emulate the best of enterprise IT and OT should be used in industrial IoT networks. In order to respond to the demands of particular applications, networks should be extremely adaptable. Given the low power needs to ensure long battery life, intelligent routing and self-awareness of network power availability should be used to maximize network-wide power usage. An implementation of differences in topology may be favored by changes in the RF environment, therefore the network should automatically adapt to these changes. The SmartMesh Network Manager from Analog Devices not only offers network security, management, and routing optimization, but it also enables users to remotely reprogram nodes if necessary, giving a path for future capabilities as customers' needs change. With distinct commercial motivations and a strong return on investment, the Internet of Things is very much an industrial phenomenon. Industrial wireless sensor networks must fulfill a high standard for intelligence, security, and long-term, dependable wire-free operation in these mission-critical applications. Wireless mesh network standards, which will be essential Industrial IoT building blocks to assist industrial clients in transforming their companies and services in the Industrial IoT age, may meet these strict criteria.

REFERENCE

1. Alkali, Y., Routray, I., & Whig, P. (2022a). Strategy for Reliable, Efficient and Secure IoT Using Artificial Intelligence. IUP Journal of Computer Sciences, 16(2).
2. Alkali, Y., Routray, I., & Whig, P. (2022b). Study of various methods for reliable, efficient and Secured IoT using Artificial Intelligence. Available at SSRN 4020364.
3. Raj, A., Sharma, V. & Shanu, A. K. (2022). Comparative Analysis Of Security And Privacy Technique For Federated Learning In IOT Based Devices. 2022 3rd International Conference on Computation, Automation and Knowledge Management (ICCAKM), Dubai, United Arab Emirates, pp. 1–5, doi: 10.1109/ICCAKM54721.2022.9990152.
4. Anand, M., Velu, A., & Whig, P. (2022). Prediction of Loan Behaviour with Machine Learning Models for Secure Banking. Journal of Computer Science and Engineering (JCSE), 3(1), 1–13.
5. Jupalle, H., Kouser, S., Bhatia, A. B., Alam, N., Nadikattu, R. R., & Whig, P. (2022). Automation of human behaviors and its prediction using machine learning. Microsystem Technologies, 1–9.
6. Ajmani, P., Sharma, V., Samuel, P., Somasundaram, K. & Vidhya, V. (2022). Patient behaviour analysis and social health predictions through IoMT. 2022 10th International Conference on Reliability, Infocom Technologies and Optimization (Trends and Future Directions) (ICRITO), pp. 1–6, doi: 10.1109/ICRITO56286.2022.9964846.
7. Nadikattu, R. R., Mohammad, S. M., & Whig, P. (2020). Novel Economical Social Distancing Smart Device for COVID-19. International Journal of Electrical Engineering and Technology (IJEET).
8. Tomar, U., Chakroborty, N., Sharma, H., & Whig, P. (2021). AI based Smart Agriculture System. Transactions on Latest Trends in Artificial Intelligence, 2(2).
9. Maurya, A. & Sharma, V. (2022). Facial emotion recognition using keras and CNN. 2022 2nd International Conference on Advance Computing and Innovative Technologies in Engineering (ICACITE), pp. 2539–2543, doi: 10.1109/ICACITE53722.2022.9823480.
10. Ali, M. A., Balamurugan, B., Dhanaraj, R. K. & Sharma, V. (2022). IoT and blockchain based smart agriculture monitoring and intelligence security system. 2022 3rd

International Conference on Computation, Automation and Knowledge Management (ICCAKM), Dubai, United Arab Emirates, pp. 1–7, doi: 10.1109/ICCAKM54721.2022. 9990243.

11. Whig, P., Kouser, S., Velu, A., & Nadikattu, R. R. (2022). Fog-IoT-Assisted-Based Smart Agriculture Application. In Demystifying Federated Learning for Blockchain and Industrial Internet of Things (pp. 74–93). IGI Global.

12. Whig, P., Nadikattu, R. R., & Velu, A. (2022). COVID-19 Pandemic Analysis using Application of AI. Healthcare Monitoring and Data Analysis Using IoT: Technologies and Applications, 1.

13. Whig, P., Velu, A., & Bhatia, A. B. (2022). Protect Nature and Reduce the Carbon Footprint With an Application of Blockchain for IIoT. In Demystifying Federated Learning for Blockchain and Industrial Internet of Things (pp. 123–142). IGI Global.

14. Murali, M. N. R. D. S. & Sharma, V. (2022). Performance analysis of DGA-driven botnets using artificial neural networks. 2022 10th International Conference on Reliability, Infocom Technologies and Optimization (Trends and Future Directions) (ICRITO), pp. 1–6, doi: 10.1109/ICRITO56286.2022.9965044.

15. Whig, P., Velu, A., & Naddikatu, R. R. (2022). The Economic Impact of AI-Enabled Blockchain in 6G-Based Industry. In AI and Blockchain Technology in 6G Wireless Network (pp. 205–224). Springer, Singapore.

16. Varghese, A. & Tandur, D. (2014). Wireless requirements and challenges in industry 4.0. In International Conference on Contemporary Computing and Informatics (IC3I), pp. 634–638.

17. Willig, A., Matheus, K., & Wolisz, A. (2005). Wireless technology in industrial networks. In Proceedings of the IEEE, vol. 93, no. 6. Institute of Electrical and Electronics Engineers Inc., pp. 1130–1151.

18. Wollschlaeger, M., Sauter, T., & Jasperneite, J. (2017). The Future of Industrial Communication: Automation Networks in the Era of the Internet of Things and Industry 4.0. IEEE Industrial Electronics Magazine, 11(1), 17–27.

19. Park, P., Ergen, S. C., Fischione, C., Lu, C., & Johansson, K. H. (apr 2018). Wireless network design for control systems: A survey. pp. 978–1013.

20. De Pellegrini, F., Miorandi, D., Vitturi, S., & Zanella, A. (may 2006). On the Use of Wireless Networks at Low Level of Factory Automation Systems. IEEE Transactions on Industrial Informatics, 2(2), 129–143.

21. Sanchez-Iborra, R. & Cano, M.-D. (may 2016). State of the Art in LP-WAN Solutions for Industrial IoT Services. Sensors, 16(5), 708. [Online]. Available: http://www.mdpi.com/1424-8220/16/5/708

22. Christin, D., Mogre, P. S., & Hollick, M. (apr 2010). Survey on Wireless Sensor Network Technologies for Industrial Automation: The Security and Quality of Service Perspectives. Future Internet, 2(2), 96–125. [Online]. Available: http://www.mdpi.com/1999-5903/2/2/96

23. Seferagic, A., Famaey, J., De Poorter, E., & Hoebeke, J. (jan 2020). Survey on Wireless Technology Trade-offs for the Industrial Internet of Things. Sensors (Switzerland), 20(2).

24. Juyal, V. et. al. (2017). Opportunistic message forwarding in self organized cluster based DTN. 2017 International Conference on Infocom Technologies and Unmanned Systems (Trends and Future Directions)(ICTUS). IEEE.

25. Uhlemann, T. H.-J., Lehmann, C., & Steinhilper, R. (2017). The Digital Twin: Realizing the Cyber-Physical Production System for Industry 4.0. Procedia Cirp, 61, 335–340.

26. Krupitzer, C., Muller, S., Lesch, V., ufle, M. Z¨, Edinger, J., Lemken, A., Schafer, ¨D., Kounev, S., & Becker, C. (2020). A survey on human machine ¨ interaction in industry 4.0. arXiv preprint arXiv:2002.01025.

27. Raj, A., Sharma, V., Rani, S., Shanu, A. K., Alkhayyat, A. & Singh, R. D. (2023). Modern Farming Using IoT-Enabled Sensors For The Improvement Of Crop Selection. 2023 4th International Conference on Intelligent Engineering and Management (ICIEM), London, United Kingdom, pp. 1–7, doi: 10.1109/ICIEM59379.2023.10167225.

28. Zhou, K., Liu, T., & Zhou, L. (2015). Industry 4.0: Towards future industrial opportunities and challenges. In 2015 12th International conference on fuzzy systems and knowledge discovery (FSKD). IEEE, pp. 2147–2152.

29. Whig, P., Velu, A., & Nadikattu, R. R. (2022). Blockchain Platform to Resolve Security Issues in IoT and Smart Networks. In AI-Enabled Agile Internet of Things for Sustainable FinTech Ecosystems (pp. 46–65). IGI Global.

30. Whig, P., Velu, A., & Ready, R. (2022). Demystifying Federated Learning in Artificial Intelligence With Human-Computer Interaction. In Demystifying Federated Learning for Blockchain and Industrial Internet of Things (pp. 94–122). IGI Global.

31. Hai, T. et al. (2023). A novel & innovative blockchain-empowered federated learning approach for secure data sharing in smart city applications. In: Iwendi, C., Boulouard, Z., Kryvinska, N. (eds) Proceedings of ICACTCE'23 — The International Conference on Advances in Communication Technology and Computer Engineering. ICACTCE 2023. Lecture Notes in Networks and Systems, vol 735. Springer, Cham. 10.1007/978-3-031-37164-6_9

32. Singh, A., Dhanaraj, R. K., Ali, M. A., Balusamy, B. & Sharma, V. (2022). Blockchain technology in biometric database system. 2022 3rd International Conference on Computation, Automation and Knowledge Management (ICCAKM), Dubai, United Arab Emirates, pp. 1–6, doi: 10.1109/ICCAKM54721.2022.9990133.

33. Whig, P., Velu, A., & Sharma, P. (2022). Demystifying Federated Learning for Blockchain: A Case Study. In Demystifying Federated Learning for Blockchain and Industrial Internet of Things (pp. 143–165). IGI Global.

34. Whig, P., Velu, A., & Nadikattu, R. R. (2022). Blockchain Platform to Resolve Security Issues in IoT and Smart Networks. In AI-Enabled Agile Internet of Things for Sustainable FinTech Ecosystems (pp. 46–65). IGI Global.

35. Whig, P., Velu, A., & Ready, R. (2022). Demystifying Federated Learning in Artificial Intelligence With Human-Computer Interaction. In Demystifying Federated Learning for Blockchain and Industrial Internet of Things (pp. 94–122). IGI Global.

36. Singh, A., et al. (2022). Blockchain: Tool for Controlling Ransomware through Pre-Encryption and Post-Encryption Behavior. 2022 Fifth International Conference on Computational Intelligence and Communication Technologies (CCICT). IEEE.

37. Whig, P., Velu, A., & Sharma, P. (2022). Demystifying Federated Learning for Blockchain: A Case Study. In Demystifying Federated Learning for Blockchain and Industrial Internet of Things (pp. 143–165). IGI Global.

38. Tao, F., Qi, Q., Wang, L., & Nee, A. (2019). Digital twins and cyber-physical systems toward smart manufacturing and industry 4.0: Correlation and comparison. Engineering, 5(4), 653–661.

39. Ali, M. A., Balamurugan, B., & Sharma, V. (2022). IoT and blockchain based intelligence security system for human detection using an improved ACO and heap algorithm. 2022 2nd International Conference on Advance Computing and Innovative Technologies in Engineering (ICACITE). IEEE.

40. Damjanovic-Behrendt, V. & Behrendt, W. (2019). An open source approach to the design and implementation of digital twins for smart manufacturing. International Journal of Computer Integrated Manufacturing, 32(4-5), 366–384.

41. Juyal, V. et. al. (2020). On exploiting dynamic trusted routing scheme in delay tolerant networks. Wireless Personal Communications, 112, 1705–1718.

42. Juyal, V. et. al. (2016). An anatomy on routing in delay tolerant network. 2016 IEEE International Conference on Computational Intelligence and Computing Research (ICCIC), Chennai, pp. 1–4. doi: 10.1109/ICCIC.2016.7919724

43. Rajasekar, V., Venu, K., Sharma, V., Saracevic, M. (2023). Algorithmic Strategies for Solving Complex Problems in Financial Cryptography. In: Seethalakshmi, V., Dhanaraj, R. K., Suganyadevi, S., Ouaissa, M. (eds) Homomorphic Encryption for Financial Cryptography. Springer, Cham. 10.1007/978-3-031-35535-6_10

44. Sharma, V., Balusamy, B., Sabharwal, M., & Ouaissa, M. (Eds.). (2023). Sustainable Digital Technologies: Trends, Impacts, and Assessments (1st ed.). CRC Press. 10.1201/9781003348313

45. Mohanraj, C. et al. (2023). Conspiracy in the stealing of electricity detection through the IOT. 2023 3rd International Conference on Innovative Practices in Technology and Management (ICIPTM), Uttar Pradesh, India, pp. 1–5, doi: 10.1109/ICIPTM57143.2023.10117849.

7 Blockchain Using Wireless Technology

Naman Mishra
Department of Economics, School of Arts and Humanities,
FS University, Shikohabad, Uttar Pradesh, India

Vandana Sharma
Department of Computational Sciences, CHRIST (Deemed
to be University), Delhi NCR Campus, India

7.1 INTRODUCTION

In today's rapidly evolving digital landscape, blockchain technology is at the forefront of innovation and has the potential to completely transform the way we do business, share information, and establish trust. Due to its decentralized and immutable nature, blockchain has generated a lot of interest and is frequently heralded as a groundbreaking technology with limitless potential. This chapter aims to explore the fundamental concepts underlying blockchain technology, delineate its useful applications, and highlight the profound impacts it will have on a wide range of businesses. Fundamentally, blockchain is a distributed ledger technology that enables the secure and transparent recording of transactions across a number of computers or nodes. Blockchain [1,2] has the ability to foster confidence and eliminate the need for intermediaries like banks or centralized agencies by providing a decentralized network where transactions may be verified and stored in an impermeable manner. This cutting-edge method of data administration has drawn interest from sectors including banking and supply chain management due to its promise to speed up processes, enhance security, and foster innovation. The decentralized nature of blockchain technology is one of the underlying principles. Blockchain disperses the data throughout a network of computers, known as nodes, as opposed to traditional databases, which store data on a central server. This ensures that no single party has complete control over the system. This decentralized architecture reduces the possibility of single points of failure or malicious assaults while simultaneously enhancing the network's security and resilience.

The immutability of blockchain is another distinguishing characteristic. A transaction or block of data is extremely impossible to change or tamper with once it is put to the blockchain. This is accomplished through cryptographic methods, where each block has a distinct hash that connects it to the one before it, creating an uninterrupted chain of data. The blockchain is extremely secure and

DOI: 10.1201/9781003389231-7

resistant to fraud or unauthorized alterations because any attempt to change a prior block would necessitate enormous processing power and consensus from the majority of the network. A wide range of businesses use blockchain technology, with banking being one of the most well-known instances. Blockchain is the underlying technology used by cryptocurrencies like Bitcoin to facilitate safe and open peer-to-peer transactions. Blockchain-based cryptocurrencies enable people to have complete sovereignty over their digital assets and promote effective cross-border transactions without the complications and expenses associated with traditional banking systems by doing away with the need for intermediaries and centralized authority. Blockchain has the potential to transform industries outside of finance by enabling complete traceability and transparency in supply chain management [3,4]. Stakeholders may follow the flow of goods from their point of origin to their destination using blockchain-based technologies, ensuring product quality and authenticity. This degree of openness not only increases consumer confidence but also makes it possible to quickly identify and address problems like product recalls or fake goods. Additionally, blockchain technology has the potential to revolutionize the healthcare sector. Blockchain can enable the easy flow of patient data between healthcare providers thanks to its secure and interoperable foundation, assuring accurate and current medical records. This can boost patient outcomes, enable personalized treatment strategies, and improve the accuracy of diagnoses. The difficulties and ramifications that come with blockchain technology should be taken into account as we learn more about its possibilities. In order to fully realize the transformative potential of blockchain, there are a number of critical concerns that must be resolved, including scalability, energy usage, and regulatory frameworks. Furthermore, while blockchain technology provides unrivaled security, the emergence of decentralized apps and smart contracts introduces new dangers and weaknesses that need to be properly controlled.

7.1.1 WIRELESS TECHNOLOGY: AN OVERVIEW

Since wireless technology eliminates the limitations of physical wires, it has become an essential component of our modern lives. Wireless technology has completely changed how we connect with devices and obtain information because of its simplicity and adaptability. We shall examine the underlying ideas, capacities, and practical uses of wireless technology in this chapter, emphasizing how they affect several facets of our daily life. Fundamentally, wireless technology includes a variety of communication strategies that send data via electromagnetic impulses across the airwaves. Without the need for physical connections, this wireless transmission enables devices to exchange data, access the internet, and communicate with one another. These technologies, such as Wi-Fi, Bluetooth, cellular networks, and other wireless protocols, have greatly increased our capacity to connect to and engage with the digital world as seen from Figure 7.1, the rapid growth of the whole infrastructure. The mobility and flexibility that wireless technology may offer is one of its primary features.

As long as they are inside the coverage area, users of wireless networks can access the internet and interact with one another from almost anywhere [5,6]. We

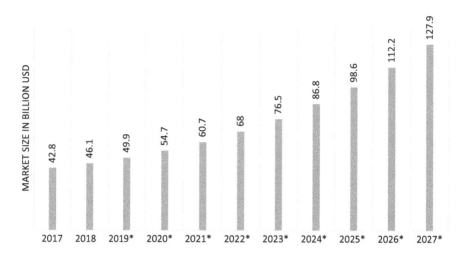

FIGURE 7.1 Wireless Connectivity Market Revenue.

Source: Statista.

may now work, learn, and socialize in a much more mobile manner because of this freedom of movement. Scalability is another benefit of wireless technology, which enables the linking of several devices to a network. Wireless connectivity makes it possible for various gadgets—be they wearable technology, computers, smart home appliances, or smartphones—to communicate and share data with one another without any issues. The Internet of Things (IoT) is built on top of this network of connected devices, where common things are given wireless capabilities to gather and exchange data, making the world more connected and effective. Additionally, by granting remote locations and underserved people access to the internet, wireless technology has significantly contributed to closing the digital divide. Individuals in rural or developing areas can now access educational materials, healthcare data, and economic opportunities that were previously inaccessible thanks to wireless networks and satellite links. Individual empowerment, inclusion, and socio-economic progress may result from this. Our auditory experiences have changed as a result of wireless technologies in the entertainment industry. We may now enjoy music and other media without being restricted by tangled cords thanks to Bluetooth speakers and headphones. Similar to how wireless streaming services and smart TVs have changed the way we watch television, they offer easy access to a wide variety of digital content.

Through location-based services, wireless technology has completely changed how we interact with our environment. GPS technology offers precise navigation, tracking, and geolocation services by using wireless signals from satellites. Wireless technology has become an essential part of our daily lives, allowing us to do everything from track the movement of commodities in supply chains to get turn-by-turn directions, discover local restaurants, and find nearby eateries. The healthcare sector has also been significantly impacted by wireless technology. Healthcare workers may remotely monitor patients, gather real-time data, and deliver prompt interventions thanks to wireless medical equipment and telehealth technologies. This optimizes patient care, permits early diagnosis of medical issues, and improves access to healthcare, particularly in isolated or disadvantaged locations. Wireless technology has many advantages, but it also has drawbacks like security and interference problems. To avoid unauthorized access or data breaches, it is essential to guarantee the privacy and protection of wireless data transfer. Additionally, to ensure dependable and quick connections as wireless networks get busier, minimizing interference and optimizing bandwidth allotment becomes more crucial.

7.1.2 Importance of Integrating Wireless Technology with Blockchain

The combination of blockchain technology with wireless technology unites two potent advancements that have the potential to transform many industries and improve our digital experiences. As we have already discussed, wireless technology allows for unimpeded connectivity and seamless communication. It offers accessibility, scalability, and mobility, enabling us to maintain connections even on the move. However, blockchain technology is a distributed ledger that guarantees data security, transparency, and immutability. It makes peer-to-peer transactions secure, decentralizes trust, and does away with the need for middlemen. We can open up a wide range of opportunities and build a more effective and reliable digital ecosystem by combining wireless technology and blockchain. The increased security and anonymity that wireless technology gives is one of the main benefits of combining blockchain technology with it. Unauthorized access and security flaws in wireless networks might jeopardize the integrity of data transmission. Wireless transactions and communications can be protected using cryptographic methods and consensus procedures by utilizing the decentralized nature of blockchain. This increases the overall security of wireless networks by making sure that the exchanged data is secure, unhackable, and private.

Decentralized applications (DApps) [7,8] and smart contracts can also be created more easily when wireless technology and blockchain are combined. Dapps (Figure 7.2) are software programmes that use the immutability and transparency of blockchain technology to operate on a decentralized network. These Dapps can function seamlessly across various devices and locations thanks to the integration of wireless connectivity, giving users a constant user experience and immediate access to blockchain-based services [9,10]. Wireless connectivity can be used to leverage smart contracts, which are self-executing contracts with predetermined rules inscribed on the blockchain, enabling automated and safe transactions without the need for middlemen. Supply chain management is a further area where the application of wireless technology and blockchain has a significant impact. IoT sensors and devices may gather and communicate real-time data about the movement and condition of commodities throughout the supply chain using wireless connectivity. Transparency and traceability may be ensured by securely storing this data on the blockchain. Stakeholders may have a clear understanding of the entire supply chain by combining wireless technology and blockchain, which also improves logistics and fosters more participant trust.

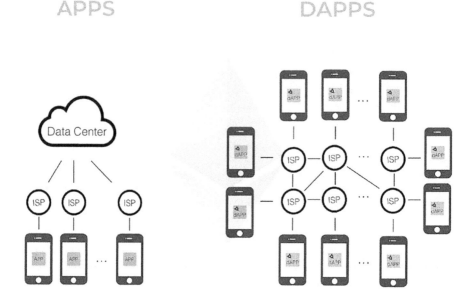

FIGURE 7.2   Normal Apps v/s D-Apps.

Additionally, combining blockchain and wireless technology can completely transform the sector of decentralized energy management. Energy usage data may be gathered in real-time with wireless sensors and smart meters and safely stored on the blockchain. Peer-to-peer energy trading, transparent and auditable energy transactions, and more effective energy distribution are made possible as a result. Individuals and communities can actively participate in energy management, promote renewable energy sources, and lower their carbon footprints by utilizing wireless connectivity.

Blockchain technology combined with wireless technology can improve financial services and make transactions more convenient and secure. Blockchain-based platforms can interact with mobile banking and payment systems without any issues, enabling quick, safe, and affordable transactions. In particular, in locations with limited access to banking services, the decentralized nature of blockchain eliminates the need for conventional financial intermediaries, facilitating financial inclusion and lowering transaction costs. Enhancing security, effectiveness, and trust across a range of businesses requires wireless technology integration with blockchain. We can build a more secure, effective, and inclusive digital ecosystem by fusing wireless connectivity with blockchain's decentralized and open nature. The combination of these technologies creates new opportunities and paves the way for a more connected and reliable digital future, from protecting wireless networks to revolutionizing supply chain management, energy management, and financial services. The following section of the chapter follows the various use cases of wireless technology in blockchain as well as the various limitations of implementing the same.

7.2 WIRELESS TECHNOLOGY IN BLOCKCHAIN APPLICATIONS

Wireless technology permits blockchain applications to function in a variety of industries, including supply chain management, banking, healthcare, and more, by providing real-time data transmission and connectivity across devices. Transparent transactions, decentralized applications, and secure peer-to-peer communication are all made possible by the combination of wireless technology and blockchain, opening up a vast array of potential applications. The significance of wireless technology is becoming more and more crucial as we go deeper into the world of blockchain applications. It drives innovation and transforms industries for a more connected and reliable digital future, following which certain applications are stated in the following:

7.2.1 INTERNET OF THINGS (IoT) DEVICES AND THEIR ROLE IN BLOCKCHAIN

Devices connected to the Internet of Things (IoT) have become crucial for the adoption and use of blockchain technology [11,12]. IoT devices are altering many businesses and the way we interact with the physical world because of their capacity to gather, exchange, and analyze enormous volumes of data. IoT devices act as participants in the distributed network and significant data sources in the blockchain world. These devices have connectivity features that allow them to interact and exchange data with other devices and blockchain networks, ranging from sensors and actuators to smart appliances and wearable technology. There are various benefits to combining IoT devices with blockchain technology. First of all, real-time data is continuously produced by IoT devices, and this data can be captured, validated, and stored on the blockchain. This improves the data's integrity and reliability by creating an unchangeable, transparent record of events.

Secondly, IoT gadgets make blockchain networks' security better. IoT devices may interact and communicate securely with the blockchain by utilizing cryptographic methods and digital signatures, preserving the integrity and validity of the data being delivered [13,14]. This reduces the possibility of unauthorized access or modification and improves the overall security of the blockchain ecosystem. Additionally, IoT devices use smart contracts to enable automated and decentralized decision-making processes. These blockchain-encoded self-executing contracts can be activated by particular circumstances or events picked up by IoT sensors. IoT devices like motion sensors and temperature sensors, for instance, can automatically initiate actions in a smart home environment based on established rules recorded in smart contracts. As a result, fewer operations require human participation and can be automated effectively.

New business models and value propositions can be created more easily thanks to IoT devices. Data can be shared and sold in a secure and open way by connecting various IoT devices to the blockchain. IoT sensors, for instance, can gather data about crop growth, soil moisture, temperature, and climate for sharing on the blockchain. Other interested parties, like farmers, academics, or food wholesalers, can then access this data and use it to make decisions based on accurate and trustworthy information. Additionally, peer-to-peer transactions and decentralized marketplaces can be established thanks to the convergence of IoT with blockchain. IoT devices can connect directly with one another and carry out transactions based on specified rules and smart contracts by cutting out middlemen. This creates possibilities for cutting-edge business models where IoT devices can independently trade resources or services without the need for centralized authorities, such as sharing economy platforms or decentralized energy grids. IoT gadgets are essential for the adoption and development of blockchain technology. Their capacity to gather, transmit, and engage with data improves the security, automation, and transparency of blockchain networks. By unleashing the potential for new applications, business models, and decentralized ecosystems, IoT and blockchain are revolutionizing industries and influencing connectivity and creativity in the future. The convergence of IoT and blockchain, which we are continuing to see emerge, will surely lead the way for a more interconnected, effective, and reliable digital world.

The combination of blockchain technology and Internet of Things (IoT) devices has created a myriad of new opportunities and the ability to completely transform a number of different sectors. Let's examine a few real-world instances:

In the area of supply chain management, IoT devices, and blockchain technology are widely used. Imagine a situation where a food distributor wants to guarantee the authenticity and freshness of its products. The distributor may track and keep an eye on the temperature conditions along the whole supply chain by giving each product an IoT device, like a temperature sensor. The blockchain securely stores the data gathered by these IoT sensors, producing an unchangeable and transparent record of temperature readings. This guarantees that the goods have been handled and delivered in the best possible way, and in the event of any inconsistencies, the distributor can easily spot and resolve the problem, retaining the goods' quality and integrity.

Energy grids (Figure 7.3) and the idea of decentralized energy generation provide yet another real-world illustration [15,16]. Imagine a neighborhood where each household's energy production and consumption are tracked by smart meters. Residents can immediately exchange excess energy by linking these IoT gadgets to an energy network built on a blockchain. Energy output and consumption are measured by smart meters, and the data is safely stored on the blockchain. Residents can automatically buy and sell energy depending on predetermined parameters thanks to smart contracts. As a result, homes can participate actively in the energy market and contribute to the general stability and sustainability of the grid, which not only encourages energy efficiency but also a feeling of communal empowerment.

Blockchain technology and IoT devices together provide revolutionary possibilities for the healthcare sector. Consider the management of patient data. Vital indicators can be continuously tracked and safely stored on the blockchain using IoT devices like wearable health trackers. This guarantees that healthcare providers have access to accurate and current health data, enabling prompt interventions and individualized treatments. Additionally, patients can have more control over their health data by giving permission for its usage and even getting involved in medical research by securely exchanging certain data with authorized researchers through blockchain-based platforms.

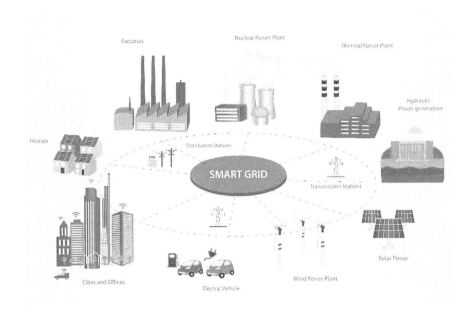

FIGURE 7.3   Smart Grid connectivity.

Another area where IoT and blockchain cross to produce novel solutions is smart cities. Imagine a city where parking spots have IoT sensors that can detect availability and occupancy. These sensors can be linked to a blockchain network, which will enable the recording and dissemination of real-time parking data to drivers looking for parking spaces. Drivers may access this data and reserve parking spaces through a decentralized application (Dapp) built on the blockchain, removing the stress of looking for parking and easing traffic congestion. The IoT devices supply the required data for a productive parking management system, while the blockchain ensures transaction transparency and trust.

These instances highlight the practical advantages and potential of fusing blockchain technology with IoT devices. The fusion of IoT and blockchain opens up a variety of options for enhanced transparency, efficiency, and automation across numerous industries, from supply chain management and energy grids to healthcare and smart cities. We can anticipate even more creative use cases that will change the way we live, work, and interact with the world around us as these technologies continue to develop and mature.

7.2.2   Cryptocurrency

A disruptive force in the world of banking and beyond, cryptocurrency is a digital form of money that runs on cryptographic principles. Advanced cryptographic methods are at the heart of cryptocurrencies, which use them to safeguard transactions and regulate the generation of new units [17–19]. Cryptocurrencies (Figure 7.4) run on decentralized networks called blockchains, in contrast to conventional currencies that are issued by central banks. These blockchains work as

FIGURE 7.4   Cryptocurrency network.

distributed ledgers, transparently and irrevocably documenting and confirming each transaction. The world was first introduced to the idea of digital currency by one of the most well-known cryptocurrencies, Bitcoin. By allowing peer-to-peer transactions without the need for middlemen like banks, Satoshi Nakamoto's creation of Bitcoin offers an alternative to conventional financial systems. Its decentralized structure and restricted supply—there are only a total of 21 million Bitcoins—affect its perceived worth and allure.

Numerous advantages and prospective benefits have been brought about by the development of cryptocurrencies. Cryptocurrencies, first and foremost, provide more security and privacy. Cryptocurrency transactions are pseudonymous, allowing individuals to execute transactions without disclosing their true identities. Additionally, transactions are protected against fraud and tampering by cryptographic mechanisms, which also guarantee the transactions' integrity. Additionally, the potential for cryptocurrencies to promote financial inclusion exists. Individuals without access to banking services or people residing in areas with a lack of a developed financial infrastructure are frequently left out of traditional banking systems. These people now have the chance to take part in the global economy thanks to cryptocurrencies, which let them send and receive money, buy things online, and conduct other financial transactions without the need for a conventional bank account. Additionally, cryptocurrencies have sparked innovation in the form of smart contracts and decentralized applications (DApps). Blockchain technology's capabilities have been enhanced by platforms like Ethereum, which enable programmers to create and deploy apps that take advantage of the transparency and security of the blockchain. Without the use of middlemen, smart contracts, self-executing agreements that are coded on the blockchain, allow for the automation of numerous activities. By optimizing processes and cutting costs, this has the potential to revolutionize sectors including finance, supply chain management, and real estate.

Initial Coin Offerings (ICOs), a fundraising technique where projects issue and sell their own tokens in exchange for recognized cryptocurrencies like Bitcoin or Ethereum, have also become a worldwide phenomenon thanks to cryptocurrencies [20,21]. Bypassing conventional venture capital channels, ICOs have given companies and entrepreneurs a way to raise money in a decentralized manner. It is crucial to remember that ICOs have additionally encountered regulatory scrutiny, difficulties with protecting investors, and difficulties in identifying fraudulent companies. The implications of cryptocurrencies extend beyond the banking industry. Supply chain management and the healthcare industry are only two areas that the underlying technology, blockchain, has the potential to transform. Blockchain-based solutions provide security, traceability, and transparency, enabling organizations to reorganize their operations, manage their data better, and build stakeholder trust. However, it's critical to be aware of the challenges and risks presented by cryptocurrencies. Due to the well-known characteristic of cryptocurrency price volatility, investors have experienced both significant gains and losses. The frameworks for law and regulation governing cryptocurrencies are still being developed, and there are still worries about money laundering, tax evasion, and unlawful behavior. Additionally, because bitcoin mining requires a lot of energy, environmental concerns have come to light. When it comes to security, privacy, and financial inclusion, cryptocurrencies have a number of distinct benefits over traditional banking systems. Blockchain technology, which underpins crypto-currencies, and their decentralized nature have opened up new avenues for creativity and economic empowerment. However, taking into account the dangers and difficulties related to cryptocurrencies, it is crucial to move cautiously through this quickly changing environment. Cryptocurrencies are likely to continue reshaping the financial industry and beyond as time goes on, spurring more innovation and altering the way we communicate, transact, and understand the concept of value.

7.2.3 Decentralized Wireless Networks and Their Potential Impact

Decentralized wireless networks, a groundbreaking idea that blends the effective-ness of wireless communication with the ideas of decentralization, are anticipated to have a significant influence on the way we use technology today. Traditional wireless networks depend on centralized infrastructure, where the network is run and controlled by a central organization. Decentralized wireless networks, in contrast, work on a peer-to-peer basis and enable direct device-to-device communication without the need for a central authority. This decentralized architecture has several benefits and creates new opportunities for networking and innovation.

Decentralized wireless networks have greater resilience and dependability as one of its main advantages. In a centralized network, network outages and interruptions may result from the failure of a central node or infrastructure point [22]. In contrast, the lack of a single point of failure in a decentralized network guarantees that the network will continue to function even if some nodes or devices fail. Decentralized wireless networks are especially well suited for mission-critical applications where continual access is crucial due to their inherent resiliency. Decentralized wireless networks also support higher levels of security and privacy. Users of centralized networks frequently have to rely on one organization to meet their communication needs, which raises questions about data privacy and the possibility of spying. Peer-to-peer communication ensures that data is shared directly between devices in a decentralized network, reducing the need for middlemen. By lowering the possibility of data breaches and unauthorized access, this peer-to-peer communication architecture gives consumers more control over their personal data. Decentralized wireless networks also have the ability to encourage inclusivity and inspire innovation. These networks liberate people and communities from the constraints imposed by conventional infrastructure providers by doing away with the requirement for centralized authorities. This has a bigger effect in underdeveloped locations where stable connectivity is harder to come by. Decentralized wireless networks give localities the ability to build their own communication infrastructure, promoting development of the local economy, chances for education, and accessibility to essential services.

Decentralized wireless networks have a huge range of potential uses. These networks can close the digital divide in outlying areas by offering reasonably priced and convenient connectivity. They have the ability to support decentralized Internet of Things (IoT) networks, facilitating seamless device connection and maximizing the potential of IoT technologies. Decentralized wireless networks can also be used for emergency communication and disaster response in situations when conventional infrastructure may be unavailable or degraded. The combination of decentralized wireless networks and cutting-edge technology like blockchain is another intriguing possibility. Blockchain technology and decentralized wireless networks can improve security, privacy, and transparency in a variety of applications. Decentralized networks built on blockchain, for instance, can provide safe and tamper-proof communication for supply chain management, identity verification, and financial transactions. Both technologies' decentralized architectures guarantee that data is transported and stored securely, promoting honesty and integrity in online interactions. Decentralized wireless networks still encounter difficulties and adoption barriers in spite of their enormous promise. To fully reap the rewards of these networks, technical challenges, legal frameworks, and scalability problems must be resolved. In order to overcome these obstacles and create an environment that will promote the expansion of decentralized wireless networks, cooperation between industry stakeholders, policymakers, and communities will be essential. Decentralized wireless networks mark a major shift in how we interact, connect, and communicate. These networks have the ability to transform our digital environment due to their innate resilience, privacy-enhancing qualities, and innovation potential. Decentralized wireless networks have the potential to revolutionize connection and usher in a future that is more decentralized, equitable, and connected through empowering people, encouraging inclusivity, and enabling secure communication.

7.3 BENEFITS AND CHALLENGES OF WIRELESS INTEGRATION

With every boon comes certain banes and as such this section of the chapter follows through the various advantages and disadvantages, that are there and that could arise in the implementation of the same.

7.3.1 ADVANTAGES

In many fields, wireless technology has changed the game. When combined with blockchain applications, these benefits can completely redefine how we interact, transact, and secure digital assets. Blockchain applications can expand accessibility to remote and underserved places by using wireless networks to get around physical infrastructure limitations. This improved accessibility empowers those who were previously shut out of the digital economy and creates new prospects for financial inclusion, decentralized applications, and digital services. Moreover, as transaction volumes rise, scaling blockchain technology has proven to be difficult. However, the incorporation of wireless technology resolves this difficulty by making use of the vast coverage and power of wireless networks. Blockchain applications can process a higher volume of transactions using wireless connectivity, resulting in effective and quick processing. Blockchain networks are appropriate for a variety of applications across industries because to their flexibility to scale and accommodate growing demand. Blockchain technology places a high priority on security, and the addition of wireless communication offers another level of defense. Wireless connections that use encryption to protect data transmission between blockchain nodes reduce the possibility of unauthorized access or modification. Data and transactions are protected by combining the built-in security features of blockchain with encrypted wireless technology, making them incredibly resilient to fraud and hacker attempts. Blockchain applications have the assurance of this strong security framework. Wireless technology improves the effectiveness of blockchain applications in addition to security. Wireless networking eliminates the need for manual intervention and delays brought on by physical infrastructure constraints by enabling real-time communication and data transfer. This has an impact on several industries, including finance, logistics, and healthcare, and leads to quicker transaction settlement, better supply chain management, and increased transparency. Processes are streamlined, operational friction is decreased, and organizations are able to optimize their workflows thanks to the seamless integration of wireless technology and blockchain. Particularly in remote or difficult environments, wireless technology is more cost-effective than conventional wired connections [23,24]. Blockchain applications can dramatically lower infrastructure expenses involved with installing physical cables or setting up centralized network hubs by utilizing wireless networks. This cost savings may be especially helpful in developing countries where a lack of resources may make it difficult to implement blockchain technology. With the use of wireless technology, businesses may adopt blockchain without having to make significant infrastructure investments, which promotes innovation and growth.

Other significant benefits of wireless technology for blockchain applications include flexibility and mobility. Blockchain devices need the flexibility of wireless communication to function in constantly changing contexts without being constrained by physical limits. Due to its adaptability, blockchain can be easily integrated into a variety of IoT devices, smart sensors, and mobile applications, facilitating real-time data interchange and automation across numerous industries. The mobility of mobile connections and transactions improves the responsiveness and agility of blockchain applications. Additionally, the combination of blockchain with wireless technologies is consistent with the increased focus on environmental sustainability. Organizations may help create a greener future by lowering their reliance on old-fashioned wired connections, which demand a lot of equipment and energy. Utilizing wireless networks for blockchain applications reduces the environmental impact of physical infra-structure, promoting sustainability efforts and ethical business practises. Combining wireless technology with blockchain applications offers a number of benefits that improve flexibility, scalability, security, efficiency, and affordability. Blockchain and wireless communication work together to break down geographical constraints, offer fast, secure transactions, and promote innovation across industries. Wireless connec-tivity and blockchain work together to create a more linked, decentralized, and profitable digital environment as wireless technology develops further.

7.3.2 Improved Accessibility and Flexibility Through Wireless Connectivity

The way we access and use technology has undergone a radical transformation, and the integration of wireless connectivity with blockchain applications has enhanced accessibility and flexibility that has the potential to revolutionize many industries. Blockchain solutions can reach remote and underserved places by expanding their reach beyond the constraints imposed by physical infrastructure by utilizing wireless networks. The ability to participate in financial transactions, decentralized software, and digital services enables people who were previously shut out of the digital economy. The flexibility that wireless connectivity in blockchain technology may offer is one of its main benefits. Wireless technology, as opposed to conventional wired connectivity, enables devices to connect and conduct transac-tions without being restricted by physical limits. Due to its adaptability, blockchain can be easily integrated into a variety of Internet of Things (IoT) gadgets, smart sensors, and mobile applications. Automation and real-time data interchange are made possible, enabling sectors like logistics, supply chain management, and healthcare to optimize their operations and base their judgements on accurate and current data. Furthermore, blockchain applications are more mobile because of wireless connectivity. Wireless networks enable mobile transactions, enabling quick and secure transfers wherever they take place. In sectors that demand dynamic operations, like transportation, field services, and retail, this mobility is especially advantageous. Organizations are empowered to streamline operations, react quickly to changing situations, and provide improved services to their clients thanks to the ability to access and transact securely in real time.

The issue of limited infrastructure is also addressed by the merging of wireless technologies and blockchain. Deploying physical infrastructure for wired connections is expensive and time-consuming in many areas. However, by utilizing current network infrastructures, wireless communication provides a cost-effective substitute. Organizations can quickly increase the scope of blockchain applications and get around infrastructure deployment challenges by minimizing their dependency on physical cables and central network hubs. Wireless connectivity also improves the robustness and dependability of blockchain networks. Traditional wired connections are susceptible to physical errors like infrastructure breakdowns or cable breakage. Wireless networks, on the other hand, are more dependable and can swiftly adjust to changing circumstances. Due to this resilience, blockchain applications may be used without interruption even under difficult conditions or during natural disasters. Organizations may ensure uninterrupted operations and reduce downtime by depending on wireless connectivity to guarantee the integrity of their transactions and data. The ability of wireless technology to support decentralized apps (dApps) is a key benefit of blockchain. Blockchain's guiding principle of decentralization is nicely complemented by wireless connectivity. Wireless networks enable peer-to-peer connection and do away with the need for middlemen, enabling people to take part in decentralized networks and contribute to the verification and upkeep of blockchain ledgers. The blockchain ecosystem benefits from increased security, trust, and openness thanks to this decentralized strategy. Wireless connectivity also improves the entire blockchain application user experience. Users can easily link their mobile or IoT devices to blockchain networks, improving the convenience and usability of transactions and providing access to digital assets. Blockchain technology is being adopted and used more widely as a result of the removal of physical links and the ability to transact from any location. The combination of blockchain applications and wireless technology improves accessibility and flexibility, which has the potential to transform a number of industries. Wireless connectivity and blockchain enable mobility, overcome physical restrictions, and uphold the decentralization tenets. Organizations may overcome infrastructure difficulties, improve resilience, and provide users with a seamless and user-friendly experience by utilizing wireless networks. The potential for more accessibility and flexibility in blockchain applications will increase as wireless technology develops, ushering in a new era of connectivity and empowerment.

7.3.3 CHALLENGES

Numerous benefits come from combining wireless technology with blockchain applications, but there are a number of issues that must be resolved if acceptance and deployment are to be effective. When merging these two technologies, reliability, security, and scalability are important factors that need to be carefully taken into account. The ability of wireless networks to maintain a steady and consistent connection is one of the fundamental difficulties. Although wireless connectivity has substantially improved over time, signal interference, network congestion, and range restrictions still exist. These elements may interfere with the efficient operation of blockchain networks, causing delays in transaction validation and perhaps resulting in inconsistent data. New wireless communication technologies, including 5 G, provide intriguing ways to lessen these difficulties. 5 G networks are more suited to enabling blockchain applications since they have higher bandwidth, lower latency, and improved reliability. Blockchain networks can offer quicker transaction processing, better network synchronization, and more overall reliability by utilizing the capabilities of 5 G technology.

Security is a key concern when mixing blockchain with wireless technology. A range of security threats, such as tampering, data interception, and unauthorized access, can affect wireless networks. The confidentiality and integrity of blockchain transactions and data must be maintained in order to foster acceptance and inspire confidence. One solution to overcome security problems is to use encryption and authentication methods. Using encryption techniques, sensitive data can be sent safely via wireless networks while maintaining its confidentiality. Strong authentication protocols, such digital signatures, can be used to verify the members' identities in a blockchain network, lowering the danger of unauthorized access and manipulation. Wireless intrusion detection and prevention systems (IDS and IPS) are another tool that may be used to find and prevent security breaches in blockchain networks. These technologies monitor network activity, identify suspect activities, and take preventative action to safeguard the security and integrity of the blockchain ecosystem.

Blockchain networks' scalability is a major challenge, especially when wireless technology is involved. The network must efficiently handle the expanding workload as the number of transactions and participants rises. Due to the consensus methods and the requirement for all nodes to validate and maintain the whole transaction history, traditional blockchain networks have difficulty scaling. Scalability now includes new complexity due to wireless technology. The number of transactions that may be processed simultaneously may be constrained by the constrained bandwidth and computational capabilities of wireless networks. Furthermore, because blockchains are decentralized, each network participant must keep a copy of the full blockchain, which can be resource-intensive for wireless devices with little storage.

Different strategies are being investigated to address these scaling problems. By processing a portion of transactions off-chain, layer 2 solutions like sidechains and off-chain transactions can reduce the load on the primary blockchain network. By lowering the computational and storage needs for wireless devices, these technologies increase scalability. Sharding is a different strategy that includes breaking the blockchain network up into smaller sections called shards. In order to enable parallel processing and boost overall scalability, each shard is in charge of handling a portion of the transactions [25,26]. To ensure data consistency, sharding in wireless blockchain networks calls for meticulous coordination and synchronization across the shards. While integrating wireless technology with blockchain technology has many advantages, issues with dependability, security, and scalability need to be resolved. The dependability and security of wireless blockchain networks can be improved through developments in wireless communication protocols, encryption, authentication techniques, and network security solutions. Additionally, investigating strategies like layer 2 solutions and sharding can aid in overcoming scaling issues. The potential of wireless technology to transform blockchain applications can be fully realized by addressing these difficulties, enabling secure, scalable, and dependable decentralized networks.

7.3.4 Environmental Issues of Blockchain

There are many benefits to combining blockchain technology and wireless internet, but it's important to think about how this integration may affect the environment. Although blockchain technology has the potential to revolutionize many different industries, issues with sustainability and environmental effect have been brought up due to its energy use and carbon footprint.

Blockchain's high energy usage is one of the main environmental problems it raises. Traditional blockchain networks, like Bitcoin, rely on a Proof of Work (PoW) [27,28] consensus method, which consumes a lot of processing power. Miners use this power-intensive procedure to validate transactions and secure the network by solving challenging mathematical puzzles. As a result, a sizable amount of electricity is used, which causes carbon emissions from power sources based on fossil fuels. For instance, according to the Cambridge Centre for Alternative Finance, the energy usage of the Bitcoin network alone is similar to that of whole nations. Blockchain networks' ongoing energy use has the potential to increase carbon emissions and the negative effects of energy production on the environment. Alternative consensus mechanisms, including Proof of Stake (PoS), are being investigated as a solution to this problem. PoS demands that each member of the network "stake" (keep) a specific amount of cryptocurrency in order to validate transactions and protect the network. Compared to PoW, this method dramatically reduces energy consumption because it does not require power-intensive mining activities. Furthermore, improvements in renewable energy sources may help to lessen the negative environmental effects of blockchain. Wireless blockchain network integration with environmentally friendly energy production, such as solar or wind power, can assist lower carbon emissions and improve the sustainability of the technology. A number of efforts have already surfaced with the goal of minimizing the environmental impact of blockchain networks by supplying them with sustainable energy.

E-waste creation is a worry for the environment associated with blockchain technology. Blockchain networks' use of wireless technology and mining machinery can see regular upgrades or obsolescence, generating a sizable amount of technological trash. Electronic waste disposed of improperly can harm the environment and result in the depletion of natural resources. Initiatives that support ethical e-waste management and recycling are essential to resolving this problem. E-waste produced by blockchain technology can be reduced by enacting rules and pushing manufacturers to build products with recyclability and longevity in mind. Additionally, looking at alternative strategies, such as blockchain-based cloud solutions, might lessen the dependency on individual devices and allay e-waste concerns. Furthermore, as more wireless connections are needed to serve blockchain applications, the current telecommunications infrastructure may become overburdened. Additional wireless infrastructure, such as cell towers and data centers, must be deployed in order to increase data transmission speeds and network coverage [29]. These facilities' development and operation may have an impact on the environment in terms of things like land use, energy use, and carbon emissions. The environmental impact of wireless infrastructure is being reduced through the promotion of energy-efficient technology and the investigation of novel solutions, such as making use of already-existing equipment or implementing shared networks. The efficiency of wireless communication can also be improved by optimizing network protocols and data transmission algorithms, which will lower the energy requirements of blockchain applications. While there are many advantages to the marriage of blockchain and wireless technology, it is crucial to address the environmental concerns that come with it. Three major issues that demand attention are high energy usage, the production of e-waste, and the strain on the telecommunications infrastructure. To achieve a more sustainable and environmentally friendly implementation of blockchain using wireless technology, it is imperative to investigate alternate consensus processes, make use of renewable energy sources, encourage responsible e-waste management, and optimize network infrastructure. We can utilize blockchain's promise while reducing its negative effects on the environment by putting environmental concerns first [30].

7.4   CONCLUSION

In conclusion, the fusion of blockchain technology and wireless technology offers both tremendous opportunities and difficult obstacles. We have discussed the benefits, drawbacks, and environmental implications of this combination throughout our conversation. Blockchain provides greater accessibility and flexibility when combined with cellular connectivity. Blockchain networks' reach is increased and users can interact in a more welcoming atmosphere thanks to the ability to access and engage in them wirelessly. This accessibility creates new opportunities for sectors like finance, supply chain, and healthcare, enabling people and organizations to interact with blockchain applications without any difficulty. The benefits of wireless technology in blockchain also include improved productivity and simplified procedures. By removing the requirement for physical connections, wireless communication enables real-time data sharing and lessens reliance on conventional infrastructure. As a result, systems become more agile and responsive. This also improves the speed and efficiency of transactions, supply chain management, and data interchange. However, we must also be aware of the difficulties with scalability, security, and reliability. Blockchain operations could be at danger due to the potential for interference, latency, and coverage issues on wireless networks. To address these issues, it is necessary to implement strong security controls, cutting-edge encryption techniques, and ongoing monitoring to guarantee the integrity and confidentiality of blockchain data. Scalability continues to be an important factor. The capacity of wireless infrastructure must keep up with the expansion of blockchain networks and the rise in demand. To increase network coverage, improve data transmission capabilities, and lessen the burden on existing infrastructure, cooperation between network providers, regulators, and industry stakeholders is crucial. We cannot ignore the environmental implications of wireless and blockchain technology. Concerns about sustainability are raised by the high energy consumption of blockchain, notably in proof-of-work consensus algorithms. Blockchain can be made more environmentally friendly and sustainable by investigating alternate consensus mechanisms like proof-of-stake and using renewable energy sources. Another issue is the constant upgrading and discarding of wireless gadgets, which results in the development of e-waste. The environmental impact can be reduced by promoting ethical e-waste management, recycling programmes, and designing gadgets with longevity and recyclability in mind. Last but not least, careful planning and optimization are required due to the load on the telecommunications infrastructure. Expanding wireless connectivity for blockchain applications can have a negative environmental impact, although shared networks, energy-efficient devices, and optimized protocols help reduce it. In conclusion, the combination of blockchain technology and wireless technology has enormous potential to revolutionize procedures and change entire sectors. Accessibility, effectiveness, and adaptability have all been improved. To assure the long-term application of this technology, however, dependability, security, scalability, and environmental impact issues must be resolved. We can maximize the advantages of wireless blockchain applications while minimizing their disadvantages by embracing creative solutions, teamwork, and ethical behavior. For wireless blockchain technology to flourish and contribute to a more connected and sustainable society, it is imperative to strike a balance between technological development and environmental stewardship.

REFERENCES

1. Zheng, Z., et al. Blockchain challenges and opportunities: A survey. International Journal of Web and Grid Services 14.4 (2018): 352–375.
2. Hai, T. et al. (2023). A Novel & Innovative Blockchain-Empowered Federated Learning Approach for Secure Data Sharing in Smart City Applications. In: Iwendi, C., Boulouard, Z., Kryvinska, N. (eds) Proceedings of ICACTCE'23 — The International Conference on Advances in Communication Technology and Computer Engineering. ICACTCE 2023. Lecture Notes in Networks and Systems, vol 735. Springer, Cham. 10.1007/978-3-031-37164-6_9
3. Monrat, A. A., Schelén, O., and Andersson, K. A survey of blockchain from the perspectives of applications, challenges, and opportunities. IEEE Access 7 (2019): 117134–117151.
4. Ali, M. A., Balamurugan, B., Dhanaraj, R. K. and Sharma, V. IoT and Blockchain based Smart Agriculture Monitoring and Intelligence Security System. 2022 3rd International Conference on Computation, Automation and Knowledge Management (ICCAKM), Dubai, United Arab Emirates, 2022, pp. 1–7, doi: 10.1109/ICCAKM54 721.2022.9990243.
5. Wang, J., et al. Blockchain-enabled wireless communications: a new paradigm towards 6G. National Science Review 8.9 (2021): nwab069.
6. Singh, A., Dhanaraj, R. K., Ali, M. A., Balusamy, B. and Sharma, V. Blockchain Technology in Biometric Database System. 2022 3rd International Conference on Computation, Automation and Knowledge Management (ICCAKM), Dubai, United Arab Emirates, 2022, pp. 1–6, doi: 10.1109/ICCAKM54721.2022.9990133.
7. Wu, K., et al. A first look at blockchain-based decentralized applications. Software: Practice and Experience 51.10 (2021): 2033–2050.

8. Singh, A., et al. Blockchain: Tool for Controlling Ransomware through Pre-Encryption and Post-Encryption Behavior. 2022 Fifth International Conference on Computational Intelligence and Communication Technologies (CCICT). IEEE, 2022.

9. Wu, K. An empirical study of blockchain-based decentralized applications. arXiv preprint arXiv:1902.04969 (2019).

10. Ali, M. A., Balamurugan, B., and Sharma, V. IoT and Blockchain based Intelligence Security System for Human Detection using an Improved ACO and Heap Algorithm. 2022 2nd International Conference on Advance Computing and Innovative Technologies in Engineering (ICACITE). IEEE, 2022.

11. Banafa, A. IoT and blockchain convergence: benefits and challenges. IEEE Internet of Things 9.2017 (2017).

12. Raj, A., Sharma, V., Rani, S., Shanu, A. K., Alkhayyat, A. and Singh, R. D. Modern Farming Using IoT-Enabled Sensors For The Improvement Of Crop Selection. 2023 4th International Conference on Intelligent Engineering and Management (ICIEM), London, United Kingdom, 2023, pp. 1–7, doi: 10.1109/ICIEM59379.2023.10167225.

13. Liang, X., et al. Towards Data Assurance and Resilience in IoT using Blockchain. MILCOM 2017-2017 IEEE Military Communications Conference (MILCOM). IEEE, 2017.

14. Mollah, M. B., et al. Blockchain for future smart grid: A comprehensive survey. IEEE Internet of Things Journal 8.1 (2020): 18–43.

15. Liu, Y., and Tsyvinski, A. Risks and returns of cryptocurrency. The Review of Financial Studies 34.6 (2021): 2689–2727.

16. Singh, A., Ali, M. A., Balamurugan, B., and Sharma, V. Blockchain: Tool for Controlling Ransomware through Pre-Encryption and Post-Encryption Behavior. In 2022 Fifth International Conference on Computational Intelligence and Communication Technologies (CCICT). IEEE, 2022, July, pp. 584–589

17. Raj, A., Sharma, V. and Shanu, A. K. Comparative Analysis Of Security And Privacy Technique For Federated Learning In IOT Based Devices. 2022 3rd International Conference on Computation, Automation and Knowledge Management (ICCAKM), Dubai, United Arab Emirates, 2022, pp. 1–5, doi: 10.1109/ICCAKM54721.2022.9990152.

18. Li, J., and Mann, W. Initial coin offering and platform building. SSRN Electronic Journal (2018): 1–56.

19. Mohanraj, C. et al. Conspiracy in the Stealing of Electricity Detection Through the IOT. 2023 3rd International Conference on Innovative Practices in Technology and Management (ICIPTM), Uttar Pradesh, India, 2023, pp. 1–5, doi: 10.1109/ICIPTM5 7143.2023.10117849.

20. Kim, M., Kerret, P. D., and Gesbert, D. Learning to Cooperate in Decentralized Wireless Networks. 2018 52nd Asilomar Conference on Signals, Systems, and Computers. IEEE, 2018.

21. Porras-Gonzalez, E. R., Martín-Martín, J. M., and Guaita-Martínez, J. M. A critical analysis of the advantages brought by blockchain technology to the global economy. International Journal of Intellectual Property Management 9.2 (2019): 166–184.

22. Dang, H., et al. Towards Scaling Blockchain Systems via Sharding. Proceedings of the 2019 international conference on management of data, 2019.

23. Schinckus, C. Proof-of-work based blockchain technology and Anthropocene: An undermined situation?. Renewable and Sustainable Energy Reviews 152 (2021): 111682.

24. Sharma, V., Balusamy, B., Sabharwal, M., and Ouaissa, M. (Eds.) Sustainable Digital Technologies: Trends, Impacts, and Assessments (1st ed.). CRC Press, 2023. 10.1201/9781003348313

25. Badea, L., and Mungiu-Pupăzan, M. C. The economic and environmental impact of bitcoin. IEEE Access 9 (2021): 48091–48104.
26. Sharma, V., Mishra, N., Kukreja, V., Alkhayyat, A. and Elngar, A. A. Framework for Evaluating Ethics in AI. 2023 International Conference on Innovative Data Communication Technologies and Application (ICIDCA), Uttarakhand, India, 2023, pp. 307–312, doi: 10.1109/ICIDCA56705.2023.10099747.
27. Ahmad, S., Mishra, S., and Sharma, V. Green Computing for Sustainable Future Technologies and Its Applications, Grima, S., Sood, K. and Özen, E. (Ed.) Contemporary Studies of Risks in Emerging Technology, Part A (Emerald Studies in Finance, Insurance, and Risk Management), Emerald Publishing Limited, Bingley, 2023, pp. 241–256. 10.1108/978-1-80455-562-020231016
28. Basheer, S., Singh, K. U., Sharma, V., Bhatia, S., Pande, N., & Kumar, A. A robust NIfTI image authentication framework to ensure reliable and safe diagnosis. Peer J Computer Science 9 (2023): e1323.
29. Durgalakshmi, K., Anbarasu, P., Karpagam, V., Venkatesh, A., Kannapiran, B., and Sharma, V. Utilization Of Reduced Switch Components With Different Topologies In Multi-Level Inverter For Renewable Energy Applications-A Detailed Review. 2022 5th International Conference on Contemporary Computing and Informatics (IC3I), Uttar Pradesh, India, 2022, pp. 913–920, doi: 10.1109/IC3I56241.2022.10073430.
30. Kokilavani, T. et al. Electric Vehicle Charging Station with Effective Energy Management, Integrating Renewable and Grid Power. 2023 3rd International Conference on Innovative Practices in Technology and Management (ICIPTM), Uttar Pradesh, India, 2023, pp. 1–5, doi: 10.1109/ICIPTM57143.2023.10118186.

8 Revolutionizing Wireless Systems
Machine Learning Tools for Tomorrow's Networks

Jagjit Singh Dhatterwal
Department of Artificial Intelligence & Data Science, Koneru
Lakshmaiah Education Foundation, Vaddeswaram,
Andhra Pradesh, India

Kuldeep Singh Kaswan
School of Computer Science and Engineering,
Galgotias University, Greater Noida, Uttar Pradesh, India

Kiran Malik
Department of Computer Science and Engineering,
Matu Ram Institute of Engineering and Management,
Rohtak, Haryana, India

8.1 INTRODUCTION TO MACHINE LEARNING IN WIRELESS TECHNOLOGY

The incorporation of machine learning (ML) techniques into wireless technology has ushered in a new age of communication system innovation and optimization [1]. Because of its ability to evaluate large and complicated datasets, machine learning has transformed the way wireless networks are planned, maintained, and operated [2]. This chapter explores the symbiotic link between ML and wireless technology in depth, offering light on the transformational potential it offers. With its pervasiveness and ever-expanding uses, wireless technology has faced issues relating to spectrum scarcity, signal interference, and resource allocation [3]. Traditional techniques frequently fall short of meeting wireless networks' dynamic and complicated nature, needing more adaptable and intelligent solutions [4]. This is where machine learning comes into play as a catalyst for altering wireless systems.

ML methods, including supervised, unsupervised, and reinforcement learning, have been used to improve signal processing, channel modeling, and resource allocation in wireless networks [5]. Deep learning approaches, including convolutional neural networks (CNNs) and recurrent neural networks (RNNs), have proven

DOI: 10.1201/9781003389231-8

outstanding proficiency in processing complicated wireless data patterns in recent years [6]. One of the primary advantages of ML in wireless technology is its capacity to forecast and adapt to changing environmental variables [7]. ML-driven predictive modeling enables wireless systems to anticipate signal fading, congestion, and interference, allowing proactive modifications to maintain optimal performance [8].

This predictive skill is especially important in dynamic contexts, such as vehicle communication networks [9]. Furthermore, ML approaches enable dynamic resource allocation, enabling efficient and equitable network resource distribution [10]. ML algorithms maximize resource use, lowering latency and improving user experience by assessing real-time traffic patterns and user needs [11]. Such resource allocation algorithms offer a lot of potential for 5G and beyond, as network densification and various services demand sophisticated resource management [12]. The incorporation of ML also solves wireless security problems [13]. Anomaly detection systems enabled by machine learning can detect illegal access, anomalous activity, and possible assaults in real time, enhancing the resilience of wireless networks [14].

Furthermore, ML facilitates the creation of adaptive encryption and authentication techniques that develop in response to evolving threats [15]. Despite these advances, there are still hurdles in using ML in wireless technologies [16]. More research is needed to ensure the dependability and interpretability of ML models, handle sparse and noisy wireless data, and address the computational challenges of real-time processing [17]. Furthermore, as ML-enhanced wireless systems grow more autonomous, ethical problems such as transparency and bias mitigation become increasingly important [18]. The combination of ML techniques with wireless technologies represents a paradigm change in communication systems [19]. This chapter offers the groundwork for a complete understanding of machine learning's revolutionary role in wireless networks, emphasizing its ability to optimize resource allocation, improve security, and adapt to changing situations [20].

8.1.1 Overview of Machine Learning and Wireless Technology Integration

The use of Machine Learning (ML) with Wireless Technology has resulted in a transformational synergy, altering how communication systems are built, maintained, and optimized. This convergence leverages the power of machine learning algorithms to extract subtle patterns from massive datasets, allowing wireless networks to adapt dynamically to changing conditions and offer improved performance. At its heart, machine learning (ML) includes the use of computational models that learn from data and then make predictions or judgments based on that learning. ML algorithms in wireless technology aid intelligent decision-making by evaluating historical and real-time data. For example, ML may be used to forecast signal fading in wireless channels, allowing network systems to modify their settings proactively for enhanced signal quality. The intrinsic complexity of wireless communication systems is determined by variables such as signal interference, channel fading, and user mobility.

ML algorithms excel at dealing with such complications. ML approaches, for example, can enhance beamforming tactics in Multiple Input Multiple Output (MIMO) systems to direct signal energy toward targeted users while avoiding interference. Furthermore, ML-driven predictive modeling is critical in resource allocation, which is a critical feature of wireless networks. ML algorithms can dynamically distribute bandwidth and transmit power by evaluating traffic patterns and user behavior, enhancing overall network performance. with environments such as the Internet of Things (IoT), where a plethora of devices with various communication requirements coexist, machine learning (ML) aids with resource prioritization based on device attributes and traffic demands. Wireless technology has expanded beyond traditional communication to include new domains such as wireless sensor networks. In these situations, machine learning improves data fusion and decision-making processes. ML techniques can enable sensor nodes to interpret data jointly, identify abnormalities, and make choices collectively, improving the overall efficiency and accuracy of sensor networks.

ML technologies have also proved their ability to handle security challenges. ML-powered anomaly detection systems can detect unwanted access attempts or strange activities in wireless networks. For example, ML algorithms can discriminate between regular and harmful network traffic patterns, improving wireless system security. Autonomous cars are an example of real-world implementation of ML-enabled wireless technologies. Real-time processing of sensor data by ML algorithms aids in activities such as image identification, object tracking, and decision-making. By identifying traffic signs, detecting people, and anticipating potential crashes, these algorithms enable cars to traverse complicated surroundings. Despite these great strides, obstacles remain. Data quality, feature engineering, and model interpretability must all be carefully considered when designing and training ML models for wireless applications. Furthermore, technical hurdles are posed by the computing needs for real-time ML processing in resource-constrained wireless devices.

8.1.2 Importance and Benefits of Using Machine Learning in Wireless Applications

The use of Machine Learning (ML) in wireless applications is critical for driving innovation and altering how communication networks work. ML provides a slew of advantages that considerably improve the performance, efficiency, and adaptability of wireless networks, contributing to a diversified range of applications across sectors. The predictive capabilities of machine learning stand out as a critical advantage in wireless applications. Consider a cellular network that must deal with changing user demands and environmental circumstances. ML algorithms may assess previous traffic patterns and forecast future demand spikes, allowing the network to distribute resources and optimize bandwidth in advance of a rise in consumption. Another significant advantage is resource optimization. The effective distribution of spectrum, power, and other resources is critical in wireless networks.

ML algorithms can continually monitor network conditions, learning from the data and allocating resources dynamically where they are most required. For example, ML can improve power distribution in a wireless sensor network to conserve energy and hence increase the network's lifetime. The capacity of machine learning to understand complicated patterns from data adds to better signal processing and interference reduction. ML algorithms can discriminate between individual users' signals and separate them from interference in a multi-user setting. This functionality assures consistent connectivity and reduces packet loss, improving the user experience. Wireless applications benefit from machine learning's ability to manage large and complicated datasets. ML algorithms can assess unique signal properties in contexts such as radio frequency (RF) fingerprinting to reliably identify and locate wireless devices. This is very useful in indoor localization for asset monitoring and navigation. In wireless communication, security is of the utmost importance. By learning typical network behavior and recognizing abnormalities that may signal malicious activity, ML assists in intrusion detection. For example, ML algorithms may identify Distributed Denial of Service (DDoS) assaults by detecting unexpected surges in traffic.

ML's automation and self-optimization skills are helpful in network administration. Autonomous base stations can adapt to changing conditions by adjusting parameters like as transmission power, beamforming, and channel allocation based on real-time input. This results in more efficient network functioning and less maintenance efforts. The significance of machine learning extends to developing wireless technologies such as cognitive radio networks. These networks use machine learning to dynamically recognize and use available frequency bands, improving spectrum usage efficiency. Cognitive radio systems may adjust in real-time to spectrum availability and user requirements, making better use of available frequencies. ML provides predictive maintenance in the context of Internet of Things (IoT) devices. ML algorithms can forecast when a machine is likely to break by evaluating sensor data from industrial equipment, allowing maintenance teams to take preemptive actions and avoid costly downtime.

Furthermore, ML enables wireless applications in automotive networks, allowing for predictive collision avoidance in self-driving cars. To predict probable collisions and trigger appropriate reactions, ML algorithms evaluate sensor data from cameras, LiDAR, and radar. The healthcare industry benefits from ML-enabled wireless apps as well. Wearable devices employing machine learning algorithms may monitor a patient's vital signs in real-time, detecting irregularities that may suggest a health problem and notifying medical personnel.

8.2   FUNDAMENTALS OF WIRELESS TECHNOLOGY

Wireless technology has changed modern communication networks, allowing for pervasive connectivity and reshaping a variety of businesses. The operation of wireless networks is based on fundamental principles such as signal propagation, modulation, multiplexing, and spectrum allocation [21]. Wireless signals are propagated via electromagnetic waves that obey physical rules. Diffraction, reflection, and refraction are features of these waves that affect their behavior as they pass through different materials [22]. A thorough understanding of signal propagation is required for the design of reliable wireless communication systems. Modulation methods are critical in encoding data onto carrier signals. Amplitude Modulation (AM), Frequency Modulation (FM), and Phase Shift Keying (PSK) techniques provide effective data transmission and reception [23].

Data speeds and spectrum efficiency are improved by advanced modulation systems such as Quadrature Amplitude Modulation (QAM). Multiplexing technologies allow several signals to be sent at the same time via the same channel. Frequency Division Multiplexing (FDM), Time Division Multiplexing (TDM), and Orthogonal Frequency Division Multiplexing (OFDM) maximize spectrum usage and support many data streams [24]. Wireless communication is based on the idea of spectrum, which is a finite and precious resource. Spectrum band distribution and management for diverse wireless services are crucial to avoiding interference and ensuring optimal usage [25]. Cognitive radio networks seek to intelligently use unused frequency bands in order to improve spectrum utilization [26].

Wireless networks are classified according to their coverage area and structure. Local Area Networks (LANs) serve local geographic areas, whereas Wide Area Networks (WANs) serve larger areas. Star, mesh, and ad hoc network topologies all have advantages in terms of scalability and fault tolerance [27]. Cellular networks are a popular wireless technology that divides geographic areas into cells that are supplied by base stations. 4G LTE and upcoming 5G cellular technologies provide high-speed data transfer, smooth handoffs, and increased spectrum efficiency [28]. The Internet of Things (IoT) is a paradigm in which networked things interact wirelessly because of the advancement of wireless technologies. IoT networks are made up of many devices ranging from sensors and actuators to smart appliances that work together to enable data-driven decision-making and automation [29].

Multiple Input Multiple Output (MIMO) technological advancements have considerably enhanced wireless network capacity and dependability. MIMO utilizes numerous antennas at both the transmitter and receiver ends, taking advantage of spatial diversity to reduce fading and increase data throughput [30]. Furthermore, wireless security is quite important. Wireless communications are protected from eavesdropping and unwanted access by encryption, authentication, and intrusion detection techniques [31]. Jamming attacks and localization-based threats provide unique security difficulties for wireless networks [32].

Table 8.1 summarizes the principles of wireless technology, which include a number of critical ideas. Signal propagation is the study of how electromagnetic waves move across media, whereas modulation is the process of putting data onto carrier signals. Multiplexing technologies allow many signals to be sent at the same time, and spectrum allocation entails regulating wireless frequencies. The structure of networks is defined by network coverage and topology, whereas cellular networks split regions into cells supplied by base stations. The Internet of Things (IoT) wirelessly links devices, and several Input Multiple Output (MIMO) improve performance by using several antennas. Data rates specify transmission speeds, whereas wireless security assures encrypted and verified connections. Wireless protocols standardize communication while channel fading and mitigation handle signal loss. Signal coverage is optimized through antenna design and propagation

TABLE 8.1

Representation of the Fundamentals of Wireless Technology

Fundamentals of Wireless Technology	Brief Description
Signal Propagation	Study of how electromagnetic waves travel.
Modulation Techniques	Encoding information onto carrier signals.
Multiplexing Methods	Transmitting multiple signals over a medium.
Spectrum Allocation	Allocating and managing wireless frequencies.
Network Coverage and Topology	LANs, WANs, and various network structures.
Cellular Networks	Dividing areas into cells served by base stns.
Internet of Things (IoT)	Interconnected devices communicating wirelessly.
Multiple Input Multiple Output (MIMO)	Utilizing multiple antennas for improved perf.
Wireless Security	Encryption, authentication, intrusion detection.
Wireless Data Rates	Transmission speeds and data throughput.
Channel Fading and Mitigation	Addressing signal degradation in wireless comm.
Wireless Protocols	Standards for communication between devices.
Antenna Design and Propagation Modeling	Designing antennas for optimal signal coverage.
Error Correction Techniques	Methods to correct errors in transmitted data.
Network Architecture	Organizing wireless devices and connections.

modeling, while data inaccuracies are corrected by error correction techniques. The core of current wireless communication systems is network architecture, which organizes wireless devices and connections.

8.2.1 WIRELESS COMMUNICATION SYSTEMS AND TECHNOLOGIES

Wireless communication systems and technologies are the foundation of modern networking, allowing for the smooth transmission of data across several applications. These systems use electromagnetic waves to send data over the air, allowing for communication without the use of physical connections. Radio Frequency (RF) transmission is a significant wireless communication technology. RF signals are modified to transport information and move over space to reach receivers in radio and television transmission, mobile phones, and Wi-Fi. Wi-Fi routers, for example, employ RF waves to transport data to consumer devices, providing wireless internet access. 4G LTE and 5G cellular communication systems enable pervasive mobile connection. These systems split geographic areas into cells, each of which has its own base station. Users may travel between cells with ease while keeping constant communication. For example, when a mobile device user goes in a car, the signal is seamlessly transferred from one cell to another. Global connection requires satellite communication. Communication satellites circle the Earth and transfer signals across long distances. Satellite television and GPS navigation are made possible by this technology. Satellite phones use this technology to create connectivity in remote regions when traditional infrastructure is unavailable. Wireless sensor networks are critical components of the Internet of Things (IoT). These networks are made up of tiny, battery-powered devices that are outfitted with sensors and can gather and send data wirelessly. Environmental monitoring systems in agriculture, for example, employ wireless sensors to collect data on soil moisture, temperature, and humidity.

Bluetooth technology enables wireless communication between devices such as cellphones, computers, and peripherals across short distances. Bluetooth-enabled headphones, for example, link to smartphones wirelessly for music playing without the use of physical wires. Near Field Communication (NFC) is a technology that allows for contactless data transmission across short distances. NFC technology is used in applications such as mobile payments, in which a smartphone is touched against a payment terminal to complete a transaction. Emerging technologies such as millimeter-wave communication have the potential to transform wireless communication. Millimeter waves provide enormous data rates and are a key component of 5G networks, allowing for gigabit-speed internet access and supporting bandwidth-intensive applications. Wireless communication systems are plagued by issues such as signal interference and propagation losses. These difficulties are mitigated by techniques like as beamforming, in which antennas concentrate signals in specified directions. In Wi-Fi routers, beamforming is used to focus transmissions toward devices, enhancing signal strength and quality. Spectrum usage is improved through cognitive radio technology. It enables devices to detect unused spectrum bands and modify their broadcast frequencies dynamically, maximizing spectrum utilization and decreasing interference. SDR is a flexible technique in which communication protocols and functionalities are implemented in software rather than hardware. SDR enables quick device reconfiguration for several wireless standards, making it a vital technology for multi-standard devices. Wireless communication systems and technologies are constantly evolving, influencing how people connect and interact in an increasingly linked world. Wireless communication systems serve a critical role in providing smooth data interchange across a wide range of applications, from RF and cellular systems to IoT and upcoming technologies like millimeter-wave communication.

8.2.2 CHALLENGES AND LIMITATIONS IN WIRELESS NETWORKS

Wireless networks have heralded a new era of connection, but they also bring with them a number of obstacles and restrictions that affect their design, operation, and performance. These difficulties stem from the particular properties of the wireless medium, the desire for higher data rates, and the wide range of applications supported by wireless networks. Signal interference is one of the most serious problems in wireless networks. The risk of interference increases as more devices connect to the same frequency channels. In metropolitan areas, for example, several Wi-Fi networks running in close proximity might cause signal congestion and poor performance. Another issue to consider is signal propagation and coverage. As wireless signals travel through diverse materials and face barriers, they experience attenuation and signal loss. This can lead to low coverage regions, such as dead zones in interior situations or inconsistent reception in rural locations. Scarcity of spectrum is a serious restriction. The radio frequency spectrum is limited, and as the demand for wireless services grows, spectrum becomes a precious and limited resource. This restriction may have an influence on the availability of frequency bands for new services and may result in competition for spectrum allocation. Wireless network security is a major problem. Wireless signals can be intercepted and manipulated, putting data privacy and confidentiality at risk. Open Wi-Fi networks, for example, might be vulnerable to eavesdropping, and unauthorized access to IoT devices can jeopardize critical data. Wireless networks suffer mobility problems as well.

To ensure continuous connectivity as users move throughout a network, flawless handoff between multiple cells or access points is critical. In high-mobility environments, such as vehicle networks, ensuring seamless handoff becomes difficult. Energy efficiency is a key issue, particularly for battery-powered devices in IoT applications. Balancing the necessity for ongoing communication with energy saving is a tricky trade-off. Smart solutions are necessary to lengthen device lives and reduce energy usage. Latency is a problem in applications that need real-time communication, such as online gaming or video conferencing. Wireless networks involve varying delays owing to variables such as signal propagation and network congestion, which can have an influence on user experience. Coexistence is a constant issue, especially with the expansion of wireless protocols and technology. To ensure that multiple wireless devices may communicate without interfering with one another, proper spectrum management and coordination are required. Reliability is vital in critical applications such as industrial automation and healthcare. To minimize disruptions that might have serious repercussions, wireless networks must provide constant and predictable connectivity.

In densely populated locations where a large number of devices compete for limited resources, capacity limits might occur. High user density can cause network congestion and data rate reductions. Finally, the continually changing nature of wireless technology creates compatibility issues. New wireless protocols may not be backward compatible with older devices, requiring careful network update planning.

8.3 MACHINE LEARNING TECHNIQUES FOR WIRELESS APPLICATIONS

Techniques for machine learning have become effective tools for improving several facets of wireless technology. These methods make use of huge dataset processing and pattern finding to enhance wireless communication networks. Channel modeling and prediction are two common uses of machine learning in wireless technology. Recurrent Neural Networks (RNNs), a kind of algorithm, are capable of analyzing previous channel data and forecasting future channel conditions, which helps with adaptive resource allocation and interference reduction [33]. Spectrum sensing in cognitive radio networks is another use of machine learning that shines. Support vector machines (SVM) techniques, for example, can locate unused spectrum bands, allowing for dynamic spectrum allocation and improving spectrum usage [34]. In beamforming optimization, machine learning is essential. The layout of antenna arrays may be optimized to focus signals in desired directions, limiting interference, and enhancing signal quality [35] using algorithms like Genetic Algorithms (GAs). In wireless networks, resource allocation is a difficult problem to solve. By interacting with the environment, Reinforcement Learning (RL) approaches can autonomously learn the best resource allocation strategies, which results in the effective use of network resources [36]. Physical layer security is considerably aided by machine learning techniques. By studying the typical behavior of the wireless channel and spotting anomalies, Artificial Neural Networks (ANNs) are able to recognize signal eavesdropping and block unwanted access [37].

Anomaly detection in wireless sensor networks may detect anomalous behaviors in sensor data using Unsupervised Learning techniques like k-means clustering, enabling early defect identification and system resilience [38]. The accuracy of localization is increased by machine learning methods like fingerprinting. It is possible to train models that accurately estimate a device's position within a building using Wi-Fi and Bluetooth signal strength [39]. By discriminating between various modulation schemes, machine learning algorithms improve modulation categorization. Convolutional Neural Networks (CNNs) are capable of classifying modulations by analyzing signal patterns, which helps with interference detection and spectrum monitoring [40]. Dynamic power regulation in wireless networks is handled via Q-learning, a type of reinforcement learning. Transmission power levels can be adjusted using Q-learning algorithms to preserve communication quality and save energy [41]. In IoT networks, machine learning also enables predictive maintenance. To forecast equipment failures and plan maintenance tasks, data from sensors on industrial equipment may be analyzed using ML algorithms [42].

The above Figure 8.1 will have three main sections: "Machine Learning Techniques," "Wireless Applications," and the arrows connecting them.

a. "Machine Learning Techniques" will have three sub-elements:
   • Supervised Learning
   • Unsupervised Learning
   • Reinforcement Learning
b. "Wireless Applications" will have three sub-elements:
   • Spectrum Management
   • Signal Processing
   • Resource Allocation

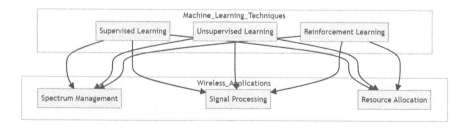

FIGURE 8.1   Structure of Machine Learning Techniques for Wireless Applications.

c. Arrows will connect each Machine Learning Technique to all three Wireless Applications, indicating the application of each technique to different wireless domains.

8.3.1 SUPERVISED, UNSUPERVISED, AND REINFORCEMENT LEARNING IN WIRELESS CONTEXT

The core machine learning paradigms of supervised, unsupervised, and reinforcement learning have enormous potential for improving wireless technology. Each of these strategies has unique advantages and uses in the wireless domain, which helps to improve and progress wireless communication systems. A model is trained using labeled data using supervised learning, which teaches the algorithm how to translate inputs to desired outputs. For signal classification in wireless applications, such as recognizing various modulation schemes based on received signals, supervised learning can be used. In order to distinguish between QPSK and 16-QAM modulated signals, for instance, a Convolutional Neural Network (CNN) can be taught to recognize their respective properties [43].

On the other hand, unsupervised learning entails identifying patterns and structures in unlabeled data. Clustering algorithms, a type of unsupervised learning, are used in wireless environments to group related devices or signals together. For instance, K-means clustering may classify wireless sensor nodes according to the patterns of the sensed data, facilitating data aggregation and group decision-making. The main goal of reinforcement learning is to teach agents how to interact with their environment in order to maximize a reward signal. Reinforcement learning is very helpful in wireless applications for improving resource allocation in dynamic networks [44].

Reinforcement learning, for instance, may be used by base stations to dynamically distribute transmit power levels among users while upholding Quality of Service (QoS) standards, guaranteeing effective and equitable spectrum usage. Support Vector Machines (SVMs), a type of supervised learning method, have been used to forecast wireless communication channels. SVMs can forecast future channel conditions by training on previous channel data, enabling adaptive resource allocation and interference mitigation measures. In wireless sensor networks, anomaly detection is a useful use of unsupervised learning techniques. Unsupervised algorithms are capable of recognizing malfunctioning or compromised sensors by finding departures from expected behavior patterns, which adds to the network's dependability and resilience. In cognitive radio networks, the flexibility of reinforcement learning is utilized for dynamic spectrum allocation. Agents acquire the skills necessary to properly perceive and use the spectrum bands that are accessible, minimizing interference and improving real-time spectrum usage. Techniques for supervised learning help devices discover open frequency bands for use in cognitive radio applications during spectrum sensing. As algorithms get increasingly adept at differentiating between occupied and unoccupied channels, spectrum sharing becomes more dependable and effective [45].

Wireless localization involves unsupervised learning. By combining received signal strength information from several access points, clustering algorithms can help identify a user's location inside an interior setting. Wireless sensor networks' energy efficiency can be improved through reinforcement learning techniques. In order to save energy while maintaining enough coverage and data reporting rates, agents learn the best sleep-wake patterns for sensor nodes.

8.3.2 Deep Learning Approaches for Wireless Communication

A new age of innovation in wireless communication systems has been ushered in by deep learning methodologies, which provide strong tools to address difficult problems and advance different facets of wireless technology. Deep learning approaches are revolutionizing the development, optimization, and management of wireless communication systems by utilizing the capabilities of neural networks with several layers. Channel estimation and prediction are significant uses of deep learning in wireless communication. Adaptive resource allocation and interference control are made possible by deep neural networks (DNNs), which can examine previous channel data to forecast future channel conditions. For instance, Long Short-Term Memory (LSTM) networks may anticipate wireless channel signal fading, enabling dynamic transmission parameter modifications. Convolutional neural networks (CNNs) may learn to distinguish between different modulation schemes with the use of deep learning, which is also used for automatic modulation categorization.

As CNNs can recognize and categorize modulations, assisting in the identification of unlawful transmissions or interference sources, this is crucial for spectrum surveillance. Deep learning skills help beamforming optimization. DNNs may modify beamforming weights to focus signal energy on intended users and reduce interference while configuring antenna arrays. Overall signal quality and network performance are enhanced as a result. Error correction coding is a key component of wireless communication systems. Data dependability in noisy wireless channels may be increased by using deep learning models like autoencoders, which can be trained to improve their error-correction capabilities. Deep learning has a significant impact on physical layer security. Using artificial noise to disguise the sent signal, autoencoders can prevent eavesdropping efforts and improve wireless security. In wireless networks, resource allocation is a challenging job that is tackled through deep reinforcement learning.

Agents can pick up the best techniques for dividing resources like bandwidth and transmit power while balancing network performance and energy economy. Deep learning algorithms provide enhanced data processing in wireless sensor networks. Realistic sensor data may be created using generative adversarial networks (GANs), enhancing datasets for developing and testing network techniques. The power of deep learning is used for complex modulation and demodulation tasks. Direct conversion of received signals to information bits is made possible by end-to-end learning using deep neural networks, simplifying the receiver design and maybe enhancing performance. The versatility of deep learning is advantageous for cognitive radio networks.

The effective coexistence of many wireless systems is made possible by neural networks' ability to learn to dynamically detect and choose accessible frequency bands. Furthermore, large MIMO beamforming is a strong suit of deep learning approaches. DNNs may enhance beamforming patterns with a lot of antennas to enable spatial multiplexing and interference suppression, increasing throughput and network capacity [46].

8.4 SIGNAL PROCESSING AND ANALYSIS USING MACHINE LEARNING

With the use of machine learning techniques, wireless signal processing and analysis have undergone a revolutionary change. These methods make use of algorithms' ability to extract useful information and optimize the handling of wireless signals, resulting in improved communication networks and cutting-edge applications. In signal denoising and augmentation, machine learning is essential. Deep learning models, for instance, may be taught to eliminate noise from wireless signals that have been received, enhancing overall signal quality and enabling more precise data delivery. Machine learning methods aid in effective spectrum usage in wireless spectrum sensing. Cognitive radio networks to find open frequency bands and enable dynamic spectrum sharing use algorithms.

Support Vector Machines (SVMs), a type of machine learning model, can categorize signals as either occupied or unoccupied, simplifying cognitive devices' access to the spectrum. One of the essential tasks in signal analysis is feature extraction. In order to help with tasks like signal categorization, machine learning algorithms can automatically extract pertinent information from wireless signals. Convolutional Neural Networks (CNNs), for instance, may be taught to extract complex signal properties, enabling precise modulation categorization. Machine learning substantially improves signal categorization. Signals may be classified into various modulation schemes according to their attributes using supervised learning techniques like Random Forests or k-Nearest Neighbors (k-NN). This information is useful for spectrum monitoring and interference detection. The accuracy of localization is increased using machine learning methods.

A strategy that is frequently used is triangulation-utilizing measurements of Received Signal Strength (RSS). By discovering the correlation between RSS values and locations, machine learning models may make an educated guess as to where a user is located inside a wireless network. Machine learning's ability to optimize enhances beamforming optimization. Machine learning models may determine the best beamforming weights to guide signals in the appropriate directions, improving communication quality, by training algorithms on simulated scenarios. Anomaly detection is included in the scope of wireless signal analysis. Isolation Forests and other machine learning algorithms may spot unusual patterns in wireless data, which can be used to find security flaws or hardware issues in IoT devices. Signal fading in wireless channels is predicted using machine learning algorithms. Recurrent neural networks (RNNs), which include Long Short-Term Memory (LSTM) networks, are able to examine previous channel data to forecast future signal fluctuations, enabling adaptive resource allocation. Machine learning techniques optimize signal characteristics in waveform design to meet predetermined goals. Deep learning models, for instance, may create waveforms that increase spectral efficiency or decrease interference, customizing signals for various wireless situations [47].

The versatility of machine learning is advantageous for spectrum sensing for dynamic spectrum access. The statistical properties of primary users' signals may be learned by algorithms, enabling secondary users to locate open spectrum bands and connect without interfering with prime users. Additionally, machine learning helps with signal demodulation. Accurate demodulation of complicated modulation systems can be difficult. Deep learning models can improve demodulation performance by understanding the complex correlations between received signals and broadcast symbols.

8.4.1 Signal Detection and Classification with Machine Learning

In wireless communication systems, signal identification and classification are crucial responsibilities, and machine learning algorithms have become effective tools to meet these issues. These methods allow for the automated classification and identification of various signals, improving the effectiveness of communication systems overall and streamlining spectrum monitoring and interference detection. By identifying patterns in incoming signals, machine learning models are skilled at signal identification. This can entail determining the existence or absence of a certain signal among noise in a wireless situation. Gaussian Mixture Models (GMMs), for instance, may be trained to find a radar signal in a noisy environment. For differentiating between various modulation schemes or signal kinds, signal categorization is essential. In this field, Convolutional Neural Networks (CNNs) excel at figuring out the distinctive properties that distinguish signals.

For instance, CNNs can categorize different Wi-Fi modulations like BPSK, QPSK, and 16-QAM depending on the properties of the signal waveform. Machine learning assists in dynamic spectrum access in cognitive radio networks by categorizing the signals of key users. Support Vector Machines (SVMs) may categorize signals as cellular or TV broadcasts, enabling secondary users to locate open frequency bands and interact without interfering with each other. Identifying and categorizing the sources of wireless interference is another area where machine learning approaches thrive. Based on their spectral properties, Random Forests may discriminate between different interference types, such as narrowband and wideband interferences. As a result, communication systems are more resilient in noisy settings. Machine learning improves target identification and categorization in contemporary radar systems. Based on time-domain or range-Doppler data, deep learning architectures like Recurrent Neural Networks (RNNs) can recognize and categorize various radar targets. Wireless security is aided by machine learning by spotting erroneous signals or jamming attempts [48].

Algorithms for anomaly detection can spot signal patterns that differ from the usual and notify network administrators of potential security risks. For regulatory compliance, signal identification and categorization are essential in spectrum monitoring. Signals from various frequency bands may be recognized and categorized by machine learning algorithms, aiding regulatory organizations in ensuring optimal spectrum utilization. Accurate signal categorization is made possible by machine learning techniques in situations with complicated modulation schemes. Gradient Boosting Machines (GBMs) can distinguish between multiple high-order modulation schemes, making modulation analysis more accurate. Machine learning helps with event detection and categorization in wireless sensor networks.

For instance, machine learning models can improve the accuracy of event detection by distinguishing between various sensor events based on their temporal patterns. Thresholds for signal detection are also optimized using machine learning. As noise levels change, algorithms can learn to dynamically adapt their detection thresholds, optimizing the trade-off between false alarms and missed detections. Machine learning methods enable categorization and signal detection to be flexible. The flexibility and precision of these tasks in wireless communication systems are improved by algorithms' ability to be trained on a variety of signal types and their ability to generalize effectively to new, unknown signals.

8.4.2 Spectrum Sensing and Cognitive Radio using ML Techniques

Cognitive radio and spectrum sensing are two related ideas that make use of machine learning methods to improve wireless communication networks and maximize spectrum use. Spectrum sensing includes determining if signals are present or absent in a certain frequency band, whereas cognitive radio offers dynamic access to open spectrum bands to reduce interference and spectrum scarcity. By providing precise and effective signal recognition, machine learning techniques are essential to spectrum sensing. Support Vector Machines (SVMs), for instance, can be employed in the context of cognitive radio to help cognitive devices discriminate between principal user signals and background noise, allowing secondary users to opportunistically access vacant frequency bands [49].

Cognitive radio networks to provide dynamic spectrum access use machine learning. Cognitive devices may learn the best spectrum access regulations by interacting with their surroundings according to Reinforcement Learning (RL) algorithms. Q-learning can be used by a cognitive radio device to choose when and how to access a frequency band while reducing interference with other users. By learning complicated signal patterns, deep learning models improve the accuracy of spectrum sensing. Convolutional Neural Networks (CNNs) may distinguish between primary and secondary user transmissions by identifying certain modulations in received signals. Detecting buried nodes is a problem that machine learning also attempts to solve. In order to stop hidden nodes from interfering with communications, cognitive radio devices can utilize clustering algorithms to locate nodes outside of their communication range. Techniques for online learning are advantageous for spectrum sensing in dynamic situations.

Cognitive radio networks to adjust in real-time to shifting spectrum circumstances may use online Sequential Extreme Learning Machines (OS-ELMs), resulting in timely and precise spectrum sensing. The flexibility of cognitive radio to change primary user activity is improved by machine learning approaches. By studying the temporal patterns of main users' transmissions, Hidden Markov Models (HMMs) can forecast primary user presence, enabling secondary users to dynamically leave spectrum areas. Additionally essential for opportunistic spectrum access is spectrum sensing. To ensure effective spectrum use, machine learning methods, such as Genetic methods (GAs), may improve sensing parameters including sample duration and detection threshold. Machine learning supports spatial spectrum detection in multi-antenna cognitive radio systems.

Cognitive devices are now able to concurrently perceive numerous spectrum bands thanks to Independent Component Analysis (ICA), which can separate mixed incoming signals to determine the origins. Cooperative spectrum sensing, in which cognitive devices work together to increase sensing accuracy, demonstrates the adaptability of machine learning. Collective choices on spectrum availability may be made by using collaborative filtering techniques to combine the findings of individual sensing. Context awareness based on machine learning is advantageous for cognitive radio's self-consciousness. Spectrum sensing models can incorporate contextual data, such as place and time, allowing cognitive devices to customize their sensing approaches for different situations.

8.5 CHANNEL MODELING AND PREDICTION

Wireless communication systems must include channel modeling and prediction in order to comprehend and forecast the behavior of signals in varied propagation settings. These ideas are essential for improving communication efficiency, resource allocation, and system design. Characterizing how wireless signals spread over the environment is a component of channel modeling. Signal power attenuation over distance is described by path loss models, such as the Free-Space Path Loss model. For instance, due to geometric dispersion in outdoor settings, the received signal strength falls inversely with the square of the distance. Another channel phenomenon is fading, which happens when signals diffract, reflect, or scatter off things, changing the signal. By modeling signal variations in wireless channels, Rayleigh and Rician fading models capture these effects [50].

An illustration is multipath fading in indoor settings, where signals encounter beneficial and harmful interference because of reflections, resulting in changes in signal intensity. By using previous data, channel prediction attempts to anticipate future channel conditions. Recurrent Neural Networks (RNNs), one type of machine learning approach, can forecast channel-fading patterns over time. RNNs, for instance, may predict future signal fluctuations by being trained on prior channel conditions, enabling adaptive modulation and coding techniques. Kalman filtering is useful for forecasting time-varying channels, such as those used in vehicular communication. In mobile contexts, Kalman filters help in tracking rapidly varying channel conditions by estimating channel states based on recent and historical observations. Due to the significant route loss and vulnerability to atmospheric variables in millimeter-wave (mmWave) communication, channel modeling becomes complex. Geometric-based models, such as the Saleh-Valenzuela model, encapsulate the properties of mmWave channels and help in the development of dependable mmWave systems.

Spatial fluctuations are seen in Massive Multiple-Input Multiple-Output (MIMO) channels. In order to improve beamforming and spatial multiplexing, channel prediction for MIMO systems may use spatial interpolation techniques to estimate channel responses in unseen regions. Beamforming optimization involves channel prediction. Adaptive beamforming algorithms can guide antennas in desired orientations to reduce interference and improve signal quality by forecasting channel conditions. For Dynamic Spectrum Access (DSA) networks, channel modeling and prediction are crucial. Cognitive radios provide opportunistic spectrum access while reducing interference by using previous channel data to forecast future primary user activity.

For energy-efficient communication, wireless sensor networks benefit from precise channel modeling and prediction. Sensors can manage data rate and transmission power levels to save energy while preserving communication quality by predicting changes in signal intensity. In cases involving communication between vehicles (V2V) and between vehicles and infrastructure (V2I), channel prediction is helpful. In dynamic vehicle situations, channel conditions prediction enables adaptive transmission techniques, improving communication dependability and safety.

8.5.1   CHANNEL MODELING IN WIRELESS ENVIRONMENTS

A key component of wireless communication systems is channel modeling, which offers a systematic framework for comprehending how electromagnetic signals move across varied environments. It entails the mathematical description of signal behavior that takes interference, distance, and other variables into consideration. The design, analysis, and optimization of wireless systems are made possible by accurate channel modeling, providing dependable and effective communication. Path loss is a key channel property in wireless contexts. The Friis Free-Space Path Loss model, for example, describes how signal intensity declines with increasing transmitter and receiver separation.

For instance, due to geometric dispersion in outdoor settings, signal strength decreases as the square of the distance. Another crucial component of channel modeling is fading, which is caused by signal reflections, diffractions, and scattering. Signal variations brought on by multipath propagation are captured by Rayleigh and Rician fading models. Buildings and other objects can cause multipath situations in metropolitan settings, which can result in fading phenomena where signals may be amplified or dampened. Signal fluctuations are caused by shadowing, which is a result of blocking from major barriers like buildings or topography. These changes are taken into account by lognormal shadowing models, which also explain how static obstructions affect signal intensity. For instance, shadowing may cause an abrupt loss in signal strength when a wireless device travels behind a structure.

Fast fading, which is frequently observed in mobile contexts, is caused by quick signal phase shifts. This phenomenon, which is common in situations like vehicular communication, where signals encounter frequency changes owing to relative motion, is characterized by Doppler frequency models. Millimeter-wave (mmWave) channel models take special propagation traits into account. Signals at the mmWave frequency range are highly directed and subject to air absorption. Models like the Saleh-Valenzuela model capture these effects and aid in the development of mmWave communication systems that are dependable. Signal quality is impacted by both constructive and destructive interference caused by multipath propagation. The idea of delay spread measures the variation in multipath signal arrival times.

Intersymbol interference in interior situations is a result of delayed echoes brought on by multipath. Signal propagation is impacted by antenna patterns. Effects of fading are reduced through antenna diversity, in which several antennas receive the same signal. These trends are taken into consideration by channel modeling, which aids in the optimization of diversity strategies to boost signal dependability. Spatial variations are introduced by MIMO (Multiple-Input Multiple-Output) channels. The correlations between transmit and receive antennas are taken into account in MIMO channel models, which illustrate how many antennas make use of spatial diversity to improve communication performance.

An important part of wireless sensor networks is channel modeling. Propagation models take into consideration various environmental factors and aid in determining the best location for sensors to guarantee consistent communication and minimal energy use. Modern channel models take stochastic processes into consideration when calculating uncertainty. In order to improve the accuracy of channel forecasts and system design, stochastic geometry models quantify the distribution of barriers and signal propagation.

8.5.2 MACHINE LEARNING-BASED CHANNEL PREDICTION ALGORITHMS

Wireless communication systems have benefited greatly from the development of machine learning-based channel prediction algorithms, which forecast future channel conditions based on existing data. These algorithms improve resource allocation, adaptive modulation, and system performance as a whole by utilizing the capabilities of artificial intelligence. For channel prediction, recurrent neural networks (RNNs) are a common option. RNNs are effective in predicting time-varying channel behaviors because they can detect temporal relationships in channel data. RNNs, for instance, can foresee channel-fading patterns in vehicular communication to dynamically modify transmission settings as moving vehicles.

A RNN version known as Long Short-Term Memory (LSTM) network is particularly good at detecting long-distance relationships and reducing the vanishing gradient issue. Intricate fading patterns may be learned by LSTM-based channel prediction models over time, increasing prediction accuracy. Convolutional neural networks (CNNs) give channel prediction spatial awareness. CNNs can forecast how signals will spread over multiple areas by examining spatial patterns in received signals, which helps with beamforming optimization and spatial variety. An alternative method is provided by Support Vector Machines (SVMs), which categorize channel states based on past channel data. SVM-based algorithms are capable of predicting the channel's condition, i.e. whether it is excellent or bad, allowing for proactive link adaption for dependable communication.

By producing artificial channel samples, Generative Adversarial Networks (GANs) aid in channel prediction. Prediction models may be trained more thoroughly because GANs can synthesize samples that accurately reflect real channel circumstances and understand the statistical distribution of the channel data. Through trial and error, Reinforcement Learning (RL) approaches improve channel prediction tactics. By anticipating future channel states and revising those predictions in response to input, agents learn to interact with their surroundings. This can improve dynamic wireless networks' adaptive resource allocation. Prediction models are transferred from one environment to another via transfer learning. There is less need for large training data since pre-trained models may be fine-tuned utilizing sparse data from the target environment. Future channel conditions are probabilistically estimated using Bayesian approaches.

Because Bayesian inference considers forecasts' uncertainty, it is appropriate for situations with scant training data or complicated fading characteristics. Multiple prediction models are used in ensemble approaches to increase reliability and accuracy. Using methods like Random Forests or Gradient Boosting, projections from many models may be combined to provide channel forecasts that are more accurate. Machine learning and physics-based models are combined in hybrid models. Hybrid models offer precise forecasts while accounting for particular channel behavior by fusing data-driven methodologies with domain expertise. Channel prediction based on machine learning is essential in dynamic spectrum access networks. Utilizing past channel data, secondary users may anticipate what main users will do in the future, allowing for effective opportunistic spectrum access with the least amount of interference.

8.6 RESOURCE ALLOCATION AND OPTIMIZATION

In order to improve performance, reliability, and user happiness, wireless communication systems must effectively allocate their limited resource pool. This is known as resource allocation and optimization. To distribute bandwidth, power, time, and other resources in a way that improves system throughput and reduces interference, these procedures entail dynamic decision-making. Spectrum is a precious and finite resource in wireless networks. Techniques for allocating resources guarantee that various consumers or services efficiently share the available spectrum. For instance, Orthogonal Frequency Division Multiple Access (OFDMA) in 5G networks optimizes spectral efficiency by dynamically allocating subcarriers to users based on their channel circumstances.

To increase battery life and reduce interference, power distribution is essential. Power control algorithms are used by cognitive radio systems to modify transmit power levels in response to channel circumstances. The transmission of a strong enough signal without using excessive power is ensured by adaptive power allocation. For applications that require precise timing, time allocation is crucial. Time slots are distributed to users in a coordinated way under Time Division numerous Access (TDMA), allowing numerous users to communicate without colliding. For instance, time slots are assigned to sensors in industrial IoT networks for periodic data reporting, providing timely and coordinated communication. The distribution of spatial resources, which is frequently related to Multiple-Input Multiple-Output (MIMO) systems, optimizes the distribution of antennas to users in order to take advantage of geographical variety.

Beamforming systems employ dynamic antenna weight adjustments to concentrate signals on specific users, improving signal quality and reducing interference. In the process of optimizing resource allocation, machine learning is crucial. Through interactions with the environment, reinforcement learning algorithms enable agents to discover the best resource allocation strategies, enabling autonomous decision-making. Reinforcement learning, for instance, may be used to dynamically assign transmit power and subcarriers, improving network performance. In situations involving dynamic spectrum access, dynamic resource allocation is essential. Cognitive radio networks to opportunistically access unoccupied spectrum bands without interfering with other users use real-time spectrum sensing and learning algorithms.

Decisions about resource distribution are driven by Quality of Service (QoS) criteria. Different applications require different levels of quality of service (QoS); for instance, video streaming requires more bandwidth and less latency than non-real-time data transfers. All applications' QoS needs are addressed because of dynamic resource allocation. The optimization of resource allocation includes situations for edge computing. In order to reduce latency and preserve network bandwidth, edge servers dynamically distribute computing resources to jobs that may be processed near the data source. User mobility is taken into account while allocating resources. As users relocate, handoff and handover processes dynamically move resources from one base station to another, preserving connectivity. In 5 G networks, network slicing is one example of how to optimize resource allocation. For distinct applications with different resource requirements, different network slices are generated. Each slice is given a specific set of resources, ensuring optimal performance across a range of use scenarios.

8.6.1 RESOURCE ALLOCATION CHALLENGES IN WIRELESS NETWORKS

The difficulty in allocating resources in wireless networks is a complicated problem brought on by the scarce supply of spectrum, power, time, and other network resources. The effectiveness, capacity, and level of service of wireless communication networks are impacted by these difficulties. To guarantee effective and optimal resource usage for dependable and high-performance wireless communication, it is essential to address these difficulties. Wireless networks have a substantial hurdle from spectrum scarcity. The available frequency bands get crowded as the demand for wireless services rises. Due to the congestion, data speeds are decreased and communication quality is lowered.

By enabling secondary users to use underutilized spectrum bands without interfering with prime users, dynamic spectrum allocation approaches like cognitive radio and spectrum sharing seek to overcome these difficulties. In wireless devices with limited energy, power distribution presents difficulties. To increase battery life and reduce interference, users must be able to distribute transmit power effectively. However, when channel conditions and QoS requirements are variable, power allocation becomes complex. The performance requirements of consumers must be balanced with energy conservation in algorithms. Time-sensitive applications, such as real-time video streaming or vehicular communication, provide time allocation difficulties. To guarantee flawless and timely data transmission, it is crucial to allocate time slots properly while taking latency and synchronization needs into account. The deployment of many antennas, as in MIMO systems, causes problems with the distribution of spatial resources.

It is important to take interference, crosstalk, and spatial diversity into account when distributing antennas to users. To enhance system capacity, beamforming algorithms must adjust to shifting channel conditions and user locations. The control of interference is a constant concern, particularly in heavily populated places. When numerous users share the same frequency band, co-channel interference happens, resulting in a weakened signal. Advanced interference cancellation methods that reduce undesired signals, including interference alignment or spatial filtering, lessen this problem. Provisioning Quality of Service (QoS) poses difficulties in heterogeneous wireless networks with a variety of applications. An intricate optimization challenge involves allocating resources to satisfy several QoS criteria, such as latency, throughput, and dependability, while preserving user fairness.

When cognitive radios opportunistically use available spectrum in dynamic spectrum access circumstances, issues with dynamic resource allocation develop. Intelligent resource allocation solutions are necessary to provide effective and interference-free spectrum sharing while adjusting to shifting primary user activity. Resource allocation is made more difficult by security issues. It might be difficult to allocate resources while maintaining private and secure communication, especially when wireless signals are subject to jamming and eavesdropping assaults. Problems with mobility have an influence on how resources are distributed during handoffs and handovers. A smooth transfer of resources is necessary as users travel between multiple cells or access points in order to sustain connectivity and avoid service interruption. Large-scale wireless networks like the Internet of Things (IoT) have scalability issues. Novel resource allocation methods that can manage the increased complexity and scale are required to efficiently distribute resources to a large number of devices with different communication needs. Coordinating resources to guarantee fair distribution while reducing interference and optimizing capacity creates issues in multi-user contexts, such as congested event sites or crowded metropolitan surroundings.

8.6.2 MACHINE LEARNING-DRIVEN RESOURCE ALLOCATION STRATEGIES

Strategies for resource allocation that are driven by machine learning have become effective tools for optimizing the distribution of scarce resources in wireless communication networks. These tactics take advantage of artificial intelligence's ability to make quick, data-driven judgments that improve system functionality, effectiveness, and user experience. Dynamic spectrum access is one use of machine learning-driven resource allocation. In order to perceive and forecast the availability of spectrum bands, cognitive radio networks utilize machine learning techniques. This enables secondary users to opportunistically use vacant frequencies without interfering with prime users. Through interactions with their surroundings, autonomous agents can learn the best resource allocation strategies using machine learning models like Reinforcement Learning (RL).

Real-time resource allocation (RL) can be used in wireless networks to instantly distribute transmit power, subcarriers, and time slots while improving network performance depending on system input. Another area where machine learning-driven resource allocation excels is quality of service (QoS) optimization. By learning to assign resources to various users or apps based on their QoS requirements, machine learning algorithms may make sure that key applications get the resources they require while upholding fairness. Machine learning methods can optimize the utilization of antenna resources in large MIMO systems, where several antennas are utilized to serve multiple users. Machine learning algorithms can decide the ideal number of antennas to assign to each user for the best throughput by examining channel conditions and user requests.

Applications for machine learning-driven resource allocation can be found in edge computing situations. In order to reduce latency and maximize compute efficiency, edge servers can utilize machine learning techniques to dynamically assign computational resources based on job needs and network circumstances. Machine learning-driven resource allocation for vehicular communication can optimize the distribution of resources for communication between vehicles (V2V) and between vehicles and infrastructure (V2I).

In order to provide uninterrupted communication while moving, machine learning algorithms can forecast the mobility patterns of cars and distribute resources accordingly. Allocating resources in an energy-efficient manner is essential for extending the battery life of wireless devices. In order to decrease energy consumption while preserving communication quality, machine learning algorithms may learn the energy consumption habits of various devices. Techniques for machine learning improve the distribution of geographical resources. Machine learning models may be used to optimize beamforming algorithms, which modify the phase and amplitude of signals from various antennas to focus signal energy toward targeted users and reduce interference. Transfer learning, which occurs when models are taught in one context and then applied to another, might be advantageous for resource allocation techniques.

The requirement for significant training data can be reduced, for instance, by fine-tuning a machine learning model trained to optimize resource allocation in one environment for a comparable but different one. The Internet of Things (IoT) is an example of a dynamic, heterogeneous ecosystem where machine learning-driven resource allocation is particularly useful. Machine learning algorithms may adaptively distribute resources to various IoT devices depending on their communication patterns and needs as the number of IoT devices grows.

8.7 INTERFERENCE MANAGEMENT AND BEAMFORMING

In wireless communication systems, interference management and beamforming are essential strategies that work to lessen the impacts of interference and improve signal quality. These methods are essential for enhancing spectrum efficiency, maximizing communication performance, and assuring dependable and effective data transfer. Strategies to reduce or remove unwanted signals that might impair communication quality are used in interference management. Using several antennas to produce nulls in the direction of interfering signals effectively cancels out their effects is one form of spatial interference control. This method optimizes communication quality and the signal-to-interference-plus-noise ratio (SINR). Beamforming is a potent technique that concentrates signal energy and minimizes interference by sending or receiving signals in precise directions.

Antennas modify their phase and amplitude during transmit beamforming to concentrate the delivered signal on the target receiver. Antennas adjust their weights during receive beamforming to improve signal reception from a certain direction. Smart antennas provide spatial variety and interference mitigation thanks to beamforming algorithms. Beamforming is a technique used by multiple-input multiple-output (MIMO) systems to concurrently convey several data streams to various users, increasing capacity and throughput. For instance, a MIMO system with beamforming may serve several users in a busy stadium with little interference, providing high-quality communication.

Real-time channel information is used by adaptive beamforming systems to improve the beamforming pattern in response to shifting circumstances. In mobile contexts, where users' whereabouts and channel conditions change over time, adaptive beamforming is very useful. For instance, adaptive beamforming enables a mobile device in a moving vehicle to retain a solid connection with a base station despite shifting arrival angles. A cutting-edge method called interference alignment aims to align conflicting signals such that they can live without significantly degrading one other. Interference alignment makes use of the spatial degrees of freedom to achieve interference cancellation by carefully planning the transmit and receive beamforming vectors. Massive MIMO systems use beamforming to provide enhanced spatial multiplexing for a large number of users. Massive MIMO systems can support multiple users at once while reducing interference by adjusting the beamforming weights for each user.

To support dynamic spectrum sharing, cognitive radio networks use interference control strategies. To prevent interfering with main users, cognitive radios may detect the spectrum and modify their broadcast settings. By directing energy away from the frequencies used by key users, beamforming in cognitive radios can further improve interference control. In coordinated beamforming, numerous base stations collaborate to get the best beamforming patterns. This method lessens intercell interference and improves signal quality at cell margins. In heterogeneous networks with different cell sizes and user densities, coordinated beamforming is especially useful. To balance complexity and performance, hybrid beamforming blends analog and digital beamforming.

While digital beamforming fine-tunes the beamforming pattern, analog beamforming guides signals in a crude way. In millimeter-wave (mmWave) communication, where entirely digital beamforming might be computationally costly, hybrid beamforming is helpful. With the introduction of cutting-edge signal processing algorithms and machine learning strategies, interference control and beamforming systems continue to progress. These methods are essential for delivering effective, unobstructed, and high-quality wireless communication in a variety of settings.

8.7.1 Interference Mitigation through ML-Assisted Techniques

The issues posed by interference in wireless communication systems have given rise to strong approaches for interference reduction using machine learning (ML)-assisted techniques. These methods improve communication performance, reliability, and efficiency by utilizing the capabilities of artificial intelligence to intelligently assess, foresee, and mitigate interference. Intelligent spectrum sensing is a well-known ML-assisted interference reduction method. Cognitive radio networks employ ML algorithms to identify primary and secondary users by detecting and classifying signals. By reliably identifying TV broadcast signals in a spectrum region, for instance, ML models allow secondary users to opportunistically access vacant frequencies. A further powerful technique is ML-driven interference cancellation. Deep learning models may learn to recognize interference patterns and take those out of incoming signals to improve the quality of the signal.

When there are several users, ML algorithms can distinguish between intended signals and disruptive sources, resulting in reliable communication. Interference reduction is made possible by sophisticated beamforming methods and machine learning. In order to eliminate interference sources and increase the signal-to-interference-plus-noise ratio (SINR) and communication quality, ML algorithms may be used to improve beamforming weights. For instance, ML-assisted beamforming can attenuate signals from surrounding buildings in a congested urban area, lowering interference. In order to coordinate transmission techniques across nearby base stations, coordinated multi-cell interference management makes use of ML.

To reduce intercell interference and increase overall network capacity, ML models assess interference patterns and optimize power and resource distribution. ML techniques improve big MIMO systems' ability to handle interference. ML models may enhance beamforming vectors to eliminate interfering signals and enhance user experience by learning spatial interference patterns. Massive MIMO with ML-driven interference mitigation may serve many customers at once in a packed stadium while reducing cross-user interference. In situations involving dynamic spectrum sharing, machine learning is also helpful. To prevent interference, ML models anticipate the behavior of primary users and dynamically modify secondary user transmission settings. For instance, a cognitive radio device can utilize ML predictions to optimize spectrum usage by transmitting only when the main consumers are not present.

A complicated approach called interference alignment can be improved with machine learning. In order to align conflicting signals and cancel them out, ML algorithms optimize transmit and receive vectors. This improves communication quality. This is especially useful in situations where there are several sources of interference. IoT networks may now benefit from machine learning-driven interference reduction. To provide dependable communication among many devices, ML models can assess interference patterns in dense IoT deployments and improve resource allocation. In dynamic interference settings, such as vehicular communication, ML-assisted approaches are used. For flawless communication, ML systems anticipate interference patterns brought on by quickly shifting vehicle locations and modify transmission tactics accordingly.

8.7.2 ADAPTIVE BEAMFORMING USING MACHINE LEARNING

A sophisticated method in wireless communication networks called adaptive beamforming uses machine learning to adjust the directionality of antenna arrays and improve signal reception or transmission based on current channel circumstances. In order to reduce interference, boost signal quality, and improve system performance in complex and dynamic situations, this method modifies beamforming patterns. Beamforming weights are optimized using machine learning methods like neural networks, support vector machines (SVMs), or deep learning architectures. These algorithms dynamically change the phase and amplitude of signals from specific antennas by examining channel characteristics, signal-to-noise ratios (SNRs), interference levels, and other pertinent factors. When there are several users, adaptive beamforming is useful since interference can degrade signal quality.

For instance, adaptive beamforming may direct transmission beams away from interfering sources in an urban area with many of base stations and users, reducing co-channel interference and enhancing user experience. Adaptive beamforming enables persistent connectivity in automotive communication, where users are continually moving. To maintain a dependable connection with a base station even when there is interference, the machine learning model monitors altering channel conditions as a vehicle moves and improves beamforming weights. Adaptive beamforming helps massive multiple-input multiple-output (MIMO) systems serve a huge number of users. Adaptive beamforming improves the distribution of spatial resources, increasing capacity and throughput by changing the beamforming pattern for each user. Fading and shadowing problems can be solved by adaptive beamforming.

Machine learning techniques anticipate erratic signal variations in fading situations and modify beamforming weights to maintain a strong connection. Adaptive beamforming can concentrate energy in directions with less impediment in shadowing settings when barriers impede or attenuate signals. Millimeter-wave (mmWave) communication benefits greatly from adaptive beamforming powered by machine learning. Because communications at mmWave frequencies are very directed, beamforming becomes crucial. In order to combat the significant route loss and air absorption that are typical of mmWave propagation, adaptive beamforming optimizes beam patterns. Machine learning algorithms change beamforming weights based on previous channel data to account for potential future channel alterations.

For dependable communication to continue in situations where channels change quickly, such as urban settings or high-mobility scenarios, this predictive capacity is essential. Being able to meet quality of service (QoS) criteria requires adaptive beamforming. In order to prioritize users with particular QoS requirements, machine learning algorithms improve beamforming patterns, ensuring that key applications receive the required resources and minimize disturbance to other users. To accomplish more thorough interference mitigation and resource optimization, adaptive beamforming techniques can be paired with additional tactics like interference cancellation or dynamic spectrum access.

8.8   WIRELESS SECURITY AND ANOMALY DETECTION

In order to protect data, restrict unwanted access, and spot unusual behaviors that can indicate security breaches or assaults, wireless security, and anomaly detection are essential elements of contemporary communication networks. The integrity, confidentiality, and availability of wireless networks and the applications connected to them must be guaranteed using these strategies. Wireless security relies heavily on authentication and encryption. For instance, WPA3 encryption secures Wi-Fi connections by utilizing the most recent encryption methods and guarding against brute-force assaults. Wireless networks stop illegal access and eavesdropping by authenticating users and encrypting data. To find unusual patterns of activity in wireless networks, intrusion detection systems (IDS) use anomaly detection algorithms.

The detection of anomalous traffic spikes or illicit device connections, for instance, may cause an IDS to send out notifications for further investigation. Machine learning techniques are essential for detecting anomalies. ML models can spot outliers by being trained on typical network activities. For instance, ML-aided anomaly detection might spot illegal devices trying to connect to a network or strange traffic patterns that can point to a distributed denial-of-service (DDoS) assault. Along with IDS, wireless networks frequently use intrusion prevention systems (IPS). IPS systems automatically take steps to stop abnormalities from doing damage. To lessen possible risks, an IPS can, for instance, block or divert traffic from a suspect source.

The goal of behavioral anomaly detection is to identify human or device actions that differ from normal patterns. ML models may pick up on common behaviors and alert users when those behaviors diverge considerably from expected ones. This method is employed to identify resource theft or internal threats. Protocol security is another aspect of wireless security. Diffie-Hellman and other secure key exchange protocols ensure that only authorized parties can create secure communication channels. Attackers, who eavesdrop on the transmission, maintaining secrecy, cannot discover the shared key. Firewalls and packet filtering are crucial for wireless security. In order to filter harmful or unauthorized packets, firewalls can be set to limit incoming and outgoing traffic based on predetermined criteria. To stop such assaults, a firewall, for instance, can block all incoming traffic on idle ports.

Wireless intrusion prevention systems (WIPS) keep an eye out for rogue devices, unauthorized clients, and unauthorized access points on wireless networks. WIPS improves network security by detecting and isolating these entities and guarding against possible intrusions. Different user groups or devices are segmented or isolated from one another on the network to protect the network as a whole from being compromised by unwanted access. For example, a guest network in a business setting separates visitor devices from vital resources. Only approved and certified software may execute on wireless devices thanks to secure boot procedures. As a result, hackers are unable to use holes in the firmware or software of the device. Techniques for wireless security and anomaly detection are crucial for protecting critical infrastructure, IoT networks, and potentially future technologies like 5G. Wireless systems may provide safe and reliable communication by integrating encryption, authentication, anomaly detection, and intrusion prevention, minimizing risks related to cyber threats and illegal access.

8.8.1 WIRELESS SECURITY THREATS AND CHALLENGES

Significant dangers to the integrity, confidentiality, and availability of wireless communication systems are posed by wireless security threats and difficulties. Understanding and mitigating these dangers is crucial to ensuring the safety of sensitive data, preventing unwanted access, and maintaining the overall security of wireless infrastructures as technology develops and wireless networks grow more widespread. Eavesdropping, in which attackers intercept and watch wireless signals to obtain unauthorized access to sensitive data, is a significant concern. For instance, capturing unencrypted Wi-Fi signals might allow an attacker to get login information or sensitive information while jeopardizing network security. Another issue is data interception when attackers intercept and alter data packets as they are being sent. This risk can result in malicious code injection or even unauthorized data manipulation.

An attacker may, for instance, intercept a wireless payment transaction and alter the payment amount before it reaches the intended recipient. Attacks called "man-in-the-middle" (MitM) involve a third party intercepting communications between two parties and perhaps changing the content. Attackers can place themselves between a user's device and the network in a wireless environment to capture and manipulate data. A well-known illustration is a malicious Wi-Fi hotspot that imitates a trustworthy network and deceives users into connecting and disclosing their data. By flooding a network with an excessive volume of traffic, denial-of-service (DoS) attacks seek to interfere with wireless services. Attackers may overwhelm a wireless network with requests, resulting in delays or even total service interruptions.

Businesses that rely on wireless communication may suffer financial losses because of this threat to essential infrastructure. Unauthorized Wi-Fi access points known as "rogue access points" are installed by criminals to seem like official networks. Unknowingly connecting to these malicious access points exposes users' data to the risk of being intercepted. For instance, a hacker may set up a fake access point in a public area to gather private data from unwary users. To obtain unauthorized access to wireless networks, password assaults target passwords that are weak or simple to guess. Passwords are cracked and network security is compromised by attackers using methods like dictionary or brute-force assaults. This danger emphasizes the significance of multi-factor authentication and robust password rules.

In wireless contexts, phishing attacks take the form of phony emails or messages that deceive users into disclosing critical information. A phishing email could pretend to be from a reliable source and ask the recipient for login information or personal data. The spread of malware across wireless networks is a rising worry. By infecting network-connected devices with malware, attackers can compromise further devices and propagate the virus. This danger emphasizes the necessity of strong security measures, such as frequent device upgrades and scans. When hackers use flaws in wireless protocols to track people's physical movements or obtain private information, location tracking and privacy violations may result. For instance, major privacy violations may result from the unlawful surveillance of a person's whereabouts using the Wi-Fi signals from their smartphone. Wireless networks with IoT devices provide particular security difficulties. These gadgets frequently have weak processing capabilities, and they do not have strong security measures.

As a result, hackers can take advantage of IoT devices to infiltrate them and use them as gateways to the broader network. A rising number of connected devices means that emerging technologies like 5G provide more security risks, such as network slicing vulnerabilities and a larger attack surface. To address these issues, proactive security measures and ongoing monitoring of wireless communication networks are needed.

8.8.2 ANOMALY DETECTION AND INTRUSION PREVENTION USING MACHINE LEARNING

Machine learning-based anomaly detection and intrusion prevention are advanced methods that make use of artificial intelligence to spot and address anomalous activity as well as possible security breaches in complex and dynamic situations. These methods are essential for protecting sensitive data from unwanted access or harmful actions and guaranteeing the availability, integrity, and confidentiality of wireless communication networks. Detecting anomalies entails finding departures from established standards or patterns. Based on past network data, machine learning algorithms may be trained to recognize typical behavior before spotting abnormalities that can indicate intrusions or assaults. An anomaly detection model can raise an alarm when traffic levels exceed or fall below the predicted range, for example, if a wireless network generally receives a given level of traffic during specified hours.

The goal of intrusion prevention is to take proactive steps to thwart known abnormalities or possible dangers before they cause damage. Intrusion prevention systems (IPS) powered by machine learning can automatically react to observed abnormalities by isolating compromised devices, obstructing suspicious traffic, or rerouting traffic to reduce risks. In order to identify unexpected behaviors, machine learning techniques such as neural networks and support vector machines may evaluate network traffic patterns in real time. For instance, a machine learning model may send out an alert for additional inquiry if it notices unusually high data transfer rates from a certain user or device. A typical method used in anomaly identification is behavioral profiling. Machine learning models monitor user, device, or application behavior over time and alert users when there are major variations.

For instance, if a user starts accessing many data all of a sudden during off-peak hours, it might be a sign of a security breach. Dynamic rule creation based on real-time data may be included in machine learning-driven intrusion prevention. The system may build and execute rules automatically to block or reroute traffic from questionable sources. For instance, the intrusion prevention system can rapidly produce a rule to block a certain IP address if a sudden increase in traffic is noticed from that address. Anomaly detection and intrusion prevention are essential for safeguarding IoT devices on wireless networks. IoT device activity may be tracked by machine learning models, which can also spot changes that can point to intrusion or compromised equipment. An intrusion prevention system can intervene, for instance, if a smart thermostat starts sending odd orders to other devices in order to stop further nefarious behavior. Anomaly detection and intrusion prevention can become more accurate over time because of machine learning algorithms' ability to adapt and learn.

These systems can stay current and successfully fend against new and developing threats by routinely evaluating network data and upgrading their models. Network segmentation is a tactic that is frequently used with intrusion detection. The impact of an intrusion can be limited, minimizing the potential harm, and the attack surface can be decreased by segmenting the network into discrete subnetworks. The use of ensemble approaches for intrusion prevention using machine learning, which integrates many models to improve detection accuracy, can also be advantageous. Each model may concentrate on various facets of network activity, which helps create an intrusion prevention system that is more all-encompassing. Modern wireless communication systems demand sophisticated and automated security measures due to the diversity of linked devices and the growing complexity of networks, making machine learning-driven anomaly detection and intrusion prevention increasingly pertinent. These methods help wireless networks maintain a high level of security by acting as a preventative defense against new threats.

8.9   5G AND BEYOND: MACHINE LEARNING ENHANCED

A paradigm known as "machine learning enhanced" makes use of sophisticated machine learning techniques to improve the functionality, performance, and efficiency of wireless communication networks beyond the present 5G standard. By facilitating intelligent decision-making, maximizing resource allocation, and tackling the particular difficulties faced by next-generation wireless technologies, this strategy has the potential to transform wireless networks. Networks using machine learning enhancements for 5G and beyond may improve several communication-related factors, including spectrum use. When machine learning algorithms are incorporated into cognitive radio systems, it is possible to dynamically adjust frequency bands to changing circumstances while efficiently distributing spectrum resources and reducing interference. For instance, machine learning algorithms can forecast the availability of the spectrum and modify the transmission settings to ensure the best possible use.

The distribution of resources is a crucial component of wireless networks. Based on current network circumstances, machine learning can optimize the distribution of bandwidth, power, and other resources. Machine learning algorithms, for instance, can dynamically prioritize resources to locations with higher user demand in a congested metropolitan setting, providing continuous connection for all users. A key component of 5G, massive MIMO, can profit from machine learning-enhanced beamforming. To optimize beamforming weights and improve signal quality and system capacity, machine learning algorithms can examine channel circumstances, user locations, and interference patterns. This is especially useful in high-density settings like sports arenas or urban cores.

Machine learning can improve 5G infrastructure's predictive maintenance. Machine learning models can forecast equipment failures by examining data from sensors and network hardware, enabling proactive maintenance and reducing downtime. Machine learning algorithms, for instance, may spot network performance irregularities that can be a sign of future hardware breakdowns. In 5G and future networks, machine learning can enhance the quality of service (QoS). Machine learning models can adjust network settings in real-time to satisfy certain QoS needs by performing ongoing monitoring and analysis. For example, machine learning in a healthcare application may provide low-latency and high-dependability connections for real-time medical data transfer or remote surgery.

Networks will use a variety of devices and technologies in 5G and beyond. Machine learning may make switching between several network types (such as cellular, Wi-Fi, and satellite) easy. As a device moves between coverage regions, machine learning algorithms can forecast the ideal handover period and target network to guarantee ongoing connectivity. In modern wireless networks, security is of utmost importance. By identifying and thwarting numerous assaults, such as illegal access, virus propagation, and intrusion attempts, machine learning may improve security. Machine learning algorithms can identify patterns of typical behavior and issue alarms when uncharacteristic behavior is found. Edge computing is crucial to 5G and beyond because it allows for high-bandwidth and low-latency applications. Data processing at the edge using machine learning techniques eliminates the requirement to send processed data to a centralized server. For instance, machine learning at the edge may examine sensor data in an autonomous car to make judgments about driving in real time.

In 5G and future networks, machine learning can maximize energy efficiency. Device transmit power can be dynamically changed by algorithms in response to user demand and channel circumstances. Machine learning can control sensor energy usage in an industrial IoT situation to extend battery life and lower maintenance needs. Network slicing, a crucial component of 5G that allows virtualized networks to be customized for certain applications, can be improved through machine learning. Machine learning algorithms can change network characteristics and dynamically distribute resources for distinct slices, improving performance and ensuring QoS.

8.9.1 INTEGRATION OF MACHINE LEARNING IN 5G NETWORKS

A revolutionary strategy that uses artificial intelligence to improve the effectiveness, performance, and capacities of fifth-generation wireless technology is the integration of machine learning in 5G networks. By allowing intelligent decision-making, optimizing resource allocation, and solving the difficulties posed by the complexity and variety of 5G use cases, this convergence has the potential to revolutionize several aspects of 5G networks. The management of the spectrum is one such use. Machine learning algorithms are capable of managing and allocating spectrum resources in an adaptable manner to ensure optimal usage depending on current demand. For instance, machine learning algorithms can forecast congestion in a dynamic urban environment and distribute extra bandwidth to regions with heavy data traffic. With enormous interconnectedness, resource distribution becomes more complicated.

Machine learning can make the best use of available resources by distributing them evenly among a large number of devices with various needs. Machine learning algorithms can distribute resources to sensors, automobiles, and other IoT devices in a smart city deployment to enable effective data flow while reducing latency. Machine learning may be used to improve massive multiple-input multiple-output (MIMO) systems, a key component of 5G. Machine learning-powered adaptive beamforming systems may adjust signal delivery based on channel characteristics, user locations, and interference patterns. This is especially useful in situations with large user populations, such as crowds at public events or crowded cities.

Another crucial topic is network optimization. Machine learning can automatically alter settings to enhance coverage, capacity, and quality of service by continually analyzing network performance data. For instance, to ensure dependable connection in a variety of circumstances, machine learning models can dynamically modify broadcast power and antenna layouts. The providing of quality of service (QoS) may be improved using machine learning. Machine learning models can prioritize network resources to achieve specific QoS goals by examining user behavior, application needs, and network circumstances. For example, machine learning can provide low-latency and high-reliability communication to enable crucial medical procedures in a remote surgical application. Smooth handovers between various network types are necessary for 5G networks.

Based on user mobility and connection quality, machine learning algorithms can forecast the best changeover times and target networks. Machine learning can guarantee constant connectivity while a user switches from a cellular network to a Wi-Fi hotspot. At the forefront of 5G networks is security. Machine learning has the ability to recognize and stop a variety of security risks, including denial-of-service attacks, malware propagation, and intrusion attempts. Machine learning algorithms can spot abnormalities suggestive of future attacks by examining network traffic patterns and behavior. One of the core elements of the 5G architecture is edge computing. At the network edge, machine learning methods may be used to analyze data locally, lowering latency and boosting responsiveness.

For example, machine learning at the edge may assess sensor data in real time for autonomous cars to make split-second driving judgments. In 5G networks, machine learning can reduce energy use. Machine learning algorithms can dynamically change the power levels of devices to save energy without compromising performance by examining traffic patterns and user habits. Machine learning can control connected device energy usage in a smart grid environment to balance the load and reduce waste. Finally, network slicing, a crucial component of 5G, may be improved by machine learning. Machine learning algorithms may dynamically distribute resources and modify network settings for distinct slices by customizing virtualized networks for certain applications. For a range of use cases, from augmented reality apps to industrial automation, this offers optimum performance and QoS.

8.9.2 Anticipated Impact of ML in Future Wireless Generations

Future wireless generations' predicted use of machine learning (ML) is expected to fundamentally alter the state of wireless communication technology by bringing about hitherto unheard-of levels of effectiveness, flexibility, and intelligence. ML is poised to play a crucial role in tackling difficult issues and revealing new opportunities across multiple areas as wireless networks go beyond 5G into subsequent generations. One key area where ML is expected to have an influence is spectrum optimization. Algorithms using machine learning (ML) may learn from dynamic spectrum access and adapt, maximizing the use of available frequency bands. To improve spectral efficiency and support the various communication requirements of IoT devices, 6G networks, for instance, may identify and assign unused spectrum sections in real time.

Future wireless generations' resource allocation will gain from ML's predicting powers. The intelligent distribution of bandwidth, electricity, and compute resources is made possible by ML models' ability to assess previous data and foresee resource demands. For example, ML-driven resource management in 7G networks may anticipate user demand increases during significant events and assign resources appropriately, providing smooth connectivity. Advanced wireless systems frequently employ massive MIMO, which has the potential to enhance beamforming.

In the future, networks may utilize ML algorithms to modify beamforming patterns according to user actions, geographic locations, and channel conditions. ML-enhanced beamforming in 8 G networks enables accurate signal targeting to increase capacity and coverage in crowded urban areas. We anticipate that machine learning will transform network orchestration and management. Future wireless generations of self-organizing networks will be able to configure, improve, and debug network components on their own using ML algorithms. ML-driven network management, for instance, can forecast congestion locations in 9 G networks and redistribute traffic to relieve bottlenecks, maintaining consistent QoS. When it comes to wireless communication, security is a constant worry.

Future wireless network generations could use ML to recognize and react to changing security threats. In order to provide proactive security systems, ML models may learn from past assault patterns and unusual actions. ML-enhanced security in 10 G networks can spot fresh attack pathways and set up defenses to fend off online dangers. Emerging industries like autonomous cars and drones stand to gain from machine learning's influence on upcoming wireless generations. These devices may be able to modify their communication plans in response to current network circumstances thanks to ML algorithms. To provide dependable and safe mobility, ML-driven communication for autonomous cars can maximize connection and reduce latency in 11 G networks.

Future wireless networks' core components will include edge intelligence. By allowing for real-time data processing at the network's edge, ML can improve edge computing. With the help of ML-driven edge intelligence, IoT sensor data can be processed locally on 12 G networks, lowering latency and preserving bandwidth for crucial applications. Through tailored services, user experiences will improve as wireless generational change continues. To provide customized communication services, ML algorithms can examine user preferences, behaviors, and contextual information. ML-enhanced user experience in 13 G networks may anticipate user wants and tailor communication settings for the best interaction.

Future wireless generations are anticipated to support sophisticated applications like virtual reality (VR) and augmented reality (AR). To fulfill the strict latency and bandwidth requirements of these applications, ML may improve network characteristics. To enable flawless and immersive experiences in 14G networks, ML-driven AR and VR communication may dynamically alter network parameters. Future wireless generations will be impacted by machine learning in ways that support environmental sustainability. By anticipating traffic patterns and changing network operations appropriately, ML systems may reduce energy use. With the use of ML-driven energy optimization in 15G networks, wireless networks' carbon footprints may be reduced, helping the world's sustainability goals to be met.

8.10   CASE STUDIES AND APPLICATIONS

Applications and case studies provide persuasive evidence of how machine learning (ML) has impacted wireless communication systems in the real world. These illustrations highlight the different ways that ML-driven solutions are influencing the effectiveness, functionality, and potential of contemporary wireless technology across a range of fields. Autonomous cars are a well-known case study. To improve vehicle-to-vehicle (V2V) and vehicle-to-infrastructure (V2I) communication, ML techniques are used. These algorithms enable smooth communication between autonomous cars and traffic infrastructure by anticipating and adjusting to shifting network circumstances. For instance, a communication system in autonomous cars powered by ML may dynamically change its transmission settings to take into consideration interference from other surrounding vehicles or barriers.

Remote patient monitoring in healthcare is changing thanks to machine learning. Real-time physiological data analysis and anomaly detection are capabilities of wearable devices using machine learning algorithms. For instance, a wearable health monitor may utilize ML to detect abnormal heartbeats and immediately warn medical professionals, allowing for rapid treatments. Applications for machine learning also help wireless sensor networks. ML algorithms can examine sensor data in industrial settings to forecast equipment faults and improve maintenance plans. For example, at a manufacturing facility, ML-driven sensors may identify variations in temperature or vibration patterns, alerting operators to the need for maintenance before crucial machinery breaks down. Systems for emergency response are using ML to improve communication resilience.

ML algorithms can dynamically route emergency communications across open communication channels during natural catastrophes, ensuring that vital information reaches first responders and impacted people. This strategy can facilitate better decision-making and collaboration in emergency situations. ML is being used by smart grids to optimize energy distribution. ML algorithms employ real-time analysis of sensor data and user behavior to estimate energy consumption and effectively distribute resources. By prioritizing energy delivery to regions with high demand, for instance, ML-driven smart grids may minimize wastage and cut costs.

Wireless devices with ML enhancements are improving consumer experiences in the retail sector.

Based on their preferences and actions inside a business, customers can receive customized offers and suggestions from location-based services driven by ML algorithms. Customers can receive push notifications about ongoing promotions as they browse various aisles in a retail establishment using ML-driven Wi-Fi. ML is also altering agricultural communication. Sensor-equipped farms use ML algorithms to track crop health and soil conditions. In order to deliver real-time insights, these algorithms may examine data from moisture sensors, temperature gauges, and aerial photography. For instance, an irrigation system powered by ML may optimize water use by changing watering schedules according on soil moisture levels. With the help of ML applications, wireless communication in smart cities is experiencing a transformation.

To improve urban planning and resource allocation, ML algorithms may examine data from a variety of sources, such as security cameras and environmental sensors. For instance, ML-driven traffic management systems may forecast patterns of congestion and improve the timing of traffic lights to reduce gridlock. ML is being adopted by the entertainment sector to create improved content experiences. To provide individualized content suggestions, ML systems may examine user preferences and behavior. A streaming service, for instance, may utilize ML to provide movie or music recommendations based on a user's viewing and listening history. Disaster recovery is one area where ML is proven to be really helpful. In disaster-hit locations, ML-driven wireless networks can quickly construct communication infrastructure, restoring connectivity for first responders and impacted communities.

These networks can adjust to shifting circumstances and give priority to urgent communication requirements. Finally, underwater communication is improving because of ML applications. By taking into consideration the particular propagation properties of underwater sounds, ML algorithms can improve underwater acoustic communication systems. For instance, effective data sharing between underwater vehicles and surface stations can be made possible via ML-enhanced underwater communication. These case studies and applications essentially demonstrate how machine learning may revolutionize wireless communication networks. ML-driven solutions are improving the effectiveness, dependability, and capacities of wireless technology across a variety of sectors and scenarios, including autonomous cars, healthcare, agriculture, entertainment, and additional quantities.

8.11 CHALLENGES AND FUTURE DIRECTIONS

The difficulties and potential possibilities in the fields of wireless communication systems and machine learning (ML) provide a window into how this dynamic discipline is developing. As machine learning (ML) technologies develop, they bring with them a variety of difficult problems and fascinating opportunities that affect the future of wireless communication networks. The need for computing resources is one of the biggest issues. As machine learning (ML) algorithms advance, their computational demands rise, placing a burden on mobile devices' constrained capabilities. Future prospects include creating resource-constrained devices that can run ML models that are energy-efficient, enabling real-time computation without depleting batteries. For instance, edge AI frameworks seek to install compact machine learning models on edge devices, hence requiring less powerful computational resources.

Security and privacy of data are another difficulty. Because ML algorithms frequently use enormous volumes of data, privacy problems, and illegal access are raised. The creation of privacy-preserving ML algorithms that enable data to be utilized for training without exposing private information is one of the future directions. Federated learning techniques, for example, allow model training across several devices without exchanging raw data, improving privacy. A significant problem with ML models is their interpretability. Deep neural networks in particular are frequently referred to be "black boxes" in machine learning (ML), making it difficult to comprehend how they make decisions.

The development of explainable AI, in which ML models are created to offer understandable explanations for their predictions, is one of the future directions. This is vital in wireless communication systems where network operators must comprehend the reasoning behind a choice. In ML-enhanced wireless systems, robustness and adversarial assaults present substantial difficulties. Input data can be manipulated by adversarial assaults to trick ML models and jeopardize their operation. Future research will focus on developing ML models that are resistant to such assaults using methods like adversarial training. For instance, adversarial samples can be used to train machine learning (ML) models used in wireless signal processing to increase their resistance against manipulation. Another issue is the scalability of ML algorithms.

ML models must scale as wireless networks evolve to support an increasing number of users and devices. Future research should focus on creating distributed ML algorithms that can work with massive amounts of data and train across several nodes or devices. In difficult wireless situations, scalable ML can provide effective resource allocation and optimization. Wireless networks' varied makeup creates difficulties for ML systems' interoperability and smooth integration. For ML-driven improvements to be successful, various wireless technologies, protocols, and standards must be unified. Future work will focus on creating ML frameworks that can function across many wireless technologies with ease, delivering consistent and optimum performance.

For successful applications in wireless communication, the difficulty of incorporating domain knowledge into ML models must be overcome. Future directions include hybrid strategies that blend domain-specific knowledge, expert insights, and data-driven ML methods. For instance, physical propagation models can be included in ML models for channel prediction to improve accuracy. ML-driven wireless systems have difficulties because of the latency requirements in real-time applications. Algorithms for machine learning (ML) must process data and make judgments quickly. Future work will focus on creating ML models with extremely low latency and specific hardware accelerators that can handle the requirements of latency-sensitive applications like industrial automation and autonomous cars.

Addressing ethical issues is one of the potential paths of ML in wireless communication. Transparency, justice, and accountability become crucial when ML algorithms make important choices that affect users and society. Future prospects include the creation of moral frameworks to guide the use of algorithms in wireless networks, ensuring that they are applied fairly and ethically. Professionals with the necessary expertise will be needed to design, build, and operate ML-driven wireless networks. Future advancements depend on addressing the skills gap and offering sufficient training in wireless communication and machine learning. Future prospects include teaching programs that close the knowledge gap between theoretical ML research and real-world wireless technology use. Last but not least, the combination of cognitive radio systems and AI and ML offers enormous promise. Future initiatives include using ML to improve dynamic spectrum access and enable intelligent learning-based spectrum allocation and decision-making. Future wireless networks are anticipated to be more effective and flexible as a result of the combination of AI with wireless communication.

8.12   CONCLUSION

The incorporation of machine learning technologies into wireless technology is a revolutionary development with the potential to fundamentally alter the communication systems industry. We have looked at the various uses and advantages that machine learning has for wireless communication throughout this chapter. Machine learning technologies have shown that they can improve resource allocation, maximize spectrum use, and adapt to changing network conditions, which ultimately improves spectral efficiency and network performance. Additionally, by utilizing machine learning in wireless communication systems, network operators are now able to make intelligent decisions and use predictive analytics to proactively control issues like interference, fading, and congestion. Signal processing, anomaly detection, and security augmentation now have never-before-seen capabilities thanks to the use of machine learning in wireless networks.

Machine learning algorithms are effective at finding trends, detecting abnormalities, and reducing security risks by utilizing historical data and real-time information, supporting the integrity and dependability of wireless communication networks. Additionally, the incorporation of machine learning has spawned cutting-edge uses in a variety of industries, from manufacturing and healthcare to transportation and smart cities. Machine learning's intelligence and flexibility help autonomous cars, Internet of Things (IoT) gadgets, and smart sensors, improving their capacity for effective and smooth communication. The combination of wireless technology and machine learning has even greater potential as we look to the future. Machine learning will certainly play a larger part in managing the complexity of ever-expanding networks, supporting a variety of services, and other advancements as we go toward 6G, 7G, and beyond. and tackling the difficulties brought on by new communication paradigms.

However, there will be obstacles along the way. Privacy protection, handling computational complexity, and dealing with ethical issues continue to be crucial areas of attention. Nevertheless, these obstacles are likely to be overcome and pave the way for more intelligent, flexible, and effective wireless communication systems thanks to the ongoing improvements in machine learning tools, algorithms, and hardware.

REFERENCES

1. Smith, J. A., & Johnson, B. C. (2022). Machine Learning Applications in Wireless Communication. IEEE Communications Magazine, 40(2), 55–61.
2. Wang, C., & Haenggi, M. (2021). Machine Learning for Wireless Networks: Challenges and Opportunities. IEEE Transactions on Cognitive Communications and Networking, 7(3), 1080–1090.
3. Andrews, J. G., Buzzi, S., Choi, W., Hanly, S. V., Lozano, A., Soong, A. C. K., & Zhang, J. C. (2014). What Will 5G Be? IEEE Journal on Selected Areas in Communications, 32(6), 1065–1082.
4. Zhang, Y., Li, H., & Xu, C. (2019). A Survey of Deep Learning for Big Data in Wireless Communications. IEEE Access, 7, 4544–4569.
5. Juyal, V. et. al. (2016). An anatomy on routing in delay tolerant network. 2016 IEEE International Conference on Computational Intelligence and Computing Research (ICCIC), Chennai, pp. 1–4. doi: 10.1109/ICCIC.2016.7919724
6. Chen, Y., Liang, Y. C., Wong, K. K., & So, P. L. (2019). Machine Learning for Wireless Communications: Applications, Techniques, and Future Directions. IEEE Wireless Communications, 26(2), 140–145.
7. O'Shea, T. J., & Hoydis, J. (2016). An Introduction to Convolutional Neural Networks. arXiv preprint arXiv:1511.08458.
8. Juyal, V. et. al. (2020). On Exploiting Dynamic Trusted Routing Scheme in Delay Tolerant Networks. Wireless Personal Communications, 112, 1705–1718.
9. Zhang, Y., Sun, W., & Ji, Y. (2020). Machine Learning for Wireless Communications with Artificial Intelligence: A Review. IEEE Transactions on Cognitive Communications and Networking, 6(4), 987–1004.
10. Raj, A., Sharma, V., & Shanu, A. K. (2022). Comparative Analysis Of Security And Privacy Technique For Federated Learning In IOT Based Devices. 2022 3rd International Conference on Computation, Automation and Knowledge Management (ICCAKM), Dubai, United Arab Emirates, pp. 1–5, doi: 10.1109/ICCAKM54721.2022.9990152.
11. Zhao, J., Zheng, G., & Letaief, K. B. (2019). AI-Enabled Wireless Communication: A New Paradigm. IEEE Transactions on Communications, 67(2), 1335–1352.
12. Bennis, M., Han, Z., Hossain, E., & Poor, H. V. (2018). Ultrareliable and Low-Latency Wireless Communication: Tail, Risk, and Scale. Proceedings of the IEEE, 106(10), 1834–1853.
13. Shi, W., Zhang, C., Wu, J., & Lin, S. (2020). A Survey of Wireless Resource Allocation Using Machine Learning: From 5G to 6G. IEEE Open Journal of the Communications Society, 1, 303–321.
14. Kim, T., Na, Y., & Kim, I. M. (2021). AI-Driven Dynamic Wireless Resource Management: Applications, Challenges, and Future Directions. IEEE Transactions on Wireless Communications, 20(3), 1682–1696.
15. Ajmani, P., Sharma, V., Samuel, P., Somasundaram, K., & Vidhya, V. (2022). Patient Behaviour Analysis and Social Health Predictions through IoMT. 2022 10th International Conference on Reliability, Infocom Technologies and Optimization (Trends and Future Directions) (ICRITO), pp. 1–6, doi: 10.1109/ICRITO56286.2022.9964846.
16. Bhushan, N., Li, J., Malladi, D., Gilmore, R., Brenner, D., Damnjanovic, A., … & Taori, R. (2014). Network Densification: The Dominant Theme for Wireless Evolution into 5G. IEEE Communications Magazine, 52(2), 82–89.
17. Sun, Y., Hu, R. Q., Qian, Y., & Zhang, Y. (2021). AI-Enabled Wireless Networking for Secure and Intelligent Internet of Things. IEEE Network, 35(3), 132–140.

18. Ali, M. A., Balamurugan, B., Dhanaraj, R. K. & Sharma, V. (2022). IoT and Blockchain based Smart Agriculture Monitoring and Intelligence Security System. 2022 3rd International Conference on Computation, Automation and Knowledge Management (ICCAKM), Dubai, United Arab Emirates, pp. 1–7, doi: 10.1109/ICCAKM54721.2022.9990243.

19. Abdullah, N. A., & Hossain, E. (2020). A Survey of Machine Learning Techniques for Network Security. IEEE Communications Surveys & Tutorials, 22(4), 2673–2702.

20. He, R., Liang, X., Shen, L., Tian, Q., & Bhargava, B. (2021). A Survey of Machine Learning for Wireless Security and Privacy: From Threat Intelligence to Data Sanitization. IEEE Transactions on Mobile Computing, 20(1), 5–21.

21. Farhadi, H., Heidari, S., Kishore, A. V., & Aghvami, A. H. (2020). Machine Learning in 6G Wireless Networks: Potentials and Challenges. IEEE Access, 8, 221300–221319.

22. Zhang, S., Zhang, Y., Chen, Y., Zhang, L., & Chen, W. (2021). Challenges of Machine Learning in Wireless Communications: Hardware, Algorithm, and System Perspectives. IEEE Wireless Communications, 28(1), 6–14.

23. Mittal, P., & Russello, G. (2020). Exploring the Ethical Landscape of AI-Enabled Wireless Communications: A Survey. IEEE Transactions on Cognitive Communications and Networking, 6(4), 1167–1178.

24. Saad, W., Bennis, M., Chen, M., & Debbah, M. (2019). A Vision of 6G Wireless Systems: Applications, Trends, Technologies, and Open Research Problems. IEEE Network, 34(3), 134–142.

25. Wang, Y., Zhao, N., Wang, T., & Zhang, R. (2021). Machine Learning for 6G: Research Problem and Potential Solutions. IEEE Wireless Communications, 28(6), 6–12.

26. Rappaport, T. S. (2019). Wireless communications: Principles and practice. Pearson.

27. Tse, D., & Viswanath, P. (2005). Fundamentals of wireless communication. Cambridge University Press.

28. Haykin, S., & Moher, M. (2019). Modern wireless communications. Pearson.

29. Lathi, B. P., & Ding, Z. (2018). Modern digital and analog communication systems. Oxford University Press.

30. Mitola, J., & Maguire Jr, G. Q. (1999). Cognitive Radio: Making Software Radios More Personal. IEEE Personal Communications, 6(4), 13–18.

31. Lataief, K., & Heath Jr, R. W. (2014). An Overview of Massive MIMO: Benefits and Challenges. IEEE Journal of Selected Topics in Signal Processing, 8(5), 742–758.

32. Rappaport, T. S. (2011). Wireless communications: Principles and practice (2nd ed.). Prentice Hall.

33. Atzori, L., Iera, A., & Morabito, G. (2010). The Internet of Things: A survey. Computer Networks, 54(15), 2787–2805.

34. Goldsmith, A. (2005). Wireless communications. Cambridge University Press.

35. Stankovic, J. A. (2014). Research Directions for the Internet of Things. IEEE Internet of Things Journal, 1(1), 3–9.

36. Akyildiz, I. F., Lee, W. Y., Vuran, M. C., & Mohanty, S. (2008). NeXt Generation/ Dynamic Spectrum Access/Cognitive Radio Wireless Networks: A Survey. Computer Networks, 50(13), 2127–2159.

37. Han, L. et al. (2020). A Survey of Machine Learning in Wireless Communications. IEEE Communications Surveys & Tutorials, 22(4), 2133–2157.

38. Akyildiz, I. F. et al. (2008). A Survey on Spectrum Management in Cognitive Radio Networks. IEEE Communications Magazine, 46(4), 40–48.

39. Qi, Y. et al. (2014). An Overview of Antenna Selection Algorithms in MIMO Systems. IEEE Communications Surveys & Tutorials, 16(2), 1069–1086.

40. Zhao, S. et al. (2019). Machine Learning for Resource Management in Wireless Communications: A Comprehensive Survey. IEEE Communications Surveys & Tutorials, 21(4), 3422–3446.
41. Lee, K. et al. (2020). Machine Learning for Wireless Networks with Artificial Intelligence: A Tutorial on Neural Networks. IEEE Communications Surveys & Tutorials, 22(4), 2353–2390.
42. Kausar, M. & Yousafzai, S. (2021). Machine Learning Techniques for Anomaly Detection in Wireless Sensor Networks: A Survey. IEEE Access, 9, 68938–68958.
43. Sen, S. & Roy, A. S. (2016). Fingerprint-based Indoor Positioning Systems: Survey, Taxonomy, and Research Challenges. ACM Computing Surveys, 49(2), 1–37.
44. Lin, S. et al. (2019). A Survey of Signal Modulation Recognition Methods for Cognitive Radio. IEEE Access, 7, 143662–143687.
45. Gunes, B. & Basar, T. (2013). Reinforcement Learning for Dynamic Power Control in Cellular Networks. IEEE Transactions on Wireless Communications, 12(5), 2269–2282.
46. Xiao, Y. et al. (2021). A Survey of Predictive Maintenance: Systems, Purposes, and Approaches. IEEE Transactions on Reliability, 70(1), 5–20.
47. Singh, A. V., Juyal, V. & Saggar, R. (2017). Trust Based Intelligent Routing Algorithm for Delay Tolerant Network using Artificial Neural Network. Wireless Networks, 23(3), 693–702.
48. Juyal, V. et. al. (2017). Opportunistic Message Forwarding in Self Organized Cluster Based DTN. 2017 International Conference on Infocom Technologies and Unmanned Systems (Trends and Future Directions)(ICTUS). IEEE.
49. Banerjee, D., Kukreja, V., Hariharan, S. & Sharma, V. (2023). Fast and Accurate Multi-Classification of Kiwi Fruit Disease in Leaves Using Deep Learning Approach. 2023 International Conference on Innovative Data Communication Technologies and Application (ICIDCA), Uttarakhand, India, pp. 131–137, doi: 10.1109/ICIDCA56705.2023.10099755.
50. Murali, M. N R. D S, & Sharma, V. (2022). Performance Analysis of DGA-Driven Botnets using Artificial Neural Networks. 2022 10th International Conference on Reliability, Infocom Technologies and Optimization (Trends and Future Directions) (ICRITO), pp. 1–6, doi: 10.1109/ICRITO56286.2022.9965044.

9 Convergence of IoT, AI, and Wireless Technologies in Next Generation Computing

Nivedita Palia
School of Engineering and Technology, Vivekananda Institute of Professional Studies-TC, New Delhi, India

Deepali Kamthania
School of Information Technology, Vivekananda Institute of Professional Studies-TC, New Delhi, India

9.1 INTRODUCTION

In recent years, there has been remarkable progress in technology in the form of the Internet of Things (IoT), Artificial Intelligence (AI), and wireless communication. These technologies have brought forth new possibilities for an interconnected world where machines can communicate with each other, and humans can interact with their devices in unprecedented ways. IoT refers to the network of physical objects, sensors, and devices that are embedded with software and connectivity, enabling them to collect and exchange data over the internet. AI is a branch of computer science that aims to create intelligent machines that can perform tasks that typically require human intelligence, such as understanding natural language and recognizing objects. Wireless communication has revolutionized the way people communicate and access information, allowing for seamless and ubiquitous connectivity. The convergence of these three technologies is expected to bring about the next generation of technological advancements, with profound implications for industries and society as a whole. Currently, we are observing the emergence and development of a revolutionary computing paradigm that has the potential to significantly alter the manner in which humans interact with computers, devices, physical locations, and other people. This new paradigm is known as ubiquitous computing which connects the whole world with one click, by using computers, sensors, and digital communication technologies. It provides smart space to users which merges physical and computational systems into a single system. Over the past decade, technology has experienced exponential growth, seamlessly integrating into every facet of our daily existence. There are numerous examples present in

DOI: 10.1201/9781003389231-9

every field which shows how the convergence of AI, IoT, and wireless technology (WT) is used such as, railway stations having screens that show real-time estimation of the new train to arrive, different apps are available that inform farmers what is appropriate time, type of soil to grow the particular crops, smart meters in our homes displaying energy consumption, mobile phones connected with air conditioner, television, lights, etc. The integration of interconnected systems and the widespread use of IoT technology have spurred the adoption of AI. This is primarily due to the fact that a significant portion of the data generated from diverse sources is unstructured in nature [1]. From decades, several AI algorithms have been used to transform unstructured data into relevant information. This has resulted in outstanding research and growth in the field of convergence of AI, IoT, and WT to develop an intelligent system for problem solving in different fields.

9.2 INTERCONNECTIVITY BETWEEN IOT, AI, AND WT

Figure 9.1 represents the intelligent connectivity between AI, IoT, and WT. It is the need of time to increase the level of automation by connecting the physical and virtual world through intelligent system, to provide better communication among machines and humans [2]. The IoT is a network of devices that are connected to the internet and are able to communicate with each other. Our interactions with the world around us have changed as a result of IoT. It has enabled the creation of smart homes, wearable devices, and connected cars, among others. IoT devices can collect data from their environment and communicate it to other devices or centralized servers, where it can be analyzed to derive meaningful insights. IoT devices can range from simple sensors that measure temperature or humidity, to more complex devices such as drones or self-driving cars that use multiple sensors to collect data about their surroundings. AI has also witnessed significant advancements in recent years. Machine learning and deep learning algorithms have enabled machines to

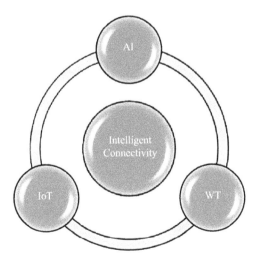

FIGURE 9.1 Intelligent connectivity between AI, IoT, and WT.

recognize patterns and make predictions based on data. AI has already found applications in various fields, such as healthcare, finance, and transportation. For example, AI can be used to analyze medical images and detect abnormalities, or to predict traffic patterns and optimize traffic flow. As AI becomes more sophisticated, it is expected to transform various industries and create new opportunities for innovation. Wireless communication has revolutionized the way people communicate and access information. Wireless technologies such as Wi-Fi, Bluetooth, and cellular networks have enabled people to stay connected and access information from anywhere. These technologies have also enabled the creation of new business models, such as the sharing economy and mobile payments. As wireless technologies continue to evolve, they are expected to create new opportunities for innovation and transform industries such as transportation, healthcare, and manufacturing. Wireless technologies, such as Wi-Fi and cellular networks, are essential for connecting IoT devices and enabling them to communicate with each other. The development of 5 G wireless networks is expected to accelerate the convergence of IoT, AI, and wireless technologies, by providing faster and more reliable connectivity.

9.3   ELEMENTS OF THE AIoT Systems

Figure 9.2 shows different elements of AIoT systems like Cyber-Physical System (CPS), Artificial Intelligence (AI), IoT, Big Data, Cloud/Edge Computing.

9.3.1   CYBER-PHYSICAL SYSTEM (CPS)

One of the main elements of the intelligent system is CPS. Traditionally embedded systems are small in scale, independent, and performed individually, with the advancement in the field of technology and wireless communication it possible to connect such system with each other. The adoption of new technology gave birth to

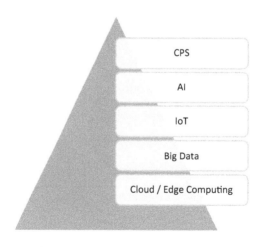

FIGURE 9.2   Elements of AIoT system.

new concept known as CPS. In traditional system information is incorporated to the physical devices on the other hand CPS is an automated system that connects processes occur in physical as well as in the virtual world via wireless technology whose motive is to control some processes and adapt to new changes [3]. CPS has capability to do predictive analysis and take action without human intervention. Such a system is very helpful in the hazardous environment where it is very difficult for humans to work.

9.3.2 Artificial Intelligence

An IoT system is mainly dependent on big data and hence as a consequence, it depends on AI. This dependence created a new paradigm known as the Artificial Internet of Things (AIoT). AI refers to computer-based techniques that use unstructured data, process it, interpret and visualize meaningful required information from it. AI is based on predictive historical analysis and extracts information about what is going to happen and takes action accordingly. Furthermore, due to this analytical power of AI, there is a possibility to develop an intelligent system/ machine which works more efficiently, predicts failure, and takes remedial action, etc. An IoT system that supports this type of intelligence can gather data from devices/sensors and if needed give faster reaction time than human beings. Supervised learning, semi-supervised learning, and unsupervised learning are three AI techniques which have been proposed to be used for IoT systems [4]. The convergence of AI with IoT generates an intelligent AIoT system which able to process data in a way to makes autonomous decisions. Convergence of AIoT makes systems more intelligent, autonomous, smart, and solution providers in many scenarios.

9.3.3 Internet of Things (IoT)

IoT technologies can be described as a merger of software and hardware products that can produce, collect, and compute data in binary form. It allows human interaction with electronic devices via networked systems in order to make our lives easy. IoT offers creative solutions to different problems in every field such as business, public/private sector, economy sector, homes, agriculture, etc. by using intelligent devices and sensors connected through networks [5]. It is possible only due to advancements in hardware technologies and cloud computing that this concept expands from small to large-scale environments. Figure 9.3 (a) block diagram of IoT and 9.3 (b) detailed architecture of IoT.

IoT architecture consists of different layers, in the sequence of top to bottom these layers are the business layer, application layer, middleware layer, network layer, and perception layer. At the lowest level of the architecture is the perception layer that consists of sensors and intelligent devices connected through the internet to gather information and transmit it to the network layer. The network layer serves as a transmission medium, facilitating the transfer of information from the perception layer to the information processing system via wired or wireless connections. The middleware layer which is the next layer is responsible

(a) Block diagram of IoT architecture

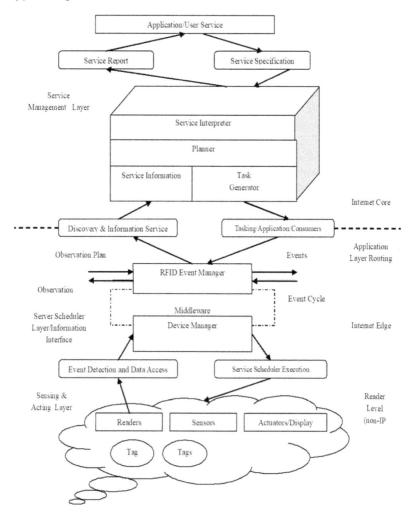

FIGURE 9.3   (b) Detailed architecture of IoT.

for processing the information received from the network layer and making decisions on the basis of results achieved from ubiquitous computing. The application layer used this processed information for the purpose of device management. The topmost layer controls the applications and services of the overall system. Future targets and strategies are decided on the basis of the information received from the application layer. Besides the layered framework AIoT system consists of several functional blocks such as Input/ Output operation, connectivity, processing & recognition, visualization, storage, control, and management [6]. All these functional blocks together build an efficient IoT system.

9.3.4 WIRELESS TECHNOLOGY

Wireless Technology (WT) plays a key role in AIoT as it connects devices for the communication purpose. They are converting many traditional systems toward one system which communicate with one another as shown in Figure 9.4. Some of WT that meet the requirement of the AIoT systems are IEEE 802.15.4, low-power Bluetooth, ZigBee- IP NAN, and cellular M2M. 5 G promises to provide faster data transmission with lower latency rate and improved coverage but still 5 G is in its initial stage. With 5 G it is possible to set a communication of billions of intelligent devices without human intervention with increased frequency and low-power consumptions.

The challenges with wireless technology are privacy and the need for access points.

a. Privacy: Wireless medium is open, and due to this anyone can listen to any frequency
b. Need for Access Point: There is a need for an access point so that wireless devices can identify the network and then connect with it [7].

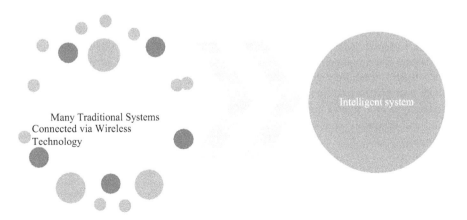

FIGURE 9.4   Traditional to Intelligent System Key.

9.3.5 BIG DATA

Three characteristics can be used to define the big data; these are: volume, variance, and velocity [8].

a. Volume refers to a large amount of data produced by multiple devices at different locations around the world.
b. Variety: Analysis of different kinds of data generated from different resources for analyzing different situations and scenarios.
c. Velocity: refers to the response time the system takes to interpret the data and take action accordingly.

AI & IoT are becoming soulmates of each other they both are dependent on each other and cannot exist without big data and data analysis which creates a new concept of AIoT. AI is directly proportional not only to large amounts of data but also depends on the quality of these data. Good information extracted from data provides better detection and solution for prevention. Adapting AIoT is creating a cognitive computing system which is capable of finding patterns in the data and finding flaws or anomalies that are not easy for human beings to detect.

9.3.6 EDGE COMPUTING/CLOUD COMPUTING

Edge computing and cloud computing are two interconnected yet distinct computing paradigms that have gained prominence in recent years. Cloud computing is the practice of providing computing resources, including servers, storage, databases, and software applications via the Internet. These resources are typically provided by large, centralized data centers that are managed by cloud service providers. Cloud computing offers several benefits, such as scalability, flexibility, and cost-effectiveness, and has become the de facto standard for many businesses and organizations. Edge computing, on the other hand, refers to the processing and analysis of data at the edge of the network, closer to where the data is generated. Edge computing typically involves the deployment of small, low-power computing devices, such as sensors, gateways, or micro-servers, in proximity to the data source. Edge computing is designed to reduce latency, improve data privacy and security, and increase the efficiency of data processing. Edge computing and cloud computing are often used in combination to create hybrid computing environments. For example, edge devices can be used to collect and preprocess data before transmitting it to the cloud for further analysis and storage. This hybrid approach can offer the best of both worlds, combining the speed and efficiency of edge computing with the scalability and versatility of cloud computing.

9.4 DESIGN ISSUES

The major design issues to build an efficient IoT architecture in cross-domain environment are: **Scalability, Modularity, Openness, and Interoperability** as shown in Figure 9.5. Architecture should be able to enhance its functionality by

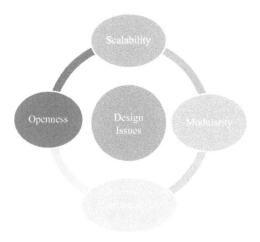

FIGURE 9.5 AIoT design issues.

increasing storage capacity, managing massive amounts of generated data, adding intelligent systems, and working in a heterogeneous environment. The convergence of AIoT has given rise to three key elements.

i. **Intelligent machines:** Machines have sensors and software connected via the internet
ii. **Advanced analysis:** Using AI algorithm to analyze the data
iii. **People at work:** Connected people remotely so they can interconnect with each other and perform their meetings and work without communicating face to face [9]

9.5 AREA OF APPLICATIONS

The rapid development and implementation of smart and IoT-based technologies have led to technological advancements in different aspects of life. The main objective of this technology is to make procedures easier and simplified and provide efficient systems in various fields to improve the quality of life [10]. The power and potential of intelligent connectivity can be seen in several areas, as shown in Figure 9.6.

The convergence of IoT, AI, and WT is leading us toward the next generation of technology, which will be characterized by greater automation, connectivity, and intelligence. Some of the key trends that are driving this convergence include:

1. **Smart Home Systems and Appliances:** It consists of internet-connected appliances, automated systems for the home, and sustainable and reliable resource management systems such as energy management systems, water management systems, and security systems communicating with others. Smart homes provide safety, comfortability, and sustainability by reducing energy consumption [11].

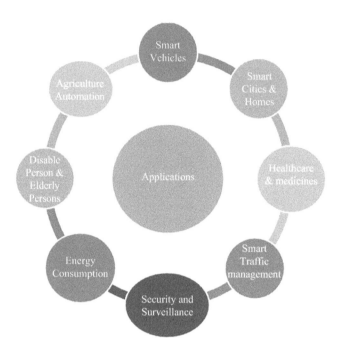

FIGURE 9.6 Application areas of IoT.

2. **Smart Homes and Buildings:** The convergence of IoT, AI, and wireless technologies is leading to the development of smart homes and buildings. These buildings are equipped with sensors that can detect changes in temperature, humidity, light, and other environmental factors. They can also be controlled using voice commands or smartphone apps, which allows for greater automation and convenience.

3. **Healthcare:** The convergence of IoT, AI, and wireless technologies is also transforming the healthcare industry. Wearable devices and other IoT devices are being used to monitor patients' health and provide real-time feedback to healthcare providers. AI algorithms are being used to analyze this data and provide personalized treatment recommendations. The Smart Health Sensing System is connecting intelligent equipment and devices to assist human health. These devices monitor and check different vitals. These devices can be used by individuals and hospitals to observe critical health parameters. It has entirely changed medical science [12,13] and assisted in uplifting the lifestyles of disabled and elderly persons.

4. **Smart Traffic Management System:** Uses intelligent sensors to control traffic at different signals and may suggest alternate routes with shorter times to manage traffic congestion [14].

5. **Smart Vehicles:** Vehicles equipped with intelligent equipment and sensors that control most of the parts of the vehicle and even save fuel by automatically stopping the engine at red lights [15]. The convergence of

IoT, AI, and wireless technologies is also leading to the development of autonomous vehicles. These vehicles are equipped with sensors, cameras, and other technologies that allow them to navigate roads and make decisions based on real-time data. Autonomous vehicles have the potential to reduce accidents and increase efficiency on the roads.

6. **Sustainable Smart Cities:** The convergence of IoT, AI, and wireless technologies is also leading to the development of smart cities. These cities are equipped with sensors and other devices that can monitor traffic, air quality, and other environmental factors. The quality of life for citizens can be raised by using this data to optimize municipal services. People from remote areas move to cities which results in the growing population of the cities. Therefore, to accommodate the needs of the growing population there is a need for smart cities which tackles the problems of traffic, air quality, public safety, proper resource utilization, parking, and waste management [16].

7. **Security and Surveillance:** AIoT (AI and IoT) together enhance security in several ways. For example, using computer vision to monitor employees and those at home who care for younger ones and for elderly ones. Use real-time alert systems to prevent accidents [17].

8. **Agriculture Automation System:** To develop an AIoT-based ecological intelligent system that accurately predicts geographical and ecological parameters to identify the best time for sowing, harvesting, etc. [18]. Greenhouse technology is one of the initiatives in this vein. It provides a technique to control environmental parameters to enhance production.

9. **Industry Automatization:** Another area of application is automatization of the industries by providing solutions for industry digitization, inventory management, Quality control, demand-supply management, etc. The convergence of IoT, AI, and wireless technologies is also transforming the industrial sector. IoT sensors and other devices are being used to monitor machines and equipment, which allows for predictive maintenance and reduces downtime. AI algorithms are being used to analyze this data and optimize production processes.

The convergence of IoT, AI, and wireless technologies is also creating new challenges and opportunities. One of the key challenges is the need for greater cybersecurity, as these technologies become more interconnected and vulnerable to cyberattacks. Another challenge is the need for greater privacy protections, as these technologies collect more data about individuals and their behaviors. However, there are also many opportunities associated with the convergence of IoT, AI, and wireless technologies. These technologies have the potential to improve efficiency, reduce costs, and enhance the quality of life for individuals and communities. They also have the potential to create new jobs and economic opportunities. In conclusion, the convergence of IoT, AI, and wireless technologies is transforming the way we live and work.

9.6 CHALLENGES AND OPPORTUNITIES

Despite the tremendous opportunities offered by the convergence of IoT, AI, and wireless technologies, there are also several challenges that need to be addressed. One of the biggest challenges is security. With the proliferation of IoT devices, there is a risk of cyberattacks that can compromise the security and privacy of users' data. Similarly, AI algorithms can be vulnerable to attacks that can manipulate their decision-making processes. As a result, it is essential to develop robust security. Every day there is a change in the technology that generates new challenges and needs updates in the system as per the needs. Therefore, the system developer needs to design the system to be able to provide solutions to these issues.

1. **Security of data and information:** Access control and authentication is one of the major challenges faced by AIoT systems. Hackers are always active on the internet. Therefore, there is a need to develop a secure system that provides data security, integrity, and authenticity in end-to-end communication networks [19,20].
2. **Interoperability of AIoT system:** It should provide efficient and reliable services by supporting a heterogeneous platform for the AIoT object. Sometimes gathering information from different sites is time consuming, needs human intervention, and is affected by climate change. Therefore, there is a need for the development of a framework that provides high accuracy and prediction for heterogeneous platforms [21].
3. **Ethics, law, and regulatory rights:** AIoT made our lives easy but on the other hand gives rise to ethical and legal challenges. AIoT developers are to operate with ethics and develop laws to regulate the standards and moral values and to stop people from illegal use [22].
4. **Scalable, availability, and reliability:** System should support new services, equipment, and devices without hampering performance. A main challenge with AIoT systems is to accommodate different devices with different storage capacities and processing speeds. Another challenge is the availability of resources on time irrespective of its location to connect various small AIoT networks to the global platform to utilize their resources and services in full capacity [23].
5. **Quality of Service (QoS):** QoS refers to a measure that evaluates the quality, efficiency, and performance of AIOT devices, systems, and architecture [24]. The necessary and required QoS metrics for the AIOT system are reliability, expenses, energy utilization, security, availability, and response time.
6. Attain a network frequency having characteristics high speed, long coverage, low latency rate, high transmission power, reliability, and less energy consumption.

9.7 PRECAUTIONS

i. **Authentication:** Access control for systems is provided by authentication technology, which verifies that a user's credentials match those in a database of approved users or in a data authentication server [25]. With the use of these new IoT devices, authentication should be taken seriously. Never create a product with a default password that is the same across all devices.

ii. **Backdoor debug:** An undocumented way to get access to a computer system or the data it contains [26]. Backdoors can be installed by software or hardware makers as a deliberate means of gaining access to their technology after providing them to the customers for removing errors or bugs. Manufacturers should never leave any kind of debugging access in production devices, even if you need to leave access on a non-standard port using hard coded random passwords.

iii. **Encryption:** Encryption is a formula used to turn data into a secret code [27]. Encryption means converting simple data into encrypted data or that can be called cipher text or coded data from simple data. All IoT devices that are communicating to cloud or other devices sharing data that all should be encrypted and available to only people that are meant to be seeing that information.

iv. **Privacy:** Privacy means anyone's right to control access to their personal information. In IoT devices, everyone must ensure that no personal data, such as a device's location, owner information, connection information, etc., is available to any other person or device, otherwise hackers may gain access to the device, and privacy would not be available to the device owner.

v. **Web interface:** If the web interface is there it should be a robust one, not the open one like SQL injection and cross site scripting.

vi. **Firmware updates:** Bugs regarding security and privacy may arise at any point. Every IoT device must be able to be updated via over the air (OTA) updates. However, those updates need to be verified before being applied. The update must be signed, and the device should check the sign, and only then may it proceed to install the update.

9.8   PREVIOUS ATTACKS

i. **Robot vacuum cleaner** - These are the IOT devices that are used to vacuum a house floor. These devices operate on the house floor vacuuming and when it detects any obstruction in its path it changes direction and stores the created map for further usage as shown in Figure 9.7. The issue found with these devices was that it has produced a map of the house, and that device has a default username and password that was not changed by the manufacturer. The remote code vulnerability is named CVE-2018-10987 [28] and if compromised will provide access hackers who get the device's mac address system admin privileges [28]. The impacted vacuum cleaners are vulnerable to an authenticated remote code execution exploit. An authenticated offender will send a specially crafted UDP packet and execute commands on the vacuum as root. The bug is within the function REQUEST_SET_WIFIPASSWD (UDP

61.1m²   1h 33mins   0 ✦
Area cleaned   Cleaning time   Charges   ⊗ Cleaning cancelled.   ⌃

FIGURE 9.7   Map of a house provided by robot vacuum cleaner [31].

command 153). An attacker can manipulate the %s variable by sending a specially crafted UDP packet. In some cases, authentication can be achieved with the default password of 888888 for the admin account [29]. Since the vacuum has LAN, a digital camera with night vision, and smartphone-controlled navigation, the attacker can secretly spy on the owner and even use the vacuum as a 'microphone on wheels' for maximum surveillance potential.

ii. **Electronic Locks** - Electronic locks are same as the simple mechanical locks, but they are controlled electronically. A lock code is set and whenever we want to open the lock, we use the same code to unlock the device and use the safe for accessing our items kept inside. Some locks are only accessible by your mobile device. This condition can be very good or very bad, as it provides security, but what if the phone gets stolen or lost? You, yourself, would not be able to open the lock. Some of these locks could be opened by just using high powered magnets around them. Another issue with smart locks that use phones to unlock and lock is firmware problems. The firmware update in 2017 caused a malfunction in smart locks produced by LockState that affected more than 500 customers. The company required affected customers to send them the lock for repairs [30]. According to the hacker convention DEF CON, around 75% of these locks are not safe and are vulnerable to attacks. These locks are vulnerable for the following reasons:

a. **Plain text passwords:** Saving the password the same as the user enters and not in any form of cryptic or hash form. The password stored in a company database should have added data, and that, too, in scrambled form, so that if anyone tries to access that password, it is irreversible and useless for others.

b. **Device spoofing:** A device is used by attackers to act as another device in a network so that that device could be used to target other devices on that network and steal their data and have access to them whenever they want.

c. **Replay attacks:** When two devices are exchanging data, the attacker tries to copy the digital signature so that it could be used as a false communication signal for the device, send malware to that device, and steal its data.

9.9 AVAILABLE SOLUTIONS

i. **Identity mixer:** Idemix is a cryptographic protocol suite that offers robust authentication and privacy-preserving features. These features include anonymity, allowing transactors to carry out transactions without disclosing their identities, and unlinkability, enabling a single identity to send multiple transactions without revealing that they originated from the same identity [32].

This is a type of cryptic message that only reveals the required information. For example, if person 1 has to prove that he is the authentic user, he can provide a digital certificate to the other user (person 2) that will only provide the necessary information for authentication, and the other information such as physical address and control over the device is not provided.

ii. **Proper authentication:** Many of the IoT devices these days do not have proper authentication, and that results in the security breaches. To ensure the security of all the devices, they must have proper authentication. Any user that tries to access the device must fulfill the authentication criteria; it should be checked every time.

iii. **Access control:** Our device should have access control so that the device is secure from attacks of other users, and other devices that communicate with our device should have controlled access, otherwise those devices can be a type of weak string in our device's security.

iv. **Encryption:** Each and every message that is sent to the device from any user or any other device should be encrypted so that the message is useful only to the user that has the proper decryption key and useless for the other users and attackers. An encrypted message is sent through the internet, and anyone can sense it, but anyone other than the user with the decryption key can use that encrypted message or signal.

v. **No backdoor debugging:** The manufacturer must ensure not to keep any sort of backdoor for further debugging that could be a potential access door for an attacker also. Backdoors are generally used by manufacturers so that in case of system failure they can access the user's device and find the reason for system failure. This kind of backdoors are generally used by attackers to hack into any device, and since all devices are connected to internet, they are all affected.

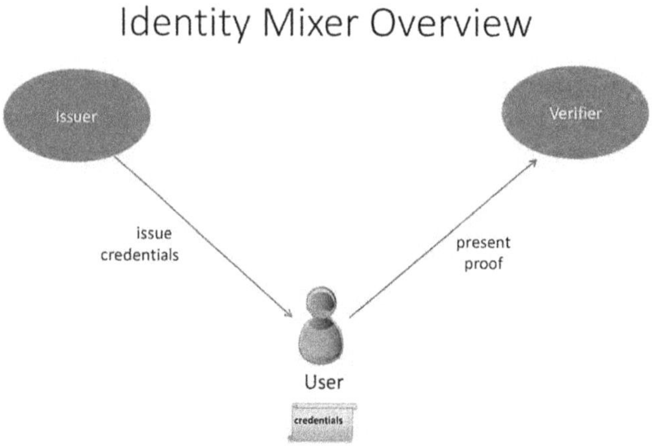

Identity Mixer Overview

FIGURE 9.8 Functioning of Identity Mixer [32].

  vi. **Provide support:** Manufacturers should provide firmware updates
      regularly so that new types of attacks do not affect our devices, and our
      devices are safeguarded from various attacks (Figure 9.8).

9.10 FUTURE SCOPE

The digital transformation forced either to develop a new system or to converge the
existing technology to achieve the solution for the existing problems. Initially, AI
and IoT emerged as individual concepts to solve problems, but the convergence of
these technique develops an intelligent system that is able to provide better
solutions then the individual one.

  1. To develop a new intelligent vehicle that communicates with another
     vehicle and with drivers using wireless technology to ensure a jam free
     journey with an enjoyable and safe driving experience [33].
  2. To develop reliable, efficient, and user-friendly system.
  3. To develop security architecture that considers the life cycle and the
     capability of AI and IoT systems. It includes development of new security
     protocols that traditional end-to-end internet protocols are not able to
     provide. System should have scalability potential so that it can serve both
     small- and large-scale needs [5].
  4. To develop an AIoT framework that supports global needs.
  5. Convergence of AI, IoT, and WT offers new business opportunities and
     new approaches for researchers to analyze the data that traditional
     techniques lack.
  6. To develop 3D models of CPS systems that perform accurately in
     hazardous environment without human intervention.

9.11 CONCLUSION

The convergence of IoT, AI, and wireless technologies is expected to bring about the next generation of technological advancements. This convergence will enable machines to communicate with each other and exchange data in real-time, allowing for seamless and intelligent decision-making. For example, self-driving cars can use sensors to collect data about their surroundings, which can be analyzed using AI algorithms to make real-time decisions about driving behavior. Similarly, smart homes can use IoT devices to collect data about the occupants' preferences and behaviors, which can be analyzed using AI algorithms to create personalized experiences. The convergence of these technologies is also expected to create new opportunities for innovation in various fields. For example, in healthcare, IoT devices can collect data about patients' health, which can be analyzed using AI algorithms to create personalized treatment plans. Similarly, in manufacturing, IoT devices can collect data about machines' performance, which can be analyzed using AI algorithms to predict maintenance needs and optimize production processes.

REFERENCES

1. Gomes, P., Magaia, N. and Neves, N. Industrial and Artificial Internet of Things with Augmented Reality. Springer Nature Switzerland AG 2020 G. Mastorakis et al. (eds.), Convergence of Artificial Intelligence and the Internet of Things, 10.1007/978-3-030-44907-0_13 pp, 323–345.
2. Posada, J., et al. Visual computing as a key enabling technology for Industrie 4.0 and Industrial Internet. IEEE Comput. Graph. Appl. 35(2), 26–40 (2015).
3. Jazdi, N. Cyber physical systems in the context of Industry 4.0. In: Proceedings of 2014 IEEE International Conference on Automation, Quality and Testing, Robotics, AQTR (2014).
4. Arsénio, A., Serra, H., Francisco, R., Nabais, F., Andrade, J., and Serrano, E.: Internet of intelligent things: bringing artificial intelligence into things and communication networks. Stud. Comput. Intell. 495, 1–37 (2014).
5. Kumar, S., Tiwari, P. and Zymbler, M. Internet of things is a revolutionary approach for future technology enhancement: a review. J Big Data. 6(111) (2019). 10.1186/s40537-019-0268-2
6. Sebastian S., and Ray P. P. Development of IoT invasive architecture for complying with health of home. In: Proc: I3CS, Shillong; 2015. p. 79–83.
7. Gilchrist, A. Industry 4.0: The Industrial Internet of Things (2016).
8. O'Leary, D. E. Artificial intelligence and big data. IEEE Intell. Syst. 28(2), 96–99 (2013).
9. Evans, P. C., and Annunziata, M. Industrial internet: pushing the boundaries of minds and machines. Gen. Electr. (2012).
10. Nizetic, S., Solic, P., Lopez-de-Ipi na Gonz alez-de-Artaza, D., and Patrono, L. Internet of Things (IoT): Opportunities, issues and challenges towards a smart and sustainable future, Journal of Cleaner Production. 274, 1–32, (2020).
11. Zhou, J., Cap, Z., Dong, X., and Vasilakos, A. V. Security and privacy for cloud-based IoT: challenges. IEEE Commun Mag. 55(1), 26–33 (2017). 10.1109/MCOM.2017.1600363CM
12. Sfar, A. R., Natalizio, E., Challal, Y., and Chtourou, Z. A roadmap for security challenges in the internet of things. Digit Commun Netw. 4(1), 118–137 (2018).

13. Jara, A. J., Zamora-Izquierdo, M. A., and Skarmeta, A. F. Interconnection framework for mHealth and remote monitoring based in the internet of things. IEEE J Sel Areas Commun. 31(9), 47–65 (2013).
14. Behrendt, F. Cycling the smart and sustainable city: analyzing EC policy documents on internet of things, mobility and transport, and smart cities. Sustainability. 11(3), 763 (2019).
15. Internet of Things. http://www.ti.com/technologies/internet-of-things/overview.html. Accessed 01 Apr 2019.
16. Alavi, A. H., Jiao, P., Buttlar, W. G., , N. Internet of things-enabled smart cities: state-of-the-art and future trends. Measurement. 129, 589–606 (2018).
17. https://www.iotforall.com/convergence-artificial-intelligence-and-iot
18. Qiu, T., Xiao, H., and Zhou, P. Framework and case studies of intelligent monitoring platform in facility agriculture ecosystem. In: Proc. 2013 second international conference on agro-geoinformatics (agro-geoinformatics), Fairfax, VA, USA, 12–16 Aug 2013. IEEE.
19. Babovic, Z. B., Protic, V., and Milutinovic, V. Web performance evaluation for internet of things applications. IEEE Access. 4(6974–92), 42 (2016).
20. Internet of Things research study: Hewlett Packard Enterprise Report. 2015. http://www8.hp.com/us/en/hp-news/press-release.html?id=1909050#.WPoNH6KxWUk
21. Van-der-Veer, H., and Wiles, A. Achieving technical, interoperability-the ETSI approach. ETSI White Paper No.3. 2008. http://www.etsi.org/images/fles/ETSIWhitePapers/IOP%20whitepaper%20Edition%203%20fnal.pdf
22. Tzafestad, S. G. Ethics and law in the internet of things world. Smart Cities. 1(1), 98–120 (2018).
23. Wu, Y., Li, J., Stankovic, J., Whitehouse, K., Son, S., and Kapitanova, K. Run time assurance of application- level requirements in wireless sensor networks. In: Proc. 9th ACM/IEEE international conference on information processing in sensor networks, Stockholm, Sweden, 21–16 April 2010. p. 197–208.
24. Temglit, N., Chibani, A., Djouani, K., and Nacer, M. A. A distributed agent-based approach for optimal QoS selection in web of object choreography. IEEE Syst J. 12(2), 1655–1666 (2018).
25. https://searchsecurity.techtarget.com/definition/authentication
26. https://www.owasp.org/images/a/ae/OWASP_10_Most_Common_pdf
27. Lantronix, Inc., Encryption and Its Importance to Device Networking, https://www.lantronix.com/wp-content/uploads/pdf/Encryption-and-Device-Networking_WP.pdf
28. https://gist.github.com/neolead/10b27c5c04bca84a5515783ca6f2ecb4#file-cve-2018-10987-txt
29. https://www.theinquirer.net/inquirer/news/3036246/smart-home-robot-vacuum-cleaners-could-spy-on-you-thanks-to-security-flaw
30. https://www.protectamerica.com/home-security-blog/safe-sound/are-smart-door-locks-safe-three-things-to-keep-in-mind_20027
31. https://www.av-test.org/en/news/robot-vacuums-undergo-a-security-check-trustworthy-helpers-around-the-house-or-chatty-cleaning-appli/
32. https://hyperledger-fabric.readthedocs.io/en/release-1.3/idemix.html#what-is-idemix
33. Liu, T., Yuan, R., and Chang, H. Research on the internet of things in the automotive industry. In: ICMeCG 2012 international conference on management of e-commerce and e-Government, Beijing, China. 20–21 Oct 2012. p. 230–233.

10 Data Modeling and Analysis for the Internet of Medical Things

Priya S. Mouna, P. Sivaprakash, and K. Arun Kumar
Rathinam College of Arts and Science, Coimbatore, Tamilnadu, India

Prithi Samuel
Department of Computational Intelligence, SRM Institute of Science and Technology, Kattankulathur, India

B. Shuriya
PPG Institute of Technology, Coimbatore, Tamil Nadu, India

Vandana Sharma
Department of Computational Sciences, CHRIST (Deemed to be University), Delhi NCR Campus, India

10.1 INTRODUCTION

Innovation in the medical field is important for enhancing the healthcare system. Nowadays, wearable devices are used for continuous monitoring of health conditions. Wearable devices such as "Biosensor contact lenses" are implemented in the medical field for collecting information about the human body in a painless manner. Biosensor contact lens enables individuals to monitor their glucose levels continuously and help treat themselves accordingly. Diabetes is increasing at an alarming rate; continuous monitoring of glucose levels is essential to manage diabetes. According to WHO, in 2019, diabetes caused direct death of 1.5 million people and 460000 died because of kidney disease caused by diabetes. Diabetes is a major cause of heart attack, kidney failure, stroke, and blindness. Regular monitoring of blood glucose levels is very crucial to managing Type 1 and Type 2 diabetes. A wearable biosensor contact lens aids the subject to monitor how their glucose level goes high and low when eating different foods and alerts them [1,2].

DOI: 10.1201/9781003389231-10

10.2   CONTACT LENS

Contact lenses were introduced in 1936 by an optometrist, William Feinbloom. Nowadays most people have deficiencies in their vision. One of the reasons for vision deficiency is diabetes. One's good vision contributes to self-confidence and overall independence for people of all ages. People with imperfect vision can be improved by treating it. Improper vision can be corrected by power glass, laser treatment, and contact lenses. People prefer using contact lenses rather than power glass and laser treatment. Early contact lenses were made of glass and hard plastic. Now technology has developed so that people can wear them in a very comfortable way. Contact lenses are placed at the top of the cornea in the eye, which makes the vision clear. People having refractive errors in the eye like farsightedness and near-sightedness are suggested to wear contact lenses to improve their vision. Nowadays, people use prosthetic lenses for cosmetic enhancement. A prosthetic contact lens is commonly called a zero-power contact lens, or a Plano contact lens. It is placed over the cornea if the cornea has become cloudy or opaque; therefore it makes the vision clear. Cosmetic contact lenses are used by people to change the color of the iris. They are translucent, enhancing the natural color of the eye and making a blue iris look deep blue. Cosmetic lenses, which are opaque, show brown eyes, blue eyes, and lavender eyes. People with disfigured irises or corneas due to ocular disease use these lenses to look normal. Even people with Myopia or Hyperopia use colored contact lenses, which are called prescribed cosmetic contact lenses. Tints are available in the contact lens to make the process of inserting and removing the contact lens easy. A tinted contact lens is nothing but a dye incorporated in the lens to look better on the eye. Mostly, tinted contact lenses are in light blue and green. Plano contact lenses are purely for cosmetic purposes and do not have lens power for vision correction. Cosmetic contact lenses are transparent and opaque. A transparent cosmetic lens permits 70% of the light to pass through it and is available in the market in different shades, and tints will be in a pattern of concentric rings. The opaque cosmetic lens absorbs or reflects the light entering the lens and completely covers the underlying eye color; they too have an iris pattern with a clear central pupil. The shape of Plano contact lenses is dotted or lined with a variety of colors so that it looks natural to the eye. The area around the pupil will have color. The center of the lens, the part over the pupil, will be clear, with no color to enhance the clarity of the vision. There are a variety of colors in contact lenses like blue, green, hazel, violet, brown, gray, and amethyst. Choosing the eye color contact lens is important; it should be chosen depending on one's hair color and skin tone. Customization of both prescribed and non-prescribed contact lenses is available in the market [3,4].

10.3   TYPES OF CONTACT LENS

- Soft contact lens
- Gas-permeable contact lens
- Extended-wear contact lens
- Disposable contact lens
- Toric contact lens. (Figure 10.1)

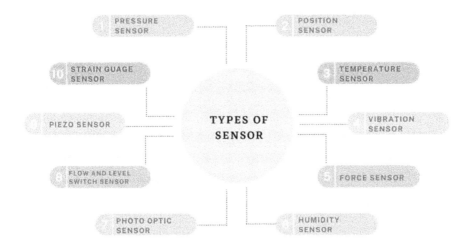

FIGURE 10.1   Types of sensor.

10.3.1   Soft-Contact Lens

The soft contact lens is very comfortable to wear. It is gel-like material and flexible plastic such as a hydrogel. As its name suggests, it is soft and comfortable to wear and allows oxygen to pass through the cornea. It is breathable and simple to wear. For long wearing hours, a soft contact lens is suitable. Silicon hydrogel lens is an advanced soft contact lens. It is more permeable, which permits oxygen to pass through it and reach the surface of the eye. Soft contact lens is used for many purposes like optical, preventive, therapeutic, cosmetic, diagnostic, and occupational. Optical contact lenses are commonly used for myopia, hyperopia, and astigmatism. To prevent chemical burns and exposure of eyes to a harmful environment, a preventive contact lens is used. For Electro retinography, a diagnostic contact lens is used. Sports persons, actors, and pilots use it for occupational purposes, hence it is called an occupational contact lens.

Advantages
- Very less chance of dislocation of contact lens
- Easy for initial comfort and easy fitting
- Used for occasional wear
- Less photophobia
- Long wearing time
- Easy to adapt to the eye
- Great for an active lifestyle.

Disadvantages
- As it is soft, it can be torn or lost easily
- Over a long time of usage may cause dryness in the eye
- Patience handling is required Soft Lens is implemented in
- Clear and colored soft lens

- Disposal and Non-Disposal soft lens
- Spherical and toric soft lens
- Multifocal soft lens.

10.3.1.1   Clear and Colored Soft Contact Lens

Soft contact lenses are available in both clear and colored forms. Clear soft contact lens is used to correct the vision and colored soft contact lens are dyed according to the user's wish and used to improve the quality of the vision.

10.3.1.2   Disposal and Non-Disposal Soft Contact Lens

They can be replaced in a day a week, or a month and longer. According to the disposal period, lenses are classified as mentioned earlier. Soft lenses are also available according to the period of disposal; they are classified as disposable and non-disposable soft contact lens.

10.3.2   GAS-PERMEABLE CONTACT LENS

PMMAs (polymethylmethacrylate) lenses are impermeable to oxygen. Earlier it was used for making contact lenses because they are inexpensive to produce. They are strong, more durable, scratch resistant, and easy to fit inside the eyes. PMMAs are rigid plastic and transparent. If there is no oxygen to the conjunctiva and cornea, then it will cause potential problems, hence why gas-permeable lenses are used. In later years, gas-permeable lenses were developed; they are oxygen-permeable but rigid materials. Chemist Norman Gaylord played a prominent role in the innovation of oxygen-permeable contact lenses. Gas-permeable contact lenses are the most durable and resist accumulation over the lens. It gives clear and crisp vision. They are easy to handle and not easily torn [5].

Advantages
- Provides excellent vision
- Allows oxygen to pass through it
- Short adaptation period
- Available in tints
- Available as a bifocal lens
- Can be worn for a long period

Disadvantages
- Consistent wear to get used to this lens
- Dislocated easily, slipped off the center of the eye
- Get scratched easily if slipped from the eye
- If debris under the eye, it causes more discomfort

10.3.3   EXTENDED-WEAR CONTACT LENS

Most of the extended-wear contact lenses are made of Silicone hydrogel. Silicone hydrogel lenses enable five times more oxygen to reach the cornea compared to regular hydrogel lenses. Silicone and regular hydrogel lenses seem to be hard when they are dry but readily absorb water. It becomes gel-like material and gets soft when hydrated. Extended-wear contact lenses can be worn continuously for six nights and seven days. With the innovation of silicone hydrogel, it is easy to allow oxygen through the lens to the eyes. People can wear an extended contact lens for 30 days straight. While sleeping, the only possibility for the cornea to get oxygen to stay healthy is from blood vessels in the eyelids. Extended-wear contact lenses are mainly used for people who have an unpredictable lifestyle, like people in military service and people with an active schedule. It is very helpful for people with binocular vision abnormalities, which include amblyopia, which is better cured with continuous vision correction [6].

Risk Factor
- Watery eyes
- Redness
- Sleeping in the contact lens may increase risk factors; it may be reduced by taking it out twice a week before sleeping
- Extended-wear contact lenses, though designed to wear during sleep, are a foreign material for the eye, so it may cause adverse reactions in the eyes

10.3.4   Disposable Contact Lens

Types of contact lenses according to the period of usage:

- Daily disposable contact lens
- Disposable contact lens
- Frequent disposable contact lens
- Conventional Lenses.

10.3.4.1   Daily Disposable Contact Lens

As its name suggests, Daily Disposable contact lenses can be used only one day. At the end of the day, it should be removed. It is considered the healthiest choice because no day-to-day debris enters under the lens. For a person with allergies, it is the best option to use.

10.3.4.2   Disposable Contact Lens

Disposable contact lenses are replaced in two weeks or before. It depends on the particular product we use. It is very popular.

10.3.4.3   Frequent Replacement Contact Lens

Frequent replacement contact lenses are replaced every month or quarter year. Monthly based replacement contact lenses are called frequent replacement contact lenses.

10.3.4.4   Conventional Lens

Conventional contact lenses or non-disposable contact lenses should be replaced every six months or longer.

10.3.5 Toric Contact Lens

Astigmatism occurs due to imperfect curvature of the cornea; the cornea does not have a spherical surface. These are the lenses that are implemented inside the eye to replace the natural lens inside the eye to improve vision. The toric lens will have different powers in the different meridians of the lens. A colored toric lens is also available. Imperfection in vision, like people having astigmatism, in some cases, cannot be treated with power glasses or contact lenses; in those cases, Toric lenses are used after surgery.

According to the surface, the toric lens is differentiated:

- Front toric lens
- Back toric lens
- Bitoric lens.

10.4 SENSOR

A sensor is a physical device that receives the input signal and transmits it through the transmitter. The input signal is a change in heat, light, humidity, motion of an object, etc. The output signal is a converted signal to human understanding, and the display at the sensor location and the output signal is transmitted over the network for further detecting and processing of the information. Sensors play a major role in the Internet Of Things. They are used to collect information about the subject and process the collected information and transmit it through the transmitter. Semsors analyze the subject and act logically on the collected data [7,8].

10.5 TYPES OF SENSORS

10.5.1 Pressure Sensor

The pressure sensor is an electronic device that converts physical data into an electronic signal. It detects and monitors pressure and converts it to the output signals. Usually, pressure is defined as the amount of force experienced per unit area. It is commonly used in Piezoelectric technology, in which the mechanical stress(pressure) is converted into electrical energy. The experienced stress is proportional to the electrical energy. There are three main pressure sensors that are widely used (Table 10.1):

- Gauge pressure
- Absolute-pressure sensor
- Differential-pressure sensor.

Gauge pressure sensors utilize the atmospheric pressure and measure the reading. It completely depends upon the atmospheric pressure, which has an effect due to the factors of altitude and humidity. Positive pressure is when the gauge sensor experiences pressure greater than the ambient atmospheric pressure. Negative pressure is when the gauge sensor experiences pressure lesser than the ambient

TABLE 10.1
Contact lens materials

Contact lens materials			
MATERIAL	MOLECULAR FORMULA	ADVANTAGE	DISADVANTAGE
Poly(methyl methacrylate) PMMA	$(C5O2H8)n$	Outstanding optical property	Low oxygen permeability
Polyethylene terephthalate PET	$(C10H8O4)n$	Excellent chemical resistance, Good thermal resistance	Low rigidity, Low surface energy
PHEMA	$(C6H10O3)n$	Good chemical and thermal conductivity, High water content	Protein deposition issues
PDMS	$(C2H6OSi)n$	Flexibility, High oxygen permeability	Restriction of water absorption, High lipid deposition
MPC	$C11H22NO6P$	Good surface wettability, High oxygen permeability	Mechanical weakness

pressure. It is used in the medical field for the monitor, the pressure inside the chamber, and controlling the pressure during the treatment. Absolute-pressure sensors measure pressure concerning absolute zero pressure. It gives the reading which does not include the atmospheric pressure. It is a pressure within the space of a vacuum. The differential sensor, which measures the difference in pressure between two pressure points, is commonly used in filtration systems.

10.5.2 Position Sensor

Position sensors detect the position of a particular desired object. They are categorized into two types:

- Linear position sensor: It simply measures the distance between two objects, referring to a point or straight line. It accurately measures the displacement of an object from one position to another. There are contacting and non-contacting linear position sensors.
- The rotary position sensor: The input for the rotary position sensor is the rotary movement of the object which converts it to the output signals. There can also be contacting and non-contacting rotary position sensors. It depends on the degree of rotation of the subject.
- In MRI and CT scans, the scanner will rely on the position sensor to obtain the imaging at the right place of the human body.
- Hospital beds use the position sensor for adjustment according to the patient's desire. In operation, theater position sensor beds are often used.

10.5.3 Temperature Sensor

A temperature sensor is an electronic device that converts the input data into electronic output data. The input can be the temperature of the environment and convert it to the output electric signals which helps to monitor the continuous change in temperature of the environment. There are different types of temperature sensors for monitoring the change in temperature. They are contact temperature sensors and non-contact temperature sensors. A contact temperature sensor requires direct physical contact with the object to be monitored. A contact temperature sensor includes thermistors and thermocouples. Thermocouple is the joining of two dissimilar metals together. When one junction is exposed to heat, the voltage generated due to the heat acts as the temperature input. This is called the thermoelectric effect. A non-contact temperature sensor usually utilizes the IR radiation emitted by the object and converts it to the output electric signals and sends it to the external electronic circuit for continuous monitoring. Examples are thermal imaging, handheld infrared industrial thermometers, human temperature measurements, and fixed infrared temperature sensors.

10.5.4 Vibration Sensor

Vibration is the mechanical oscillation above the equilibrium position of the component. It is simply a back-and-forth motion of the machine or component. A vibration sensor is a device that measures the frequency of vibration in the machine. The vibration may denote the imbalance or breakdown in the assert. A vibration sensor may physically attach to the machine, or it may be wireless that will detect the vibration in the machine depending upon the type of the sensor. The recent advancement in the Internet of Things has necessitated vibration sensors for enhancement in the medical field. Even in the sound environment, the vibration sensor detects the vibration of the heart sound and the abdominal sound of the human through skin vibration.

10.5.5 Force Sensor

A force sensor determines the amount of force applied to an object. The applied force can be determined by calculating the change in the resistance value of the sensing resistor. Force sensors convert the applied mechanical energy such as weight, pressure, load, and compression to the electric signals as an output. The force sensor is used in the hospital for bed occupancy, so there's no need of checking the patient frequently, hence it can be easily monitored through the computer. The force sensor is very useful in fluid detection such as infusion pumps. These sensors make the flow of fluid detection easy and alert the respective medical professional if there is any error. It is used by physicians by implanting the force sensor in the shoes, whether the pressure is evenly applied on it or the patient is having any abnormality in the way of walking.

10.5.6   HUMIDITY SENSOR

As its name suggests, it measures the humidity in the environment and converts it to the correspond- ing electrical signals as an output. It measures and reports the humidity of the air and it determines the amount of water vapor present in the air. In the hospital, the ventilator is used to make the patient feel comfortable and warm, wet air is circulated in the ventilator so that the humidity of the wet air can be accurately sensed by the humidity sensor. A thermistor sensor is used for measuring the temperature and humidity in the anesthesia machine to make the patient feel comfortable breathing. The humidity sensor is used in sterilizers, incubators, and pharmaceutical processing equipment. A humidity sensor is installed in the hospital for maintaining the temperature in the hospital, humidity should be consistently monitored to ensure the safety against harmful germs, thus it prevents the spread of disease.

10.5.7   PHOTO OPTIC SENSOR

A photo optic sensor is a device that converts the incident light on it to the electrical signal as an output. It produces the electrical signal proportional to the incident light on the active area of the photo optic sensor. A photo optic sensor can be a wearable device, it is an optical biosensor that can measure the heart rate, temperature, blood pressure, and oxygen saturation level of the human body. It can detect human movement in a room and differentiate between everyday activity and sudden cases, for instance, a sudden fall of a patient can be detected by the photo optic sensor, hence there is no need for the nurse to be with the patient all the time.

10.5.8   FLOW AND LEVEL SWITCH SENSOR

The level sensing method is used for the detection of fluid leak and the level measurement in industrial, domestic, food, beverages, and agricultural fields. This sensor is installed to monitor the flow of gas or liquid in various cases such as anesthesia equipment for detecting the amount of flow of medicine, and gas mixing during surgery in the operation theater. The respiratory rate of the patient can be monitored. It plays a vital role in electrosurgery, such as cutting off the tumor, and coagulation. In modern agriculture, sensors are essentially used for monitoring the flow of liquid fertilizer and the nutrition supply to irrigation equipment.

10.5.9   PIEZO SENSOR

Piezo Electric sensors convert the applied mechanical energy in the environment into electrical energy as an output. It is commonly used in measuring moment, force strain, acceleration, and vibration. They are customized into different shapes according to their usage, such as disks, piezo plates, piezo tubes, and piezo strips (Figure 10.2).

10.5.9.1   Piezoelectric Pressure Sensor
The Piezoelectric pressure sensor utilizes the change in pressure in the environment, such as pressure exerted by gas or liquid. The automobile uses a piezoelectric

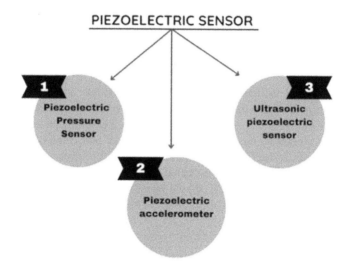

FIGURE 10.2   Piezoelectric sensor.

pressure sensor for measuring engine combustion and for measuring the blast and explosion of bombs. Thus, the generated electrical signals are used to produce the equivalent mechanical response, which is needed to adopt the pressure change.

10.5.9.2   Piezoelectric Accelerometer

It determines the change in vibration, acceleration, or shock into the measurable output as an electric signal. Piezoelectric accelerometers produce an electrical signal as an output which is proportional to the force applied.

10.5.9.3   Ultrasonic Piezoelectric Sensor

The ultrasonic Piezoelectric sensor converts the electrical pulses to the mechanical vibration, and the mechanical vibration in return is converted into electric energy for the detection of ultrasound. It is based on the Piezo effect, which converts the electrical energy into ultrasonic energy and vice versa. A Piezoelectric transducer is used as an ultrasonic dental scaler to remove plaque. It is more efficient than the traditional method. It usually operates in the very low range of 24 to 32 kilohertz. They are used to detect the distance between two objects, the liquid level, and the flow of liquid. The ultrasonic Piezoelectric sensor is comprised of two elements: the transmitter and the receiver; this is collectively called a Piezoelectric transducer. The transmitter part of the sensor transmits the ultrasonic pulses, which are received from the sensor and converted to electrical signals.

10.5.10   STRAIN GAUGE SENSOR

The precise mechanical strain can be determined using the strain gauge sensor. In the medical field, a strain gauge sensor is used for maintaining accuracy. In hospitals, a strain gauge sensor is used in mammography machines; this machine is used for detecting breast tumors and other related conditions. This machine determines the physical force that is applied to the patient by the machine, taking an accurate image so that this strain gauge sensor is implanted in this machine. It is used in patient lift systems in hospitals. Monitoring the fluid flow in the insulin pump requires the lightweight strain gauge sensor to monitor the insulin flow out of the pump. It is further divided according to the non-contacting sensor [8,9].

10.5.10.1   Non-Contacting Senor

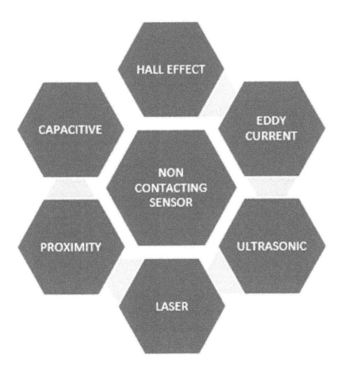

FIGURE 10.3   Non-Contacting Senor.

10.6   NON-CONTACTING SENSOR 6 BIOSENSOR

It is an integrated device that provides us the quality information about the analyte, which is to be tested, is in spatial contact with the biological element, and the biological response is converted into electrical signals by the transducer element. A biosensor consists of two components:

- Biological
- Electronic

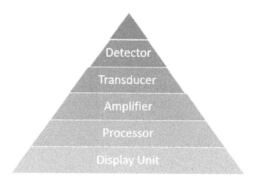

FIGURE 10.4   Elements of Biosensor.

10.6.1   Elements of Biosensor

- Detector
- Transducer
- Amplifier
- Processor
- Display unit (Figure 10.4).

10.6.1.1   Detector

It is the first segment of the sensor that is in physical contact with the analyte. It is the biochemical receptor. It interacts with the analyte in the biological body. The detector detects the concentration of the analyte in the biological body [10].

10.6.1.2   Transducer

Interaction between the analyte and the biochemical receptor produces a chemical change that is detected by the transducer. The electrical signal is generated concerning the composition of the analyte. A transducer converts the biochemical event to an electrical signal. The electrical signal is passed to the next segment of the sensor. A bio transducer consists of two parts, which, acting together, convert a biochemical signal to an electronic or optical sign:

- Bio recognition layer
- Physicochemical transducer.

10.6.1.3   Types of Transducers

- Electrical transducer
- Optical transducer
- Thermal transducer
- Magnetic transducer
- Chemical transducer.

10.6.1.4   Amplifier

The received electrical signals are amplified by the amplifier. It sends the amplified signal to the processor.

10.6.1.5   Processor

Convert the electrical signal into analyte concentration present in a solution. It filters and interrupts the electrical signal into a clinically meaningful value that is present.

10.6.1.6   Display Unit

The display unit displays the value as a digital readout.

10.6.2   Working Principle of Biosensor

Biological receptors or biologically sensitive elements interact with the analyte in the biological body. The concentration of biochemical is converted into the electrical response in the form of the signal by the transducer. When the analyte interacts with the immobilized biological material, it will produce the biochemical reaction, and ultimately components of the system covert the biochemical changes into a digital output [11,12].

10.6.2.1   Types of Biological Elements

Protein including enzymes and antibodies

1. Nucleic acid
2. Antibody-based biosensors, commonly called immunosensors
3. Plant protein or lectins
4. Tissue slices
5. Microorganisms and organelles.
   - Output of the transducer can either be current or voltage.
   - If the output of the transducer is voltage, then it is converted into current using an operational amplifier, based on current to voltage converter, before further proceeding with the process.
   - Amplifier in the sensor is used to amplify the voltage; if the amplitude of the voltage is very low then it is superimposed to a higher amplitude by the amplifier.
   - Signal processing units will filter and process the amplified signal and pass it to the next segment of the sensor.
   - The output will be displayed in the display.

10.6.3   Classification of Biosensor

10.6.3.1   Electrochemical Biosensor

An electrochemical biosensor is a study of the relationship between resistance, capacitance, current, voltage, and chemical/ biological change. It is the reaction of

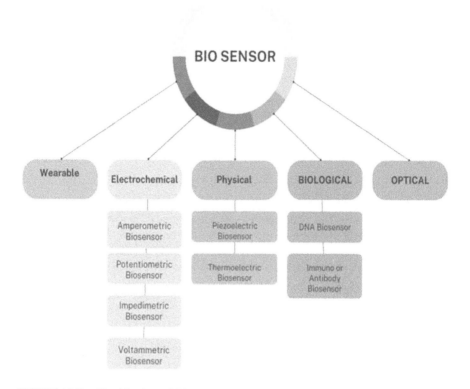

FIGURE 10.5   Classification of Biosensor.

enzymatic catalysts that generates electrons or consumes electrons. The electrochemical biosensor consists of three electrodes:

- Counter
- Reference
- Working type.

Reference electrodes are kept at a distance from the reaction to maintain the stable potential, and it is made of silver and silver chloride. Working electrodes act as the transducer element in the biochemical reaction. Counters electrodes/trigger electrodes in which a chemical reaction takes place and the current is generated, which is proportional to the concentration of the analyte [13].

10.6.3.1.1   Amperometric Biosensor
A glucose amperometric biosensor (glucometer) uses glucose oxidase as an enzyme to convert the glucose to H2O2 and oxidize it. Glucose oxidase will react with the working electrode inside the glucometer. Once you have glucose in the sample, glucose oxidase will convert the glucose into gluconic acid and

H_2O_2. The current from H_2O_2 oxidation is proportional to the glucose concentration. If there is more glucose, there will be more hydrogen oxide, which increases the amount of electrons. The glucose level in the blood will be indicated by the flow of electrons in the glucometer. This is how the glucometer works [14].

10.6.3.1.2 Potentiometric Biosensor

In our daily lives, several liquids are necessary, including water, drinks, and pharmaceuticals. The chemical properties of certain liquids define their quality, which helps with various measuring principles like PH measurement. The biological reaction is converted to an electrical response using ions in electrodes in accordance with the potential metric concept. Both solid-state electrodes and pH meter glass electrodes are frequently used electrodes. The possible variation between the system of reference and the system being measured is used to compute the pH value. If the concentration of hydrogen ions is the same on both sides, there is no potential difference, and the tested solution has a pH of 7, then it is neutral. If the potential difference is bigger, the measuring system is described as acidic, and its pH value is less than 7, whereas if it is lower, the measurement solution is described as basic, and its pH value is higher [15].

10.6.3.1.3 Conductimetric Biosensor

It is also called a thermal detection biosensor. It measures the change in temperature of the analytic solution, and the enzyme action takes place, which interprets the analyte concentration in the solution. Then the analytic solution is made to pass into the container containing the immobilized enzyme. Now the temperature of the solution is measured using a separate thermistor when the solution enters and leaves the container.

10.6.3.1.4 Impedimetric Biosensor

An impedimetric biosensor works on the principle of measuring the difference in the impedance when the sinusoidal voltage is applied. The difference or change in impedance is measured by measuring the change in current, in ampere. Impedance can be calculated by the voltage divided by the current in the circuit.

10.6.3.1.5 Voltametric Biosensor

Voltametric biosensors detect the analyte by measuring the changes in the current corresponding to the voltage that we are applying. They measure current as well as potential. They are classified into three types

- Anode stripping voltammetry (ASV)
- Cathodic stripping voltammetry (CSV)
- Adsorbing stripping voltammetry (ASV).

10.6.3.2 Optical Biosensor

The optical biosensor is a device that makes use of the optical measuring principle, such as fluorescence, chemiluminescence, and absorbance. They make use of optoelectronic transducers and fiber optics. The words optical and electrode are combined to form the word optrode. As the main transducing components of optical biosensors, enzymes, and antibodies are used [16]. The remote sensing of material using optical biosensors is secure and non-electrical. They do not need a reference sensor, which is another benefit. The same light source as the sampling sensor can produce a comparative signal.

The fiber optic lactate biosensor, which is based on fluctuations in the molecular oxygen content, is one of the crucial optical biosensors. By measuring the counting influence of oxygen on a fluorine dye, it is possible to see that when the concentration of lactate in the reaction rises, oxygen is used up and the counting effect decreases proportionally. This increases the luminous output that can be measured. The assessment of glucose is crucial for managing diabetes. For this, a straightforward method utilizing a paper strip and reagent is employed. A portable reflectance meter may be used to test the color's intensity after dyeing. The fluorescence approach can be used to determine the infection itself.

10.6.3.3 Physical Biosensor Piezoelectric Biosensor

The foundation of piezoelectric biosensors is acoustics (sound). Also known as acoustic biosensors.

Piezoelectric biosensors are built on piezoelectric crystals. Positive and negative charges cause a crystal to vibrate at specific frequencies. The interaction between the Piezoelectric material and the surface as a result of its oscillation on the Piezoelectric effect principle is known as an affinity interaction. The resonance frequency of a crystal may be detected by electrical equipment when a particular molecule is absorbed on the surface of the crystal. Due to the crystal's inability to fully oscillate in a viscous liquid, it is highly challenging to utilize a Piezoelectric biosensor to evaluate the chemical in a solution (Figure 10.6).

When pressure is applied on an object, voltage is generated due to the deformation of the object (Figure 10.7).

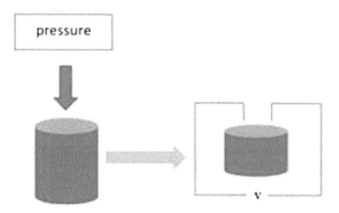

FIGURE 10.6   Pressure on crystal.

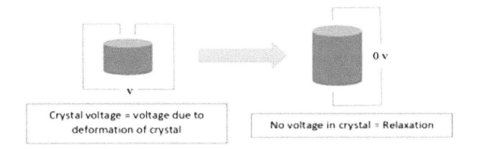

FIGURE 10.7   Relaxation of crystal.

10.6.3.3.1   Thermometric Biosensor

Thermometric Biosensor detects the heat/energy absorbed and heat evolved during the biochemical reaction. A thermometric biosensor is used for the detection and estimation of cholesterol levels in the biological body. When cholesterol gets oxidized by the enzyme called cholesterol oxidase, heat energy is evolved which can be measured by a thermometric biosensor [17].

Advantages
- Long-lasting stability – If no physical contact between the transducing element and the chemical sample, then there will be no damage to the thermistor.
- Cost efficient – They are available at low cost.
- Accuracy – The accuracy can be maintained. It is not disturbed by varying optical and chemical sample characteristics.

Disadvantage
- Very sensitive – They consist of a very sensitive element.
- Not recommended – Due to the Nonspecific heating effect.

10.6.3.4   Biological Element DNA Based Biosensor

DNA-based biosensor is basically the attraction between the single strand DNA which compliment each other. Mostly DNA based biosensors are used in food industries. If there is a pathogen that is harmful, its genetic material is collected and then broke down. This sensor has a complementary sequence that can easily attract the genetic material of the pathogen and can be identified. Let us consider an analyte which is single-stranded DNA, and the electrodes used which act as a transducer. The immobilized single-stranded DNA on the electrode is further processed by adding a sample; if there is a complimentary DNA sequence to the existing immobilized single-stranded DNA then it binds together. The transducer knows it by mechanical changes or by vibration and sends the signal [18,19].

10.6.3.4.1   Immunobiosensors

The immunobiosensor, also known as an immunological biosensor, operates on the basis of im- munological specificity and measurement using a biosensor with an amperometric or potentiometric response. The main theme of the human immune system is to provide immunity to the body. The immune system recognizes each cell in the biological entities as harmful or not. If any antigen (foreign substance) is present in our system then our immune system will provide immunoglobulin which binds the antigen. As the name suggests, the Immunobiosensor is working in the concept of the immune system of the human body. It utilizes the antibody as a bio-receptor for recognizing the antigen and forms a stable immunocomplex. The immunobiosensor, also called an immunological biosensor, works by measuring the reaction of a biosensor with an amperometric or potentiometric response based on immunological specificity. The activity of the enzyme bound to the immunobio-sensor is corresponding to the relative concentration of the labeled and unlabeled enzyme. The determination of the immunocomplex is done by coupling this reaction to the transducer, which converts the chemical signals into electrical signals that can be viewed in the display as the output [20,21].

10.6.3.4.2   Characteristics of the Immunobiosensor
- Recognizes the antigen quickly
- Creates immunocomplex without the help of supplementary products
- Output will be more accurate.

10.6.3.4.3   Piezoelectric Immunosensor Is Used in Many Fields Because of the Following Characteristics
- High resistivity
- Specificity
- Reaction is quick
- No need for supplementary product for generating immune complex.

10.6.3.4.4   Thermometric Immunosensor
It is used to determine the change in heat absorption and heat evolved during the process of reaction between the antibody/antigen reactions. Variation in the temperature is directly converted into electrical signals. Then, with the output electrical signals, the temperature is determined by the thermometric immuno-sensor. Benefits of thermometric immunobiosensors are:

- Cost of operating is low.
- They do not fluctuate easily and can be applied in many sensing.

10.7   BIOSENSOR IN CONTACT LENS

Diabetes mellitus is reported to be caused by genetic factors. Diabetes has become a common disease in modern society. The World Health Organization picked diabetes as a key challenge for global healthcare. Diabetes is an incurable disease that has to be managed for life. This is why this smart lens that makes diabetes management and treatment more convenient will revolutionize the field of diabetes care. People will benefit if they are able to monitor their glucose level via mobile rather than picking up a strip and making a self-assessment with a glucometer. Glucose testing through a glucometer is a more painful and uncomfortable process relative to biosensor contact lenses. This is the more convenient strategy to get the glucose level [22].

10.7.1 CATHETER INSULIN PUMP

Type 1 and Type 2 diabetes patients can use an insulin pump to regulate their blood glucose levels. An insulin pump is a battery-operated device that eliminates the need for routine injections by delivering active insulin to the blood through a catheter. The components of the technology include a battery-operated pump, a disposable insulin reservoir, and a microchip set up to administer exact doses to assist and maintain a constant blood glucose level. It is possible to plan ahead for continuous insulin administration throughout the day. Your level of blood sugar can be rapidly adjusted with the use of an insulin pump. To account for the number of carbohydrates as soon as you consume, you can also set the pump to give an insulin bolus just prior to eating. An insulin pump allows you to live a more adaptable life and helps you to keep a consistently stable blood sugar level. If you need to check your blood sugar with a glucometer, you can program your pump to deliver the right amount of insulin into the body. Insulin is delivered from the pump through an infusion set that includes a flexible tube attached to a soft plastic that is inserted just under the skin. According to studies, maintaining a steady glucose level and checking it regularly can help avoid long-term complications from diabetes including blindness, renal disease, heart disease, and stroke [23,24].

10.7.2 BIOSENSORS CONTACT LENS

Biosensors are wearable device that are highly integrated circuits replacing traditional devices such as catheter insulin pumps for the measurement of glucose level. It is a time-consuming method. Expanding insulin pump while performing integration into the contact lens and integrated sensor on a transparent substrate that is compatible material. Uric acid is used as a biomarker that can measure tears; this is the way to measure if you have renal disease. The benefit of using a sensor, since it is transparent, is the integration of many sensors on a contact lens is easy; it can be right in the middle where the pupil is going to be looking out through the contact lens, and that way the integration of many more contents into the contact lens. Indium gallium zinc oxide is used. Potentially 2000 sensors are used in a square millimeter on the contact lens. This will help with a lot of disease diagnostics. Google has introduced a smart Biosensor Contact lens for the determination of glucose levels. In the past contact lenses integrated with electronics were stiff and potentially harmful to the sensitive human eye. But here the components are all flexible, and most important they are transparent. The glucose sensor has an antenna, LED display, and glucose sensor, rectifier embedded, and soft contact lenses that are embedded in the silicon hybrid substrate that sits on the top of the breathable contact lens. It utilizes tears for the detection of glucose levels in the human body. The lens can stretch up to 30% and around 90% transparent. The lens is powered wirelessly through antenna circles, with the pupil preventing obstruction of sight. If the glucose level rises to a predetermined amount the LED pixel turns on [25].

10.7.3 Electrical Components In Biosensor

- Wireless communicator: The wireless system for communicating the signals is an essential part of the wearable contact lens enhancement instead of employing the traditional method. Advanced techniques are employed in smart biosensors for eliminating the usage of cable which is inconvenient in the transmission of signals. So that RFID referred to as the Radiofrequency Identification technique is implemented. RFID is a wireless system that uses radio waves at different frequencies to transfer data. RFID is one of the fundamental components of the Internet of Things. The basic RFID system includes an RFID reader and an RFID tag. RFID readers are devices that consist of one or more antennae that emit radio waves and receive a signal from the RFID tag. An RFID tag is attached to assert to transmit stored data to the antenna, the antenna received the stored data from the tag and transmits the data to the RFID reader, and, finally, the final data is transmitted into the RFID database where it can be stored and evaluated [26–28] (Figure 10.8).

10.7.3.1 Application of RFID

- Tracking the patient's location along with their medical records
- Real-time tracking assets, which include checking the locations and availability of the wheelchair in the hospital
- Drug authentication, which involves checking drug stock and also ensuring the patient receives the correct drug on time
- For patient tracking, RFID wristbands are used; this is especially useful for newborn babies to avoid mismatching and kidnapping
- RFID sensor used in a surgical instrument for tracking them; this prevents a serious issue where the device has been accidentally kept inside the human body during surgery
- RFID-embedded medical devices reduce the time to diagnose the disease; these devices consist of preloaded symptom file, and with the help of these

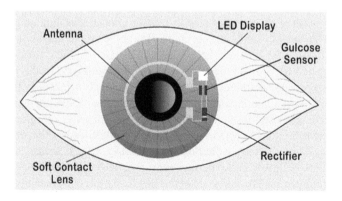

FIGURE 10.8 Electrical components in biosensor.

files the device performs various tests and acquires data that is stored on the cloud for further analysis
- RFID data can be stored managed and shared online this is easy for maintaining the electronic medical records and asset management application.

The user may access the required information and view the patient's worldwide record in real-time by linking the RFID reader to the internet. A micro-loop antenna is a good choice for smart contact lenses. For wireless communication, it ensures particular electromagnetic waves. It can transform electrical signals into power signals, allowing the charging of the digital contact lens as it functions as a communicator.

- Power supply: The power supply is required for the smart contact lens for monitoring the biomarkers for a long period of time. The capacitor is a device that is used to store electrical charge. The capacitor which is used in the contact lens is very small, and it is used for energy storage, but it is limited because they are small in size. There are two ways to extend the energy of the sensor: one is to minimize the dissipated power so it tries reduce the power consumption and increases the operating efficiency of the system. Adorners harvest power from the environment in order to extend the energy autonomy of the sensor. The effect of all the sensors on the environment is very important when a wireless communication network with thousands of sensors is taken into account. Any time the gadget requires power, we can supply it. The gadget may use this power to charge the capacitor and operate without a battery if two cables are put next to each other and an AC current is sent through one of them. This induces an electric current in the other coil through magnetic field coupling. Although this power is insufficient to drive the motors, it is adequate to read some information from the gadget, which is why RFID is so well-liked [29]. Passive RFID is used here (Figure 10.9).

A reader for an RFID system may be seen on the left, and a tag or transponder can be seen on the right. The tag contains a low-power chip and coil or antenna that can store some perfect data and transmit it back to the reader when needed. It successfully offers the gadget a reliable power source by coordinating three components. In order to create an efficient electric current, the body itself creates

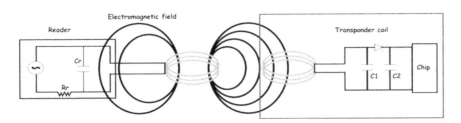

FIGURE 10.9 Power supply.

chemical compounds like glucose that react with the conducting anode or cathode in the contact lenses. This technique makes it possible to power smart contact lenses with biological batteries. Although ascorbic acid is abundant in the human body, it has no effect on the tear glucose, which has to be calculated and may be transformed into electromagnetic energy to power the smart contact lens.

10.8 GLUCOSE SENSOR

A glucose sensor essentially measures the amount of glucose in the body. There are two types of glucose sensor:

- Glucometer blood glucose meter, also called continuous glucose. The glucometer monitor measures a Snapshot of the glucose giving a fixed number at one point in time.
- CGM measures the glucose level periodically, often every five minutes along with the current level. We can also identify which direction the glucose is going and how fast it is going in that direction.

How do they work? Glucose sensors are essentially biosensors. Biosensors are devices that use living organisms or biological molecules to detect. The presence of chemicals in the biosensor for detecting glucose levels consists of several components. First is the analyte, which is the substance we are trying to measure; in our case, the analyte is glucose. Second is the bio-receptor, which is a molecule that specifically recognizes the analyte, and third is the transducer, which converts one form of energy into another. Modern devices use electrochemical methods for detecting the glucose level more specifically. They use an amperometric type of sensor that monitors current when electrons or changed between a biological system and an electrode. Finally, the electronic system processes the transducer signal and preparation for the display, and the display generates numbers or curves understandable by the user [30].

10.8.1 BIORECEPTOR

Enzyme-based receptors are the most prevalent kind. The two enzyme families that make up the majority of glucose biosensors are glucose oxidase (GOx) and glucose dehydrogenase (GDH). These enzymes delay the cofactor selectivity of redox potentials for glucose. Commercial production of the GOx enzyme is based on a fungal reaction sequence for the enzyme, which catalyzes the oxidation of glucose by oxygen to create gluconic acid and hydrogen peroxide while also needing the redox cofactor FAD. FAD serves as the first electron acceptor and is reduced to FADH2, after which the cofactor is restored by interacting with oxygen to produce hydrogen peroxide, which is subsequently oxidized at the anode. The electrode quickly identified the number of electron transfers, and this electron flow is inversely correlated with the blood glucose concentration.

10.9 ELECTRON MEDIATOR

Since oxygen and glucose concentrations might vary, oxidized-based electronics that rely on oxygen as an electron acceptor are prone to inaccuracy. By substituting GDH for GOx, the oxygen demand problem may be avoided. Since there is no need for an oxygen cofactor, we also switch out the oxygen with a synthetic electronic acceptor that can transport electrons to the electrode.

10.9.1 BLOOD GLUCOSE VERSUS SENSOR GLUCOSE

Glucose is a carbohydrate and the main source of energy for our cells, we acquire glucose from food which then makes its way from our digestive track to the bloodstream and then the interstitial fluid, which is the fluid that surrounds all cells in the body. From this fluid, glucose then moves into cells. A blood glucose meter measures the amount of glucose from a finger prick using single-use enzyme-coded test strips. Although a continuous glucose monitor usually monitors the glucose in saliva, urine, and interstitial fluid. Tear fluid, however, provides an effective illustration of blood replenishment. Tear glands, which are present in the eyes of all mammals, release tear fluid. Lipids, proteins, enzymes, and electrolytes are all present in the multilayer of the basal tear fluid. Basal tear protects, cleans, and lubricates the eye. The compositional difference between the blood and the tear flow is caused by the separation of the blood and the tear. Blood metabolism leaks into the tears as it travels through the blood-brain barrier to reach the brain. From this, the relationship between the blood and the tear is established. The analyte may be continually monitored over an extended length of time utilizing the bio-receptor in the eye without the pain of using any strips.

10.9.2 IMPEDIMENTARY BIOSENSOR VERSUS FIELD EFFECT SENSOR

Glucose concentration, which is measured in the tears, is low; its order of magnitude is lower than glucose measured in blood or interstitial fluid. Using colloidal nanosphere lithography to minimize the size of the semiconductor, which is scalable, is how the sensitivity of the sensor is increased. Instead of the electrochemical method, field effect sensing is used to measure the change in the electric field near the surface, and an electric field is going to change the conductivity of the semiconductor in the lens. The main advantage of using field defects in contact lenses is if it is scaled smaller, and if it is smaller the current will increase. The smaller size is a very important factor in making contact lenses. If the impedimetric biosensor is scaled smaller and smaller, then the electric current decreases.

10.10 MEDICATIONS THROUGH SMART CONTACT LENS

The smart lens used to diagnose diabetes is constructed of two soft lenses joined together by an electronic circuit whose source code resides in the body. As the blood sugar level rises above a specified threshold, the microprocessor chip receives

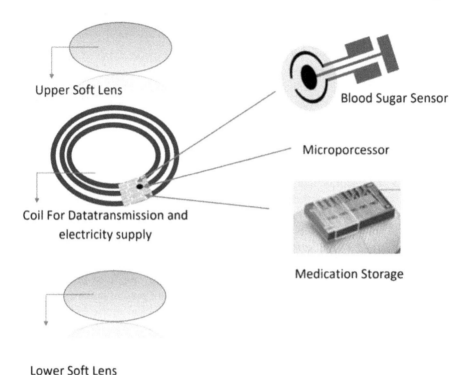

Upper Soft Lens

Blood Sugar Sensor

Microporcessor

Coil For Datatransmission and
electricity supply

Medication Storage

Lower Soft Lens

FIGURE 10.10   Medication through contact lens.

the measurement from the sensor and sends a signal to release the medicine. A minuscule storage compartment for medication is located right next to the chip. When the chip generates a signal and current flows to the compartment, the metallic cover dissolves and the drug is administered to the eye (Figure 10.10).

10.11   FUTURE FOR SMART CONTACT LENS

Imagine being able to capture images, film videos, and zoom in on items instantly, without the use of an external device. Imagine being able to read the news anywhere, at any time, with a lens that provides vision better than 20 out of 20 long into old age. Specifically, it is what scientists want to do using smart contact lenses. With robotic contact lenses developed by University of California, San Diego researchers, all you have to do to zoom in by up to 32% and blink twice while wearing the lenses. Incredibly, the lens doesn't require batteries because it gets its energy from a certain eye movement. They are exposed to mechanical motion and kinetic energy when they blink, and this kinetic energy is converted into electrical power. Beyond current capabilities, intelligent contact lens technology may improve human vision. Researchers have created a bionic lens that could be able to correct someone's vision forever. The amount of water required by a Bionic Lens is less than 1% of that required by the natural eye. This implies that your eyes won't be tired from focusing all day. Years ago Google developed Google Glasses to allow us to take photos or videos of our surroundings all with voice commands. Unfortunately, as cool as the technology was, the person wearing a device looked not so cool. Many people just couldn't get behind the aesthetic. Still, the idea was great, and its been reimagined in the form of smart contact lenses.

Sony is working on smart contact lenses that would let you snap pictures or videos in the blink of an eye. The user may manage the gadget without being concerned about it capturing arbitrary pictures since the sensor in the lens can distinguish between voluntary and involuntary blinks. Smart contact lenses continue to assist us in viewing and recording reality. A smart contact lens with an integrated camera and blink-activated sensors has been patented by Samsung. They concentrate on providing an augmented reality perspective of the world. The sensor will be able to overlay information on the real environment by including cameras, motion sensors, and transmitters. An outside menu, as an illustration. Boot camps may be replaced with smart contact lenses to make security and law enforcement personnel safer. These can improve military operations, including providing surgeons with improved eyesight and instant feedback. On vital signs as well as removing the patient with a chronic condition so that symptoms may be watched, there is little question that the smart contact lens will soon be widely used with all the innovation taking place.

10.11.1 Application

- Glucose sensor is great for people with diabetes; it allows them to live more carefree.
- It allows the doctor to make a better treatment decision.
- Athletes can also determine how their diet and exercise affect their glucose level and performance.

REFERENCE

1. Moreddu, R., Vigolo, D., Yetisen, A. K. (2019). Contact lens technology: from fundamentals to applications. Advanced Healthcare Materials, 8(15), 1900368.
2. Nicolson, P. C., Vogt, J. (2001). Soft contact lens polymers: an evolution. Biomaterials, 22(24), 3273–3283.
3. Donshik, P. C. (2003). Extended wear contact lenses. Ophthalmology Clinics of North America, 16(3), 305–309.
4. Barnett, M., Mannis, M. J. (2011). Contact lenses in the management of keratoconus. Cornea, 30(12), 1510–1516.
5. Vishnu, S., Ramson, S. J., Jegan, R. (2020, March). Internet of medical things (IoMT)-An overview. In 2020 5th international conference on devices, circuits, and systems (ICDCS) (pp. 101–104). IEEE.
6. Shichiri, M., Yamasaki, Y., Kawamori, R., Hakui, N., Abe, H. (1982). Wearable artificial endocrine pancreas with needle-type glucose sensor. The Lancet, 320(8308), 1129–1131.
7. Katz, J., Schein, O. D., Levy, B., Cruiscullo, T., Saw, S. M., Rajan, U., …Chew, S. J. (2003). A randomized trial of rigid gas permeable contact lenses to reduce the progression of children's myopia. American Journal of Ophthalmology, 136(1), 82–90.

8. Jain, S., Nehra, M., Kumar, R., Dilbaghi, N., Hu, T., Kumar, S., ...Li, C. Z. (2021). Internet of medical things (IoMT)-integrated biosensors for point-of-care testing of infectious diseases. Biosensors and Bioelectronics, 179, 113074.

9. Balusamy, B., et al. (2024). Design control and management of intelligent and autonomous nanorobots with artificial intelligence for Prevention and monitoring of blood related diseases. Engineering Applications of Artificial Intelligence, 131, 107798.

10. Senapati, A., et al. (2024). Artificial intelligence for diabetic retinopathy detection: A systematic review. Informatics in Medicine Unlocked, 101445.

11. Sharma, V., et al. (2023). Predicting the Cerebral Blood Flow Change Condition during Brain Strokes using Feature Fusion of FMRI Images and Clinical Features." 2023 14th International Conference on Computing Communication and Networking Technologies (ICCCNT). IEEE.

12. Raj, A., Kumar, A., Sharma, V., Rani, S., Shanu A. K. and Bhardwaj H. K (2023). Decipherable for Artificial Intelligence in Medicare: A Review, 2023 4th International Conference on Intelligent Engineering and Management (ICIEM), London, United Kingdom, pp. 1-6, doi: 10.1109/ICIEM59379.2023.10165690

13. Davis, J., Vaughan, D. H., Cardosi, M. F. (1995). Elements of biosensor construction. Enzyme and Microbial Technology, 17(12), 1030–1035.

14. Singh, A., Dhanaraj, R. K., Ali, M. A., Balusamy, B., Sharma, V. (2022). Blockchain Technology in Biometric Database System. 2022 3rd International Conference on Computation, Automation and Knowledge Management (ICCAKM), Dubai, United Arab Emirates, pp. 1–6, doi: 10.1109/ICCAKM54721.2022.9990133.

15. Davis, G. (1985). Electrochemical techniques for the development of amperometric biosensors. Biosensors, 1(2), 161–178.

16. Trivedi, U. B., Lakshminarayana, D., Kothari, I. L., Patel, N. G., Kapse, H. N., Makhija, K. K., ...Panchal, C. J. (2009). Potentiometric biosensor for urea determination in milk. Sensors and Actuators B: Chemical, 140(1), 260–266.

17. Kim, S., Baek, D., Kim, J. Y., Choi, S. J., Seol, M. L., Choi, Y. K. (2012). A transistor-based biosensor for the extraction of physical properties from biomolecules. Applied Physics Letters, 101(7), 073703.

18. Karmakar, N. C., Amin, E. M., Saha, J. K. (2016). Chipless RFID sensors.

19. Pfeiffer, E. F. (1990). The glucose sensor: the missing link in diabetes therapy. Hormone and metabolic research. Supplement Series, 24, 154–164.

20. Paladhi, A. G., Pal, K., Vallinayagam, S., Packirisamy, A. S. B., Bashreer, V. A., Nandhini, R. S., Ukhurebor, K. E. (2022). Novel electrochemical biosensor key significance of smart intelligence (IoMT IoHT) of COVID-19 virus control management. Process Biochemistry.

21. Yang, Z., Mansouri, K., Moghimi, S., Weinreb, R. N. (2021). Nocturnal variability of intraocular pressure monitored with contact lens sensor is associated with visual field loss in glaucoma. Journal of Glaucoma, 30(3), e56.

22. Ma, X., Ahadian, S., Liu, S., Zhang, J., Liu, S., Cao, T., ...Khademhosseini, A. (2021). Smart contact lenses for biosensing applications. Advanced Intelligent Systems, 3(5), 2000263.

23. Bamgboje, D., Christoulakis, I., Smanis, I., Chavan, G., Shah, R., Malekzadeh, M., ...Tzallas, A. (2021). Continuous non-invasive glucose monitoring via contact lenses: Current approaches and future perspectives. Biosensors, 11(6), 189.

24. Kim, J., Cha, E., Park, J. U. (2020). Recent advances in smart contact lenses. Advanced Materials Technologies, 5(1), 1900728.

25. Mirzajani, H., Mirlou, F., Istif, E., Singh, R., Beker, L. (2022). Powering smart contact lenses for continuous health monitoring: Recent advancements and future challenges. Biosensors and Bioelectronics, 197, 113761.

26. Jihad, A. J., Mathew, S. S., Paul, S., Pushpalatha, D. P. (2016, November). Continuous Health Monitoring Using Smartphones—A Case-study for Monitoring Diabetic Patients in UAE. In 2016 12th International Conference on Innovations in Information Technology (IIT) (pp. 1–5). IEEE.
27. Kim, J. (2019). Development of Wearable and Transparent Smart Contact Lenses for Wireless Ocular Diagnostics.
28. Park, J., Kim, J., Kim, S. Y., Cheong, W. H., Jang, J., Park, Y. G., …Park, J. U. (2018). Soft, smart contact lenses with integrations of wireless circuits, glucose sensors, and displays. Science Advances, 4(1), eaap9841.
29. Basheer, S., Singh, K. U., Sharma, V., Bhatia, S., Pande, N., & Kumar, A. (2023). A robust NIfTI image authentication framework to ensure reliable and safe diagnosis. PeerJ Computer Science, 9, e1323.
30. Ajmani, P., Sharma, V., Samuel, P., Somasundaram, K., Vidhya, V. (2022). Patient Behaviour Analysis and Social Health Predictions through IoMT. 2022 10th International Conference on Reliability, Infocom Technologies and Optimization (Trends and Future Directions) (ICRITO), pp. 1–6, doi: 10.1109/ICRITO56286.2022.9964846.

11 6G/5G Cellular Networks Empowering Wireless Technologies

*M. Aathira, P. Riashree, M. Saumiya, G. Ananthi,
and A. Malini*
Thiagarajar College of Engineering, Madurai,
Tamil Nadu, India

11.1 INTRODUCTION

Our society is swiftly progressing toward a future characterized by comprehensive automation and remote management systems. The rapid advancement of various emerging technologies, including Artificial Intelligence (AI), Virtual Reality (VR), Three-Dimensional (3D) media, and the Internet of Everything (IoE), has resulted in an unprecedented surge in data traffic [1]. To put this into perspective, global mobile data traffic amounted to 7.462 exabytes per month in 2010, and projections indicate that it will reach a staggering 5016 exabytes per month by 2030 [2]. These numbers underscore the critical need for enhancements in our communication systems.

Autonomous systems are gaining prominence across various sectors of society, including industry, healthcare, transportation, maritime, and even space exploration. To enable a smarter, more automated way of life, millions of sensors will be integrated into urban infrastructure, vehicles, residences, factories, agricultural processes, consumer products, toys, and countless other environments.

5G networks, while offering significant advancements over existing systems, will likely fall short of meeting the demands of a fully automated and intelligent network that delivers everything as a service and provides a completely immersive experience [3]. Although upcoming 5G communication systems will bring notable improvements, they may not adequately cater to the needs of future emerging intelligent and automation systems beyond the next decade [4].

5G technology will introduce various enhancements, including new frequency bands like millimeter wave (mmWave), utilization of optical spectra, advanced spectrum management, and the integration of licensed and unlicensed frequency bands [4]. These improvements will undoubtedly result in better quality of service (QoS) compared to fourth-generation (4G) communications [5–8].

However, the rapid growth of data-centric and automated systems could potentially outstrip the capabilities of 5G wireless systems. Certain devices, such as virtual reality

DOI: 10.1201/9781003389231-11

(VR) devices, will require data rates exceeding what 5G can offer, necessitating the development of Beyond 5G (B5G) technologies capable of delivering a minimum of 10Gbps data rates [1]. Consequently, with 5G approaching its limits by 2030, research into the design goals for its successor is already underway in the scientific literature.

To address the limitations of 5G and meet the evolving challenges, the development of a sixth-generation (6G) wireless system becomes imperative, offering a host of novel features. 6G will build upon the foundations of previous generations, integrating network densification, high throughput, high reliability, low energy consumption, and extensive connectivity into a cohesive framework.

In addition to these core elements, 6G will continue the trajectory of previous generations by introducing new services and technologies. These novel services encompass artificial intelligence (AI), smart wearables, implants, autonomous vehicles, immersive computing reality devices, advanced sensing capabilities, and three-dimensional mapping [9]. Perhaps the most critical requirement for 6G wireless networks is their ability to efficiently handle massive volumes of data and provide extremely high-data-rate connectivity per device [1]. This will be central to meeting the demands of emerging applications and technologies in the future. The forthcoming 6G system is poised to usher in a significant leap in performance, elevating user Quality of Service (QoS) to levels several times greater than those achievable with 5G, and it will introduce a range of exciting features. A paramount focus of 6G will be the robust protection of the system's integrity and the security of user data, ensuring a secure and comfortable user experience [10].

6G is envisioned to become a global communication infrastructure, and it is anticipated that in many scenarios, per-user data rates will reach an astonishing 1 terabit per second (Tb/s) [1,11]. This represents a substantial increase compared to 5G. Furthermore, 6G is expected to provide simultaneous wireless connectivity that is a thousand times more robust than what 5G can offer.

In addition to these advancements, 6G aims to enable ultra-long-range communication with latency as low as 1 millisecond (ms) [12], opening up new possibilities for real-time applications and services.This chapter presents the system model for Reconfigurable Holographic surface representation and capacity analysis is implemented.

11.2   ARCHITECTURE OF 6G COMMUNICATIONS

In this section, we present a prospective architectural framework for 6G, as depicted in Figure 11.1, encompassing the concepts of Future massive MIMO systems will be enabled and enhanced via combining other innovative technologies, architectures, and strategies such as

- Intelligent Omni Surfaces
- Intelligent reflecting surfaces
- Artificial intelligence
- THz communications
- cell free architecture
- Internet of things

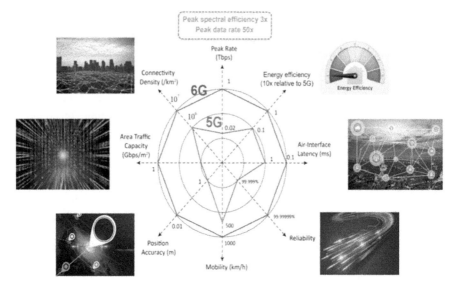

FIGURE 11.1   6G Architecture.

- augmented reality
- virtual reality
- automated driving
- achieves higher data rate
- provides wider coverage
- provides higher energy efficiency
- provides lower latency

11.2.1   6G WIRELESS COMMUNICATIONS

The physical layer (PHY) in wireless communication systems encounters a myriad of challenges, encompassing hardware issues like amplifier distortion, local oscillator leakage, as well as channel-related complications such as fading and interference. Achieving reliable and efficient communication amidst these hardware and channel impairments necessitates the harmonized optimization of numerous design parameters. Historically, the complexity involved has made comprehensive end-to-end optimization in wireless systems impractical. Consequently, conventional methods break down the entire system into multiple independent blocks, each relying on simplified models that fall short of capturing the complexities of real-world systems.

AI technologies bring forth exciting possibilities for achieving comprehensive optimization spanning the entire physical layer, from the transmitter to the receiver. We foresee the emergence of an "intelligent PHY layer" paradigm within the context of 6G, where the entire system can autonomously learn and enhance its performance. This vision becomes attainable through the application of advanced sensing techniques, data collection methodologies, AI technologies, and specialized signal processing approaches tailored to the specific domain. Remarkably, recent research has demonstrated the feasibility of employing deep neural networks (DNNs) to train the transmitter, channel, and receiver as an integrated auto-encoder system, thus facilitating the joint optimization of transmitter and receiver functions.

11.2.2 6G Hardware Setup

The rise of novel radio access technologies and the growing prevalence of IoT devices will exert significant influence on the design of 6G networks, with hardware limitations playing pivotal roles in shaping this evolution. On one front, as radio communication progresses into millimeter-wave (mmWave) and Terahertz bands, the substantial costs and power consumption associated with hardware components will have a profound impact on both the architecture of transceivers and the development of algorithms. On the other hand, IoT devices are characterized by constraints such as limited storage capacity, finite energy resources, and restricted computing capabilities. These resource-constrained platforms necessitate a holistic approach that encompasses communication, sensing, and inference to effectively address their unique challenges.

11.2.2.1 Case Study

Let's take the example of mmWave hybrid beamforming as an illustration. This approach stands as a cost-effective means of attaining significant beamforming gains. It achieves this by reducing the requirement for a large number of radio frequency (RF) chains, resulting in substantial reductions in both hardware costs and power consumption. Nevertheless, within the current hardware setup, a notable number of phase shifters are still essential. Phase shifters operating at mmWave frequencies are typically costly, underscoring the need to minimize their quantity. A novel hardware-efficient hybrid structure, as depicted in Figure 11.2, offers a solution to this challenge. This structure demands only a limited number of phase shifters, each set at a fixed phase. Consequently, hardware modifications

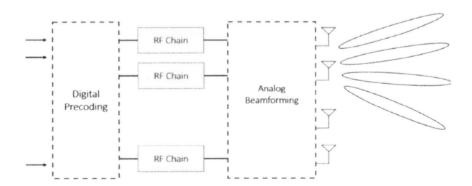

FIGURE 11.2 Hybrid beamforming structures.

are confined to the analog network, allowing the fundamental design principles for hybrid beamforming to remain applicable. This innovative approach can achieve performance levels approaching that of fully digital beamforming, all while utilizing far fewer phase shifters than other existing hybrid beamforming configurations.

11.2.3 SIMPLIFIED STRUCTURE OF 5G/6G NETWORK

Creating a system model for 5G/6G network empowering wireless technology involves outlining the key components, principles, and capabilities that define these advanced network generations. In what follows is a simplified system model for such networks:

Wireless Infrastructure:

- Base Stations:
  Centralized and decentralized base stations equipped with advanced antennas, including massive MIMO (Multiple-Input Multiple-Output) arrays.
- Small Cells:
  Distributed small cell nodes for improved coverage, especially in densely populated areas.
- Satellite Integration (6G):
  Integration of low-earth orbit (LEO) satellites for global coverage and low-latency communication.

Network Architecture:

- Core Network:
  Evolved Packet Core (EPC) for 5G, and a more flexible and dynamic core architecture for 6G.
- Network Slicing:
  Ability to create virtual networks tailored to specific applications and services.
- Edge Computing (6G):
  Integration of edge computing resources for ultra-low latency and real-time processing.

Spectrum Bands:

- 5G:
  Utilization of sub-6 GHz and mmWave bands.
- 6G (Projected):
  Exploitation of terahertz (THz) and higher frequency bands for extreme data rates.

Key Technologies:

- Massive MIMO:
  Utilization of a large number of antennas for improved spectral efficiency and coverage.
- Beamforming:
  Precise control of signal direction for efficient communication.
- Network Function Virtualization (NFV):
  Virtualizing network functions for flexibility and scalability.
- Software-Defined Networking (SDN):
  Centralized network control for optimized resource allocation.
- AI/ML Integration:
  Intelligent algorithms for network optimization, security, and predictive maintenance.

Wireless Devices:

- Smartphones, IoT Devices:
  Compatible with 5G and 6G standards, capable of high-speed data transmission and low-latency communication.
- 6G Devices (Projected):
  Terahertz band support, advanced AI integration, and holographic communication capabilities.

Applications and Use Cases:

- Enhanced Mobile Broadband (eMBB):
  High-speed internet access, 4K/8K video streaming, and augmented/virtual reality (AR/VR).
- Ultra-Reliable Low Latency Communication (URLLC):
  Critical applications like autonomous vehicles, remote surgery, and industrial automation.
- Massive Machine Type Communication (mMTC):
  IoT deployments at an unprecedented scale.
- Holographic Communication (6G):
  Immersive and realistic 3D communication experiences.
- Global Connectivity (6G):
  Worldwide access to data and services via satellite integration.

Security and Privacy:

- End-to-End Encryption:
  Ensuring data security during transmission.
- AI-Powered Threat Detection:
  Real-time monitoring and response to security threats.

- Privacy-Preserving Techniques:
  Protecting user data and identities.

Regulation and Policy:

- Spectrum Allocation:
  Governments and regulatory bodies allocate spectrum bands for 5G and 6G use.
- Privacy and Data Protection:
  Developing regulations to safeguard user data and privacy.
- Global Standards:
  Collaboration on international standards to ensure interoperability.

Research and Development:

- Continuous Innovation:
  Ongoing research and development to advance 6G technologies and applications.
- Testbeds and Prototyping:
  Testing and validating new concepts in real-world scenarios.

This system model provides a high-level overview of the components and principles that underpin 5G and anticipated 6G networks, highlighting their capabilities in empowering wireless technology for a wide range of applications and industries. It serves as a foundation for understanding the evolving landscape of wireless communication technology.

Regulation and Policy:

Spectrum Allocation:
- Regulatory bodies allocate specific frequency bands for 5G and 6G use based on auction mechanisms and interference considerations.

Capacity and Throughput:

Spectral Efficiency:
- The ratio of data rate to bandwidth, often measured in bits per second per Hertz (bps/Hz).

Propagation Delay and Latency:

Propagation Time:
- Calculation of the time taken for a signal to travel from the sender to the receiver based on the propagation speed.

End-to-End Latency:
- Summation of various delays in the network, including propagation, processing, and queuing delays.

Network Slicing:

Queueing Theory:
- Mathematical models for analyzing queue behavior in network slices.

Resource Allocation Algorithms:
- Optimization techniques to allocate resources (e.g. bandwidth, processing power) among network slices.

Beamforming and Antenna Arrays:

Array Factor:
- Mathematical representation of the radiation pattern of antenna arrays.

Beamforming Algorithms:
- Optimization equations for steering beams toward specific users or directions.

Interference Management:

Interference Coordination:
- Mathematical models for managing interference in dense networks, including interference cancellation techniques.

Interference Alignment:
- Techniques to align interference in multiuser scenarios.

Edge Computing:

Queueing Models:
- Analyzing the performance of edge servers using queueing theory.

Optimization Models:
- Mathematical frameworks for optimizing resource allocation at the network edge.

Security and Privacy:

- Cryptography:
  Mathematical algorithms for encryption and decryption, such as RSA or AES.

- Probability and Statistics:
  Tools for modeling security threats and assessing risks.
- Game Theory:

Modeling strategic interactions among security players in a network.

Resource Management and Optimization:

- Linear and Non-linear Programming:
  Techniques for optimizing network resource allocation, such as bandwidth or power.
- Convex Optimization:

A specialized mathematical framework for convex optimization problems common in wireless resource allocation.

Artificial Intelligence and Machine Learning:

- Regression and Classification Models:
  Predictive modeling for network optimization and predictive maintenance.
- Reinforcement Learning:
  Algorithms for autonomous network management and control.

Holographic Communication (6G):

- Holography Equations:
  Mathematical equations that describe the generation and reconstruction of holographic images.

This framework provides a foundation for modeling and analyzing various aspects of 5G and anticipated 6G networks, encompassing signal propagation, capacity, latency, resource management, security, and emerging technologies like terahertz communication and holographic communication. Researchers and engineers can use these mathematical tools to design, optimize, and analyze wireless networks to meet the diverse requirements of future wireless applications and services.

11.3 RECOMMENDATIONS

Within this section, we present actionable recommendations for addressing the challenges and obstacles that have emerged within the realm of 6G, harnessing the power of machine learning techniques, as depicted in Figure 11.3. As two primary pathways converge, a novel generation takes shape: 1) a technological trajectory that advances cutting-edge technologies to a mature state, and 2) a societal trajectory that facilitates the adoption of innovative services that existing technology finds challenging to deliver efficiently. Our journey commences with the

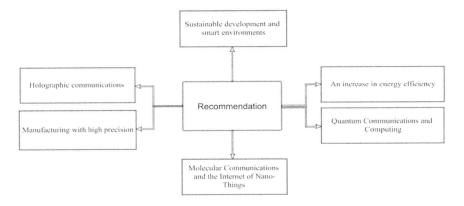

FIGURE 11.3   Categories of Motivation.

introduction of pioneering services, followed by a detailed exposition of the indispensable drivers necessary for their realization.

11.3.1   Holographic Communications

In conjunction with holographic communications, it is envisaged that 5D communications and services, which integrate all human sense information (sight, hearing, touch, smell, and taste), will emerge, resulting in a totally immersive experience [13]. In order to implement holographic communications using multiple-view cameras, data rates on the order of terabits-per second will be required [14], which will be insufficient for 5G.

11.3.2   Achieving Precision Manufacturing

Within the framework of Industry 4.0, a fundamental goal is to reduce human intervention in industrial processes by implementing automated control systems and advanced communication technologies. In the sphere of high-precision manufacturing, this pursuit entails achieving remarkably high levels of reliability, typically ranging from 1 to 10^9, and extremely low latency, with round-trip times spanning from 0.1 to 1 millisecond [15]. Additionally, within the domain of industrial control networks, there is a critical need for real-time data transmission characterized by exceptional determinism. This translates to an extraordinarily low delay jitter, typically in the order of 1 nanosecond.

11.3.3   Sustainability in Wireless Intelligent Environments

Information and communication technologies (ICTs), encompassing wireless communications, cloud computing, and the Internet of Things (IoT), are poised to play a pivotal role in advancing global sustainability efforts and enhancing the overall quality of life. These technologies have the potential to make significant contributions, particularly in domains such as healthcare enhancement and the development of smart cities. The concept of smart cities encompasses the establishment of intelligent transportation and energy distribution infrastructures. To achieve these objectives, the deployment of a pervasive sensing framework and a distributed decision and actuation system becomes imperative.

6G is anticipated to exert substantial influence in this domain, relying on 3D communication platforms that can enable almost instantaneous distributed edge cloud functionalities, including distributed decision-making processes. In critical scenarios like autonomous driving, prioritizing safety measures is of paramount importance to minimize the risk of accidents. This requires exceptionally high levels of communication reliability, surpassing 99.9999%, and minimal end-to-end latency below 1 millisecond. Moreover, facilitating seamless communication between vehicles and between vehicles and roadside equipment will be vital in reducing collision risks, necessitating high-speed data connections.

11.3.4 ENHANCING ENERGY EFFICIENCY

Sustainable progress undeniably demands a sharp focus on energy consumption. Consequently, 6G must develop communication strategies that not only deliver effectiveness but also prioritize energy efficiency. The overarching objective is to enable communication that operates without depleting batteries whenever possible, with the aim of achieving communication efficiency within the range of 1 picojoule per bit (1 pJ/b). It's worth noting that specific key performance indicators (KPIs), such as delay jitter and energy per bit, did not receive significant emphasis in the context of 5G, but they will gain paramount importance as primary KPIs in the context of 6G.

11.3.5 QUANTUM COMMUNICATIONS AND COMPUTING

To address heightened security demands compared to current technologies, 6G is poised to embrace quantum communications to a greater extent. Quantum communications leverage the principles of the quantum no-cloning theorem and the uncertainty principle, providing robust security through the use of quantum keys [16]. In quantum communications, any attempts by eavesdroppers to observe, measure, or replicate data result in the disturbance of the quantum state, making eavesdropping activities readily detectable. In theory, quantum communications offer the potential for complete security.

While the challenges of achieving terabits-per-second (Tb/s) data transmission and comprehensive applications/scenarios present obstacles for wireless computing in 6G, they also bring exciting opportunities [17]. Unlike traditional computing, which operates on binary 0–1-b operations, quantum computing harnesses the power of quantum superposition and entanglement, significantly enhancing computing capabilities through the use of qubits and unitary transformations.

11.3.6 MOLECULAR COMMUNICATIONS AND THE INTERNET OF NANO-THINGS (MOLECULAR COMMUNICATIONS AND THE INTERNET OF NANO-THINGS)

Advanced nanotechnology holds the potential to enable the development of nanoscale devices, including nano-robots, implantable chips, and biosensors, all of which have significant applications in fields such as nanoscale sensing and biomedicine [17]. The adoption of nanotechnology, particularly in biomedicine, has generated substantial interest due to its potential to perform tasks such as precise drug distribution within blood vessels and continuous monitoring of bodily organs. These capabilities have the potential to greatly enhance healthcare outcomes for individuals. Realizing effective communication and information transmission can be achieved by connecting these nanodevices to the internet or by establishing networks, often referred to as the Internet of Nano-Things (IoNT). Similar work on interplanetary communications is referred in [18–21].

11.4 SYSTEM MODEL

From the system model of Figure 11.4, we can observe that the signal transmitted from the transmitter is sent to the respective user through the RHS element [4]. As the input signal is greatly affected due to fading in this wireless environment because of the various obstacles in the environment, the signal strength tends to fluctuate. So, using the RHS elements, the input signal is directed to the respective receiver antenna with maximum signal strength.

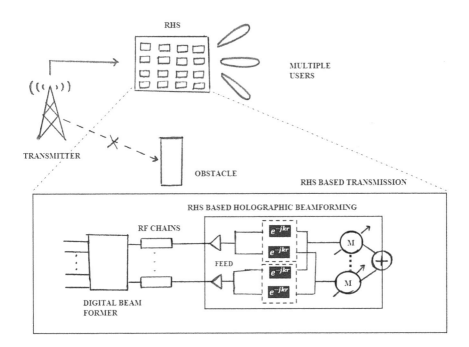

FIGURE 11.4 RHS based Multiuser Communication System.

Before transmitting the signal we first precode the signal. Precoding is done to ensure that the signal reaches the correct recipient without mismatch. Precoding is also called beamforming. It consists of Digital beam Former, RF chains, and the feed. These are the in-built structures that constitute the array of RHS elements. These structures help increase the overall directivity, which in turn has a larger impact on the channel capacity. Thus, such a RHS based multiuser communication system utilizes the bandwidth of the channel effectively and thus has a higher channel capacity.

11.5   MULTIUSER CAPACITY ANALYSIS

Let the transmitted signal from the base station be,

$$x = W \wedge S \tag{11.1}$$

Where, S is the transmitted signal vector for k values.

The Expectation of this signal with its hermitian matrix is given as,

$$E[SS^H] = \frac{P}{k}I_k \tag{11.2}$$

Here, P is the transmitted power.

Also, At the base station, the signals are assumed to be transmitted under a normalized power allocation matrix $\wedge$ which satisfies $Tr[\wedge \wedge^H] = 1$

The normalized precoding matrix W is given by,

$$W \in C^{M \times K} \tag{11.3}$$

Due to zero forcing by the RHS based transmission, the received signal can be written as,

$$y = GW \wedge S + n \tag{11.4}$$

Where, G is the radiation amplitude of each radiation element

$$G = \frac{Re\{\varphi_{intf}(r^*_{m,n}, \theta_o, \varphi_o)\} + 1}{2} \tag{11.5}$$

For zero forcing precoding, the kth column of W can be written as,

$$W_k = \frac{V_k}{\|V_k\|_F} \tag{11.6}$$

Where, V_k is the kth column of matrix V

$$V = G^H (GG^H)^{-1} \qquad (11.7)$$

Consequently, with zero forcing precoding, the signal to noise ratio for user k can be expressed as,

$$r_k = \frac{P\wedge_K}{k\sigma^2} (g_k \ w_k)(g_k \ w_k)^H \qquad (11.8)$$

Where, g_k is the kth row of G and

$$\wedge_K = [\wedge\wedge^H]_{k,k} \qquad (11.9)$$

Here, we assume that the channel state information is perfectly obtained by the base station and thus $\wedge$ is assumed to be a constant in the following which can be obtained by water filling algorithm.

Using above notations, we can express the data rate for user k as,

$$r_k = E[log_2(1 + r_k)] \qquad (11.10)$$

The multiuser capacity can be achieved by,

$$C = E \sum_k log_2 \left(1 + \frac{P\wedge_K}{k\sigma^2}[GG^H]_{k,k}\right) \qquad (11.11)$$

11.6   RESULTS AND DISCUSSION

The theory and practical curves for the number of RHS elements versus the total channel capacity is plotted. The plot is done for three SNR values of 10dB, 20dB and 30dB and it is clearly seen that as the signal to noise ratio increases, the channel capacity also increases. Along the horizontal axis, the number of RHS elements are increased in a scale of order of 4th power of 10. From the curve characteristics, it's inferred that as the number of RHS elements increases, the channel capacity also increases in the units of bits/seconds (also denoted in the units of Hz). Also the graph is simulated both theoretically and practically and it's inferred from the graph that both the theory and practical curve overlaps each other.

From this Figure 11.5, it is clear that the increased number of RHS elements that are used as reflecting surfaces in the 6G wireless channel will greatly increase the capacity of the channel and the overall multiuser communication is enhanced by the use of these reflecting surfaces.

Figure 11.6 shows the transmitted signal can be expressed as a function of the symbol index. Received signal is represented as a function of symbol index (inclusive of noise).

Figure 11.7 shows the throughput and latency plots as a function of time.

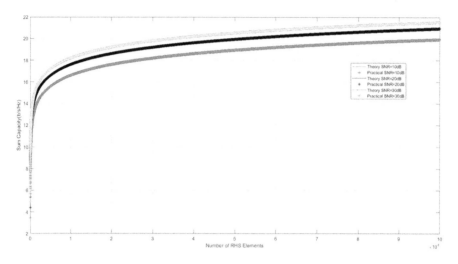

FIGURE 11.5   Capacity versus number of RHS elements.

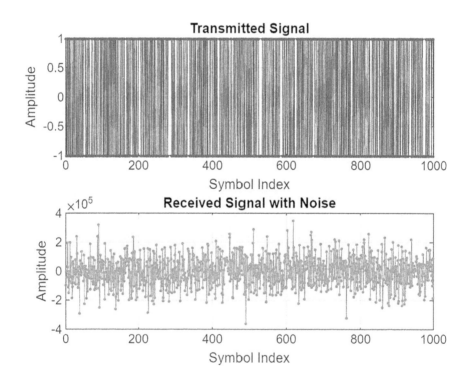

FIGURE 11.6   Transmit-receive signal as a function of symbol index.

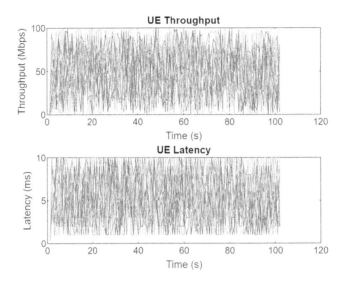

FIGURE 11.7   Throughput and latency as a function of time.

11.7   CONCLUSION

Multiuser communication is improved with the help of RHS elements. The communication becomes more efficient as it reflects the signal exactly to the respective recipient with a maximum achievable power. Also, with increased SNR and with the increased number of RHS elements, channel capacity is greatly increased and helps us get a desired communication between the transmitter and the receiver. The holographic technology finds its immense use case in the implementation of reconfigurable surfaces that can help in achieving a higher directivity. And in turn, these RHS elements find their application in wireless communication in 6G mobile phones where they can be used to provide highly reliable multiuser communication with increased channel capacity.

REFERENCES

1. S. Mumtaz et al., "Terahertz communication for vehicular networks," IEEE Transactions on Vehicular Technology, vol. 66, no. 7, pp. 5617–5625, July 2017.
2. ITU-R M.2370-0, IMT traffic estimates for the years 2020 to 2030, Jul. 2015.
3. S. J. Nawaz, S. K. Sharma, S. Wyne, M. N. Patwary, and M. Asaduzzaman, "Quantum machine learning for 6G communication networks: state-of-the-art and vision for the future," IEEE Access, vol. 7, pp. 46317–46350, 2019.
4. Giordani et al., "Towards 6G networks: use cases and technologies."
5. M. Shafi et al., "5G: a tutorial overview of standards, trials, challenges, deployment, and practice," IEEE Journal on Selected Areas in Communications, vol. 35, no. 6, pp. 1201–1221, Jun. 2017.
6. D. Zhang, Z. Zhou, S. Mumtaz, J. Rodriguez, and T. Sato, "One integrated energy efficiency proposal for 5G IoT communications," IEEE Internet of Things Journal, vol. 3, no. 6, pp. 1346–1354, Dec. 2016.

7. M. Jaber, M. A. Imran, R. Tafazolli, and A. Tukmanov, "5G backhaul challenges and emerging research directions: a survey," IEEE Access, vol. 4, pp. 1743–1766, Apr. 2016.

8. J. G. Andrews, S. Buzzi, W. Choi, S. V. Hanly, A..Lozano, A. C. K. Soong, and J. C. Zhang, "What will 5G be?," IEEE Journal on Selected Areas in Communications, vol. 32, no. 6, pp. 1065–1082, Jun. 2014.

9. W. Saad, M. Bennis, and M. Chen, "A vision of 6G wireless systems: applications, trends, technologies, and open research problems."

10. 123 Seminars Only. (2019). 6G mobile technology. [Online]. Available: http://www. 123seminarsonly.com/CS/6G-Mobile-Technology.html.

11. K. David and H. Berndt, "6G vision and requirements: is there any need for beyond 5G?," IEEE Vehicular Technology Magazine, vol. 13, no. 3, pp. 72–80, Sept. 2018.

12. F. Tariq et al., "A Speculative Study on 6G," arXiv:1902.06700

13. K. David and H. Berndt, "6G vision and requirements: Is there any need for beyond 5G?," IEEE Veh. Technol. Mag, vol. 13, pp. 72–80, 2018.

14. R. Li, "Towards a new internet for the year 2030 and beyond," In Proceedings of the 3rd Annu. ITU IMT-2020/5G Workshop Demo Day, Geneva, Switzerland, 18 July 2018; pp. 1–21.

15. G. Berardinelli, N. H. Mahmood, I. Rodriguez, and P. Mogensen, "Beyond 5G wireless IRT for industry 4.0: Design principles and spectrum aspects," In Proceedings of the 2018 IEEE Globecom Workshops (GC Wkshps), Abu Dhabi, United Arab Emirates, 9–13 December 2018; pp. 1–6.

16. P. Botsinis, D. Alanis, Z. Babar, H. V. Nguyen, D. Chandra, S. X. Ng, and L. Hanzo, "Quantum search algorithms for wireless communications," IEEE Commun. Surv. Tutor, vol. 21, pp. 1209–1242, 2018.

17. O. B. Akan, H. Ramezani, T. Khan, N. A. Abbasi, and M. Kuscu, "Fundamentals of molecular information and communication science," Proc. IEEE, vol 105, pp. 306–318, 2016.

18. V. Juyal et. al., "On exploiting dynamic trusted routing scheme in delay tolerant networks." Wireless Personal Communications, vol. 112, pp. 1705–1718, 2020.

19. V. Juyal et. al., "An anatomy on routing in delay tolerant network," 2016 IEEE International Conference on Computational Intelligence and Computing Research (ICCIC), Chennai, 2016, pp. 1–4. doi: 10.1109/ICCIC.2016.7919724

20. V. Juyal et. al., "Opportunistic message forwarding in self organized cluster based DTN," 2017 International Conference on Infocom Technologies and Unmanned Systems (Trends and Future Directions)(ICTUS). IEEE, 2017.

21. V. Juyal et. al., "Performance comparison of DTN multicasting routing algorithms-opportunities and challenges," 2017 International Conference on Intelligent Sustainable Systems (ICISS). IEEE, 2017.

12 Software Defined Network Based Artificial Intelligence Empowered Internet of Medical Things (SDN-AI-IoMT) to Predict COVID-19

Evolution and Challenges

S. Kavi Priya
Department of Computer Science and Engineering,
Mepco Schlenk Engineering College, Sivakasi,
Tamil Nadu, India

N. Saranya
Department of Computer Science and Engineering,
Sri Krishna College of Technology, Coimbatore,
Tamil Nadu, India

12.1 INTRODUCTION

As years progress, the way the world communicates with us improves. Internet of Things (IoTs) is blooming in the medical field in past few years, as a result, there is a technological progression in low-power networked systems and healthcare devices [1]. IoT technology has evolved into a critical advancement with a wide range of applications. It describes any set of machines that get as well as share information over Wi-Fi without the need of user intercession [2]. The medical industry is undergoing a substantial shift, with digitalization manipulating how practitioners communicate with their patients. Patients are now able ability to see their crucial symptoms and assist doctors immediately. IoT as its name infers that it is the interconnection of things or devices. Things in IoT can be of any kind, from a smart device with much artificial intelligence that can interact with other things effectively to a dumb thing that does not interact, for the healthcare application IoMT (Internet of Medical Things) is developed.

DOI: 10.1201/9781003389231-12

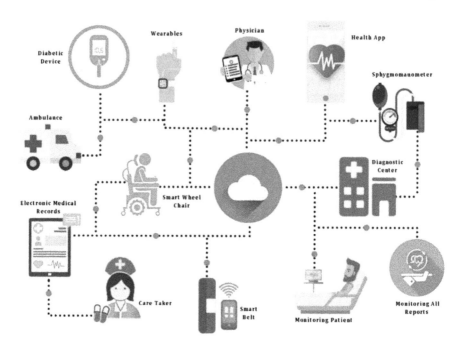

FIGURE 12.1   Architecture of IoMT [7].

IoMT consists of healthcare equipment or sensors that can distribute information over a web that does not need individual-individual or individual-machine communication [3]. An IoMT based healthcare system consists of various stages. Initially, the healthcare data is acquired from the patient's body using sensors attached to them. These data are then sent over the next stage for analysis or prediction using AI based technique. The analysis results are then sent back to the patients' smart phones or doctors in serious cases. An instance of IoMTs in which victims' physiological parameters are accumulated using various devices and directed toward IoMT apps via the web is depicted in Figure 12.1.

Because IoMT devices are distributed, network control is distributed; that incurs risks when executed on traditional networks. In such a case, SDN has become a feasible option because it provides a centralized perspective on the network, which conceals management challenges and provides network control. The software-defined network (SDN) framework has received the most attention recently since it offers a more consistent, versatile, and secure network environment [4]. SDN comprises of planes such as data pane, control plane, and application plane. SDN tries to incorporate network intelligence in a single connected device by isolating the data and control plane [5].

In the healthcare sector, an early disease prediction will enhance a patient's lifetime. Artificial Intelligence techniques aid doctors to predict diseases as early as possible. Machine learning (ML) is a capability of a machine to gain and integrate knowledge through large-scale observations, as well as to improve and expand automatically by acquiring fresh information, instead training with that data [6].

The online and smartphone-based applications for disease diagnosis deliver assistance in remote regions where hospitals have limited health monitoring capabilities. Learning starts with findings or data, which consists of examples, real observation, or training, to search for trends in information and subsequently create finer findings entirely based on the instances that we offer.

The primary benefit of this paper is as follows:

1. This article establishes a single framework for a device-to-device interaction to address the drawbacks of the COVID-19 pandemic in the healthcare sectors.
2. The articles discussed SDN that used multiple controllers to minimize packet loss, fragmenting networks, and mainly handles load balancing.
3. The authors also used the AI-SDN-IoT framework to communicate data healthcare applications safely and effectively, ensuring system reliability during COVID-19.

Section 2 describes the related work. Section 3 describes the methodologies used in the proposed work. Section 4 describes the results and discussion, and Section 5 concludes the work.

12.2 RELATED WORK

This section explores the works of SDN, IoMT, and AI. Various researchers used different artificial intelligence models such as machine learning, deep learning, and ensemble modeling to predict distinct types of diseases. In IoMT various sensors are deployed, and it constantly gathers data and sends it to the successive layers for processing. In SDN network security is the primary concern, and most of them focus on load balancing and privacy.

12.2.1 IN ARTIFICIAL INTELLIGENCE

The following table explains the research papers published related to Artificial Intelligence in the prediction of various diseases (Table 12.1).

12.2.2 IN INTERNET OF MEDICAL THINGS

The following table details the works related to the Internet of Medical Things (IoMT) in the prediction of various diseases (Table 12.2).

12.2.3 IN SOFTWARE DEFINE NETWORKING (SDN)

The following table details the works related to the Software Define Networking (SDN) (Table 12.3).

TABLE 12.1

Literature works on AI

S. No	Authors	Title	Methodologies	Merits	Demerits
1	Tommi et al [8]	Using artificial intelligence tools to detect chest x-rays with no significant findings in a primary healthcare setting in oulu, Finland	Chestlink – a software is used to analyze the X-rays.	Maximizes the sensitivity by reducing the error in the dataset	Comparison with ground truth and not able to fully access the patient's demographic information
2	Chiu et al [9]	Machine learning for emerging infectious disease field responses.	The cases of Coronavirus in a hospital with limited number of medical resources is predicted using machine learning technologies	Decision Tree (DT) technique suits well for this problem compared to Deep Neural Network and Logistic Regression	The influenza diagnosis is confirmed for the cases without confirmation from the lab tests and used only one database for prediction.
3	Bhargava et al [10]	Machine learning-based automatic detection of novel coronavirus (COVID-19) disease	Fuzzy c-means clustering is used for segmenting and various features are extracted & classified using machine learning algorithms	SVM achieves higher accuracy of 99.14%	Computational time and cost are higher
4	Pyrros et al [11]	Validation of a deep learning, value-based care model to predict mortality and comorbidities from chest radiographs in COVID-19	Predicts the mortality of patients suffered from Covid-19 using CNN	CNN achieves higher accuracy	Labeling is difficult because of high noise present in the dataset
5	Kogilava ni et al [12]	COVID-19 Detection Based on Lung Ct Scan Using Deep Learning Techniques	Features are extracted from the deep encoder model and classified using SVM technique	Polynomial SVM works better than linear and Gaussian SVM.	The model is not able to correctly identify the affected areas in images

TABLE 12.2
Literature works on IoMT

S. No	Author	Title	Methodologies	Merit	Demerit
1	Jiang et al [13]	Toward an Artificial Intelligence Framework for Data-Driven Prediction of Coronavirus Clinical Severity	Build Artificial Intelligence structure & machine learning model to predict the severity of coronavirus	Detect cases with mild severity effectively	Size of the dataset is small, and the model achieves only 70-80% accuracy only.
2	Dwivedy et al [14]	LMNet: Lightweight multi-scale convolutional neural network architecture for COVID-19 detection in IoMT environment	LMNet model is used to detect COVID-19 in CXR images	By using LMNet model the integration of IoMT devices will be easy	Focusing on single label classifier and not on multi-label classification
3	Yildrim et al [15]	Real-time internet of medical things framework for early detection of Covid-19	IoMT structure has been used to diminish the effect of COIVD-19	Gradient Boosting Tree (GBT) achieves 100% precision, 92% recall and 95% F1 score	Privacy and security issues are not addressed.
4	Singh et al [16]	A secure energy-efficient routing protocol for disease data transmission using IoMT	OptiGeA protocol is used for detecting communicable infectious diseases	OptiGeA protocol surpasses the state-of-the methods by employing mobile sink approaches to reduce the transmission distance	Considerable number of instructions cannot be professionally managed
5	Hossen et al [17]	Federated Machine Learning for Detection of Skin Diseases and Enhancement of Internet of Medical Things (IoMT) Security	Novel CNN with federated learning technique to solve the privacy issues	Proposed model shows higher precision with 86%, 43%, and 60% for acne, eczema, and psoriasis	Model works more efficiently if the training data and class labels will increase

TABLE 12.3

Literature works on SDN

S. No	Author	Title	Methodologies	Merit	Demerit
1	Trosicia et al [18]	Scalable OneM2M IoT Open-Source Platform Evaluated in an SDN Optical Network Controller Scenario	This work validates and discusses the functionality of OneM2M-Compliant server	OneM2M frameworks scalability is better and flexible	The study doesn't consider the reliability and security aspects in larger networks
2	Ke et al [19]	SDN-based Privacy and Functional Authentication Scheme for Fog Nodes of Smart Healthcare	SDN gateway is established in fog nodes to lower the computational capacity of the IoT nodes	Storage cost is minimum compared to other existing methods	Didn't focus on the authentication between fog and IoT nodes
3	Babbar et al [20]	Intelligent Edge Load Migration in SDN-IIoT for Smart Healthcare	SDN-IIoT technology for migrating heavily loaded controller to lightly loaded controller	Efficient load balancing and attacks are prevented	Load migration is not focused, and malicious activities are not considered
4	Aslam et al [21]	Adaptive Machine Learning Based Distributed Denial-of-Services Attacks Detection and Mitigation System for SDN-Enabled IoT	Adaptive Machine Learning based SDN-enabled Distributed Denial-of-Service s attacks Detection and Mitigation (AMLSDM) framework to mitigate DDoS attacks	Higher accuracy and lower false alarm rate	Mitigation of DDoS and phishing attacks have to be explored more deeply
5	Paliwal et al [22]	Effective Flow Table Space Management Using Policy-Based Routing Approach in Hybrid SDN Network	In this work a hybrid network scenario of SDN and legacy switching function is proposed	Hybrid of IP and SDN makes low cost	Controllers are limited to three and subnets are fixed

12.3 METHODOLOGIES

This work focuses on predicting chronic diseases in patients. Overall 200 countries were affected globally from the first occurrence of COVID-19. In this perplexing battle, science and technology played a significant role. A variety of experts, including technical experts whom emphasized discovering appealing patients via the development of diagnostic images such as X beams and CT filters, employ AI to uncover new drugs and therapies.

12.3.1 INTERNET OF MEDICAL THINGS (IOMT)

A majority of the traditional hospital uses human/individual administrating and updating of patient statistical information such as past cases, lab tests, therapy, accounting, and medicines maintenance, that further results in manual failures and also warily influences victims. Intelligent healthcare built on the Internet of Things (IoT) avoids human errors and aids clinicians in promptly and accurately recognizing disorders by combining all critical characteristics tracked by different sensors throughout the web with an analysis assistance system. The Internet of Medical Things (IoMT) encompasses medical equipment which can send data over an internet devoiding any interaction.

It was utilized in the healthcare sector such as tracking the health status of elder patients, smart hospitals, diagnosing diseases, emergency warning, etc. In the period of COVID-19, there is an increase in remote patient monitoring strategies due to social distancing rules that require clinicians to monitor patients far off via IoMT devices [23]. These devices focus on services such as diagnosing the severity of coronavirus, tracking the location of the infected and vulnerable patients.

The incorporation of the internet into the surroundings of our lives has set the stage for IoMT applications, and it has become a segment of our day-to-day life. The majority of IoMT systems are organized into four layers, such as sensor layer, gateway layer, cloud layer, and visualization layer [24]. These layers incorporate various techniques, equipment, sensors, and computers that are linked via wired or wireless links.

The sensor layer is designed to gather vital parameters from the patients such as heart rate, temperature, blood pressure, etc. These parameters acquire the patients' vital values and transfer these values to the next phase. Various sensors are utilized to acquire the patients' vital parameters. The network layer provides an individual interface for both patients and physicians, complete with modules that collect health history along with some other information, which is then retained in a secure IoT-based cloud database. See Figure 12.2.

For a reliable, real-time healthcare framework, it serves as the core for IoMT architecture. The application layer is focused on intelligent healthcare management, with personalized interfaces for predicting diseases. This component manages patient consults administration, accurate diagnosis, and other supplementary analyses.

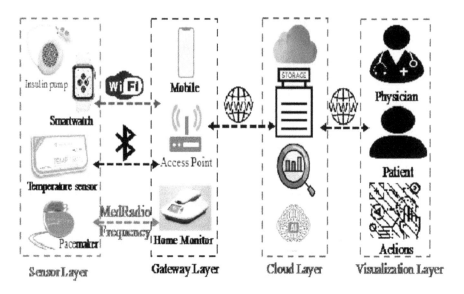

FIGURE 12.2 IoMT different types of layers [24].

12.3.2 SOFTWARE DEFINED NETWORK (SDN)

The primary function of IoT systems is to gather information from environments and render that data available and useful if required. The features of IoT mentioned such as privacy, network connectivity and huge volumes of data and devices present challenges in developing a quick, stable, and convenient network infrastructure. Tackling these issues necessitates novel applications of SDN technology beyond its existing use in data centers and core networks.

SDN appears to be the most successful and potential technology widely used in many areas. In SDN architecture there are three stages such as application plane, control plane, and data plane. With programmability of networks, the SDN model has simplified networking management to a client-free framework [25] (Figure 12.3).

SDNs emerged as a new networking conceptual framework as the control plane and data plane were separated. Due to its original and assuring structure, the entire control logic has been routed to a centralized control plane. Its resilience and prospects are built on its centralized architecture and intellectual capacity. To collect data from connected nodes, an SDN controller employs the southbound protocol. The most essential protocol used is the southbound protocol, which is in charge of data transfer between the controller and connected nodes. One of the most prominent southbound protocols is OpenFlow, a widely used networking connection developed by the Open Networking Foundation (ONF). This interface enables provision for nodes such as switches and routers to transfer or acquire data.

SDN was initially intended to be utilized in the basic network and data centers, in which extremely skilled routers or switches are used to optimize the consumption of various resources. IoT networks are further varied and propagated than mobile networks, and controlling and tracking the servers as well as the network gets more

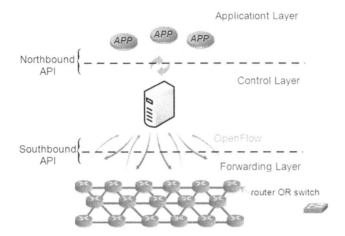

FIGURE 12.3   Basic Architecture of SDN [26].

challenging as the amount of gadgets and apps develops opening up a new domain in which SDN might be effective.

Because the SDN controller is incorporated at centralized node, it is appropriate for configuration and control of sensor nodes or linked nodes. Moreover, depending on its comprehensive perception, the controller optimizes routing according to the application specifications. If an instance has various kinds of sensors that meet application standards, the SDN controller can choose the one it wants to trigger. This allows modules to be utilized by multiple services without having to be rebuilt, leading to a more sustainable and constantly growing monitoring environment.

12.3.3   ARTIFICIAL INTELLIGENCE BASED HEALTHCARE

The capability of software to accomplish activities or understand in a manner that we connect with brains among people is referred to as AI [27]. AI and related technologies have grown more ubiquitous in business and administration, and they are beginning to be employed in the medical field. A plethora of studies have already found that AI can function more effectively than humans in the medical sector such as disease diagnosis. Physicians or researchers can now diagnose cancer more quickly and earlier than ever before, by identifying diseases before they mutate, and deducing genetic disorders by employing AI based systems.

Unlike the initial era of AI technologies, which depended on professional collection of clinical experience and the synthesis of rules, latest AI study has used machine learning techniques to recognize patterns in data that can contribute to complex interactions [28]. Artificial intelligence benefits both physicians and patients. Ehealth and its software solutions have received increasing attention in recent years. They employ various algorithms, some of which gather data from sensing devices such as fitness trackers.

AI techniques are majorly divided into two classifications. The first classification incorporates machine learning techniques to inspect structural data such as numerical

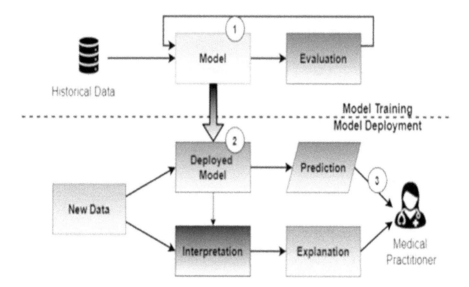

FIGURE 12.4 Working of AI systems of humans by detecting trends and inferring conclusions using the available information [29].

data, imaging data, etc. The second classification incorporates Natural Language Processing (NLP) techniques to inspect unstructured data such as lab tests, physician's note, etc.

The healthcare data are high-dimensional, where it consists of a substantial number of attributes recorded for every inference and it could be greater than the overall amount of instances. Most of the data are noisy and statistically ineffective. As a result, machine learning approaches can be utilized to tackle problems with large datasets. Machine learning is an element of artificial intelligence (AI) that seeks to mimic human behavior (Figure 12.4).

The importance of data in machine learning cannot be overstated. There is a large amount of data available in all kinds of sectors such as healthcare, education, and transportation. These data provide insight which can help people in decision making. Machine Learning symbolizes more advanced arithmetic features than traditional statistics, and it leads to improved performance in forecasting a result that is ascertained by a diverse set of instances.

ML algorithms are most likely classified into three types: unsupervised, supervised, and reinforcement learning. Supervised machine learning is a decision-making technology that trains from information. Unsupervised machine learning requires individuals making decisions to analyze undetected trends in data that have not been labeled. Reinforcement machine learning is a strategy that encourages suitable behavior while punishing incorrect behavior.

12.3.4 Challenges Faced by Healthcare

The abrupt automation of the medical industry has resulted in the generation of massive amounts of medical data. This trove of data includes case records, test results, MRI scans, sensor data, bioinformatics, and various other types of information. In the extent that information systems have been able to cope with the growth of ever massive manual supports, it faces a growing need for systems to manage them. The privacy of that information becomes challenging in medical fields, and it will be insufficient to ensure safety not only from outside threats, as well as from intruders within organizations to misuse one's power.

As more intelligent technologies hit the market, we will require suitable rules and surveillance technologies to ensure systems security and data safety while assimilating such equipment or gadgets into smart healthcare. An even more limitation to implementing such technologies is data overload. We will be required to develop methods to convert enormous amounts of victim's data into appropriate information so that doctors can act on such information by analyzing it and providing timely action.

Considering these challenges, the work focuses on integrating AI, SDN, and IoMT. By using these technologies, the analysis will be efficient, accurate, and on-time. Figure 12.1 depicts a workflow of the AI-SDN-IoMT. In this work, sensors that senses various symptoms are deployed. These sensors detect and transfer data to SDN switches, which then transmit it to the Health controller. If the user's condition is critical after predicting from sensed data, the required indicator is conveyed to the user. The primary goal of this work is to predict the presence of COVID-19 by analyzing vital features. As a result, it is critical to identify the best ML algorithm for the hypothetical situation. We use a COVID dataset to investigate a person's health response and forecast if the person has COVID using ML algorithms (Figure 12.5).

The proposed model comprises three layers as application layer, the control layer, and the data layer. In the data layer communication devices and sensors are present to gather information from the patients. In the control layer, SDN switches and controllers are present to efficiently utilize the sensors by enhancing their performance. In the application layer, an intelligent system is present that accurately diagnoses the disease using ML algorithms.

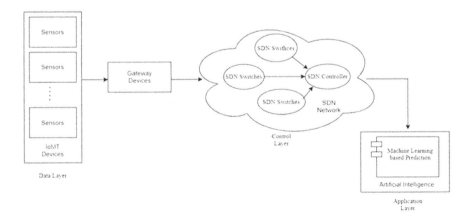

FIGURE 12.5 Flowchart of the proposed system.

12.4   RESULTS AND DISCUSSION

12.4.1   DATASET DESCRIPTION

The informational database for this work was obtained from the Kaggle website
[30]. It consists of ten attributes and 5434 instances. Among them, 4383 patients
affected with coronavirus and 1051 are not. The attributes describe the symptoms
experienced by the Covid-19 affected patients. The attributes present in this dataset
are breathing problem, fever, sore throat, dry cough, hypertension, Travel overseas,
interaction with COVID-19 patients, attendance at substantial amount of events,
trips to open accessible areas, and relatives functioning in vulnerable locations.

12.4.2   EVALUATION PARAMETERS

Accuracy, precision, recall, F1 Score, and ROC-AUC are the assessment metrics
employed in this paper. The parameters values are calculated using the following
notations such as true positive (tp), false positive (fp), true negative (tn), and false
negative (fn).

12.4.2.1   Accuracy
It counts how many positive and negative observations were correctly classified.

$$\text{Accuracy} = \frac{tp = tn}{tp + tn + fp + fn} \tag{12.1}$$

12.4.2.2   Precision
Precision is determined by dividing the total number of true positives across all
classes by the sum of true positives and false positives.

$$\text{Precision} = TP/(TP + FP) \tag{12.2}$$

12.4.2.3   Recall
The ratio of total true positives across all classes and the sum of true positives and
false negatives is used to calculate recall.

$$\text{Recall} = \frac{tp}{tp + fn} \tag{12.3}$$

12.4.2.4   F1 Score
By computing the mean of the two, it combines precision and recall into a single
measure.

$$\text{F1 score} = 2 \times \frac{Precision \times Recall}{Precision + Recall} \tag{12.4}$$

Several types of machine learning techniques such as XGBoost, Random Forest (RF), Decision Tree (DT), Support Vector Machine (SVM), Naïve Bayes (NB), Logistic Regression (LR) and are used to predict coronavirus in victims.

12.4.2.4.1 Logistic Regression

Despite its name, logistic regression is a classification technique rather than a regression model [30,31]. It is a more straightforward and effective method. It is straightforward to set up and produce outstanding outcomes with independently distinct classes. It is a popular classification method in the business world. It is a technique based on statistics for classifying binary data that can be extended to the classification of multiple classes.

12.4.2.4.2 Naïve Bayes

The Bayes hypothesis underpins the Naive Bayes classifier. They have a foundation in probabilistic classifiers [32,33]. Because these classifiers are easy to develop, they are widely employed in machine learning classification. The following Eq. expresses the Bayes theorem.

$$P(A \mid B) = P(A \mid B)*P(A)/P(B)$$

12.4.2.4.3 Support Vector Machines

Support Vector Machine is a supervised machine learning approach for both regression and classification. The fundamental principle of SVMs is the concept of determining an appropriate hyperplane using support vectors, i.e., the coordinates of each class located at the edge [34,35]. Points that are nearest to the boundary are called support vectors. The aim of the SVM is to maximize the distance between the hyperplane and the support vectors.

12.4.2.4.4 Decision Tree

The decision tree is a supervised technique that may categorize information files by using specified criteria during decisions. It is a well-known efficient method which is widely utilized in many different kinds of applications such as image processing, machine learning, data mining, and pattern recognition. The DT structure is made up of branches and nodes, with each of them carrying a set of numerical values that indicate the class of interest for every record within a comparable node [36,37].

12.4.2.4.5 Random Forest

Random forest (RF) is a popular ensemble method that has been impacted by randomized substructure and randomized split selection. The conventional RF relies on bootstrap datasets and is divided using the CART algorithm [38,39]. RF has been widely used in many areas, including image processing and text mining, due to its outstanding efficiency and rapid training process.

12.4.2.4.6 XGBoost

In 2001, Friedman developed the gradient-boosting decision tree technique. The gradient descent approach is used to produce trees that are based on all prior trees

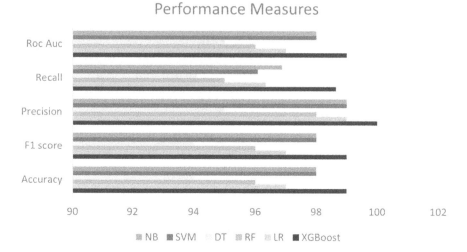

FIGURE 12.6   Performance measures of various models.

while keeping the objective function as minimal as possible [40,41]. The maximal gradient boosting decision tree, or XGBoost, is a classification and regression tree ensemble model. To forecast the output, the XGBoost model [42,43] begins with a collection of base learners xi = f1,f2,f3 fk, where fk is a distinct tree structure, and K is the number of additives units. At iteration t, the objective function can be reduced by investigating all base learners/functions and selecting one that reduces the loss.

The dataset is primarily divided into both testing and training sets using the tenfold cross validation test. The datasets are subjected to ML methods, and performance measures are calculated.

The performance metric comparisons are depicted in Figure 12.6. From the figure, it is inferred that XGBoost is more accurate than other models. XGBoost has a higher accuracy 99%. SVM and NB attained equal accuracy 98% next to XGBoost. Then LR has 97%, RF has 96%, and at last, DT attained 94% accuracy.

From these results, it is inferred that out of the other five models, XGBoost performs well. Table 12.4 shows the total time required by the model to execute. The results exhibit that XGBoost executes faster than other models in 0.010 seconds.

TABLE 12.4

Execution time comparison

S. No	Algorithm	Computational Time (seconds)
1	XGBoost	0.010
2	LR	0.064
3	RF	0.533
4	DT	0.354
5	SVM	0.328
6	NB	0.024

Random Forest executes slow, and next to random forest Decision Tree executes in 0.354 seconds[44].

12.5 CONCLUSION

We suggested an integrated AI-SDN-IoMT architecture in this paper to forecast COVID-19 in patients. The sensors in IoMT equipments communicate with the smart system via the SDN network. To anticipate diseases, a machine learning-based forecasting model is constructed. Different machine learning models are implemented, and XGBoost stands out in regard to performance measures like Accuracy, Precision, Recall, F1 score, and ROC-AUC score. Furthermore, it is quicker to execute than other techniques.

We will add more machine learning models in the future, and multi-criteria decision making will be used to select the best model. In addition, we will look into privacy and security concerns.

REFERENCES

1. J. G. Ko, C. Lu, M. B., Srivastava, J. A. Stankovic, A. Terzis, and M. Welsh, "Wireless Sensor Networks for Healthcare," Proceedings of the IEEE, Vol. 98, No. 11, Nov. 2010, 10.1109/JPROC.2010.2065210.
2. M. M. Khan, S. Mehnaz, A. Shaha, M. Nayem, and S. Bourouis, "IoT- Based Smart Health Monitoring System for COVID-19 Patients", Computational and Mathematical Methods in Medicine, Vol. 2021, 1–11, 2021, 10.1155/2021/8591036.
3. S. Vishnu, S. R. Jino Ramson, R. Jegan, "Internet of Medical Things (IoMT) – An Overview," 2020 5th International Conference on Devices, Circuits and Systems (ICDCS), 2020.
4. M. W. Nadeem, H. G. Goh, V. Ponnusamy and Y. Aun, "DDOS Detection in SDN using Machine Learning Techniques," Computers, Materials & Continua, Tech Science Press, Vol. 71, No.1, 2022, DOI: 10.32604/cmc.2022.021669.
5. V. Juyal et al. "On Exploiting Dynamic Trusted Routing Scheme in Delay Tolerant Networks," Wireless Personal Communications, vol. 112, 1705–1718, 2020.
6. M. Pal, S. Parija, R. K. Mohapatra, S. Mishra, A. A. Rabaan, A. A. Mutair, S. Alhumaid, J. A. Al-Tawfiq, and K. Dhama, "Symptom-based COVID 19 Prognosis through AI-Based IoT: A Bioinformatics Approach", Biomed Research International, Vol. 2022, 1–12, 2022, 10.1155/2022/3113119.
7. A. Raj, V. Sharma, and A. K. Shanu, "Comparative Analysis Of Security And Privacy Technique For Federated Learning In IOT Based Devices," 2022 3rd International Conference on Computation, Automation and Knowledge Management (ICCAKM), Dubai, United Arab Emirates, 2022, pp. 1–5, doi: 10.1109/ICCAKM54721.2022. 9990152.
8. Juyal, V. et al., "An Anatomy on Routing in Delay Tolerant Network," 2016 IEEE International Conference on Computational Intelligence and Computing Research (ICCIC), Chennai, 2016, pp. 1–4. doi: 10.1109/ICCIC.2016.7919724
9. M. Y. Shaheen, "AI in Healthcare: medical socio-economic benefits and challenges," ScienceOpen Preprints, 2021, 10.14293/S2199-1006.1.SOR-.PPRQNI1.v1.
10. R. C. Deo, "Machine Learning in Medicine," Circulation, vol. 132, 1920–1930, 2015.
11. A. Agah Medical applications of artificial intelligence, 1st edn. Taylor & Francis Group, Baton Rouge.

12. T. Keski-Filppula, M. Nikki, M. Haapea, N. Ramanauskas, O. Tervonen, "Using artificial intelligence to detect chest X-rays with no significant findings in a primary health care setting in Oulu, Finland",arXiv, 2022, 10.48550/arXiv.2205.08123.

13. M. N. R. D. S. Murali and V. Sharma, "Performance Analysis of DGA-Driven Botnets using Artificial Neural networks," 2022 10th International Conference on Reliability, Infocom Technologies and Optimization (Trends and Future Directions) (ICRITO), 2022, pp. 1–6, doi: 10.1109/ICRITO56286.2022.9965044.

14. A. Maurya and V. Sharma, "Facial Emotion Recognition Using Keras and CNN," 2022 2nd International Conference on Advance Computing and Innovative Technologies in Engineering (ICACITE), 2022, pp. 2539–2543, doi: 10.1109/ICACITE53722.2022.9823480.

15. H. Y. R. Chiu, C. K. Hwang, S. Y. Chen et al., "Machine Learning for Emerging Infectious Disease Field Responses," Sci Rep, vol. 12, 328, 2022. 10.1038/s41598-021-03687-w.

16. A. Bhargava, A. Bansal and V. Goyal, "Machine Learning-based Automatic Detection of Novel Coronavirus (COVID-19) Disease," Multimed Tools Appl, vol. 81, 13731–13750, 2022, 10.1007/s11042-022-12508-9.

17. A. Pyrros, J. Rodriguez Fernandez, S. M. Borstelmann, A. Flanders, D. Wenzke, et al., "Validation of a Deep Learning, Value-based Care Model to Predict Mortality and Comorbidities from Chest Radiographs in COVID-19," PLOS Digital Health, vol. 1, no. 8, e0000057, 2022. 10.1371/journal.pdig.0000057.

18. S. V. Kogilavani, J. Prabhu, R. Sandhiya, M. S. Kumar, U. S. Subramaniam, A. Karthick, M. Muhibbullah, and S. B. S. Imam, "COVID-19 Detection Based on Lung Ct Scan Using Deep Learning Techniques", Computational and Mathematical Methods in Medicine, Vol. 2022, 1748-670X, 2022, 10.1155/2022/7672196.

19. V. Dwivedy, H. D. Shukla, and P. K. Roy, "LMNet: Lightweight Multi-scale Convolutional Neural Network Architecture for COVID-19 Detection in IoMT Environment", Computers and Electrical Engineering, 2022, 108325, 10.1016/j.compeleceng.2022.108325.

20. E. Yildirim, M. Cicioğlu and A. Çalhan, "Real-time internet of medical things framework for early detection of Covid-19," Neural Comput & Applic, 2022. 10.1007/s00521-022-07582-x.

21. X. Jiang, M. Coffee, A. Bari, J. Wang, X. Jiang et al., "Towards an Artificial Intelligence Framework for Data-driven Prediction of Coronavirus Clinical Severity," Computers, Materials & Continua, vol. 63, no.1, 537–551, 2020.

22. S. Singh, A. S. Nandan, G. Sikka, A. Malik, and A. Vidyarthi, "A Secure Energy-efficient Routing Protocol for Disease Data Transmission using IoMT," Computers and Electrical Engineering, Vol. 101, 108113, 2022, 10.1016/j.compeleceng.2022.108113.

23. Beverly Park Woolf, Chapter 7 - Machine Learning, Editor(s): Beverly Park Woolf, Building Intelligent Interactive Tutors, Morgan Kaufmann, 2009, Pp 221–297.

24. B. Ramasubramanian and G. Anitha, "An Efficient Approach for the Detection of New Vessels in Diabetic Retinopathy Images," Int. J. Eng. Innov. Technol, vol. 2, no. 3, pp. 240–244, 2012.

25. L. M. Koonin et al., "Trends in the Use of Telehealth during the Emergence of the Covid-19 Pandemic – United States, January – March 2020", Morb. Mortal. Wkly. Rep., Vol. 69, pp. 1595–1599, 2020.

26. A. A. Toor, M. Usman, F. M. Younas, A. C. Fong, S. A. Khan, S. Fong, "Mining Massive E-Health Data Streams for IoMT Enabled Healthcare Systems," Sensors, vol. 20, no. 7, 2131, 2020. 10.3390/s20072131.

27. P. Ajmani, V. Sharma, P. Samuel, K. Somasundaram and V. Vidhya, "Patient Behaviour Analysis and Social Health Predictions through IoMT," 2022 10th International Conference on Reliability, Infocom Technologies and Optimization (Trends and Future Directions) (ICRITO), 2022, pp. 1–6, doi: 10.1109/ICRITO56286. 2022.9964846.

28. A. Ghubaish, T. Salman, D. Ünal, A. Al-Ali, and R. Jain, "Recent Advances on the Internet of Medical Things (IoMT) Systems Security," IEEE Internet of Things Journal. PP. 10.1109/JIOT.2020.3045653.

29. W. Bekri, R. Jmal, and L. Chaari Fourati, "Internet of Things Management Based on Software Defined Networking: A Survey," Int J Wireless Inf Networks, vol. 27, 385–410, 2020. 10.1007/s10776-020-00488-2.

30. M. N. Hossen, V. Panneerselvam, D. Koundal, K. Ahmed, F. M. Bui, and S. M. Ibrahim, "Federated Machine Learning for Detection of Skin Diseases and Enhancement of Internet of Medical Things (IoMT) Security," in IEEE Journal of Biomedical and Health Informatics, doi: 10.1109/JBHI.2022.3149288.

31. M. Troscia, A. Sgambelluri, F. Paolucci, P. Castoldi, P. Pagano, and F. Cugini, "Scalable OneM2M IoT Open-Source Platform Evaluated in an SDN Optical Network Controller Scenario," Sensors, vol. 22, no. 2, 431, 2022. 10.3390/s22020431.

32. C. Ke, Z. Zhu, F. Xiao, Z. Huang, and Y. Meng, "SDN-based privacy and functional authentication scheme for fog nodes of smart healthcare," in IEEE Internet of Things Journal, doi: 10.1109/JIOT.2022.3161935.

33. H. Babbar, S. Rani, and S. A. Alqahtani, "Intelligent edge load migration in SDN-IIoT for smart healthcare," in IEEE Transactions on Industrial Informatics, doi: 10.1109/TII.2022.3172489.

34. M. Aslam, Y. Dengpan, A. Tariq, M. Asad, M. Hanif, D. Ndzi, S. A. Chelloug, M. A. Elaziz, M. A. A. Al-Qaness, and S. F. Jilani. "Adaptive Machine Learning Based Distributed Denial-of-Services Attacks Detection and Mitigation System for SDN-Enabled IoT," Sensors, vol. 22, no. 7, 2697, 2022. 10.3390/s22072697.

35. M. Paliwal and K. K. Nagwanshi, "Effective Flow Table Space Management Using Policy-Based Routing Approach in Hybrid SDN Network," in IEEE Access, vol. 10, pp. 59806–59820, 2022, doi: 10.1109/ACCESS.2022.3180333.

36. S. Abdulhamit, "Classification examples for healthcare", Practical Machine Learning for Data Analysis using Python, Academic Press, 2020, pp. 203–322.

37. P. Suresh, K. Logeswaran, P. Keerthika, R. Manjula Devi, K. Sentamilselvan, G. K. Kamalam, H. Muthukrishnan, "Contemporary survey on effectiveness of machine and deep learning techniques for cyber security", in Cognitive Data Science in Sustainable Computing, Machine Learning for Biometrics, Academic Press, 2022, pp. 177–200.

38. A. Rani, N. Kumar, J. Kumar, J. Kumar, and N. K. Sinha, "Machine learning for soil moisture assessment", in Cognitive Data Science in Sustainable Computing, Deep Learning for Sustainable Agriculture, Academic Press, 2022, pp. 143–168.

39. C. S. Lee, P. Y. S. Cheang, and M. Moslehpour, "Predictive Analytics in Business Analytics: Decision Tree", Advances in Decision Sciences, Vol. 26, Iss. 1, 1–29, Mar 2022.

40. P. Shaowei, Z. Zheng, Z. Guo, and H. Luo, "An Optimized XGBoost Method for Predicting Reservoir Porosity using Petrophysical Logs", Journal of Petroleum Science and Engineering, Vol. 208, Part C, 109520, 2022.

41. N.-H. Nguyen, J. Abellán-García, S. Lee, E. Garcia-Castano, and T. P. Vo, "Efficient estimating compressive strength of ultra-high performance concrete using XGBoost model", Journal of Building Engineering, Vol. 52, 104302, 2022.

42. J. Bai, Y. Li, J. Li, X. Yang, Y. Jiang, and S.-T. Xia, "Multinomial Random Forest", Pattern Recognition, Vol. 122, 108331, 2022.

43. V. Juyal et al., "Opportunistic Message Forwarding in Self Organized Cluster Based DTN." 2017 International Conference on Infocom Technologies and Unmanned Systems (Trends and Future Directions)(ICTUS). IEEE, 2017.
44. V. Juyal et al., "Performance Comparison of DTN Multicasting Routing Algorithms-Opportunities and Challenges." 2017 International Conference on Intelligent Sustainable Systems (ICISS). IEEE, 2017.

13 Exploring Toroidal Link in Honeycomb Mesh Network Using Genetic Algorithm

Neetu Faujdar and Reeya Agrawal
Dept of Computer Engineering and Application,
GLA University, Mathura, Uttar Pradesh, India

Akash Punhani
Dept of Computer Science and Engineering, SRM Institute
of Science and Technology, Delhi NCR Campus, Modinagar,
Ghaziabad, Uttar Pradesh, India

13.1 INTRODUCTION

13.1.1 MESH NETWORK TOPOLOGY

In this mesh topology, all the nodes(computers) are connected in a network where each and every node is connected to each other via network (cable/wire). In other words, every device is connected to every other device in mesh topology [1]. There is a point to point link between the connected devices. We can calculate the number of links by the formula n(n-1)/2 where n is equal to the number of devices. There are some advantages of using mesh topology. The most important advantage being no traffic problems due to point to point or direct link between the two communicating devices. Hence, being a reliable and secure network system. Moreover, detecting any fault in the network is easier in mesh topology. You may also find some disadvantages of using mesh topology. Like the number of wires required is more so it sometimes becomes a tedious task. Scalability problems are more regular in mesh topology [2].

A mesh topology can be of two types: full mesh topology and partially connected mesh topology. In a full mesh topology, each node or computer in the system has an association with every different node or computer in that network [3]. The number of associations in this topology can be determined using the formula, where n is the number of computers or nodes in the network. In a partially connected mesh topology, any of two of the nodes or computers in the $(n)/2n - 1$ network have associations with multiple other computers or nodes in the network; it is a modest way to execute repetition in a system [4].

13.1.2 FEATURES OF MESH NETWORK TOPOLOGY

13.1.2.1 Physical Parameters

There are various parameters associated with the direct interconnection network on which we identify interconnection: [5].

    I. Diameter
   II. Bisection Width
  III. Node Degree
  IV. Edge Length

13.1.2.2 Functional Parameters

Interconnection networks can be examined on the different QoS compels which are listed here.

    I. Throughput
   II. Latency
  III. Load factor
  IV. Traffic Patterns
     a. Bit-Complement Traffic
     b. Uniform Distributed Traffic
     c. Tornado Traffic Pattern
     d. Neighbor Traffic

13.2 PROPOSED METHODOLOGY

13.2.1 HEXAGONAL NETWORK

13.2.1.1 Honeycomb 2D Mesh Network

Honeycomb mesh network is a type of mesh network in which the mesh network connection exists in the form of hexagons joined together to form a honeycomb mesh topology [6]. Honeycomb mesh representation can be seen in Figure 13.1:

13.2.1.2 Honeycomb 3D Mesh Network

Honeycomb 3D mesh network is formed by connecting the extreme nodes on both the vertical sides with each other. And similarly repeating the same procedure for extreme nodes on the horizontal axis [7]. By doing this, a torus-like structure can be obtained that is known to be a honeycomb 3D mesh interconnection network [8]. Figure 13.2 shows the structure obtained:

The Omnet++ software has been used as stated earlier. It is a simulation tool based on C++ [9]. We implemented all the codes in C++. Initially had made some

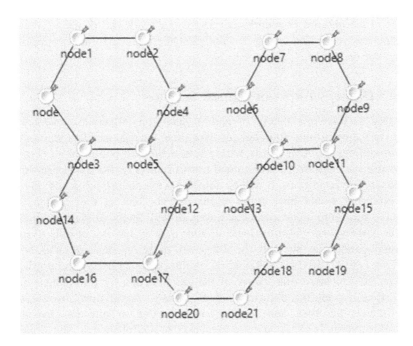

FIGURE 13.1   Honeycomb 2D Mesh Network.

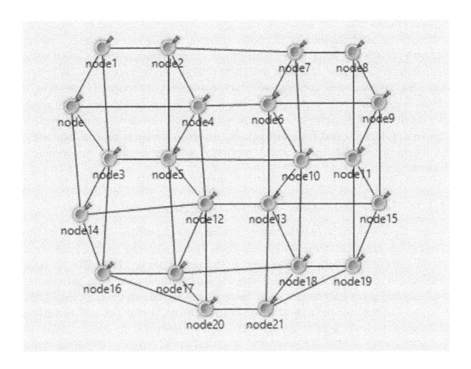

FIGURE 13.2   Honeycomb 3D Mesh Network.

changes in the libraries in routing part as per our needs and demands. When the simulator was ready for testing we designed the topologies and started implementing our codes [10].

13.2.2 DARWIN'S THEORY OF NATURAL SELECTION

According to Darwin's theory of natural selection, organisms changed with other external environmental changes over time. Change to adapt, according to the surroundings. In other words, nature selects the best photos of all organisms able to survive even in the worst conditions of all [11]. So if an organism can tolerate adverse conditions, it will be able to have more offspring and obviously these offspring would have traits of the parents, and so they will have the stamina of surviving in the worst conditions as well. So the offspring will also be fittest as parents, and with time these options may or may not be able to survive in adverse conditions, but only the fittest will carry the survival chain forward [12]. This type of survival is known as evolution by natural selection. Darwin has been able to prove the theory of natural selection by providing evidence from different scientific domains and disciplines. As of now, we know that nature selects the best, and the organisms evolve to suit the environment needs of survival [13]. So natural selection brings change in the organisms and organisms evolve. The evolution of organisms may be in the form of change in color, change in behavior, change in size, and many other minute changes. These minute changes over a period of time lead to the evolution of any organism rather than the whole species. Some organisms mutate or get defects in the genetic formulations of the body [14]. As we all know, genetic makeup is known for overall behavior or appearance of any species, so the fittest of all have different genetic makeup that helps them to survive [15]. We have been able to take the concept of Darwin's theory of natural selection in networking, which has further been able to give a conclusion that if you only have the fittest traffic patterns giving the best possible results you can be made to achieve low latency and high throughput. So we have been able to implement this theory on 2D hexagonal mesh topology, and we have got an optimized result set [16].

13.2.3 GENETIC ALGORITHM AS OPTIMIZATION ALGORITHM

Genetic algorithm is a search based optimization technique. It works on the principle of genetics and natural selection. It has derived its principle from Darwin's theory of natural selection as discussed above. Basically, it is an optimization technique that we are using for optimizing our data set, introducing new links that gives best results [17]. These things are known to be toroidal links. So in our chapter, we have optimized the hexagonal 2D network and hexagonal 3D network to form a new 2D and 3D toroidal networks. In optimization, we have a set of inputs that are processed to give a set of outputs [18]. Best output can be obtained by varying inputs. Genetic algorithm is a part of an evolutionary computation. In this algorithm, a pool of possible solutions is present which are further mutated to form a recombination. The further recombination is mutated to produce new offspring. And this process goes on repeat till the best possible solution is obtained [19]. Fitness value is assigned based on the objective function. Fitter individuals are given chances to produce fitter individuals. This phenomenon is supported by Darwin's theory of survival of the fittest. At this point the evolution takes place. And the process of evolution occurs until we reach a stopping criteria. Genetic algorithms are randomized in nature [20]. It exploits historical information. So here are the advantages of the genetic algorithm:

1. There is no derivative information required.
2. It is a faster and very efficient means of optimization.
3. Genetic algorithms are known to exhibit good parallel capabilities.
4. It gives the list of solutions and not just a single solution.
5. It is good when search is large and when many parameters are involved.
6. Optimization is based on continuous functions, discrete functions, or multi objective functions.

Beside advantages it also has some limitations. These limitations include:

1. It is not at all suited for simple problems like derivatives.
2. Fitness value is repeatedly calculated so it is an expensive procedure.
3. There is no guarantee of an optimized solution.
4. It requires a proper implementation.

13.2.4 ADJACENCY MATRIX

Adjacency Matrix Representation
Advantages

1. Easy to implement.
2. Easy to follow.
3. Removing an edge takes $O(1)$ time.
4. Queries are efficient and can be performed $O(1)$.

Drawbacks

1. More space complexity- $O(V^2)$.
2. Even in a sparse graph, the same space is consumed.
3. Adding a single vertex requires $O(V^2)$ time

This matrix is passed as the parameter to the genetic algorithm to get the desired number and position of links to be placed [21].

Arr1(3D) [ ]=

This array is passed as a parameter for obtaining 2d toroidal structure.

Arr22D [ ]=

$$
\begin{aligned}
[\,&[0, 1, 0, 1, 0, 0, 0, 0, 0, 0, 0, 0, 0, 0, 0, 0, 0, 0, 0, 0, 0, 0], \\
&[1, 0, 1, 0, 0, 0, 0, 0, 0, 0, 0, 0, 0, 0, 0, 0, 0, 0, 0, 0, 0, 0], \\
&[0, 1, 0, 0, 1, 0, 0, 0, 0, 0, 0, 0, 0, 0, 0, 0, 0, 0, 0, 0, 0, 0], \\
&[1, 0, 0, 0, 1, 1, 0, 0, 0, 0, 0, 0, 0, 0, 0, 0, 0, 0, 0, 0, 0, 0], \\
&[0, 0, 1, 1, 0, 0, 0, 0, 0, 0, 0, 0, 0, 0, 0, 0, 0, 0, 0, 0, 0, 0], \\
&[0, 0, 0, 1, 0, 0, 1, 0, 1, 0, 0, 0, 0, 0, 0, 0, 0, 0, 0, 0, 0, 0], \\
&[0, 0, 0, 0, 0, 1, 0, 1, 0, 0, 0, 0, 0, 0, 0, 0, 0, 0, 0, 0, 0, 0], \\
&[0, 0, 0, 0, 0, 0, 1, 0, 0, 1, 0, 0, 0, 0, 0, 0, 0, 0, 0, 0, 0, 0], \\
&[0, 0, 0, 0, 0, 1, 0, 0, 0, 1, 0, 1, 0, 0, 0, 0, 0, 0, 0, 0, 0, 0], \\
&[0, 0, 0, 0, 0, 0, 0, 1, 1, 0, 0, 0, 0, 0, 0, 0, 0, 0, 0, 0, 0, 0], \\
&[0, 0, 0, 0, 0, 0, 0, 0, 0, 0, 0, 1, 0, 1, 0, 0, 0, 0, 0, 0, 0, 0], \\
&[0, 0, 0, 0, 0, 0, 0, 0, 1, 0, 1, 0, 1, 0, 0, 0, 0, 0, 0, 0, 0, 0], \\
&[0, 0, 0, 0, 0, 0, 0, 0, 0, 0, 0, 1, 0, 0, 1, 0, 0, 0, 0, 0, 0, 0], \\
&[0, 0, 0, 0, 0, 0, 0, 0, 0, 0, 1, 0, 0, 0, 1, 1, 0, 0, 0, 0, 0, 0], \\
&[0, 0, 0, 0, 0, 0, 0, 0, 0, 0, 0, 0, 1, 1, 0, 0, 0, 0, 0, 0, 0, 0], \\
&[0, 0, 0, 0, 0, 0, 0, 0, 0, 0, 0, 0, 0, 1, 0, 0, 1, 0, 1, 0, 0, 0], \\
&[0, 0, 0, 0, 0, 0, 0, 0, 0, 0, 0, 0, 0, 0, 0, 1, 0, 1, 0, 0, 0, 0], \\
&[0, 0, 0, 0, 0, 0, 0, 0, 0, 0, 0, 0, 0, 0, 0, 0, 1, 0, 0, 1, 0, 0], \\
&[0, 0, 0, 0, 0, 0, 0, 0, 0, 0, 0, 0, 0, 0, 0, 1, 0, 0, 0, 1, 0, 1], \\
&[0, 0, 0, 0, 0, 0, 0, 0, 0, 0, 0, 0, 0, 0, 0, 0, 0, 1, 1, 0, 0, 0], \\
&[0, 0, 0, 0, 0, 0, 0, 0, 0, 0, 0, 0, 0, 0, 0, 0, 0, 0, 0, 0, 0, 1], \\
&[0, 0, 0, 0, 0, 0, 0, 0, 0, 0, 0, 0, 0, 0, 0, 0, 0, 0, 1, 0, 1, 0]\,]
\end{aligned}
$$

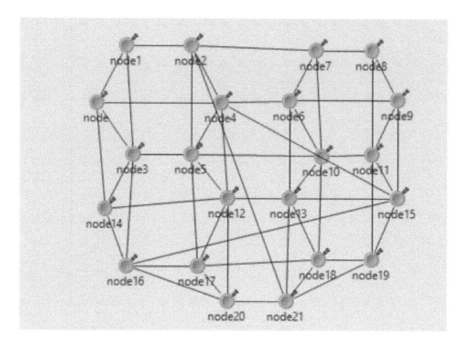

FIGURE 13.3   Honeycomb 3D toroidal structure.

13.2.5   HONEYCOMB TOROIDAL STRUCTURES

The toroidal structure is a special form of structure where extra links are introduced based upon the results from the genetic algorithm [22]. The links that are known to give better efficiency are added to the original structure or topology which will in turn lead to better results [23]. The following figures are obtained by introducing the new links in order to optimize the previous structure and produce better efficiency [24]. The first figure depicts the 2d toroidal structure, and the second figure depicts the obtained 3d toroidal structure after applying genetic algorithms [25] (Figures 13.3 and 13.4).

13.3   RESULT AND ANALYSIS

Omnet++ has been used to simulate the designed topologies. Further simulation has been done on the basis of different traffic patterns. The outcomes have also been analyzed with respect to different traffic patterns. The results have been seen improving with the advancement by using different algorithms along with some optimizations in sub sequential designs. These have led us to have totally different conclusions by introducing new links to the different mesh interpretations. Consequently, there has been an improvement in efficiency and that has led us to observations that have proved the betterment of toroidal networks over simple mesh and hexagonal mesh networks.

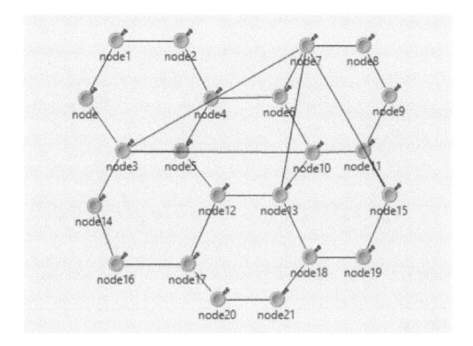

FIGURE 13.4   Honeycomb 2D toroidal structure.

13.3.1   HONEYCOMB 2D VERSUS HONEYCOMB 3D

In all aspects, it has been observed that the honeycomb 3D interconnection network has proved to be giving better efficiency as compared to the honeycomb 2D interconnection network.

13.3.1.1   Uniform Traffic Pattern

13.3.1.1.1   Latency

Latency has been found to be improving in the honeycomb 3D interconnection network, which has been found by analyzing the readings at different inter packet arrival delays [26]. This has been shown in Figure 13.5. The Table 13.1. is a comparison of the latencies observed in two different design patterns at the given inter packet arrival delay, i.e. time interval in simpler words in uniform traffic pattern. So the maximum improvement in latency has been observed at 20.50μs with the percentile improvement of 27.47% and the minimum improvement is observed at 5.12μs with a percentile improvement of 14.90%.

13.3.1.1.2   Throughput

Throughput has been found to be improving in the honeycomb 3D interconnection network, which has been found by analyzing the readings at different inter packet arrival delays [27]. This has been shown in Figure 13.6. The Table 13.2. is a comparison of the throughputs observed in two different design patterns at the given inter packet arrival delay, i.e. time interval in simpler words in uniform traffic

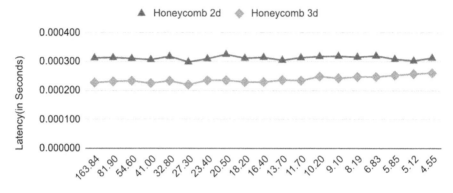

FIGURE 13.5 Latency (Honeycomb 2D versus Honeycomb 3D)-Uniform traffic pattern.

TABLE 13.1

Honeycomb 2D and Honeycomb 3D Latency in Sec

	Latency(In Seconds)		
Inter Packet Arrival Delay(in μs)	Honeycomb 2d	Honeycomb 3d	Improvement
163.84	0.000312	0.000227	27.24%
81.90	0.000313	0.000231	26.20%
54.60	0.000310	0.000233	24.84%
41.00	0.000306	0.000225	26.47%
32.80	0.000317	0.000233	26.50%
27.30	0.000298	0.000220	26.17%
23.40	0.000309	0.000235	23.95%
20.50	0.000324	0.000235	27.47%
18.20	0.000311	0.000229	26.37%
16.40	0.000314	0.000229	27.07%
13.70	0.000304	0.000236	22.37%
11.70	0.000313	0.000234	25.24%
10.20	0.000317	0.000248	21.77%
9.10	0.000318	0.000242	23.90%
8.19	0.000315	0.000247	21.59%
6.83	0.000319	0.000247	22.57%
5.85	0.000308	0.000252	18.18%
5.12	0.000302	0.000257	14.90%
4.55	0.000312	0.000260	16.67%

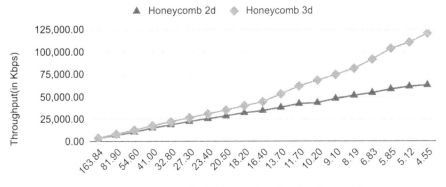

FIGURE 13.6   Throughput (Honeycomb 2D versus Honeycomb 3D)-Uniform traffic pattern.

TABLE 13.2
Honeycomb 2D and Honeycomb 3D Throughput in Kbps

	Throughput(In Kbps)		
Inter Packet Arrival Delay(in μs)	Honeycomb 2d	Honeycomb 3d	Improvement
163.84	3,570.00	4,090.00	14.57%
81.90	7,130.00	8,630.00	21.04%
54.60	10,700.00	13,000.00	21.50%
41.00	15,200.00	17,900.00	17.76%
32.80	18,800.00	22,200.00	18.09%
27.30	22,500.00	26,700.00	18.67%
23.40	25,600.00	31,000.00	21.09%
20.50	28,700.00	35,400.00	23.34%
18.20	32,200.00	40,300.00	25.16%
16.40	34,700.00	44,600.00	28.53%
13.70	38,400.00	53,300.00	38.80%
11.70	42,500.00	62,100.00	46.12%
10.20	43,500.00	68,500.00	57.47%
9.10	48,100.00	74,800.00	55.51%
8.19	51,600.00	81,700.00	58.33%
6.83	54,500.00	91,700.00	68.26%
5.85	58,600.00	104,000.00	77.47%
5.12	61,600.00	111,000.00	80.19%
4.55	63,200.00	121,000.00	91.46%

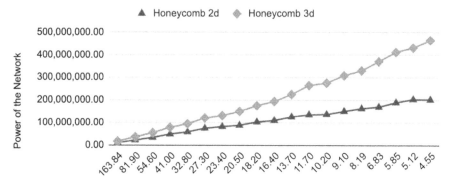

FIGURE 13.7   Power (Honeycomb 2D versus Honeycomb 3D)-Uniform traffic pattern.

pattern. So the maximum improvement in throughput has been observed at 4.55μs with a percentile improvement of 91.46% and the minimum improvement is observed at 163.84μs with a percentile improvement of 14.57%.

13.3.1.1.3   Power of the Network

Power of the network has been found to be improving in the honeycomb 3D interconnection network, which has been found by analyzing the readings at different inter packet arrival delays [28]. This has been shown in Figure 13.7. The Table 13.3. is a comparison of the power of the networks observed in two different design patterns at the given inter packet arrival delay, i.e. time interval in simpler words in uniform traffic pattern. So the maximum improvement in power of the network has been observed at 4.55μs with the percentile improvement of 129.75% and the minimum improvement is observed at 163.84μs with a percentile improvement of 57.46%.

13.3.1.2   Bit-Complement Traffic Pattern

13.3.1.2.1   Latency

Latency has been found to be improving in the honeycomb 3d interconnection network, which has been found by analyzing the readings at different inter packet arrival delays [29]. This has been shown in Figure 13.8. Table 13.4 is a comparison of the latencies observed in two different design patterns at the given inter packet arrival delay, i.e. time interval in simpler words in bit-complement traffic pattern. So the maximum improvement in latency has been observed at 16.40μs with a percentile improvement of 42.57% and the minimum improvement is observed at 4.55μs with a percentile improvement of 15.70%.

13.3.1.2.2   Throughput

Throughput has been found to be improving in the honeycomb 3d interconnection network, which has been found by analyzing the readings at different inter packet

TABLE 13.3

Power of the Network Honeycomb 2D and Honeycomb 3D

	Power of the Network		
Inter Packet Arrival Delay(in µs)	Honeycomb 2d	Honeycomb 3d	Improvement
163.84	11,442,307.69	18,017,621.15	57.46%
81.90	22,779,552.72	37,359,307.36	64.00%
54.60	34,516,129.03	55,793,991.42	61.65%
41.00	49,673,202.61	79,555,555.56	60.16%
32.80	59,305,993.69	95,278,969.96	60.66%
27.30	75,503,355.70	121,363,636.36	60.74%
23.40	82,847,896.44	131,914,893.62	59.23%
20.50	88,580,246.91	150,638,297.87	70.06%
18.20	103,536,977.49	175,982,532.75	69.97%
16.40	110,509,554.14	194,759,825.33	76.24%
13.70	126,315,789.47	225,847,457.63	78.80%
11.70	135,782,747.60	265,384,615.38	95.45%
10.20	137,223,974.76	276,209,677.42	101.28%
9.10	151,257,861.64	309,090,909.09	104.35%
8.19	163,809,523.81	330,769,230.77	101.92%
6.83	170,846,394.98	371,255,060.73	117.30%
5.85	190,259,740.26	412,698,412.70	116.91%
5.12	203,973,509.93	431,906,614.79	111.75%
4.55	202,564,102.56	465,384,615.38	129.75%

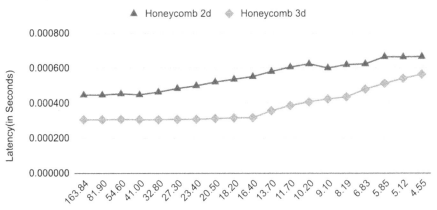

FIGURE 13.8   Latency (Honeycomb 2D versus Honeycomb 3D)-Bit-Complement traffic pattern.

TABLE 13.4
Latency Honeycomb 2D and Honeycomb 3D

	Latency(In Seconds)		
Inter Packet Arrival Delay(in µs)	Honeycomb 2d	Honeycomb 3d	Improvement
163.84	0.000447	0.000306	31.54%
81.90	0.000447	0.000306	31.54%
54.60	0.000454	0.000308	32.16%
41.00	0.000448	0.000306	31.70%
32.80	0.000464	0.000306	34.05%
27.30	0.000484	0.000308	36.36%
23.40	0.000500	0.000308	38.40%
20.50	0.000521	0.000312	40.12%
18.20	0.000537	0.000316	41.15%
16.40	0.000552	0.000317	42.57%
13.70	0.000581	0.000357	38.55%
11.70	0.000606	0.000386	36.30%
10.20	0.000624	0.000407	34.78%
9.10	0.000601	0.000424	29.45%
8.19	0.000620	0.000436	29.68%
6.83	0.000624	0.000480	23.08%
5.85	0.000665	0.000513	22.86%
5.12	0.000663	0.000541	18.40%
4.55	6.66E-04	5.65E-04	15.17%

arrival delays [30,31]. This has been shown in Figure 13.9. The Table 13.5. is a comparison of the throughputs observed in two different design patterns at the given inter packet arrival delay, i.e. time interval in simpler words in bit-complement traffic pattern. So the maximum improvement in throughput has been observed at 8.19µs with the percentile improvement of 141.75% and the minimum improvement is observed at 163.84µs with a percentile improvement of 21.38%.

13.3.1.2.3 Power of the Network

Power of the network has been found to be improving in the honeycomb 3d interconnection network, which has been found by analyzing the readings at different inter packet arrival delays. This has been shown in Graph 4.1.2.3. Table 4.1.2.3. is a comparison of the power of the networks observed in two different design patterns at the given inter packet arrival delay, i.e. time interval in simpler words in bit-complement traffic pattern. So the maximum improvement in power of the network has been observed at 10.20µs with a percentile improvement of 253.4% and the minimum improvement is observed at 163.84µs with a percentile improvement of 77.31%. Similar work is referred to in [32–35] (Figure 13.10) (Table 13.6).

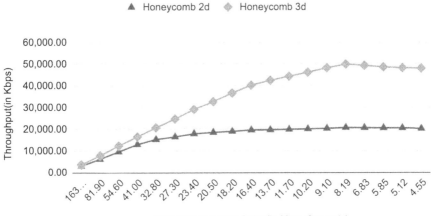

FIGURE 13.9 Throughput (Honeycomb 2d versus Honeycomb 3d)-Bit-Complement traffic pattern.

TABLE 13.5

Throughput (Honeycomb 2d versus Honeycomb 3d)-Bit-Complement traffic pattern

	Throughput(In Kbps)		
Inter Packet Arrival Delay(in μs)	Honeycomb 2d	Honeycomb 3d	Improvement
163.84	3,040.00	3,690.00	21.38%
81.90	6,220.00	7,860.00	26.37%
54.60	9,590.00	12,300.00	28.26%
41.00	12,900.00	16,400.00	27.13%
32.80	15,200.00	20,600.00	35.53%
27.30	16,400.00	24,600.00	50.00%
23.40	17,800.00	29,000.00	62.92%
20.50	18,400.00	32,600.00	77.17%
18.20	18,900.00	36,600.00	93.65%
16.40	19,500.00	40,200.00	106.15%
13.70	19,600.00	42,400.00	116.33%
11.70	19,800.00	44,300.00	123.74%

13.3.1.3 Tornado Traffic Pattern

13.3.1.3.1 Latency

Latency has been found to be improving in the honeycomb 3d interconnection network, which has been found by analyzing the readings at different inter packet

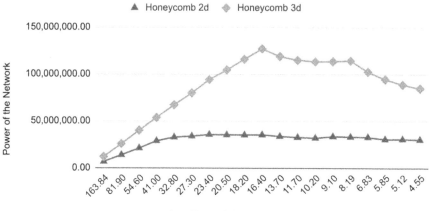

FIGURE 13.10   Power (Honeycomb 2d versus Honeycomb 3d)-Bit-Complement traffic pattern.

TABLE 13.6

Power (Honeycomb 2d versus Honeycomb 3d)-Bit-Complement traffic pattern

	Power of the Network		
Inter Packet Arrival Delay(in μs)	Honeycomb 2d	Honeycomb 3d	Improvement
163.84	6,800,894.85	12,058,823.53	77.31%
81.90	13,914,988.81	25,686,274.51	84.59%
54.60	21,123,348.02	39,935,064.94	89.06%
41.00	28,794,642.86	53,594,771.24	86.13%
32.80	32,758,620.69	67,320,261.44	105.50%
27.30	33,884,297.52	79,870,129.87	135.71%
23.40	35,600,000.00	94,155,844.16	164.48%
20.50	35,316,698.66	104,487,179.49	195.86%
18.20	35,195,530.73	115,822,784.81	229.08%
16.40	35,326,086.96	126,813,880.13	258.98%
13.70	33,734,939.76	118,767,507.00	252.06%
11.70	32,673,267.33	114,766,839.38	251.26%
10.20	32,051,282.05	113,267,813.27	253.40%
9.10	33,610,648.92	113,443,396.23	237.52%
8.19	33,225,806.45	114,220,183.49	243.77%
6.83	32,852,564.10	102,500,000.00	212.00%
5.85	30,676,691.73	94,541,910.33	208.19%
5.12	30,769,230.77	88,909,426.99	188.96%
4.55	30,180,180.18	84,778,761.06	180.91%

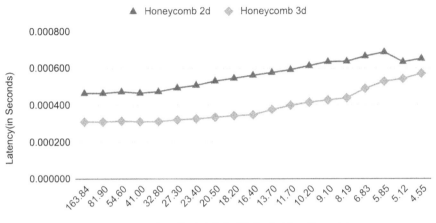

FIGURE 13.11 Latency (Honeycomb 2d versus Honeycomb 3d)-Tornado traffic pattern.

arrival delays. This has been shown in Figure 13.11. Table 13.7 is a comparison of the latencies observed in two different design patterns at the given inter packet arrival delay, i.e. time interval in simpler words in tornado traffic pattern. So the maximum improvement in latency has been observed at 16.40μs with a percentile improvement of 38.15% and the minimum improvement is observed at 4.55μs with a percentile improvement of 12.31%.

13.3.1.3.2 Throughput

Throughput has been found to be improving in the honeycomb 3d interconnection network, which has been found by analyzing the readings at different inter packet arrival delays. This has been shown in Figure 13.12. Table 13.8. is a comparison of the throughputs observed in two different design patterns at the given inter packet arrival delay, i.e. time interval in simpler words in tornado traffic pattern. So the maximum improvement in throughput has been observed at 4.55μs with a percentile improvement of 170.86% and the minimum improvement is observed at 41.00μs with a percentile improvement of 30.40%.

13.3.1.3.3 Power of the Network

Power of the network has been found to be improving in the honeycomb 3d interconnection network, which has been found by analyzing the readings at different inter packet arrival delays. Similar work is referred in [36–38]. This has been shown in Figure 13.13. The Table 13.9 is a comparison of the power of the networks observed in two different design patterns at the given inter packet arrival delay, i.e. time interval in simpler words in tornado traffic patterns. So the maximum improvement in power of the network has been observed at 8.19μs with

TABLE 13.7

Latency(Honeycomb 2d versus Honeycomb 3d)-Tornado traffic pattern

	Latency(In Seconds)		
Inter Packet Arrival Delay(in μs)	Honeycomb 2d	Honeycomb 3d	Improvement
163.84	0.000465	0.000310	33.33%
81.90	0.000465	0.000310	33.33%
54.60	0.000473	0.000314	33.62%
41.00	0.000466	0.000310	33.48%
32.80	0.000473	0.000311	34.25%
27.30	0.000493	0.000320	35.09%
23.40	0.000507	0.000325	35.90%
20.50	0.000530	0.000334	36.98%
18.20	0.000545	0.000342	37.25%
16.40	0.000561	0.000347	38.15%
13.70	0.000576	0.000376	34.72%
11.70	0.000591	0.000399	32.49%
10.20	0.000613	0.000415	32.30%
9.10	0.000634	0.000427	32.65%
8.19	0.000636	0.000438	31.13%
6.83	0.000664	0.000489	26.36%
5.85	0.000686	0.000528	23.03%
5.12	0.000633	0.000542	14.38%
4.55	0.000650	0.000570	12.31%

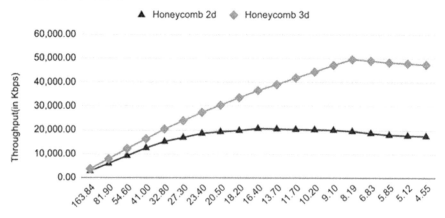

FIGURE 13.12 Throughput (Honeycomb 2d versus Honeycomb 3d)-Tornado traffic pattern.

TABLE 13.8

Throughput (Honeycomb 2d versus Honeycomb 3d)-Tornado traffic pattern

Inter Packet Arrival Delay(in μs)	Throughput(In Kbps)		
	Honeycomb 2d	Honeycomb 3d	Improvement
163.84	2,770.00	3,690.00	33.21%
81.90	5,990.00	7,860.00	31.22%
54.60	9,220.00	12,200.00	32.32%
41.00	12,500.00	16,300.00	30.40%
32.80	15,200.00	20,400.00	34.21%
27.30	16,900.00	23,900.00	41.42%
23.40	18,600.00	27,400.00	47.31%
20.50	19,300.00	30,400.00	57.51%
18.20	19,800.00	33,600.00	69.70%
16.40	20,700.00	36,600.00	76.81%
13.70	20,500.00	39,100.00	90.73%
11.70	20,300.00	41,900.00	106.40%
10.20	20,200.00	44,400.00	119.80%
9.10	20,000.00	47,200.00	136.00%
8.19	19,500.00	49,600.00	154.36%
6.83	18,700.00	49,000.00	162.03%
5.85	18,000.00	48,300.00	168.33%
5.12	17,700.00	47,900.00	170.62%
4.55	17,500.00	47,400.00	170.86%

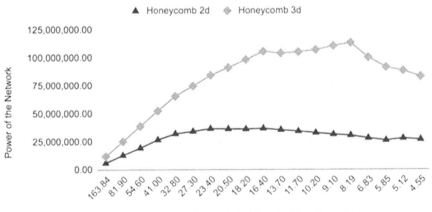

FIGURE 13.13 Power (Honeycomb 2d versus Honeycomb 3d)-Tornado traffic pattern.

TABLE 13.9

Power(Honeycomb 2d versus Honeycomb 3d)-Tornado traffic pattern

	Power of the Network		
Inter Packet Arrival Delay(in µs)	Honeycomb 2d	Honeycomb 3d	Improvement
163.84	5,956,989.25	11,903,225.81	99.82%
81.90	12,881,720.43	25,354,838.71	96.83%
54.60	19,492,600.42	38,853,503.18	99.32%
41.00	26,824,034.33	52,580,645.16	96.02%
32.80	32,135,306.55	65,594,855.31	104.12%
27.30	34,279,918.86	74,687,500.00	117.88%
23.40	36,686,390.53	84,307,692.31	129.81%
20.50	36,415,094.34	91,017,964.07	149.95%
18.20	36,330,275.23	98,245,614.04	170.42%
16.40	36,898,395.72	105,475,504.32	185.85%
13.70	35,590,277.78	103,989,361.70	192.18%
11.70	34,348,561.76	105,012,531.33	205.73%
10.20	32,952,691.68	106,987,951.81	224.67%
9.10	31,545,741.32	110,538,641.69	250.41%
8.19	30,660,377.36	113,242,009.13	269.34%
6.83	28,162,650.60	100,204,498.98	255.81%
5.85	26,239,067.06	91,477,272.73	248.63%
5.12	27,962,085.31	88,376,383.76	216.06%
4.55	26,923,076.92	83,157,894.74	208.87%

the percentile improvement of 269.34% and the minimum improvement is observed at 41µs with a percentile improvement of 96.02%.

13.3.1.4 Neighbor Traffic Pattern

13.3.1.4.1 Latency

Latency has been found to be improving in the honeycomb 3d interconnection network, which has been found by analyzing the readings at different inter packet arrival delays [39,40]. This has been shown in Figure 13.14. Table 13.10. is a comparison of the latencies observed in two different design patterns at the given inter packet arrival delay, i.e. time interval in simpler words in neighbor traffic patterns. So the maximum improvement in latency has been observed at 18.20µs with a percentile improvement of 33.57% and the minimum improvement is observed at 4.55µs with a percentile improvement of 7.14%.

13.3.1.4.2 Throughput

Throughput has been found to be improving in the honeycomb 3d interconnection network, which has been found by analyzing the readings at different inter packet arrival delays. This has been shown in Figure 13.15. The Table 13.11. is a

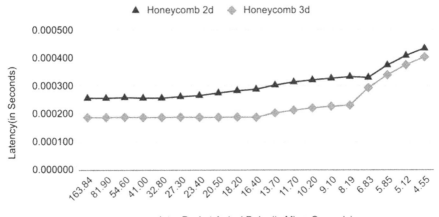

FIGURE 13.14 Latency (Honeycomb 2d versus Honeycomb 3d)-Neighbor traffic pattern.

TABLE 13.10

Latency (Honeycomb 2d versus Honeycomb 3d)-Neighbor traffic pattern

	Latency(In Seconds)		
Inter Packet Arrival Delay(in μs)	Honeycomb 2d	Honeycomb 3d	Improvement
163.84	0.000257	0.000187	27.24%
81.90	0.000257	0.000187	27.24%
54.60	0.000259	0.000188	27.41%
41.00	0.000257	0.000187	27.24%
32.80	0.000257	0.000187	27.24%
27.30	0.000262	0.000188	28.24%
23.40	0.000266	0.000187	29.70%
20.50	0.000275	0.000187	32.00%
18.20	0.000283	0.000188	33.57%
16.40	0.000288	0.000187	35.07%
13.70	0.000303	0.000203	33.00%
11.70	0.000314	0.000213	32.17%
10.20	0.000321	0.000221	31.15%
9.10	0.000327	0.000227	30.58%
8.19	0.000333	0.000231	30.63%
6.83	0.000330	0.000293	11.21%
5.85	0.000374	0.000339	9.36%
5.12	0.000408	0.000375	8.09%
4.55	0.000434	0.000403	7.14%

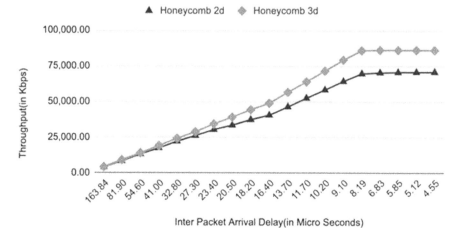

FIGURE 13.15   Throughput (Honeycomb 2d versus Honeycomb 3d)-Neighbor traffic pattern.

TABLE 13.11
Throughput (Honeycomb 2d versus Honeycomb 3d)-Neighbor traffic pattern

	Throughput(In Kbps)		
Inter Packet Arrival Delay(in μs)	Honeycomb 2d	Honeycomb 3d	Improvement
163.84	4,010.00	4,300.00	7.23%
81.90	8,380.00	9,130.00	8.95%
54.60	13,200.00	14,100.00	6.82%
41.00	17,500.00	19,200.00	9.71%
32.80	22,200.00	24,300.00	9.46%
27.30	26,200.00	28,900.00	10.31%
23.40	30,400.00	34,400.00	13.16%
20.50	33,500.00	39,200.00	17.01%
18.20	37,400.00	44,500.00	18.98%
16.40	40,600.00	49,000.00	20.69%
13.70	46,500.00	56,600.00	21.72%
11.70	52,500.00	64,000.00	21.90%
10.20	58,300.00	71,500.00	22.64%
9.10	64,300.00	79,200.00	23.17%
8.19	69,700.00	85,900.00	23.24%
6.83	70,400.00	86,200.00	22.44%
5.85	70,700.00	86,200.00	21.92%
5.12	70,800.00	86,200.00	21.75%
4.55	70,800.00	86,100.00	21.61%

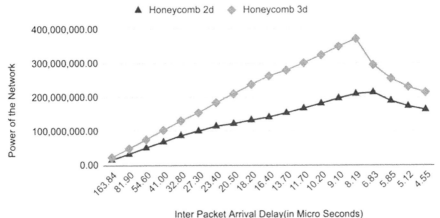

FIGURE 13.16   Power (Honeycomb 2d versus Honeycomb 3d)-Neighbor traffic pattern.

comparison of the throughputs observed in two different design patterns at the given inter packet arrival delay, i.e. time interval in simpler words in neighbor traffic patterns. So the maximum improvement in throughput has been observed at 8.19μs with a percentile improvement of 23.24% and the minimum improvement is observed at 163.84μs with a percentile improvement of 7.23%.

13.3.1.4.3   Power of the Network
Power of the network has been found to be improving in the honeycomb 3d interconnection network, which has been found by analyzing the readings at different inter packet arrival delays. This has been shown in Figure 13.16. Table 13.12 is a comparison of the power of the networks observed in two different design patterns at the given inter packet arrival delay, i.e. time interval in simpler words in neighbor traffic patterns. So the maximum improvement in power of the network has been observed at 16.40μs with a percentile improvement of 85.87% and the minimum improvement is observed at 4.55μs with a percentile improvement of 30.96%.

13.3.2   Honeycomb 3D Versus Honeycomb 3D Toroidal

In all aspects, it has been observed that the honeycomb 3d toroidal interconnection network has proved to be giving better efficiency as compared to the honeycomb 3d interconnection network.

13.3.2.1   Uniform Traffic Pattern

13.3.2.1.1   Latency
Latency has been found to be improving in the honeycomb 3d toroidal inter-connection network, which has been found by analyzing the readings at different inter packet arrival delays. This has been shown in Figure 13.17. The maximum

TABLE 13.12

Power(Honeycomb 2d versus Honeycomb 3d)-Neighbor traffic pattern

	Power of the Network		
Inter Packet Arrival Delay(in μs)	Honeycomb 2d	Honeycomb 3d	Improvement
163.84	15,603,112.84	22,994,652.41	47.37%
81.90	32,607,003.89	48,823,529.41	49.73%
54.60	50,965,250.97	75,000,000.00	47.16%
41.00	68,093,385.21	102,673,796.79	50.78%
32.80	86,381,322.96	129,946,524.06	50.43%
27.30	100,000,000.00	153,723,404.26	53.72%
23.40	114,285,714.29	183,957,219.25	60.96%
20.50	121,818,181.82	209,625,668.45	72.08%
18.20	132,155,477.03	236,702,127.66	79.11%
16.40	140,972,222.22	262,032,085.56	85.87%
13.70	153,465,346.53	278,817,733.99	81.68%
11.70	167,197,452.23	300,469,483.57	79.71%
10.20	181,619,937.69	323,529,411.76	78.14%
9.10	196,636,085.63	348,898,678.41	77.43%
8.19	209,309,309.31	371,861,471.86	77.66%
6.83	213,333,333.33	294,197,952.22	37.91%
5.85	189,037,433.16	254,277,286.14	34.51%
5.12	173,529,411.76	229,866,666.67	32.47%
4.55	163,133,640.55	213,647,642.68	30.96%

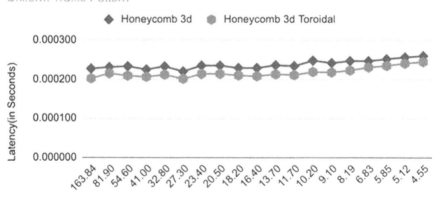

FIGURE 13.17   Latency (Honeycomb 3d versus Honeycomb 3d toroidal)-Uniform traffic pattern.

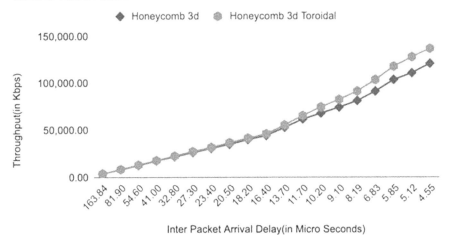

FIGURE 13.18   Throughput (Honeycomb 3d versus Honeycomb 3d toroidal)-Uniform traffic pattern.

improvement in latency has been observed at 10.20µs with a percentile improvement of 11.69% and the minimum improvement is observed at 4.55µs with a percentile improvement of 5.77%.

13.3.2.1.2   Throughput

Throughput has been found to be improving in the honeycomb 3d toroidal interconnection network, which has been found by analyzing the readings at different inter packet arrival delays. This has been shown in Figure 13.18. The maximum improvement in throughput has been observed at 6.83µs with a percentile improvement of 13.41% and the minimum improvement is observed at 81.90µs with a percentile improvement of 3.36%.

13.3.2.1.3   Power of the Network

Power of the network has been found to be improving in the honeycomb 3d toroidal interconnection network, which has been found by analyzing the readings at different inter packet arrival delays. This has been shown in Figure 13.19. The maximum improvement in power of the network has been observed at 8.19µs with a percentile improvement of 24.46% and the minimum improvement is observed at 81.90µs with a percentile improvement of 11.05%.

13.3.2.2   Bit-Complement Traffic Pattern

13.3.2.2.1   Latency

Latency has been found to be improving in the honeycomb 3d toroidal interconnection network, which has been found by analyzing the readings at different

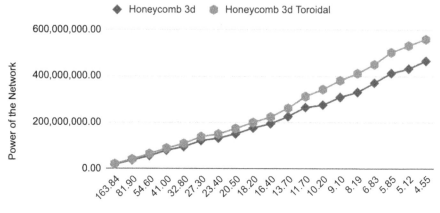

FIGURE 13.19   Power (Honeycomb 3d versus Honeycomb 3d toroidal)-Uniform traffic pattern.

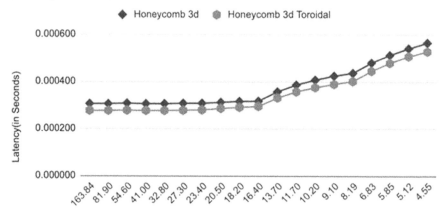

FIGURE 13.20   Latency (Honeycomb 3d versus Honeycomb 3d toroidal)-Bit-Complement traffic pattern.

inter packet arrival delays. This has been shown in Figure 13.20. The maximum improvement in latency has been observed at 54.60µs with a percentile improvement of 9.74% and the minimum improvement is observed at 5.12µs with a percentile improvement of 6.28%.

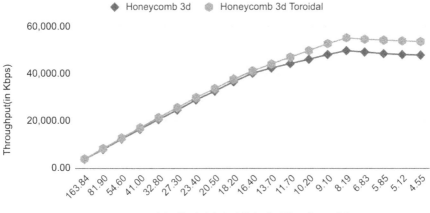

FIGURE 13.21 Throughput (Honeycomb 3d versus Honeycomb 3d toroidal)-Bit-Complement traffic pattern.

13.3.2.2.2 Throughput

Throughput has been found to be improving in the honeycomb 3d toroidal interconnection network, which has been found by analyzing the readings at different inter packet arrival delays. This has been shown in Figure 13.21. The maximum improvement in throughput has been observed at 5.12μs with a percentile improvement of 12.27% and the minimum improvement is observed at 16.40μs with a percentile improvement of 2.49.

13.3.2.2.3 Power of the Network

Power of the network has been found to be improving in the honeycomb 3d toroidal interconnection network, which has been found by analyzing the readings at different inter packet arrival delays. This has been shown in Figure 13.22. The maximum improvement in power of the network has been observed at 8.19μs with a percentile improvement of 20.74% and the minimum improvement is observed at 16.40μs with a percentile improvement of 10.13%.

13.3.2.3 Tornado Traffic Pattern

13.3.2.3.1 Latency

Latency has been found to be improving in the honeycomb 3d toroidal interconnection network, which has been found by analyzing the readings at different inter packet arrival delays. This has been shown in Figure 13.23. The maximum improvement in latency has been observed at 13.70μs with a percentile improvement of 11.97% and the minimum improvement is observed at 5.12μs with a percentile improvement of 7.93%.

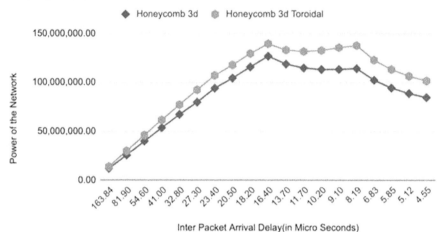

FIGURE 13.22 Power (Honeycomb 3d versus Honeycomb 3d toroidal)-Bit-Complement traffic pattern.

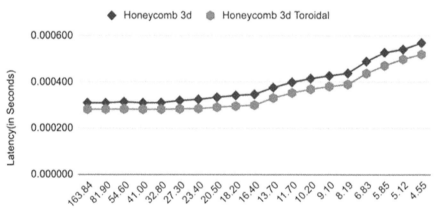

FIGURE 13.23 Latency (Honeycomb 3d versus Honeycomb 3d toroidal)-Tornado traffic pattern.

13.3.2.3.2 Throughput

Throughput has been found to be improving in the honeycomb 3d toroidal interconnection network, which has been found by analyzing the readings at different inter packet arrival delays. This has been shown in Figure 13.24. The maximum improvement in throughput has been observed at 4.55μs with a percentile

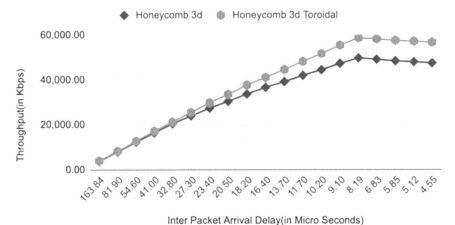

FIGURE 13.24 Throughput (Honeycomb 3d versus Honeycomb 3d toroidal)-Tornado traffic pattern.

improvement of 19.62% and the minimum improvement is observed at 32.80μs with a percentile improvement of 3.92%.

13.3.2.3.3 Power of the Network

Power of the network has been found to be improving in the honeycomb 3d toroidal interconnection network, which has been found by analyzing the readings at different inter packet arrival delays. This has been shown in Figure 13.25. The

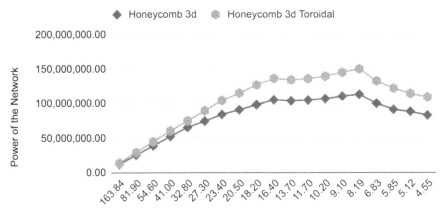

FIGURE 13.25 Power (Honeycomb 3d versus Honeycomb 3d toroidal)-Tornado traffic pattern.

maximum improvement in power of the network has been observed at 5.85μs with a percentile improvement of 33.45% and the minimum improvement is observed at 132.80μs with a percentile improvement of 14.61%.

13.3.2.4 Neighbor Traffic Pattern

13.3.2.4.1 Latency

Latency has been found to be improving in the honeycomb 3d toroidal inter-connection network, which has been found by analyzing the readings at different inter packet arrival delays. This has been shown in Figure 13.26. The maximum improvement in latency has been observed at 8.19μs with a percentile improvement of 23.81% and the minimum improvement is observed at 4.55μs with a percentile improvement of 11.66%.

13.3.2.4.2 Throughput

Throughput has been found to be improving in the honeycomb 3d toroidal interconnection network, which has been found by analyzing the readings at different inter packet arrival delays. This has been shown in Figure 13.27. The maximum improvement in throughput has been observed at 4.55μs with a percentile improvement of 14.52% and the minimum improvement is observed at 54.60μs with a percentile improvement of 2.84%.

13.3.2.4.3 Power of the Network

Power of the network has been found to be improving in the honeycomb 3d toroidal interconnection network, which has been found by analyzing the readings at

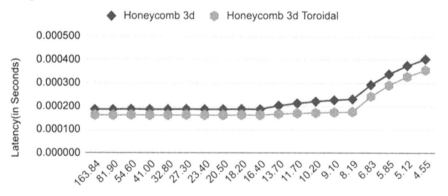

FIGURE 13.26 Latency (Honeycomb 3d versus Honeycomb 3d toroidal)-Neighbor traffic pattern.

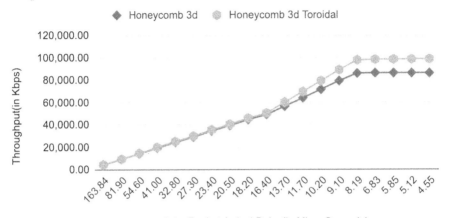

FIGURE 13.27 Throughput (Honeycomb 3d versus Honeycomb 3d toroidal)-Neighbor traffic pattern.

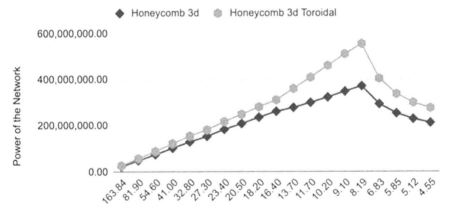

FIGURE 13.28 Power (Honeycomb 3d versus Honeycomb 3d toroidal)-Neighbor traffic pattern.

different inter packet arrival delays. This has been shown in Figure 13.28. The maximum improvement in power of the network has been observed at 8.19μs with a percentile improvement of 49.28% and the minimum improvement is observed at 54.60μs with a percentile improvement of 18.61%.

13.4   HONEYCOMB 2D TOROIDAL VERSUS HONEYCOMB 3D TOROIDAL

In all aspects, it has been observed that the honeycomb 3d toroidal interconnection network has proved to be giving better efficiency as compared to the honeycomb 2d toroidal interconnection network.

13.4.1   UNIFORM TRAFFIC PATTERN

13.4.1.1   Latency

Latency has been found to be improving in the honeycomb 3d toroidal interconnection network, which has been found by analyzing the readings at different inter packet arrival delays. This has been shown in Figure 13.29. The maximum improvement in latency has been observed at 9.10µs with a percentile improvement of 26.85% and the minimum improvement is observed at 4.55µs with a percentile improvement of 19.67%.

13.4.1.2   Throughput

Throughput has been found to be improving in the honeycomb 3d toroidal interconnection network, which has been found by analyzing the readings at different inter packet arrival delays. This has been shown in Figure 13.30. The maximum improvement in throughput has been observed at 4.55µs with a percentile improvement of 65.26% and the minimum improvement is observed at 163.84µs with a percentile improvement of 8.48%.

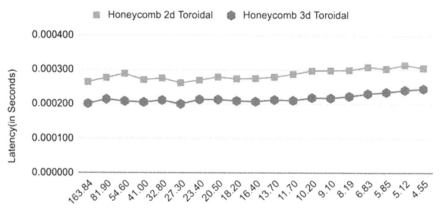

FIGURE 13.29   Latency (Honeycomb 2d toroidal versus Honeycomb 3d toroidal)-Uniform traffic pattern.

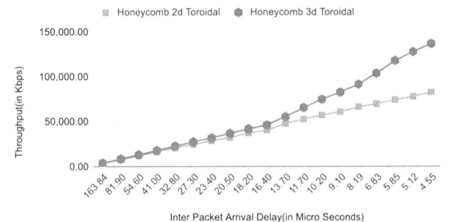

FIGURE 13.30   Throughput (Honeycomb 2d toroidal versus Honeycomb 3d toroidal)-Uniform traffic pattern.

13.4.1.3   Power of the Network

Power of the network has been found to be improving in the honeycomb 3d toroidal interconnection network, which has been found by analyzing the readings at different inter packet arrival delays. This has been shown in Figure 13.31. The

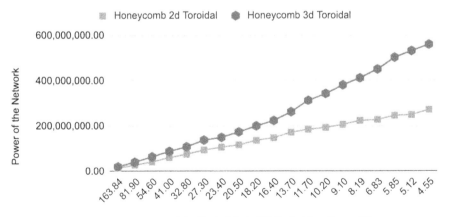

FIGURE 13.31   Power (Honeycomb 2d toroidal versus Honeycomb 3d toroidal)-Uniform traffic pattern.

maximum improvement in power of the network has been observed at 5.12µs with a percentile improvement of 113.26% and the minimum improvement is observed at 23.40µs with a percentile improvement of 40.14%.

13.4.2 TRAFFIC PATTERN2BIT-COMPLEMENT

13.4.2.1 Latency

Latency has been found to be improving in the honeycomb 3d toroidal interconnection network, which has been found by analyzing the readings at different inter packet arrival delays. This has been shown in Figure 13.32. The maximum improvement in latency has been observed at 18.20µs with a percentile improvement of 27.43% and the minimum improvement is observed at 4.55µs with a percentile improvement of 10.51%.

13.4.2.2 Throughput

Throughput has been found to be improving in the honeycomb 3d toroidal interconnection network, which has been found by analyzing the readings at different inter packet arrival delays. This has been shown in Figure 13.33. The maximum improvement in throughput has been observed at 8.19µs with a percentile improvement of 43.26% and the minimum improvement is observed at 41µs with a percentile improvement of 12.50%.

13.4.2.3 Power of the Network

Power of the network has been found to be improving in the honeycomb 3d toroidal interconnection network, which has been found by analyzing the readings at

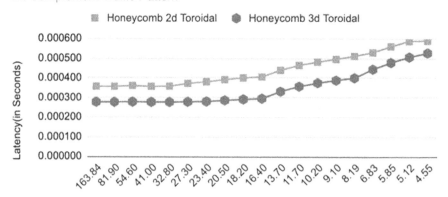

FIGURE 13.32 Latency (Honeycomb 2d toroidal versus Honeycomb 3d toroidal)-Bit-Complement traffic pattern.

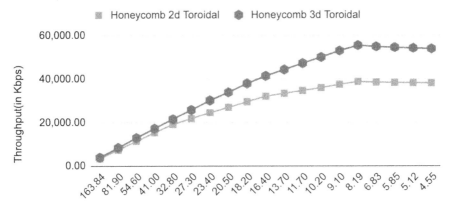

FIGURE 13.33 Throughput (Honeycomb 2d toroidal versus Honeycomb 3d toroidal)-Bit-Complement traffic pattern.

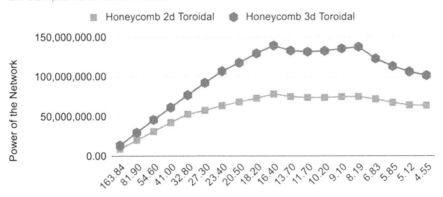

FIGURE 13.34 Power (Honeycomb 2d toroidal versus Honeycomb 3d toroidal)-Bit-Complement traffic pattern.

different inter packet arrival delays. This has been shown in Figure 13.34. The maximum improvement in power of the network has been observed at 8.19µs with a percentile improvement of 82.92% and the minimum improvement is observed at 41µs with a percentile improvement of 44.99%.

13.4.3 Tornado Traffic Pattern

13.4.3.1 Latency

Latency has been found to be improving in the honeycomb 3d toroidal inter-connection network, which has been found by analyzing the readings at different inter packet arrival delays. The Figure 13.35. is a comparison of the latencies observed in two different design patterns at the given inter packet arrival delay, i.e. time interval in simpler words in tornado traffic pattern. The maximum improvement in latency has been observed at 16.40μs with a percentile improvement of 27.71% and the minimum improvement is observed at 4.55μs with a percentile improvement of 15.45%.

13.4.3.2 Throughput

Throughput has been found to be improving in the honeycomb 3d toroidal interconnection network, which has been found by analyzing the readings at different inter packet arrival delays. This has been shown in Figure 13.36. The maximum improvement in throughput has been observed at 4.55μs with a percentile improvement of 101.78% and the minimum improvement is observed at 32.80μs with a percentile improvement of 10.99%.

13.4.3.3 Power of the Network

Power of the network has been found to be improving in the honeycomb 3d toroidal interconnection network, which has been found by analyzing the readings at different inter packet arrival delays. This has been shown in Figure 13.37. The maximum improvement in power of the network has been observed at 8.19μs with a percentile improvement of 147.05% and the minimum improvement is observed at 32.80μs with a percentile improvement of 40.51%.

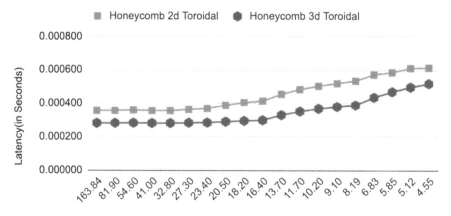

FIGURE 13.35 Latency (Honeycomb 2d toroidal versus Honeycomb 3d toroidal)-Tornado traffic pattern.

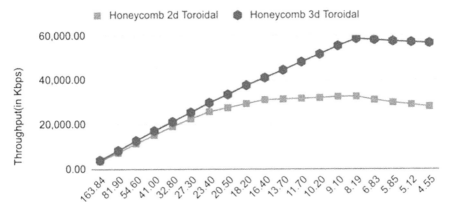

FIGURE 13.36   Throughput (Honeycomb 2d toroidal versus Honeycomb 3d toroidal)-Tornado traffic pattern.

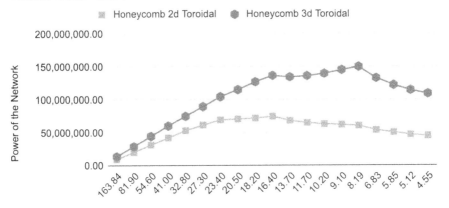

FIGURE 13.37   Power (Honeycomb 2d toroidal versus Honeycomb 3d toroidal)-Tornado traffic pattern.

13.4.4   NEIGHBOR TRAFFIC PATTERN

13.4.4.1   Latency

Latency has been found to be improving in the honeycomb 3d toroidal interconnection network, which has been found by analyzing the readings at different inter packet arrival delays. This has been shown in Figure 13.38. The maximum

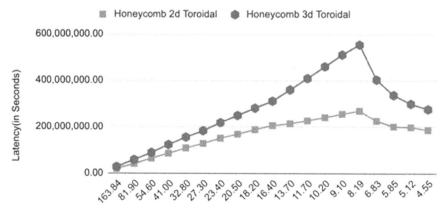

FIGURE 13.38 Latency (Honeycomb 2d toroidal versus Honeycomb 3d toroidal)-Neighbor traffic pattern.

improvement in latency has been observed at 8.19μs with a percentile improvement of 38.46% and the minimum improvement is observed at 4.55μs with a percentile improvement of 14.22%.

13.4.4.2 Throughput

Throughput has been found to be improving in the honeycomb 3d toroidal interconnection network, which has been found by analyzing the readings at different inter packet arrival delays. This has been shown in Figure 13.39. The maximum improvement in throughput has been observed at 5.12μs with a percentile improvement of 27.10% and the minimum improvement is observed at 54.60μs with a percentile improvement of 3.57%.

13.4.4.3 Power of the Network

Power of the network has been found to be improving in the honeycomb 3d toroidal interconnection network, which has been found by analyzing the readings at different inter packet arrival delays. This is shown in Figure 13.40. the maximum improvement in power of the network has been observed at 8.19μs with a percentile improvement of 105.92% and the minimum improvement is observed at 54.60μs with a percentile improvement of 38.52%.

13.5 CONCLUSION

After having a complete set of results we have found honeycomb 3d toroidal is giving the best results. This is known to provide the best efficiency and high fault

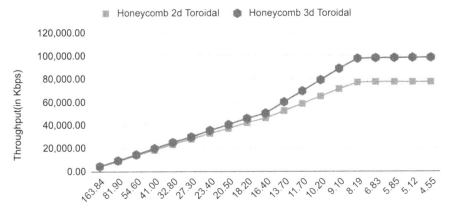

FIGURE 13.39 Throughput (Honeycomb 2d toroidal versus Honeycomb 3d toroidal)-Neighbor traffic pattern.

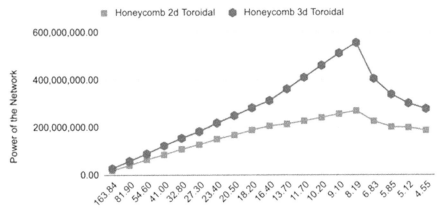

FIGURE 13.40 Power (Honeycomb 2d toroidal versus Honeycomb 3d toroidal)-Neighbor traffic pattern.

tolerance. Further, we have some outcomes based upon traffic patterns as well. This is known to provide a wider scope of discussion.

From the results obtained from the simulation it is clear that the proposed topology honeycomb 3D mesh is better in comparison to proposed topology honeycomb 2D mesh.

The purpose of our methodology was to increase throughput and decrease the latency of honeycomb mesh so as we have worked on 4 traffic patterns those are Bit-complement traffic, Uniform Distributed traffic, Tornado traffic, and Neighbor traffic in all of the traffic patterns the throughput of honeycomb 3D mesh is more than honeycomb 2D mesh and latency of honeycomb 3D mesh is less than honeycomb 2D mesh. We have also introduced more fault tolerant links in honeycomb 3D mesh as earlier there were very less fault tolerant links in honeycomb 2D mesh which is a disadvantage, due to which it was not fault tolerant. Thus, with increased throughput and fault tolerance also with decreased latency honeycomb 3D mesh is far better than honeycomb 2D mesh.

The massive increase in the number of connected devices with the advent of the Internet of Things are calls for self-organizing and dynamic networks. The state-of-the-art wireless mesh networking protocols provide self-organizing networks that do not address the demands of 5 G networks such as low latency and high reliability. In this demonstration, we exhibit how we build a reliable low latency network out of a chaotic and dynamic mesh network. We combine the principles of opportunistic routing and network coding to achieve this. We let the audience interact with the nodes of the wireless mesh networks, i.e. causing node failures, link changes, etc. We demonstrate how our mesh network retains all of its flows intact without any service interruption despite flows intact without any service interruption despite these interactions and node failures.

REFERENCES

1. A. Punhani, Nitin and P. Kumar, "A modified diagonal mesh interconnection network," 2014 Annual IEEE India Conference (INDICON), Pune, 2014, pp. 1–6.
2. W. J. Dally, and B. Towles, Principles and practices of interconnection networks, San Francisco, CA, USA: Morgan Kaufmann, 2004.
3. Y.-g. Wanga, H.-m. Dub, and X.-b. Shena, "Topological properties and routing algorithm for semidiagonal torus networks", The Journal of China Universities of Posts and Telecommunications, vol. 18, Issue 5, pp. 64–70. October 2011.
4. C. D. Thompson, "Area-time complexity," In Proc. Eleventh Annu. ACM Symp. The Theory of Computing, Apr. 1979, pp. 81–88.
5. B. Grot, J. Hestness, S. W. Keckler, and O. Mutlu, "Express cube topologies for on-chip interconnects," 2009 IEEE 15th International Symposium on High Performance Computer Architecture, Raleigh, NC, 2009, pp. 163–174.
6. A. Punhani, and P. Kumar Nitin, "Diagonal connected T mesh," Indian J. Sci. Technol, vol. 9.32, pp. 1–7, 2016.
7. C. Decayeux, and D. Seme, "3D honeycomb network: modeling, topological properties, addressing scheme, and optimal routing algorithm," in IEEE Transactions on Parallel and Distributed Systems, vol. 16, no. 9, pp. 875–884, Sept. 2005.
8. A. Punhani, P. Kumar, and Nitin, "A horizontal fat mesh interconnection network," 2017 Tenth International Conference on Contemporary Computing (IC3), Noida, 2017, pp. 1–5.
9. A. Varga and R. Hornig. "An overview of the OMNeT++ simulation environment," 60, 2008. 10.1145/1416222.1416290.
10. S. Yadav and C. R. Krishna, " CCTorus: A new torus topology for interconnection networks," in Int'l Conference on Advanced Computational Technologies & Creative Media (ICACTCM'2014), Pattaya (Thailand), Aug. 14-15, 2014, pp. 8–14.

11. Nitin and D. S. Chauhan, "Comparative analysis of traffic patterns on k– ary n–tree using adaptive algorithms based on burton normal form," The Journal of Supercomputing, vol. 59, no. 2, pp. 569–588, 2012.

12. K. W. Tang, and S. A. Padubidri, "Diagonal and toroidal mesh networks", IEEE Transactions on Computers, vol. 43, no. 7, pp. 815–826, 1994.

13. K. W. Tang and S. A. Padubidri, "Routing and diameter analysis of diagonal mesh networks," in Proc. Inr. Conf Parallel Processing, St. Charles, IL, Aug. 17-21 1992, pp. 1–143-150.

14. J. Duato, S. Yalamanchili, and L. Ni, "Interconnection Networks—An Engineering Approach," Morgan Kaufmann, 2002.

15. K. Feng, Y. Ye, and J. Xu, "A formal study on topology and floor plan characteristics of mesh and torus-based optical networks-on-chip" Elsevier Journal of Microprocessors and Microsystems, 2012. DOI:10.1016/j.micpro.2012.06.010

16. L. K. Arora, and R. Kumar, "Alternatives of XY-routing for mesh," – in: Special Issue of International Journal of Computer Application ICNICT, 2012, pp. 6–8.

17. Y. Wang, H. Du, and X. Shen, "Topological properties and routing algorithm for semi-diagonal torus networks," – J. China Univ. Posts Telecommunication, vol. 18, no 5, pp. 64–70, 2011.

18. J. Carle and J. F. Myoupo, "Topological properties and optimal routing algorithms for three dimensional hexagonal networks," Proc. Int'l Conf. High-Performance Computing in the Asia-Pacific Region (HPC-Asia 2000), 2000, pp. 116–121.

19. M. S. Chen, K. G. Shin, and D. D. Kandlur, "Addressing, routing and broadcasting in hexagonal mesh multiprocessors," IEEE Trans. Computers, vol. 39, no. 1, pp. 10–18, Jan. 1990.

20. J.-F. Myoupo, H. NDamas, and D. Seme, "Hexagonal mesh: A new addressing scheme and an optimal routing algorithm," Proc. Int'l Symp. Parallel and Distributed Computing and Networks, PDCN '02, 2002.

21. I. Stojmenovic, "Honeycomb networks: Topological properties and communication algorithms," IEEE Trans. Parallel and Distributed Systems, vol. 8, no. 10, pp. 1036–1042, Oct. 1997.

22. P. Gratz, B. Grot, and S. W. Keckler. "Regional congestion awareness for load balance in networks-on-chip," in International Symposium on High-Performance Computer Architecture, February 2008, pp. 203–214.

23. H.-S. Wang, X. Zhu, L.-S. Peh, and S. Malik, Orion: a PowerPerformance Simulator for Interconnection Networks. International Symposium on Microarchitecture, November 2002, pp 294–305.

24. R. Mullins, A. West, and S. Moore. "Low-latency virtual channel routers for on-chip networks," in International Symposium on Computer Architecture, June 2004, pp. 188–197.

25. J. Duato, S. Yalamanchili, and L. M. Ni, Interconnection networks: An engineering approach, Morgan Kaufmann, 2003.

26. A. Punhani, P. Kumar, and Nitin, "Routing for Center Concentrated Mesh", International Journal of Intelligent Engineering and Systems, vol. 10, no. 1, pp. 86–94, Feb. 2017.

27. T. W. James, Dally; Brian Patrick, Principles and Practices of Interconnection Networks Elsevier, 2004.

28. C. Sun, C-HO Chen, G. Kurian, et al., "DSENT—a tool connecting emerging photonics with electronics for opto-electronic networks-on-chip modeling. 2012 IEEE/ACM Sixth Int," Symp. Networks-on-Chip, IEEE, 2012, pp 201–210.

29. R. M. Francis, Exploring networks-on-chip for FPGAs. Ph.D. diss., University of Cambridge, 2009.

30. Z. Zhang, A. Greiner, and S. Taktak, "A reconfigurable routing algorithm for a fault-tolerant 2D- Mesh Network-on-Chip," Proc Des Autom Conf, 2008, pp. 441–446.

31. V. Juyal et al., "On exploiting dynamic trusted routing scheme in delay tolerant networks," Wireless Personal Communications, vol. 112, pp. 1705–1718, 2020.

32. M. N. R. D. S. Murali, and V. Sharma, "Performance analysis of DGA-driven botnets using artificial neural networks," 2022 10th International Conference on Reliability, Infocom Technologies and Optimization (Trends and Future Directions) (ICRITO), 2022, pp. 1–6, doi: 10.1109/ICRITO56286.2022.9965044.

33. V. Juyal et al., "Opportunistic message forwarding in self organized cluster based DTN," 2017 International Conference on Infocom Technologies and Unmanned Systems (Trends and Future Directions)(ICTUS). IEEE, 2017.

34. V. Juyal et al., "Performance comparison of DTN multicasting routing algorithms-opportunities and challenges," 2017 International Conference on Intelligent Sustainable Systems (ICISS). IEEE, 2017.

35. V. Juyal, A. V. Singh, and R. Saggar, "Message multicasting in near-real time routing for delay/disruption tolerant network," 2015 IEEE International Conference on Computational Intelligence & Communication Technology, Ghaziabad, India, 2015, pp. 385–390, doi: 10.1109/CICT.2015.79.

36. V. Juyal, N. Pandey, and R. Saggar, "Impact of varying buffer space for routing protocols in delay tolerant networks," 2016 International Conference on Communication and Signal Processing (ICCSP), Melmaruvathur, India, 2016, pp. 2152–2156, doi: 10.1109/ICCSP.2016.7754562.

37. V. Juyal, N. Pandey, and R. Saggar, "A heuristic light weight security algorithm for resource constrained DTN routing," 2016 IEEE International Conference on Computational Intelligence and Computing Research (ICCIC), Chennai, India, 2016, pp. 1–4, doi: 10.1109/ICCIC.2016.7919695.

38. A. Raj, V. Sharma and A. K. Shanu, "Comparative analysis Of security and privacy technique for federated learning In IOT based devices," 2022 3rd International Conference on Computation, Automation and Knowledge Management (ICCAKM), Dubai, United Arab Emirates, 2022, pp. 1–5, doi: 10.1109/ICCAKM54721.2022.9990152.

39. P. Ajmani, V. Sharma, P. Samuel, K. Somasundaram, and V. Vidhya, "Patient behaviour analysis and social health predictions through IoMT," 2022 10th International Conference on Reliability, Infocom Technologies and Optimization (Trends and Future Directions) (ICRITO), 2022, pp. 1–6, doi: 10.1109/ICRITO56286.2022.9964846.

40. M. A. Ali, B. Balamurugan, R. K. Dhanaraj, and V. Sharma, "IoT and Blockchain based smart agriculture monitoring and intelligence security system," 2022 3rd International Conference on Computation, Automation and Knowledge Management (ICCAKM), Dubai, United Arab Emirates, 2022, pp. 1–7, doi: 10.1109/ICCAKM54721.2022.9990243.

14 Open Research Challenges in Wireless Technologies Case Study

M. Yogeshwari
Department Information Technology, School of Computing Sciences, Vels University, VISTAS, Chennai, Tamil Nadu, India

A. Prasanth
Department of Electronics and Communication Engineering, Sri Venkateswara College of Engineering, Sriperumbudur, Tamil Nadu, India

14.1 INTRODUCTION

The wireless network spread its wings in the late 1970s. The growing number of mobile and handheld communication devices act as a backbone in the growth of the wireless network. These networks provide the facility of ubiquitous computing and information sharing regardless of users' locations. Wireless networks are broadly classified as "infrastructure" and "infrastructure-less" networks. The infrastructure wireless networks have definite access points connected through wires. The mobile users are connected to these access points through a wireless communication medium. Cellular networks are an example of such networks. The infrastructure-less wireless networks have no fixed gateway for the communication path. These networks are known as "wireless ad hoc networks (WANET)." They can change their locations and configure themselves on the fly, also known as "mobile ad hoc networks (MANET)."

14.1.1 Wireless Ad Hoc Network

The wireless ad hoc networks have no fixed infrastructure. Ad hoc network is a group of autonomous devices communicating with one another deprived of the aid of any central authority and fixed infrastructure [1,2]. Figure 14.1 represents a wireless ad hoc network.

In these networks, every node functions as end point, and a router forwards data to every alternative node that might well be multiple hops away from one another [3]. And the nodes might well be mobile in nature, making it look like a very dynamically changing topology in the network [4].

DOI: 10.1201/9781003389231-14

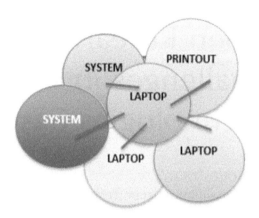

FIGURE 14.1   "Wireless Ad hoc Network".

14.1.1.1   Historical Review

The WANETs are classified into four generations. The first generation starts in 1972. The DARPA ("Defense Advanced Research Projects Agency") started exploration and analysis on the practicability of involving "packet-switched radio" communications technology to produce consistent computer communications [5]. The packet radio network (PRNET) in amalgamation with "ALOHA (Arial Locations of Hazardous Atmospheres)" and "CSMA (Carrier Sense Medium Access)" has evolved through the years (1973–987) to be a reliable, robust, and operational experimental network [6].

The 2nd generation of ad hoc network evolved in the late years of 1980s. The "Survivable Adaptive Radio Networks (SURAN)" program gears the development of ad hoc networks. These enhancements and improvements in the ad hoc networks have considerably provided an atmosphere for mobile nodes on the battlefield [7]. This had made the mobile nodes to survive even without the availability of fixed infrastructure. The 2nd generation of ad hoc network has taken along an exponential growth in the performance of radios by reducing them to smaller and inexpensive networks and by making them highly robust to attacks.

In the late years of the 1990s and in early 2000, the 3rd generation of wireless ad hoc networks brought the concept of commercialization of ad hoc network with the rapid enhancements in mobile technology [8]. In the meanwhile, the revolutionary idea of the grouping of mobile nodes was put on the table at several research conferences and seminars. Mobile ad hoc network was revived as a potential technology in the field of computer communications. And looking at the possible growth and vast adaptability of the technology, "Mobile ad hoc network" working committee was organized by the "Internet Engineering Task Force (IETF)" in the mid years of 1990s in order to standardize the protocols of networking for the recently accepted wireless technology [9,10].

The 4th generation of communication networks that came into picture in 2010 are actually an "Integrated Global Network," which is basically based on the approach of open-systems. Such integrated network is an intelligent concept that makes all wireless networks assemble with the wired backbone networks and converge all the multimedia, data traffic, and voice over a core network, which is based on a single IP.

14.1.1.2 Characteristics

- **Autonomous functions:** In a wireless ad hoc network, each node is autonomous. Every node functions as a host as well as a router. The absence of fixed infrastructure and central authority compels node to perform router functionality in addition to its basic operations as a host.
- **Distributed operation:** These networks are self-organizing in nature. In these networks, the central authority is also absent, hence the administration of the network is respectively distributed in between the nodes, which then collaborates amongst themselves and implements functions like routing and security in the network.
- **Routing with multiple hops:** The range of transmission of wireless nodes is fixed. The node that does not appear in the direct range of transmission of the destination node has to forward the packets to the intermediate nodes for communication.
- **Dynamic topology:** The nodes can change their positions, and that is why they move within network with varying speed and direction. Therefore the network topology changes dynamically and randomly. So the nodes' connectivity may vary with time. The mobility pattern of nodes is considered in routing and other management activities of the network.
- **Inconsistent medium parameters:** The wireless medium has high bit-error rates. The medium in which the nodes communicate is prone to noise, interference, and signal weakening and has limited bandwidth compared to a wired network. In a few stations, the physical link between the users has numerous connecting links, and additionally, the available links are often diversified.

14.1.1.3 Applications

Wireless ad hoc networks have increased their applicability in various fields as these networks can be deployed at any place at any time with limited or no communication infrastructure. The following are some of its important applications.

a. **Tactical Networks:** The wireless ad hoc network was initially developed for military applications. Military applications require "on-the-move" communications. WANETs comply with "on-the-move" condition because of infrastructure-less architecture and fast deployment [11,12]. MANETs are used in army "hopping" mines, in platoons, and anywhere troops communicate in unfamiliar territory to provide them an advantage in the battlefield. Tactical MANETS frequently take on their shapes automatically throughout the task, so when the mission is finished or deactivated, the network "disappears." Typically, it is referred to as a "on-the-fly" wireless tactical network.

b. **Emergency Services:** Another important application area of ad hoc network is emergency services like search rescue and search operation during the disaster recovery process [13,14].

For example, suppose an aeroplane has an emergency landing due to some mechanical fault at some unreachable place like in a forest or in water and the airline has provided wireless device attached to life jacket under each seat. Then the search and rescue team finds it easier to locate the victim's exact positions.

Similarly, in the case of natural disasters like earthquakes, floods, etc., where the disaster may destroy existing communication infrastructure, the emergency response groups will create ad hoc networks to swap the destroyed infrastructure and enable the groups to better synchronize their efforts.

The use of wireless sensor networks in the healthcare system is extremely important. The patient health may be monitored 24×7 through sensor devices for efficient diagnosis. It displays the application of a wireless ad hoc network in healthcare services.

c. **Commercial and Civilian environment:** Ad hoc networks also have vast uses in the commercial and civilian environment. In the field of business, remote database access, mobile office, electronic payment, virtual meeting, and many more concepts become possible because of these networks. There are numerous other examples of application in these networks, like applications related to transport and vehicular services such as transmission of road, road or accident support, and weather conditions predicting application [15].

Similarly, a different kind of commercial network can be set up anytime and anywhere like a network of visitors at the airport, taxi-cab network, a network within a sports stadium, virtual classrooms, ad hoc communication during conferences, meetings, or lectures, etc.

14.1.1.4 Classification of Wireless Ad Hoc Network

WANETs are infrastructure-less; they can be fully or partially mobile and can be flexibly designed as per requirement. Therefore, the ad hoc network is of a different type depending on its applications [16].

14.1.1.4.1 Mobile Ad Hoc network (MANET)

A type of wireless ad hoc network called a mobile ad hoc network may change its position and setup itself instantly [17,18]. MANET is a group of mobile hosts that are well equipped with wireless communication devices. The communication among the nodes is broadcast or multicast in nature. The mobile hosts can advance randomly and may switch on or goes off while not acknowledging alternative hosts. Mobility and autonomy leads to dynamic topology within network [19,20].

14.1.1.4.2 Wireless Mesh Network (WMN)

A WMN is a communication network of nodes structured in an exceedingly mesh topology. It is conjointly a sort of WANET. A mesh implies rich interconnection among the devices or nodes. Wireless mesh networks usually encompass "mesh routers, clients, and gateways." The mobility of nodes is not too recurrent. The clients inside the network are usually laptops, mobile phones, and different wireless equipment. The mesh network transmits data to and from the wireless devices which can, however needn't, be connected to the internet.

14.1.1.4.3 Wireless Sensor Network (WSN)

Wireless sensor networks imply that they rely on wireless connectivity and spontaneous development of networks in order that sensor information is transported through wireless medium. WSNs are spatially located sensors to analyze the environmental parameters like "Temperature, Sound, Pressure, etc." and to synchronously collect information to the central locations. Some of its uses include monitoring the environment and habitats, underwater sensing (seismic/oil spills), battlefield surveillance, and wireless sensors in enterprise-led networks.

14.1.1.4.4 Vehicular Ad hoc Network (VANET)

VANET implies a network build in an ad hoc manner wherever different mobile vehicles and alternative joint devices are available to connect over a wireless medium and communicate helpful data with each other. A tiny network is made at the same instance within the vehicles and alternative devices acting as nodes within the network. A vehicular Ad Hoc Network allows information exchange among vehicles and also between vehicles and "road-side base stations" with an objective of managing proficient and harmless transportation.

14.1.1.5 Challenges of Wireless Ad Hoc Network

14.1.1.5.1 Autonomous and Infrastructure-less

WANET is independent of conventional structure. There is no fixed infrastructure. All devices connect through a wireless medium and play the role of an independent router and generate independent data because it functions in a dispersed P2P style. All nodes are autonomous in nature. Due to the necessity of dispersing network administration throughout the nodes, fault identification and management become challenging.

14.1.1.5.2 Dynamic Topology

The nodes in a Wireless Ad hoc Network can move randomly at any interval. Therefore the topology of the network of MANET may modify randomly and quickly at undefined times. This makes routing tough as a result of the topology is consistently dynamic and nodes cannot be assumed to possess determined data storage. In the worst case, it is unpredictable whether or not the node can stay because it may leave the network at any time.

14.1.1.5.3 Physical Layer Limitations

Collisions, hidden terminals, interference, uni-directional link, and higher packet loss due to constant path breaks because of movement of nodes are some of the physical layer limitations faced by wireless ad hoc networks.

14.1.1.5.4 Restricted Bandwidth and Quality

The networks have limited link bandwidth and its quality is also low as compared to the wired networks. Wireless link has a lower capacity than a wired network. These networks have very high levels of fading, numerous accesses, and interference conditions, which leads to limited throughput.

14.1.1.5.5 Dissimilarity in Link and Node Capabilities

All nodes in wireless ad hoc networks are autonomous and have different capabilities and link capacity. The heterogeneous radio abilities of node create an irregular link. Nodes might have additional interfaces that have variable sending or receiving power and may operate in varying frequency bands.

In addition to this, the nodes may have varying processing capability due to different software/hardware configuration. The designing of protocols and algorithms for such a diverse network can be complicated. The variation in "power consumption," "traffic load," "channel conditions," "congestion," "traffic distribution," etc. should be kept in mind while building schemes for these networks.

14.1.1.5.6 Energy-Constrained Operation

All or few of the nodes in a wireless network could also be powered by batteries. As batteries have limited power so the processing power of the node is restricted, this successively reduces applications and services which will be supported by each node. It this state of affairs, the foremost vital system criterion for optimization may be energy conservation.

14.1.1.5.7 Network Robustness and Reliability

Wireless ad hoc networks are less robust than wired network because of wireless medium, dynamic topology, and energy constrained devices. This limits the reliability of the network. Limited wireless transmission is term to be responsible for less reliability of wireless ad hoc networks. Because of the broadcast nature of wireless medium, errors occur like packets loss, hidden and exposed node, etc. The characteristics of wireless links are time dependent in nature. There are transmission impediments that occur, like "signal path loss," "fading," "blockage," and "interference." Therefore, the reliability of wireless transmission is resisted by various factors.

14.1.1.5.8 Network Security

Compared to a wired network, wireless ad hoc networks are much more susceptible to security problems. So, security is one of the critical challenges for these networks. The data from one device to different devices should be transported safely, securely, and without missing even a single bit of data. Because of infrastructure-less organization and lack of centralized observance control, these networks are susceptible to a variety of attacks.

14.1.1.5.9 Quality of Services

In Mobile wireless ad hoc networks, the environment changes constantly, so it is very challenging to provide different quality of service levels [21–23]. The random nature in the quality communication of MANET makes it troublesome for the server to ensure a good service to the devices. To enable multimedia system services, adaptive service quality is frequently imposed on traditional resources.

14.1.1.6   Vulnerabilities of WANET

Wireless ad hoc networks have intrinsically diverse characteristics than wired networks. The wireless medium, mobile nodes, dynamic topology, and an exhaustive power supply create different security vulnerabilities to these networks. WANET faces threats from nodes outside the network that are unauthorized to involve within the network and also from nodes inside the network that has the authorization credentials to be active within the network. As shown in Figure 14.2, the threats may be categories on the source of location into external and internal threats and on the basis of behavior into active and passive threats or attacks. Similar attacks and its related routing algorithms is referred to in Figure 14.2 [24–26].

The external threats may range from "passive eavesdropping," where the malicious node only listens to transmit signals to "active interference," where the enemy interrupts the network by sending misleading or corrupted signals or data. In passive eavesdropping, the adversaries only intercept the message transmitted in the network without disturbing the transmission. The objective behind this is that the adversary will be able to analyze the valuable information like network topology, and the identity of more heavily used nodes to perform further attacks. Eavesdropping is also a problem to maintain location privacy. Similar works and their application are referred to in [27–29].

The main menace from active interference could be an ignorance of service attack. This attack causes stopping within the wireless communication medium or broken communications. The duration for which the attack is active and the routing protocol in use determines the actual effects of such attacks. The reactive routing protocol interpret non-acceptance of service to be a link breaks whereas the proactive routing protocol does not answer instantly to the undelivered information.

The internal threats posed by the participating nodes exert more impact as internal nodes have the essential data to involve in network management operations. The misbehaving internal nodes are categorized into four types "failed nodes,"

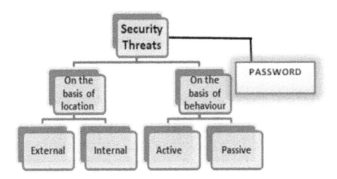

FIGURE 14.2   Classification of security threats.

TABLE 14.1

Security attacks on different layers of the TCP/IP protocol stack

TCP/IP PROTOCOL STACK LAYERS	SECURITY ATTACKS
Application layer	"Malicious coding, Corruption of data, Viruses and Worms"
Transport layer	"Hijacking of session, SYN Flooding Attack"
Network layer	"Blackhole, Wormhole, Sinkhole, Link Spoofing, Rushing Attack, Replay Attacks, Link Withholding (Misuse), Resource Consumption, and Sybil Attack"
Data link layer	"Selfish misbehavior, Traffic analysis, Dishonest behavior"
Physical layer	"Passive interference-Eavesdropping, Active interference"

"badly failed nodes," "selfish nodes," and "malicious nodes." "Failed" and "selfish" nodes are those that restrict themselves from performing any bound operation as specified compulsion by the protocol.

The failed node does so due to some unforeseen failure, like power failure and environment events. Whereas, the selfish nodes only main reason to do this is to save power. They could perform operations that are inaccurate, thus passing wrong and deceptive information. Malicious nodes could disorder the network by employing diversity of attacks, like "flooding attack, black-hole attack, packet-modification attack, gray-hole attack, energy based attacks, packet delay attack, sybil attack" are some of the threats to the security of a network. Other related measures for various applications are defined [30,31].

These attacks pierce all levels of the protocol. Table 14.1 lists the various attacks on different layers. Spread-spectrum methods, frequency hopping, interleaving, or other security measures are employed for lower levels, whereas cryptography is one of the greatest solutions to stop these threats at higher layers.

14.1.2 APPLICATIONS OF WSN

WSN applications are classified into two types:

Category 1: Mesh based WSN with multi-hop transmission and dynamic routing
Category 2: point to point with single hop transmission and single hop routing

The sensors deployed in typical applications like data collection, environmental monitoring, structural monitoring, military surveillance, and medical telemetry consider energy consumption levels as an important criteria which can hinder system lifetime.

Due importance is given to SHM applications which monitor civil structures like Bridges and Multistorey application. The goal of SHM is to develop smart structures which can self-diagnose the problems and raise alerts if there is any damage in the structure. For instance, in earthquake prone zones routine mild tremors give rise to hidden cracks that may not cause visible damage to structural condition of the building.

Generally wired seismic accelerometers are used to measure movement in a structure, but they are expensive, and cumbersome to install and maintain. This limits the number of sensors that can be deployed, which in turn affects the building's structural integrity using wired sensor networks. If sensors of low cost and wireless type are available, dense packs of sensors can be deployed to monitor those critical structures.

Smart Dust Motes developed by UC Berkeley engineers can measure true structural condition using below the skin measurement. Tiny mote is a battery operated WN. It is a low cost mote which can sense a wide variety of factors like light, temperature and Civil Engineering dynamic responses. UC Berkeley smart dust motes helps in more accurate finite element analysis, which is a computer modeling method to represent a structure's behavior in a given condition.

14.1.3 IMPORTANCE OF WIRELESS SENSOR NODE LOCATION

To monitor an environment, WNs are distributed throughout the area. But random distribution of WNs has many drawbacks, such as;

- difficulty in tracking of WNs
- lack of security
- difficulty in managing and monitoring a WSN.

In applications like SHM, a WN should be deployed in a location which has rich information content. Deploying WNs in crack prone locations helps in monitoring the structure effectively rather than deploying randomly.

A few algorithms to find out this optimal information-rich locations are analyzed in detail and a new efficient algorithm is proposed in this thesis. Fixing WNs only in these optimal locations helps in achieving higher information quality from the given structure.

14.1.4 RESEARCH QUESTIONS

The purpose of this research is to give a deeper understanding on both the sensor node location and energy optimization techniques available in SHM applications. To fulfill the purpose the following research questions were addressed.

- What is the importance of sensor node location while deploying a WSN?
- How the energy consumption of each WN can be optimized?
- Are these optimization techniques helpful in improving the overall system lifetime and information quality?

14.1.5 NEED FOR RESEARCH

Sensor node location prioritizing information quality is not yet a popular technique in the SHM industry. If a WN's deployment location is chosen wisely then it helps in reducing the number of sensors which in turn reduces the cost and weight of the system. In addition, to increase the deployed WN's lifetime, energy efficient routing protocols should be designed. Hence, in this process, both sensor node location and energy optimization techniques are explored in detail.

14.1.6 PROBLEM STATEMENT

WSN is widely used for SHM applications to detect mild cracks which when unattended may result in huge damage to human lives and the economy.

Normally WNs are deployed randomly to monitor a specified environment. This random deployment method is inappropriate, as a higher number of WNs are needed to monitor the entire structure which, in turn, increases the cost and weight of the monitoring system. So, to reduce the number of WNs, information-rich locations in the structure should be identified to deploy WNs only in these locations.

The WNs are deployed on each floor of a nine storey building. The height of each floor is assumed to be 3.33 m. Considering the distance between each floor, a WN is deployed at each floor. This in turn helps to get accurate information about each floor. Instead of placing nine WNs, one on each floor, the entire structure can be monitored with six or seven WNs by deploying WNs only at the information-rich locations. Concrete floors in between each floor may have impact on the wireless transmission and the design of network topology. However such limitations are not considered in this thesis. In the future, while deploying the WSN in real world with the necessary hardware, these limitations should be considered.

Fisher Information Matrix (FIM) is used as an evaluation metric to identify the information-rich locations in the structure. Only the locations which have higher information quality are chosen with the help of FIM out of all the available locations in the structure.

There are many algorithms available in the literature like SPEM and GA, which use the FIM matrix to find the optimal information-rich sensor locations. But they typically select the optimal sensor locations consuming more time or with low information quality. So, in this thesis, an attempt is made to design an efficient algorithm HIOGA which can find these optimal sensor locations quickly with higher information quality. Once, these optimal sensor locations are found the WNs are deployed in these locations alone and not in a random fashion.

14.1.6.1 Case Study I

The objective here is to select only six or seven optimal WNs among the available nine WNs to monitor a 9-storey building. If it is possible to monitor the entire structure with the required information quality even with seven WNs, it will be efficient in terms of both cost and weight. Hence a new HIOGA algorithm is proposed to find out this optimal number of WNs.

These WNs require some energy to transmit the information available to the sink node. If the information transmission occurs repeatedly, the WNs deployed in these optimal information-rich locations soon die away, as they are battery operated.

So, there is a need to design an energy efficient algorithm which considers remaining energy available in a WN, energy arrival rate, the energy consumed by the WN to transmit the information, the distance of the WN from the sink node as additional parameters, in addition to the information quality while selecting the WN locations.

Upon surveying the literature available in this field there are algorithms like LEACH, ICSHS claimed to give better energy optimization. All these algorithms results can be improved further by designing the system with efficient clustering techniques. So, in this thesis, an energy efficient CHRIGEON algorithm is proposed in Chapter 4, whose performance is analyzed using case study II.

14.1.6.2 Case Study II

The objective here is to select CHs from the available hundred WNs, which are deployed randomly to monitor a given area of 200×200 m^2. The CHs duty is to aggregate the information available with its associated member WN's information and transmit it to a remote sink node.

CHRIGEON algorithm proposed optimizes energy. HIOGA algorithm proposed in Chapter 3 chooses WNs' optimal location and related information quality. A new HIEOGA algorithm proposed in Chapter 6 applies the CHRIGEON algorithm to the result of HIOGA algorithm, which optimizes both energy and information quality.

A WN consists of the following components:

1. Power Unit
2. Processing Unit
3. Sensing and Actuation Unit
4. A Communication Unit and other application-dependent units

14.1.6.2.1 *Power Unit*

To make the WNs operable for many years an efficient energy supply should be used. Generally, WNs are battery-operated, which make power consumption an important challenge. As once deployed in a remote environment, these nodes cannot be reached easily again for recharging or replacement. Either two AA alkaline cells or a Li-AA cell are used as battery for a WN. WN has limited power sources which are less than 500mAh, 1.2 V.

To manage the power available with the WNs and to conserve the available power, energy efficient protocols should be designed. A WN's power consuming functions are to detect unusual events, process the data, and then transmit it to a remote sink node. While transmitting the data available to a remote sink node, a WN either collects the information and processes it or relay the available data. Relaying the information collected from other nodes to remote sink node also requires additional power. An energy efficient optimization algorithm is proposed in this thesis to route available data to the remote sink node. Energy optimization helps in increasing the system's network lifetime.

14.1.6.2.2 *Processing Unit*

WNs are typically embedded systems whose processor's capability ranges from an 8-bit micro controller to a 64-bit microprocessor. It stores information ranging from 0.01 to 100 GB.

14.1.6.2.3   Sensing and Actuation Unit

An event happening in the environment can be sensed by this unit and it reacts according to that sensed value. Humidity, sound, acceleration, temperature, and pressure sensors are available to sense the environment.

14.1.6.2.4   Communication Unit

Modulation techniques, network topologies, transmission rangeand routing techniques are important areas of concern while transmitting the sensed information to the remote sink node. Transmission distance ranges from a few meters to a few Kilometers. Throughput ranges from 10 to 256 kbps.

Network of WNs forms a WSN. WNs are distributed in a special domain called sensor field to collect the information, process and route it to a remote sink node. In this thesis, a group of non-CH WNs forward their sensed data to a CH node. Each CH node forwards its own information along with information collected by its associated nodes to a remote sink node in multi-hop fashion. This technique of selecting a CH node for each cluster of WNs is known as clustering.

14.1.6.2.5   Multi Hop Routing

Selecting the shortest paths from the CHs to the remote sink node is essential to maximize the network lifetime. Every CH node identifies its neighbor CH node and transmits its data to it. The neighbor node aggregates this with its own data and transmits it to the CH near the sink node (or) to the sink node directly, whichever is closer.

The information collected by a single WN hops multiple times to reach a remote sink node establishing a path. This path cost should be minimized to help the information from a WN reach the remote sink node consuming less energy. A shortest path algorithm like Dijkstra is used to find the shortest path between each CH and the remote sink node. The path cost depends not only on the distance between CHs but also on remaining energy available with each CH node and the energy consumed by a CH node for transmitting its aggregated data to remote sink node.

14.2   CLUSTERING

Designing energy efficient routing protocols for WSN considering the power and resource limitations of the network helps in improving the lifetime of the system. Clustering is a type of routing protocol in which WNs are grouped based on its location and then selecting a WN, which has more available remaining energy as CH nodes from the group. Using this technique total energy consumption in a network is greatly reduced, which in turn extends the system's lifetime. The aggregated data by the CH nodes are then transmitted to a remote sink node, either in single hop or multi-hop fashion generally.

Clustering technique is used as a routing protocol. The WNs that have higher energy arrival rates, closer to the sink, are selected as CH node. The nodes associated with the CHs reserve a portion of their harvested energy. This saved energy will be used by the same node when they are selected as CH in any future round. In this thesis, Multi-hop routing technique is used to transmit the aggregated data to the remote sink node.

14.2.1 Optimization Techniques

A sensor network is defined from information point of view, as a WSN graph G_{WSN} comprising a set $\{V_e, L_i\}$ where, V_e ($1 \le e \le n$) and n is the number of WNs. V_e specifies WN in a WSN and L_i($1 \le i \le n^2$) represents a link between two vertices with its associated costs.

A graph G_{WSN} is having vertices as V_e and links between them as L_i. A link is incident at both vertices which are adjacent to each other. Edges are of two types:

Parallel: Two links with same vertices
Loop: A link with same end points

Graphs with no parallel edges or loops are called Simple graph. Complete Graph is a simple graph with a path existing in between every pair of vertices. The link cost for each node may vary depending on the remaining energy available, distance from the sink node, and energy consumption by each WN. The ultimate goal is to find an optimal path formed by linking a set of nodes with the minimum total cost associated with it. To find this optimal path there are many optimization techniques available in the literature.

The following are some of the techniques available to optimize the path:

14.2.1.1 Minimum Spanning Trees

It is a collection of edges of a connected, undirected graph without any cycles, connecting all the vertices together, with minimum total edge weight.

A telecommunication firm is planning to lay cable in a new area. The constraint here is to lay the cables only along the road side. Here, an undirected graph is established in that area containing all the houses. Some paths might be more expensive than others based on the length of the cable required to establish a connection. These expensive connections are assigned with larger weights than the connections that are cheaper. A minimum spanning tree in this case is a subset of those paths, which connects every house with lowest total cost and no cycles.

14.2.1.2 Shortest Path Algorithms

A route R in a graph G_{WSN} is a sequence $V_1, L_1, V_2, \ldots L_m, V_m$, where each V_e is a vertex and each link is L_i for $1 < e < m$, the ends of L_i are V_{e-1} and Ve. One of the objectives of this thesis is to find the route for information transmitted by each node to a distant sink node with minimum energy consumption. To satisfy the objective a directed graph is used. For example, if one wishes to make a street map table of minimum driving distance from one place of a city to every other street corner in the city obeying the directions one-way, then there are many possible ways to do that. This can be regarded as a directed graph, as one-ways are also to be considered.

A directed graph Gr has a disjoint set of V_e, L_i and functions related to each link like head and tail. It means each link L_i has two vertices with an associated direction. In the above example the street map of the city is a digraph whose vertices represent the street corners. There is an arc for each section of street joining the corners and for each direction in which it is legal to drive along it. The following are some of the differences of digraph in comparison with undirected graph.

     i. Parallel: If a digraph's links have same head and tail
     ii. Simple: A digraph which has no loops or parallel arcs

A route in which all links are forward is called a directed path. The vertex c can be reached from each vertex by traversing different paths. This traversing cost may vary depending on its location and other factors. In this thesis, the objective of reaching the sink node through the shortest path available is achieved using the directed graph. The shortest path is calculated considering the distance of each node from sink node, remaining energy available and energy consumption for transmission as factors influencing the link cost. Based on the overall path cost a comparison is made for each route and that route which gives the minimum value is chosen as an optimal solution. Dijikstra's shortest path algorithm is used in this thesis to evaluate the shortest path to reach a sink node from each vertex.

14.2.1.3   Dijkstra's Shortest Path Algorithm

This algorithm finds the shortest path between a CH node to all other CH nodes or to the sink node available in the network, whichever is closer.

14.2.1.3.1   Steps
     1. Set of CH nodes which are not visited is formed.
         The initial CH node is kept as current node and then assigns tentative cost which is zero for the initial node, infinity for the remaining nodes.
     2. Considering all the unvisited neighbors calculate the tentative cost of current node with respect to the neighbor node and update it with the smaller one.
     3. After all the unvisited nodes are considered, mark them as visited.
     4. Stop the algorithm when the destination node is marked as visited.
     5. Else select the unvisited node and set this as a current node and go to step 3.
         This algorithm helps in finding the optimal path from each CH node to the remote sink node.
         The initial CH node is kept as current node and then assigns tentative cost which is zero for the initial node, infinity for the remaining nodes.
     6. Considering all the unvisited neighbors calculate the tentative cost of current node with respect to the neighbor node and update it with the smaller one.
     7. After all the unvisited nodes are considered, mark them as visited.
     8. Stop the algorithm when the destination node is marked as visited.
     9. Else select the unvisited node and set this as a current node and go to step 3.

This algorithm helps in finding the optimal path from each CH node to the remote sink node.

14.3 CONCLUSION

The fundamentals of wireless sensor networks and its usage in SHM Applications are briefly discusses the hardware components involved in WSNs, how to route sensed data to the remote sink node using clustering technique and optimization technique used in WSN. Surveys the literature available in the field of WSN energy optimization and sensor node location optimization technique in SHM Applications. The sensor node location optimization with proposed Higher Information Oriented Genetic Algorithm (HIOGA) and compares its results with the existing exhaustive search, Genetic Algorithm, SPEM algorithms. The sensor nodes energy optimization with the proposed Cluster Head Routing in Geographic Energy Optimized Network (CHRIGEON) protocol and compares its results with existing LEACH and Cuckoo based clustering algorithms. The conclusion of the above work based on their performance in terms of both sensor nodes location and energy optimization.

REFERENCES

1. N. Mast, S. Khan, M. I. Uddin, Y. Y. Ghadi, H. K. Alkahtani, S. M. Mostafa, "A Cross-Layer Solution for Contention Control to Enhance TCP Performance in Wireless Ad-Hoc Networks", IEEE, Volume 11, 2023.
2. M. Girmay, V. Maglogiannis, D. Naudts, M. Aslam, A. Shahid, I. Moerman, "Technology Recognition and Traffic Characterization for Wireless Technologies in ITS Band", ELSEVIER, Vehicular Communications, Volume 39, 2023.
3. S. G. Rahul, N. K. Kumar, R. Kushwaha, "7 - Smart Structural Health Monitoring System using IoT and Wireless Technology", Elsevier, Recent Advancement of IoT Devices in Pollution Control and Health Applications, Pages 85–108, 2023.
4. N. Temene, C. Sergiou, C. Georgiou, V. Vassiliou, "A Survey on Mobility in Wireless Sensor Networks", ELSEVIER, Volume 125, 2022.
5. G. Kirubasri, G. Kirubasri, D. Pandey, B. K. Pandey, V. K. Nassa, P. Dadheech, "Software-Defined Networking-Based Ad hoc Networks Routing Protocols", Springer, Software Defined Networking for Ad Hoc Networks, Pp. 95–123, 2022.
6. V. Kumar, J. Yu, F. Li, J. Zhang, F. Ye, S. Karri, G. Subramanyam, "Seamless Wireless Communication Platform for Internet of Things Applications", IEEE Xplore, 2022.
7. A. S. Parihar, S. K. Chakraborty, "A Cross-Sectional Study on Distributed Mutual Exclusion Algorithms for Ad Hoc Networks", Springer, Pattern Recognition and Data Analysis with Applications, pp. 29–38, 2022.
8. M. Ali Jamshed, K. Ali, Q. H. Abbasi, M. Ali Imran, M. Ur-Rehman Challenges, "Applications, Future of Wireless Sensors in Internet of Things: A Review", IEEE Xplore, Volume 22, Issue 6, 2022.
9. K. Gulati, R. S. K. Boddu, D. Kapila, S. L. Bangare, N. Chandnani, G. Saravanan, " A Review Paper on Wireless Sensor Network Techniques in Internet of Things (IoT)", ELSEVIER, Volume 51, Pp. 161–165, 2022.
10. U. Srilakshmi, S. A. Alghamdi, V. A. Vuyyuru, N. Veeraiah, A. Youseef, "A Secure Optimization Routing Algorithm for Mobile Ad Hoc Networks", IEEE, Volume 10, 2022.

11. F. A. Butt, J. N. Chattha, J. Ahmad, M. U. Zia, M. Rizwan, I. Haide, "On the Integration of Enabling Wireless Technologies and Sensor Fusion for Next-Generation Connected and Autonomous Vehicles", IEEE, Volume 10, 2022.

12. A. Prasanth, "Certain Investigations on Energy-Efficient Fault Detection and Recovery Management in Underwater Wireless Sensor Networks", Journal of Circuits, Systems, and Computers, Vol. 30, 2150137:1–18, 2021.

13. O. S. Puleko, O. Vlasenko, V. Chumakevych, "Software Model for Studying the Features of Wireless Connections in Flying Ad-Hoc Networks (FANETs)", Journal of Physics, 2020.

14. A. Bahaa, I. Alyani, Aduwati, "Electro-textile Wearable Antennas in Wireless Body Area Networks: Materials, Antenna Design, Manufacturing Techniques, and Human Body Consideration—A Review", Textile Research Journal, 1–18, 2020.

15. D. N. Bradley, S. K. Salil, W. Yvonne, G. O. Keat, August 16, Wireless Technologies, 2020.

16. S. J. Prasanth, "A novel multi-objective optimization strategy for enhancing quality of service in IoT enabled WSN applications", Peer-to-Peer Networking and Applications, Vol.13, 2020.

17. A. Prasanth, S. Pavalarajan, "Implementation of efficient intra- and inter-zone routing for extending network consistency in wireless sensor networks", Journal of Circuits, Systems, and Computers, Vol.29, 2020.

18. M. Yogeshwari, G. Thailambal, "Automatic segmentation of plant leaf disease using improved fast fuzzy C means clustering And adaptive Otsu thresholding (IFFCM-AO) algorithm," European Journal of Molecular & Clinical Medicine, volume 7, issue 3, pp 5447–5462, 2020.

19. Dr. M. Yogeshwari, Dr. R. Varalakshmi, "A review on plant leaf disease identification and classification image," JARDCS, volume 11, issue 8, pp 1463–1475, 2019.

20. P. Paruthi Ilam Vazhuthi, A. Prasanth, S. P. Manikandan, K. K. Devi Sowndarya, "A hybrid ANFIS reptile optimization algorithm for energy-efficient inter-cluster routing in Internet of Things-enabled Wireless Sensor Networks," Peer-to-Peer Networking and Applications, 1–29, 2023.

21. P. Vazhuthi, S. P. Manikandan, A. Prasanth, "An energy-efficient auto clustering framework for enlarging quality of service in internet of things-enabled wireless sensor networks using fuzzy logic system," Concurrency and Computation: Practice and Experience, volume 34, 1–28, 2022.

22. V. Juyal et al., "Opportunistic message forwarding in self organized cluster based DTN," 2017 International Conference on Infocom Technologies and Unmanned Systems (Trends and Future Directions)(ICTUS). IEEE, 2017.

23. V. Juyal et al., "Performance comparison of DTN multicasting routing algorithms-opportunities and challenges," 2017 International Conference on Intelligent Sustainable Systems (ICISS). IEEE, 2017.

24. V. Juyal et al., "On exploiting dynamic trusted routing scheme in delay tolerant networks," Wireless Personal Communications, volume 112, 1705–1718, 2020.

25. V. Juyal et al., "An Anatomy on Routing in Delay Tolerant Network," 2016 IEEE International Conference on Computational Intelligence and Computing Research (ICCIC), Chennai, 2016, pp. 1–4. doi: 10.1109/ICCIC.2016.7919724

26. A. Maurya, V. Sharma, "Facial Emotion Recognition Using Keras and CNN," 2022 2nd International Conference on Advance Computing and Innovative Technologies in Engineering (ICACITE), 2022, pp. 2539–2543, doi: 10.1109/ICACITE53722.2022.9823480.

27. D. Banerjee, V. Kukreja, S. Hariharan, V. Sharma, "Fast and Accurate Multi-Classification of Kiwi Fruit Disease in Leaves using deep learning Approach," 2023 International Conference on Innovative Data Communication Technologies and

Application (ICIDCA), Uttarakhand, India, 2023, pp. 131–137, doi: 10.1109/ICIDCA56705.2023.10099755.

28. M. N. R. D. S. Murali, V. Sharma, "Performance Analysis of DGA-Driven Botnets using Artificial Neural networks," 2022 10th International Conference on Reliability, Infocom Technologies and Optimization (Trends and Future Directions) (ICRITO), 2022, pp. 1–6, doi: 10.1109/ICRITO56286.2022.9965044.

29. A. Raj, V. Sharma, A. K. Shanu, "Comparative Analysis Of Security And Privacy Technique For Federated Learning In IOT Based Devices," 2022 3rd International Conference on Computation, Automation and Knowledge Management (ICCAKM), Dubai, United Arab Emirates, 2022, pp. 1–5, doi: 10.1109/ICCAKM54721.2022.9990152.

30. P. Ajmani, V. Sharma, P. Samuel, K. Somasundaram, V. Vidhya, "Patient Behaviour Analysis and Social Health Predictions through IoMT," 2022 10th International Conference on Reliability, Infocom Technologies and Optimization (Trends and Future Directions) (ICRITO), 2022, pp. 1–6, doi: 10.1109/ICRITO56286.2022.9964846.

31. M. A. Ali, B. Balamurugan, R. K. Dhanaraj, V. Sharma, "IoT and Blockchain based Smart Agriculture Monitoring and Intelligence Security System," 2022 3rd International Conference on Computation, Automation and Knowledge Management (ICCAKM), Dubai, United Arab Emirates, 2022, pp. 1–7, doi: 10.1109/ICCAKM54721.2022.9990243.

Index

Milton Keynes UK
Ingram Content Group UK Ltd.
UKHW031128141024
449569UK00006B/364